URBAN ECOLOGY AS THE BASIS OF URBAN PLANNING

Edited by
H. Sukopp, M. Numata and A. Huber

SPB Academic Publishing bv, The Hague, The Netherlands

CIP-DATA KONINKLIJKE BIBLIOTHEEK, DEN HAAG

Urban

Urban ecology as the basis of urban planning / ed. by H.
Sukopp, M. Numata and A. Huber. - The Hague : SPB
Academic Publishing. − Ill.
With index, ref.
ISBN 90-5103-096-7
Subject headings: urban ecology.

© 1995 SPB Academic Publishing bv, P.O. Box 11188
         1001 GD Amsterdam, The Netherlands

ISBN 90-5103-096-7

TABLE OF CONTENTS

FOREWORD

Towns and cities as they have developed through history not only represent important forms of human coexistence but also relationships between man and nature. Urban ecology investigates the biosphere with the same ecological methods as other branches of ecology their fields, particularly with the anthropocentric viewpoint. Today it is the obviously inadequate adaptation of *human* societies to their surroundings which places ecology at the centre of the environmental discussion. Ecological statements about the relationship between our society and its environment, based on the knowledge of natural living conditions are becoming more and more urgent. This is especially true of urban ecology, since the various forms of towns and cities as they have developed through history represent not only important forms of human coexistence, but also of relationships between man and nature. Although scientific research demonstrates the importance of wild plant and animal life for man, practical measures together with a strategic planning instrument are needed for effectively protecting and reintroducing nature into urban areas.

Today city planning is an established discipline. It not only is taught at universities, it is also represented in the administrations of most cities and towns. The task to integrate the various requests concerning structural and functional as well as social, cultural, historical and ecological issues is to be tackled on different levels. This book, a compilation of 13 manuscripts by different authors, focusses on the ecological foundations for urban planning.

While habitat mapping already is quite a common procedure in Europe, the ecological data gained in detailed investigations only rudimentally are used in the planning process. The deficiencies in connecting the different fields of study imply the necessity to develop a method for considering and processing the scientific data systematically in a reconstructable procedure. It is not the intention of this volume to do this, but rather to give an insight into some recent studies suitable for being integrated into the planning process.

Next to a conceptual article about a theory of urban biocoenoses the volume contains some concrete examples of basic research and inventory work about faunistic, floristic and vegetational topics. They show the different grades of human influence and its effects on the ecosystems of cities and villages. Other articles contain suggestions for the translation of the inventory work into planning and development. A review about approaches to the study of spontaneous urban flora and vegetation in Central Europe rounds the selection of manuscripts. They are arranged in five blocs: 'theory and methodology', 'cities', 'villages', 'green spaces' and 'human ecology'.

The manuscripts were submitted in 1992. Most of them are the drafting of the talks held at the INTECOL Congress in Yokohama, Japan, in 1990. Others are related papers, one is the translation of a doctoral thesis. Remarkable with the latter is, that the investigated small village near Antalya, Turkey, does not exist in this form anymore, so that the investigation records a meanwhile historical state.

We wish to thank all people associated with the preparation of this volume and the organisation of the symposium of 1990. In particular we thank Professor Dr. Akira Miyawaki (Organising Committee of the Congress), Mrs. Almut Huber (redactor) and Mrs. Christel Maubach (secretarial work).

Herbert Sukopp
Makoto Numata

Theory and methodology

TOWARDS A THEORY OF URBAN BIOCOENOSES

Some hypotheses and research questions

LUDWIG TREPL

Institut für Ökologie der Technischen Universität Berlin, FG Ökosystemforschung und Vegetationskunde, Schmidt-Ott-Straße 1, 12165 Berlin, Germany

Introduction

This text is partly a result of preparatory work for a workshop on urban ecology ('First Meeting of an Intecol and UNESCO-MAB International Network for Urban Ecology', Berlin, June 18–20th, 1991), and partly of the evaluation of discussions during this workshop and a Second Meeting (Warsaw, December 15–17th, 1992). The main reason for the meetings were certain problems in the MAB 11-programme, indicating more stress was needed on theoretical and conceptual aspects. The purpose of this paper is to state hypotheses and pose questions for further research.

Urban ecology started to establish itself some twenty years ago and soon became an expanding field of research. Many of the problems confronting it today are the product of its beginnings as a world-wide, organized programme (especially within the MAB-framework) aimed at solving applied rather than scientific problems (despite remarkable theoretical attempts in earlier research, *e.g.* Falinski 1971). It thus lacks a theoretical basis accompanied by a body of data, arising it instead from 'functionalized research', (sensu Böhme *et al.*, 1973). Moreover, those findings which could have served as the basis were from research of non-urban ecological systems. Whether these findings can always be applied to urban conditions is not at all clear.

We assume that the development of urban ecology as a subdiscipline of ecology will be useful. This would require urban ecology to develop a theoretical core of its own (*cf.* Falinski 1971, Sukopp 1973) which would generate questions so that questions did not only arise from external requirements, *i.e.*, from 'practice'. The subject matter of the theory would be the structure and functioning of urban ecosystems, *i.e.*, the theory would have to provide an answer to what are the specifics of such ecosystems (the difference with regard to other ecosystems) and what the systematic relation of their characteristics is.

Today there are tentative approaches to this. It is possible to collect and collate the questions and hypotheses discussed in urban ecology and in the overall field of ecology which are relevant to urban ecosystems. This paper attempts to do so with a relatively small yet strategically important section of everything which a theory on urban ecology would have to encompass. It is hoped that others will follow the example with other sections. If not 'a Theory on Urban Ecology', at least a framework of coherent questions and trial answers could result to which papers on urban ecology field projects could be orientated.

If you talk about the 'theory on urban ecology' today you have to explain what is actually meant by this, much more than has been the case for ecology as a whole. For, annoyingly, '(urban) ecology' is not only a name for what has been called ecology in the scientific community for more than a hundred years, but is also a name – especially in public political phraseology – for what is called 'urban environmental planning'. This encompasses everything that can be used for this purpose including ideology, technological and socio-technological rules, and philosophical consideration of this 'urban ecology' as a whole. This is a (not clearly defined) system of action but not science. However, since a number of sciences with ecology among them, are included, we are faced with the awkward situation that almost nobody knows what is meant, not only when we talk about (urban) ecology but also when we talk about it explicitly as a science.

Urban Ecology as the Basis of Urban Planning, p. 3–21
edited by H. Sukopp, M. Numata and A. Huber
© 1995 SPB Academic Publishing bv, Amsterdam, The Netherlands

In this text urban ecology is to be understood as part of the science 'ecology', *i.e.*, a part of biology. Leaving aside all discussions on practical relevance of ecology for planning or politics, it is not only legitimate but necessary to regard urban ecology as a part of the biological science of ecology, *i.e.*, an empirical-analytical science, not a normative one. The question here is not: What should people *do* to live better in cities? but: What do we *know* about structure and functioning of ecological systems in urban and industrialized regions? All reference to practical usefulness in this context is best avoided.

The main issue is: What are the peculiarities of urban ecological systems; how are they different to non-urban ecosystems? The answer is relevant for the following question: Is it possible to develop urban ecology from a diffuse field of research into a subdiscipline of ecology like *e.g.*, limnology? This seems to be possible only if urban ecosystems have similar differences from non-urban ones that limnic ecosystems have when compared with terrestrial ones, and that we will be able to describe this. Only then a consistent, coherent, well-circumscribed subdiscipline with a certain degree of theoretical and methodological autonomy may develop, comparable to limnology. Otherwise all efforts to institutionalize urban ecology, *e.g.*, through an 'International Network', will fail, I fear.

I'm not sure that this will be possible. Between limnic and terrestrial ecosystems there are sharp boundaries. You will find no benthos or metalimnion in terrestrial ecosystems. But it seems to me that (nearly?) all characters of urban ecosystems can be found in some non-urban ecosystems too, and not only in man-made agricultural ones. Most of the community or ecosystem characters mentioned in the following text are characters of highly disturbed systems in general, and not only of the special case of urban ecosystems. But there are differences to *most* of the non-urban ecosystems, and in order to set up the framework of urban ecology, it is essential to specify them.

As mentioned above, there has been work to describe the special nature of urban ecosystems for some decades. This work mostly stressed the matter-and-energy aspect and the abiotic aspect of ecosystems, *e.g.*, the well-known work in Brussels (Duvigneaud & Denaeyer-de Smet 1975). I decided, in contrast, to focus on the biocoenological or community aspect. I believe, by doing so it will be possible to draw a more differentiated picture.

We have to distinguish between different kinds of urban (or urban-industrial) ecosystems, biocoenoses or communities,[1] in particular:

1. typical urban biocoenoses, *e.g.*, those of vacant industrial land, not those biocoenoses situated in the city having a more natural or a rural character (*e.g.*, remnants of forests, arable lands, meadows, 'encapsulated rural landscape');
2. all biocoenoses within the limits of the city regardless of whether they are specifically urban or not;
3. biocoenoses with special characteristics due to their location in a city (*e.g.*, the large proportion of ruderal species even in forests or meadows in urban territory);
4. biocoenoses which owe their existence to the special 'city' complex of factors;
5. biocoenoses which owe their existence to the special 'industry' complex of factors (even if located in the countryside).

Which of the above variants is meant in what follows must depend on the context.

---

[1] I use the term 'ecosystem' in the following sense: an ecosystem is a (syn-)ecological subject, *i.e.*, a 'community', regarded in terms of systems theory (*cf.* Stöcker 1979). 'Ecosystem' as 'not only the living organisms, but also their abiotic environment' does not make sense. There is no abiotic environment unless as related to the (organisms and their) community, and research in abiotic factors therefore is a *part* of community ecology – otherwise 'abiotic environment' would be a typical non-concept (*cf.* Hard 1973). 'Biocoenosis' and 'community' are often used as synonyms in literature. But sometimes the term community is used in a more general sense than 'biocoenosis'.

Within the framework of the biocoenotic aspect some questions and hypotheses are presented (items 1 to 42) which are generated from each other and which are related to each other. *These are not necessarily my hypotheses,* I do not always defend them. You find them in literature, although rarely in literature on urban ecology. Correspondingly, the papers quoted deal mainly with ecological questions in general; here these hypotheses will be related to special urban conditions only. To me they seem to be worth examining because they are closely related to the problems which have been playing the key role on the (general) ecological research front. In other words: In this paper little can be found about the structure and function of urban ecological communities, rather about the assertions – very tentative assertions in most cases – of the ecologists.

Questions and hypotheses

The questions and hypotheses concern the following three subjects:
– integration
– succession
– invasion

I. Integration

1. If you ask for the main characteristics of urban ecosystems – or of ecosystems subject to generally strong urban industrial effects – most ecologists would agree with the following hypothesis: the most important differentiating characteristics of urban ecosystems compared with most non-urban ones is their *low degree of integration* (or organization, or connectivity, or similar terms; for definitions see *e.g.*, Ulanowicz 1986, 1990, contributions in Higashi & Burns (eds.) 1991).

2. This will immediately be followed by a question and you will notice that this hypothesis is based on another. The question is: what is meant by 'degree of integration'? The hypothesis is that the degree of disintegration of ecological systems be correlated with increasing anthropogenic influence. First the question as to the meaning of '(degree of) integration'. There are as many meanings as uses of the term. We will list some of the problems which result of this lack of clarity.

3. First of all, each answer primarily depends upon the *ecosystem (or community) definition* chosen. Above all, two fundamentally different concepts are used (*cf.* Ravera 1984):
   3a. An ecosystem (or: community) is understood to be all living things (and their environment) within a continuous space limited as naturally as possible ('s-ecosystem', 's' for space). The living things in this space need not necessarily be linked by causal or functional relations or interactions and some of them may maintain closer relations with living things of other ecosystems than with their neighbours in the ecosystem. – This view has developed mainly out of the geobotanical and limnological tradition (*cf. e.g.*, Ellenberg 1973) which has held that it is beyond doubt that – with regard to site conditions and physiognomic aspects – the spatial connection has to be decisive for the definition of ecological units. An ecosystem for example is a forest or a lake, or it is the system which results from the abstraction of the ecological aspects ('the ecosystem of the, or this particular, forest').
   3b. An ecosystem is understood to be all living things (and those environmental factors relevant to them) more or less closely linked to each other by causal or functional relations independent of their proximity in the space ('f-ecosystems', 'f' for func-

tion). Such an ecosystem can include in its spatial limits organisms which do not belong to it and vice versa, and the system can be geographically dispersed (migrating
birds!)[2]. Such a view developed primarily out of animal ecology where it plays a major role today mainly in the research of 'micro-ecosystems' like plant-insect complexes.[3]

4. In the case of s-ecosystems a *completely disintegrated ecosystem* is conceivable as a borderline
case. The elements − if the species are understood to be elements of the system − do not
maintain 'ecological' relations (predation, parasitism, mutualism, in some respects also competition) among themselves (decomposing may be caused outside the ecosystem). The hypothesis would have to be examined that this especially occurs in the cities and industrialized areas, or that urban ecosystems are, in broad terms, more likely to match this model of
complete disintegration than others.

5. Sparse plant populations are frequent in extreme conditions. Here, single plants do not
influence one another. For urban conditions the hypothesis can be put forward that, because of the increased variability in time of environmental factors and the historic uniqueness of their combination (see below, chapter III) compared with other extreme environments, *e.g.*, arctic or arid zones, it is more likely that animals maintain no (or at least no obligatory) ecological relation either with each other or with plants of the same space (*i.e.*, in
the 's-ecosystem'). At least the first (no or poor development of plant-animal relations) is
proven in case of stands of plants of alien origin (Kennedy & Southwood 1984, Kowarik
1986, Lohmeyer & Sukopp 1992, see also Turcek 1961). If urban ecosystems are understood to be f-ecosystems, complete disintegration would be excluded by definition. Of
course, there, too, the relations within the system may become very weak. Where the relations are most weak, there is the borderline of the ecosystem.

6. If it is true that urban ecosystems are only poorly integrated because of the low number
and intensity of relations between the elements, especially of obligatory relations, and if the
space-time dynamics of the particular species are relatively independent of each other, this
has *consequences for the classification* of synecological units based on similarities and differences
in the combination of species and in the structure of relations between the organisms involved.[4] With regard to ecological space structures ('Raumgliederungen'), in cities and outside them, one usually assumes classifications to be based on vegetational science (in Central
Europe: on plant sociology in the narrow meaning). Under the condition of poor integration you obtain a different 'map' for each taxonomically determined 'community'. Only in
cases of marked integration could one assume that the structures coming from different
groups of organisms would match.
What are the practical consequences for data collection? The largest impetus for ecological
stock-taking in the cities was presumably brought about by the city biotope maps (see *e.g.*,
Sukopp & Weiler 1986, accounts in Sukopp *et al.*, 1990). The recording of 'biotopes' is
generally the registration of ecosystems, which are more or less of the s-ecosystem type, and
at the same time are supposed to be functional units. The main aspect of differentiation is

---

[2] With regard to the s-ecosystem-concept the term ecotope was coined; for f-ecosystems this term makes no
sense.
[3] The difference in use between the terms 'biocoenose' (which corresponds to a 'biotope') and 'community'
basically corresponds to the difference between those concepts of ecosystems, at least atmospherically; an un-
ambiguous distinction is not drawn.
[4] Only this can reasonably be called an ecosystem classification. A classification which is based on abiotic
factors or which includes them as 'equal' either already tacitly assumes organisms as a reference system, or it is
based on an outright classical nonsensical concept of 'environment' (*cf.* Hard 1973).

usually the vegetation. In view of what has just been said, what is the biological meaning of biotope maps, the meaning with regard to ecosystems and biocoenoses?

7. Defining the ecological structure of urban spaces based on the strength of functional relations between elements of the ecosystem is an important task. It would first be about s-ecosystems which are similar to f-ecosystems but eventually also about a purely ecological-functional subdivision of the city. Only then one would have isolated those systems which react to interventions as ecological units.

8. The question about the internal urban (f-)ecosystem boundaries (= ecological subdivisions of the city) would have to be followed by the question as to the boundaries of urban f-ecosystems with regard to other, non-urban ecosystems, or as to the ecological boundaries with regard to the surrounding countryside. At the same time this question considers the *meaning of terms like 'the city as an ecosystem'* (as opposed to 'the ecosystems in the city'). Is it true that all the ecosystems of a city together build an (f-)ecosystem so that you can talk of the city as an ecosystem in the sense of an ecological-functional unit? Maybe there is a zone in the outskirts of the city where the interrelations of elements (= organisms) are interrupted while within it and outside it the connections are comparatively firm (*cf.* Kunick 1982)? Can this functional unit – if it is one, at all – be ascribed self-organizing abilities? Or is the unity of urban ecosystems merely characterized by the dependence of their living elements on abiotic environmental conditions (*e.g.*, the unique urban climate) without these elements being held together by closer relations and thus being distinguished from non-urban ecosystems or the city surroundings (the hypothesis of the lower degree of integration of urban ecosystems would suggest just this)? Is that which is distinct in whatever form from surrounding ecosystems an f-ecosystem or is it an agglomeration of several ecosystems which are merely spatially adjacent (because the sites are adjacent)?

9. This suggests that in questioning the importance of '(the degree of) integration' you have to become involved in an old debate: the debate between *holism and reductionism,* organismic and individualistic concepts, 'ecosystem orientated' and 'population orientated' approaches (*cf.* McIntosh 1985, Trepl 1987). The basic proposition of each of the first mentioned schools of thought was or is, that the ecosystems or communities are highly integrated, that subsequently they are units acting and reacting as 'entities' (or 'wholes') and that their unity is brought about by the (more or less obligatory) interaction of the elements (species). The opponents of these theories have held that the elements are only loosely connected, separable and otherwise combinable accumulations of elements which form 'communities' only because of the same requirements as to the abiotic site conditions and due to random dispersal; the interactions are weak or non-specific ones (*cf.* item 23).

10. If the initial hypothesis of the low degree of integration of urban ecosystems were true, the following would apply: *the propositions of the reductionistic, individualistic and population orientated tradition would better apply to urban ecosystems* as 'disintegrated' systems. The dispute between the opposing positions which has gone on for decades would turn out to be an argument which, at least in important aspects[5], has taken for absolute some views which in fact correspond to two different types of real ecosystems. Most urban and industrial ecosystems or biocoenoses would be characteristic of one of the two, namely the individualistic one.

11. The terms, theories and methods developed for each of the two traditions of theory which have been thought to be contrary rather than complementary could each be employed more usefully for one of the two types. Conclusions would be for example:

---

[5] For the differences between aspects which can be decided on empirical grounds and those which cannot with regard to this question see Schoener 1986a, Trepl 1992.

11a. Urban and industrial ecosystems have *no or little 'cybernetic character'* (*cf.* the relevant general controversy in Engelberg & Boyarsky 1979, Patten & Odum 1981); self-regulatory processes and negative feedback play only a minor role. But: Suppose the human community of a city (or parts of it) can be described as a self-regulating or self-organizing system: What would be the consequences for urban ecosystems, which are, of course, influenced by those self-regulating processes of the human community? Are they forced to show such self-regulatory characters in some respect too? And how shall we apply such an idea?

11b. The urban communities are *non-equilibrium systems* (*cf.* e.g. Chesson & Case 1986) since, under the set conditions, there can hardly be any interaction structures between the species which are required to have the community return to its original combination of species after changes of the biotic composition due to disturbances (*cf.* e.g., Price 1984, Hubbell & Foster 1986). Interaction structures can therefore not generate equilibrium conditions. At least it will often be impossible to maintain the system homeostasis, because the compensating function of parallel trophic chains and other 'ecosystem reserve structures' is weakened by decrease of species numbers under strong urban and industrial pressure (*cf.* Trojan 1984).

11c. Generally all those *characteristics* which in the ecological literature normally are *associated more closely with systems of the individualistic type* or with non-equilibrium systems would be expected in urban rather than in non-urban conditions. This would mean for example: higher importance of physical processes than biological ones; major influx of resources from outside the system (does this also apply to the particular urban ecosystems?); high species turnover; high degree of niche overlapping; coexistence instead of character displacement; minor importance of population density-related factors; predomination of stochastic processes over deterministic processes; stability type resilience rather than resistance (sensu Orians 1975); predominantly 'limes-convergens'-boundary-situations (*cf.* van Leeuwen 1966); more frequent occurrence of species with r-strategy than those with K-strategy (with implications like: the life of the species of urban systems is usually shorter, the species are comparatively mobile, the populations are generally far from the theoretical carrying capacity, *i.e.*, food is no limiting factor in most cases, etc.) (on the general discussion of the difference between such types of communities and ecosystems *cf.* Schoener 1986b, Wiens 1984, Price 1984, Hengeveld 1989, and many more). – Such assertions must be empirically tested. Yet with regard to a large number of characteristics of ecosystems and communities it is unclear – because the relevant theories lead to contradictory conclusions – what would be hypothetically required for urban conditions, *e.g.*: the relevance of competition as opposed to predation; the relation of scarce and common species; species richness of the particular biotope which is relatively homogeneous in itself (Schoener 1986 mentions 11 different and partly conflicting causes for large numbers of species; see also Solbrig 1991).

11d. *Methods and theoretical approaches* which would be better applied to research into urban ecosystems would be those more rooted in the individualistic tradition, *e.g.*: island theory, patch dynamics approaches, models on disequilibria, theories on succession as processes of a historical, non-deterministic character. On the other hand models of equilibria, theories of self-regulating systems, cycle models, models of deterministic succession etc. would be more suitable for non-urban conditions (but possibly some urban ecosystems are more self-regulated than some agricultural or even some natural ones).

11e. The individualistic tradition has doubted the possibilities and the usefulness of classifications (*e.g.*, Gleason 1926), and the development of *ordination methods* has taken place. With regard to urban ecosystems it would in consequence be sensible to be critical of the adoption of classification methods (especially those of plant sociology) which have been developed anyway in non-urban conditions.

12. If we assume that urban ecosystems in particular do not conform to holistic-organismic concepts, then we may conclude that the criteria for the assessment of whether an ecosystem is intact, harmed or destroyed will not be found in the ecosystem itself. Therefore, *talking of ecosystems as if they could be 'ill'* (Ulanowicz 1986)[6] is even *less appropriate* here than it is with regard to non-urban conditions. It is only reasonable to say that ecosystems are not efficient with regard to certain external requirements. Whether urban ecosystems are to be called 'intact' or not depends completely on these requirements. Depending on which of these requirements is being considered the same system may be regarded as intact or destroyed. Unlike ecosystems of higher integration, it makes no sense to say that urban ecosystems are per se intact (destroyed) (unless one takes the former as standard and then establishes the terminological rule that urban ecosystems are to be called destroyed a priori). Accordingly, there are presumably no stabilizing interactive structures (see item 11) and, consequently, no conditions of equilibrium are created by them.

13. The term '(level of) integration' – in the sense of the creation of superordinated units by means of more or less numerous and strong relations between the components – includes many diverse elements. We have to inquire about the distinctions that may be made between different urban ecosystems and between urban and non-urban ones when considering *different kinds of interactions*.
The term integration of ecosystems, as something which can be high or low, is widely used in the phraseology of ecology, even though not always in these precise terms (*e.g.*, sometimes 'complexity' is used correspondingly). However, nobody will contest that it is something totally different if for example the relations between the elements, which are seen as the cause of integration, are those of competition or whether the relationship is characterized by the use of an element as a resource (predation, parasitism) – whether the relations are of 'cooperative' (mutualism, symbiosis) or of 'antagonistic' nature (competition, predation). It is hard to tell what the biologic sense is of adding up this on the basis of the lowest common denominator, *i.e.*, that all this constitutes relations between elements. It is similarly problematic that, on the one hand integration is said to progress with any increase in the number and intensity of relations (complexity) but that on the other hand, the term also implies the *self-referential* termination of relations, which is obviously something *qualitatively* different which cannot simply be added to what was mentioned above.
A number of further questions and hypotheses could be generated out of the question about the meaning and importance of the '(degree of) integration'. I cannot do this here, however. I only refer you to comprehensive, general ecological literature on the respective subjects, for example on the discussion on the relevance of certain types of interaction, such as competition and predation, on the relation between diversity, stability and productivity or between diversity and complexity, or on holism, inter alia (*cf. e.g.*, articles in Saarinen 1982, Strong *et al.* 1984, Trojan 1984, Kikkawa & Anderson 1986, Gray *et al.* 1987, Roughgarden *et al.* 1989, Solbrig 1991). This literature should be read only from our specific point of view.

14. As already alluded to above (see item 2), the hypothesis of a low degree of integration of urban ecosystems is bases on another hypothesis which holds that the *degree of disintegration correlates with increasing anthropogenic influence.* ★

15. One may doubt this hypothesis in view of the fact that another, similarly firm view was formulated over species diversity (and biological diversity in general). The view was held

---

[6] The term 'illness' presupposes a self-referential character: the sick person – in this case the sick ecosystem – itself feels unwell. This is independent of whether he, she or it renders services to others or not.

(and is still held, *e.g.*, Solbrig 1991), that anthropogenic influences in general have an impoverishing effect. Obviously things are more complicated than that: (anthropogenic) disturbances seem to have an enriching effect, and only lead to impoverishment if they become very strong (*e.g.*, Westhoff 1968, Sukopp 1972, Connell 1978; an example for a special urban community – Collembola –: Kuznetzova 1992). But it seems that there are remarkable differences between the effects of the anthropogenic influence (or the 'urban pressure') on species richness and degree of integration with regard to different subsystems and structural units of the ecosystem. Thus, urban and industrial pressure may cause a decrease in the numbers of zoophages and saprophages, but an increase in phytophages (*cf.* Trojan 1984). Perhaps the view that anthropogenic influences in general have an impoverishing and disintegrating effect, is based on the metaphysical conviction that human actions per se are hostile to life.

16. Since a very strong anthropogenic influence leads to disintegration[7] in any case, one should at least examine whether the relation between the two is of a linear kind or whether moderate influence is likely to bring about the opposite effect, just as in case of species diversity. Furthermore, the relation between species diversity and integration should be made clear. After all, the likelihood of connections increases as the number of species rises.

17. What are we to make of the *city fringe areas*, which are remarkably *rich in species*? Are they rich in species which are completely unrelated (under dynamic environmental conditions complexity – in the sense of number of relations between elements – is said to be decreasing with a rising number of species, see Kikkawa 1986), or are their communities not only diverse but also complex, and are they 'highly integrated'? Methods of testing this need developing.

18. Would it be appropriate at all (and if so, in which respect) to *combine all anthropogenic factors in one variable* which could increase or decrease (perturbation, load, hemerobia ...) or is "the impact of man on nature (...) an empty concept, which does not mean anything (...)"? (Kostrowicki 1979). How can one differentiate between anthropogenic influences, so that different types of influences can be established for urban ecosystems? What are city-specific (combinations of) factors? What is the ecological difference between increasing anthropogenic influence in general and urbanization in particular? Accordingly, what is the sense in differentiating between the ecology of ecosystems which are subject to a strong anthropogenic influence (highly-burdened ecosystems) and urban ecology? 'Urban ecology' is obviously not only an 'ecology of ecosystems which are subject to a high anthropogenic influence', for cities regularly hold in addition other ecosystems which are certainly not of the character ascribed to urban ecosystems (*e.g.*, ecosystems of some old parks). Questions like these are crucial in distinguishing between urban ecology and the ecology of systems subject to anthropogenic disturbance (or pressure) in general, and between the ecology of systems disturbed by man and perturbed ecosystems in general. Probably the answer will not be found by considering the more or less homogenuous single communities. The very city-specific is more likely to be found if one examines the *spatial arrangement* of the different groups of environmental factors and, accordingly, the spatial arrangement of urban ecosystems (mosaic structure etc.).

---

[7] This is nothing but tautology, for the relations between the elements already constitute part of what is called 'community'. Hence any disturbance of the *community* of organisms can only impair the relationships. The relationships may be multiplied or intensified by lesser disturbance. This is permissible within the meaning of the term. At the end, however, when disturbances become extreme, the relationships must be broken up; otherwise, it would make no sense to talk of a 'disturbance'.

II. Succession

19. When only minor changes occur in abiotic environmental factors (including anthropogenic ones), changes in the biocoenosis must, logically, be caused or controlled mainly by internal factors. In this case, there are some reasons to believe that successions (the term is used in its broadest sense here) are deterministic (in the sense the term is usually used in the discussion on ecological successions, see Drury & Nisbet 1973 and other publications), *i.e.*, they are directional, repeatable and predictable, and in their course they are independent of the initial composition of the community (see Odum 1969, Margalef 1968, Patten 1985, and other literature on deterministic successional concepts cited *e.g.*, in Drury & Nisbet 1973).

20. In comparison, successions in biocoenoses which are subject to strong and extremely variable anthropogenic influences are of a historical rather than a merely dynamic character (see item 23). Hence these *successions are not deterministically directed* (*i.e.*, directed according to the functional laws applying to the interrelation of elements) towards a pre-determined state (climax); they are *unpredictable* and not repeatable.[8]

This is a trivial difference: While we can rather successfully predict the succession of a fallow meadow in the countryside into a forest of a certain type, thereby excluding human interventions (in many cases, the succession would take place almost exactly as predicted), such an undertaking would be rather futile in case of fallow urban areas. In any case, the succession would soon be interrupted here by an intervention which, if at all, may only be predicted on the basis of social-scientific and not ecological studies.

In principle, the *historic uniqueness* of urban situations, *i.e.*, of combinations of environmental factors and of organisms, differentiates urban ecosystems from most natural ones, even those subject to strong disturbance. Therefore any evolutionary adaptation to the special urban combination of environmental (biotic and abiotic) factors can hardly exist (or urban ecosystems have no "evolutionary experience", which is necessary to "counteract new agents" (Trojan 1984)).

21. Hence the science of ecology alone is not sufficient to predict satisfactorily concrete ecological events in cities. Ecological science only formulates, so to speak, models which remain out of touch with reality. To put it another way: in more natural ecosystems, even those subject to very variable external influences, ecology itself is largely able to include the peripheral conditions which must be known in addition to ecological laws (according to the Hempel-Oppenheim formula) in order to explain and predict ecological events. This does not apply to urban ecosystems since they are mostly exposed to a stronger anthropogenic influence, *i.e.*, influence of categorially different systems. Urban ecosystems are to a large degree playthings of non-ecological systems.

22. Furthermore, urban environmental conditions are subject to strong, irregular temporary changes. Hence one has to expect here, more than in the countryside, that the peripheral conditions may change in a way which was not predictable at the time the prognosis was made. *This makes predictions impossible in principle* (*cf.* Trepl 1987). Anyway, our prognostic capacity is limited to the slow periods of (re)construction which follow disruptions ("history telling"). The short periods of the disturbances themselves ("history making"), however, are irregular and are thus beyond predictability (Margalef 1984). In urban ecosystems, however, the periods of disturbance quickly follow each other.

---

[8] Of course, all real events are unrepeatable. What is meant here is the fact that – within the deviations predefined as being 'negligible' – specific and defined abstract characteristics (*e.g.*, the composition or number of species) recur and are also predictable under certain conditions.

23. Changes in urban biocoenoses are not predictable (as can be inferred from knowledge of the structure and functioning of the biocoenosis itself) since they are highly dependent on changes in abiotic environmental factors. According to Sanders 1969, they are 'physically controlled' rather than 'biologically accommodated'; according to Richardson 1980, such systems show an individualistic character. Furthermore they are highly dependent on immigrations which – from the point of view of the system of the biocoenosis – arrive by chance (see chapter III, invasion). Here, therefore, only *little use may be made of the 'successional rules* which have repeatedly been established, for example as to the development of productivity or diversity (see *e.g.* Odum 1969), and which are said to have proven their usefulness for the management of forest ecosystems, for example (Thomasius 1988). No reasonable approximation to climax conditions exists. Unlike some cases of non-urban systems (see *e.g.*, Horn 1976), the further course of successions is always dependent on the historic event which caused them. The initial species composition remains relevant in further development. Under the same environmental conditions, essentially different communities develop depending on the local availability of colonising species.

24. There are divergent opinions on successional development. Some say that successions are 'community controlled', others say that they are *externally controlled* in the sense mentioned above and that species replacement is the result of *migrational effects* (views already held by Darwin, Wallace and Gleason, later *e.g.*, by Drury & Nisbet 1973, Harper 1977, Grime 1979, Hubbell & Foster 1986). In the case of urban ecosystems, the latter view is to be favoured in general. Here, perhaps, one of the main differences between urban and most of the non-urban ecosystems is to be found.

25. Communities may be classified into communities which emerged from a co-evolutionary development and *communities produced by successive invasions* (for a catalogue of differences between the two groups, see Rummel & Roughgarden 1983). Urban biocoenoses are an extreme example of the latter group. They are characterized by a high degree of recruitment of foreign members (*cf.* Schoener 1986b, also see chapter III, invasion). Here, the old concept of the ecological community (represented by the 'climax') as a self-reproducing entity (Clements 1916) applies even less than elsewhere.

26. A number of *successional mechanisms* have been distinguished in relevant literature (see *e.g.*, Egler 1954, Horn 1976, Connell & Slatyer 1977, Miles 1987). As to their importance for urban ecosystems, the following may be assumed, at least with regard to vegetation: The classical 'obligatory succession' (Horn 1976), which is based on the assumption that one species or a group of species prepares – more or less literally speaking – the ground for the following ones ('reaction', Clements 1936), is of even less importance here than it is anyway. In comparison, the concept of 'initial floristic composition' (Egler 1954) which says that all species are established before the start of the succession or that they colonize within the first few years may be of relative importance. Due to the mosaic structure of urban biotopes, the propagules of very different community types are available to spread rapidly after site disturbance. Correspondingly, the tolerance model (Connell & Slatyer 1977) or competition hierarchy model (Horn 1976) according to which the species gradually colonize during the course of a succession and replace the ones existing may be of lesser importance. In a sense, however, this concept is of special relevance for cities, since here, foreign species invade in rapid succession and very often turn succession in a certain direction. However, this is not part of the subject 'succession' (see chapter III, invasion). The inhibition model (Connell & Slatyer 1977) according to which dominant species suppress further development may well play some role (especially under nutrient-rich conditions), but it is more typical of certain succession under non-urban conditions (*e.g.*, on fallow grasslands of better soil).

27. The peculiarities of succession have methodological consequences for urban ecology. Here, perhaps more than in general (Horn 1976), it seems appropriate to examine successions from the standpoint of *'adaptation of individual species'* rather than *'emerging characteristics of communities'*. Research on successions must, inevitably, consist more of a description of individual historical examples (*cf. ibid.*); it should be an 'historical research' rather than a 'system research'.

28. Urban ecology is essentially *'historical research'* also for the following reason: ecology has developed in history as an 'actualistic' science, to distinguish itself precisely as such from evolutionary biology (Reiter 1885, *cf.* Trepl 1987). Commonly a distinction is made between ecological time and evolutionary time and there is a type of theory in which the terms equilibrium and reversibility are of prime importance. All this is possible because it makes sense to a certain degree to neglect the real historical changes (evolutionary changes of species and the 'geological' changes, *i.e.*, the irreversible and on principle unpredictable ones), since they are brought about in the long term. Now, abiotic factors − *i.e.*, those factors corresponding to 'geological changes' - change extremely quickly under urban-industrial conditions. As to the species and their changes, the term ecological time which implies that the species remain unchanged makes no sense in cities. There are processes of speciation here, but the change of species due to genetic change (which is designated by the term evolutionary time) is replaced by the steady and (in comparison with more natural conditions) extremely quick change in species composition due to invasion and extinction. In some respect, therefore, the methodology of urban ecology must resemble that of historical ecology (which studies 'geological' periods of time), although urban ecology only takes very recent or short-term events into account.

29. With regard to *methodology*, this means above all that "Many resource variables must be measured, as many different variables may be important to different species, in different places, at different times. Because components of the community may vary independently of one another, repeated sampling will be necessary (...)" (Wiens, 1984, on non-equilibrium communities). In contrast, the following applies: "Under conditions of equilibrium and saturation, the common practice of measuring only a few resource variables can be justified (...) True patterns can be revealed by taking only single samples (...)" (*ibid.*). Under urban-industrial conditions, changing peripheral conditions are hence of greater methodological importance than general rules.

III. Invasion

30. A major reason for the (relative) unpredictability of successions in urban ecosystems is the high degree of invasion or immigration[9]. Urban biocoenoses are not only 'open communities' in the general sense, *i.e.*, communities "whose recruits (...) are produced at great distances from the community's place" (Schoener 1986b), but also in the bio-geographical sense, *i.e.*, they are *extremely rich in species of foreign origin* (Sukopp 1983, Sukopp & Werner 1987). A number of reasons may be given for this. However, little is known about their relative importance.

31. In principle, *two main causes* may be distinguished: (1) The main cause for the richness

---

[9] The term invasion mostly refers to what has long been researched in the field of 'anthropo-' or 'hemerochoria' and its consequences (Thellung 1918/19, and many others, *cf.* Trepl 1990a). However, the term places emphasis on purely biological aspects, *i.e.*, it insists on the bio-geographical foreignness of the invaders rather than on the *anthropogenic* surmounting of dispersal barriers. 'Immigration' (or also 'colonization') is often used in a similar sense, yet it is mostly not linked to the condition of bio-geographical foreignness. Hence it is the more comprehensive term in this respect.

of urban ecosystems in alien species possibly lies in the character of urban ecosystems themselves, *i.e.*, in their *high invasibility*, or vice versa, in their low resistance to the invasion of species. (2) The main reason may also lie in the fact that the propagules of alien species are transported to a greater extent to urban rather than to non-urban ecosystems. Consequently, the *conditions of dispersal* (introduction, transportation) and not of naturalisation would then be decisive.

32. Answering this question is a prerequisite for answering the further ones. It is presumably the most important question with regard to the future of urban communities (and, thus, of the most rapidly expanding part of ecosystems and communities all over the world), since it concerns far more extensive ecological (biocoenological) changes than may be brought about in the cities by future site changes. The question is: To what value will the species number increase as an effect of the introduction of alien species to cities? The starting-point for an answer are the following reflections (*cf.* Trepl & Sukopp 1993).

32a. In all or most parts of the world, the habitat or site conditions (in the sense of abiotic factors which are not modified by living things) would allow far more species to exist than can be found there at present. Thus, we have no reason to believe that the majority of species of the North American and East Asian temperate mixed deciduous forests, or those of the Colchis (*i.e.*, the nemoral zone) are excluded from the Central European flora and fauna for climatic or edaphic reasons (even though the climatic factors which are relevant for the species are less similar than could be expected from the corresponding annual average values, Jäger 1988). But also a very great number of species from other biogeographic areas are able to live in the Central European climate, as is made especially clear by the way in which exotic plants flourish in outdoor cultivation (*e.g.*, in botanic gardens).

32b. Their invasion was obstructed by geographic barriers most of which had existed since the early tertiary period. With the beginning of world-wide transport around the year 1500, these barriers have been removed for many species (Elton 1958). Now, the decisive question in our context is: For how many (and for which) species will the barriers be removed in the medium- and long-term? And is the removal of the dispersal barriers sufficient to facilitate the establishment of species in areas of favourable abiotic environmental conditions? To put it in extreme terms: Do we have to expect that in the long-term (and what is meant by long-term?) all bio-geographical realms which have been separated since the tertiary period will be (re-) mixed completely (*cf.* Elton 1958), so that on all sites more or less all species will be found which could live under the respective habitat conditions? Despite the world-wide extinction of a great number of species, this would end in a considerable increase in their local and regional numbers. The present decrease in the number of species – on the local and regional level! – would be of temporary nature.

32c. The removal of dispersal barriers presumably has far-reaching consequences especially for cities and settlements. The following reflection may show this: the vast majority of species are animals. The most important habitat elements for animals are – directly or indirectly speaking – plants. Therefore it seems reasonable to assume that animal species are kept away from climatically favourable areas (provided possibilities of introduction exist) by unsuitable vegetation: The necessary resources for relatively specialized species are not sufficiently provided by the plants. The possible number of animal species depends to a high degree on the number of plant species (besides, of course, their qualitative composition). Yet, the real number of plant species remains far below the number which would be possible under the site (climate) conditions. This is not only due to the dispersal barriers but also to interactions, especially competition. In urban settlements, however, less dispersion barriers exist and, in addition, the diversity of the species of the vegetation is (more or less) not limited by interspecific competition between plants. Wild grown plants (at least in Central European Cities, the increase of species caused by invasion far exceeds the loss due to extinction) and, above all, useful and ornamental plants considerably increase the number of plant species which are (potentially) relevant for anmimals. There are examples which show how exotic plants take the first steps in building up 'their' community by dragging behind them parts of the food chain beginning with them, mostly at intervals of decades (see e.g., Wilson 1937 on *Rhododendron ponticum*). That is to say that time has been too short as yet for most of the alien plant species presently found in the cities to 'drag behind' a greater number of animal species. Think of the enormous differences in number between animals living on indigenous plants and those living on alien ones (see e.g., Zwölfer 1973, Kennedy & Southwood 1984, Kowarik 1986). So there are many reasons to believe that there will be a considerable increase in the number of species in settlements. It will presumably exceed by far the result expected outside settlements as a consequence of the world-wide mixture of species. Under certain conditions, a substantial increase may have to be expected.

33. The weak point of such a prognosis is that we still have not found the answer to the above question (item 31) about the main cause of the urban communities' richness in alien species (conditions of naturalisation and of immigration). For our prognosis, this means:

1.   We do not know to what extent interaction between animals – i.e., biotic resistance – forces the possible maximum number of animal species below the upper limit determined by the climate and the vegetational component alone of the habitat.

2.   We can only speculate on the time the process of invasion will take until the world-wide intermixture – in so far as it is permitted by the anthropogenic surmounting of dispersal barriers – will be completed (hypothetically).

34. *The greatest gaps in research concern the process of transportation.* In particular, we do not know whether the process of introduction, i.e., the surmounting of dispersal barriers in general, has already reached its climax or not. There are diametrically opposed opinions on this. Some say that the immigration of alien species passed its climax in the last century. This was proved to be true of ferns and flowering plants, not only with regard to Central Europe but also to other industrialized zones; only in agricultural and industrial areas developed later its immigration still increasing (Jäger 1988). Others, in contrast, say: "Biological invasion is soon likely to acquire an even greater frequency, because of the current transportation systems and the forthcoming climatic change" (Di Castri 1990). The way our knowledge stands now, arguments for and against both opinions can be given (*cf.* Trepl & Sukopp 1993).

35. Hence we are not even in a position to predict approximately the value to which the number of species will rise. Neither can we substantiate the thesis that the figure will be reached within a few decades, nor the antithesis which says that it will only be reached after such a long time that one cannot reasonably assume that human settlements will exist under ecologic conditions similar to those existing today.

36. If we assume that the main reason for the great number of alien species in urban ecosystems is to be found in the conditions of immigration, then we may ask: What goes to make up those better conditions of immigration? What role does transport play in general? What roles do certain types of transportation of goods play? What consequences will their (foreseeable) modifications have on future transportation of species? What role do changes in the structure of space, like the formation of habitat islands, creation of linear structures

(transport routes) and (for dispersal over shorter distances) homogenisation of landscape play?

37. In contrast, the great number of alien species in urban ecosystems could be attributed mainly to properties of these ecosystems, *i.e.*, to the *conditions of naturalisation*. What are these properties?

    37a. A widely accepted view is that urban ecosystems are subject to strong *disturbances* and that disturbances generally *increase invasibility*. Accordingly, 'ideal invaders' would be species which are particularly suited to adapt themselves to disturbed areas ('ideal weed', Baker 1965, r-strategists, ruderals, Grime 1979). Yet this opinion is also contradicted, inter alia with reference to the fact (?) that the majority of the successful invaders are specialists rather than generalists, as would have to be expected under the above conditions (Newsome & Noble 1986).

    37b. Another widely supported theory says that a great *diversity of species increases the community's resistance to invasion* (*e.g.*, Elton 1958, Fox & Fox 1986, Brown 1989). This opinion is disputed as well (*e.g.*, Simberloff 1986, 1989, *cf*. Trepl 1993). What would this mean for urban ecosystems against the background that cities (but not the single ecosystem of the urban mosaic) are generally richer in species than those of the surroundings of cities? Before answering this question, the correlation between species diversity and resistance must be made plain. The most important types of interaction (competition, herbivory, predation, parasitism, mutualism) would have to be examined as to their importance for biological invasion (see *e.g.*, Crawley 1987, Brown 1989, Pimm 1989, Trepl 1994).

38. The contradictions mentioned may be put down to the fact that there are different (types of) communities responding differently to the invasion of alien species and that especially *disturbances and species diversity in different communities have a different effect on the possibilities of successful immigration* or the prevention of it. Accordingly, there would be no 'good' or 'bad' invaders among the alien species but rather 'functional groups' showing good or bad colonizing abilities in different (types of) communities (Newsome & Noble 1986, Noble 1989).

    38a. Following the distinction underlined by Schoener (1986b, 1986c), we have to differentiate above all between two basic situations: assuming that the resources competed for are divisible (*e.g.*, different parts of a plant serve different insects as food) and competition is consequently specific, we may well believe that a loss of certain species (and thus a reduction in the number of species) would result in niche gaps which very often or usually cannot be filled with species already present in community, but perhaps by invaders which are particularly suited to the respective niches (*cf* Lawton 1984, Trepl 1990b).

    38b. In the opposite case, the resources are homogenous and indivisible. This is to say that more or less all species compete for the same resources. Competition, thus, is non-specific ('diffuse'). This is especially the case with plants which all compete mainly for the same resources (light, water, nutrients), although differences in demand have partly developed, which reduce competition (Richardson 1980). Under these circumstances, the loss of certain species, *i.e.* the reduction of the number of species, is not to the benefit of the invaders. In this case the neighbours already present are in a position to close the gap themselves – since they have the same niche and, consequently, can make use of the same resources which were used by the lost species (example: decline of *Castanea dentata*, Woods & Shanks 1959). In principle, invaders could also become established in the gaps – communities of the mentioned type can never be 'saturated' or 'immune'. However, the establishment of invaders is less probable since they are not immediately close at hand, as a rule. With regard to plants, hence, the thesis could be formulated that open space as a result of destruction of the biomass constitutes the only general and real resistance-reducing factor (Rejmanek 1989), and not poverty in species (*cf.* Trepl 1990b, 1994).

38c. Following Bazzaz (1986), the characteristics of the invading species (*i.e.*, rules of invasion), may only be predictable in case of invasions in disturbed communities, and not in undisturbed ones. This can be explained on the basis of what has been described above. The situation in which disturbance facilitates invasion corresponds to a large degree to that of 'unspecific competition': the disturbance creates the necessary gaps in the closed population and most disturbances do not in the main affect only one or a few particular species. The examples of successful invasion in undisturbed communities, however, are mostly cases of 'specific competition' (except the invaders concerned are generally dominant in competition, *i.e.*, apt to replace indigenous species even without prior disturbance, *e.g.*, in the course of vegetative spread). The characteristics of the invaders complement those of the species already present. Therefore, you find a combination of plant species well suited to one another.

39. Starting from the assumption that urban ecosystems show the above characteristics (chapter I), *i.e.*, that there are comparatively few relations between the elements and – in particular – hardly any co-evolutionary developments, we may then conclude that a successful *invasion in urban communities would be less of the niche-specific, complementary type.* Further, we may conclude that unspecific disturbance would increase the possibility of invasion, that general characteristics of 'good invaders' could be indicated and that the number of species would not be a resistance-increasing factor (for the latter *cf.* Kuznetzova 1992).

40. Consequently, the fact that there is a particularly large *decrease* in the number of *indigenous species* in urban areas (*cf. e.g.*, Auhagen & Sukopp 1982) may *not* be considered (by and large) as *the reason for* the large *increase in the number of aliens* (in the sense that they fill the gaps in the niche produced by the losses). However, the factors causing the decrease in indigenous species (to a certain extent, they may also be included as 'disturbances') constitute, at the same time, an important reason for the increase in aliens.

41. According to what is said above (item 31), one of the most important tasks consists in assessing the relative importance of the conditions under which immigration or introduction takes place and the invasibility or resistance of the target ecosystems (*cf.* Erkamo 1961). Yet this is very difficult, since it is very often the case that exactly in those areas where an increasing rate of disturbance (perhaps the most important factor increasing invasibility within the communities) can be observed, an increasing rate of immigration can be expected, as well. This is true of most ecosystems with a particularly high number of alien species, *e.g.*, ecosystems of oceanic islands, river valleys and, especially, cities.

42. What is *necessary* here are *tests showing the community's influence on the chances of establishment* (or the effects of the particular species' inclination to becoming established). To this end, equal rates of immigration must be provided for in experiments, or situations must be found in which these conditions are expected to be fulfilled. In order to prove the relevance of immigration conditions, it is necessary to examine real or experimentally created situations which show great differences as to the introduction of species under similar conditions in the target objects, or in which particular species only differ from one another with regard to their possibility to reach new home areas (and not with regard to their possibilities of becoming established after arrival).

Acknowledgements

For helpful comments I am very grateful to John Celicea, Paris, George Barker, Peterborough, Frank Golley, Georgia, Franz Rebele, Berlin, Herbert Sukopp, Berlin, Wang Rusong, Beijing, Wolfgang Haber, München, and Almut Huber, Berlin. For discussion I wish to thank the participants of the 'First Meeting on an International Network for Urban Ecology' in Berlin 1991: Axel Auhagen, Germany, David Goode, United Kingdom, Dimitri Kavtaradze, USSR, Akira Miyawaki, Japan, Pedro Palomo, Spain, Uwe Starfinger, Germany, and Pzemyslaw Trojan, Poland.

References

Augagen, A. & Sukopp, H. 1982. Auswertung der Roten Liste der wildwachsenden Farn- und Blütenpflanzen von Berlin (West) für den Arten und Biotopschutz. Landschaftsentwicklung und Umweltforschung 11: 5–18.

Baker, H.G. 1965. Characteristics and modes of origin of weeds. In: Baker, H.G. & Stebbins, G.L. (eds.) 1965: The genetics of colonizing species. New York, London, pp. 149–169.

Bazzaz, F.A. 1986. Life history of colonizing plants: Some demographic, genetic, and physiological features. In: Mooney, H.A. & Drake, J.A. (eds.) 1986: Ecology of biological invasions of North America and Hawaii. Ecological Studies 58: 96–110.

Böhme, G., Daele, W. van den, & Krohn, W. 1973. Die Finalisierung der Wissenschaft. Zeitschr. f. Soziologie 2 (2): 128–144.

Brown, J.H. 1989. Patterns, modes and extents of invasions by vertebrates. In: Drake, J.A., Mooney, H.A., di Castri, F., Groves, R.H., Kruger, F.J., Rejmánek, M., Williamson, M. (eds.) 1989: Biological invasions: A global perspective. Chichester, New York, Brisbane, Toronto, Singapur, pp. 85–109.

Chesson, P.L. & Case, T.J. 1986. Overview: nonequilibrium community theories: chance, variability, history and coexistence. In: Diamond, J. & Case, T.J. (eds.): Community ecology. New York, pp. 333–343.

Clements, F.E. 1916. Plant succession. An analysis of the development of vegetation. Carnegie Institution of Washington, Publ. No. 242.

Clements, F.E. 1936. Nature and structure of the climax. J. Ecol. 24: 252–284.

Connell, J.H. & Slayter, R.O. 1977. Mechanisms of succession in natural communities and their role in community stability and organisation. American Naturalist 111: 1119–1144.

Connell, J.H. 1978. Diversity in tropical rain forests and coral reefs. Science 199: 1302–1310.

Crawley, M.J. 1987: What makes a community invasible? In: Gray, A.J., Crawley, M.J. & Edwards, P.J. (eds.): Colonization, succession and stability. Oxford, pp. 429–454.

Di Castri, F. 1990. On invading species and invaded ecosystems: the interplay of historical chance and biological necessity. In: Di Castri, F., Hansen, A.J. & Debussche, M. (eds.): Biological invasions in Europe and the Mediterranean Basin. Dordrecht, pp. 3–16.

Drury, W.H. & Nisbet, I.C.T. 1973. Succession. Arnold Arbor. J. 54 (3): 331–368.

Duvigneaud, P. & Denaeyer-de Smet, S. 1975. L'écosystéme urbain. Application à l'agglomération bruxelloise. Colloque international organisé par l'Agglomération de Bruxelles, Bruxelles.

Egler, F.E. 1954. Vegetation science concepts. I. Initial floristic composition: a factor in old-field vegetation development. Vegetatio 4: 412–417.

Ellenberg, H. 1973. Versuch einer Klassifikation der Ökosysteme nach funktionalen Gesichtspunkten. In: Ellenberg, H. (ed.): Ökosystemforschung. Berlin, Heidelberg, New York.

Elton, C.S. 1958. The ecology of invasions by animals and plants. London.

Engelberg, J. & Boyarsky, L.L. 1979. The noncybernetic nature of ecosystems. Am. Nat. 114: 317–324.

Erkamo, V. 1961. Über die Synanthropen in der finnischen Flora. Fennia 85: 82–85.

Falinski, B. (ed.) 1971. Synanthropisation of plant cover II: Synanthropic flora and vegetation of towns connected with their natural conditions, history and function. (Poln., engl. summary). Mater. Zakl. Fitosoc. Stos. U.W. Warszawa-Bialowieza 27: 1–317.

Fox, M.D. & Fox, B.J. 1986. The susceptibility of natural communities to invasion. In: Groves, R.H. & Burdon, J.J. (eds.) 1986: Ecology of biological invasions: An Australian perspective. Canberra, pp. 57–66.

Gleason, H.A. 1926: The individualistic concept of the plant association. Bull. Torrey Bot. Club 53: 7–26.

Gray, A.J., Crawley, M.J. & Edwards, P.J. (eds.) 1987. Colonization, succession and stability. The 26th Symposium of the British Ecological Society held with the Linnean Society of London. Oxford etc.

Grime, J.P. 1979. Plant strategies and vegetation processes. Chichester, New York, Brisbane, Toronto.

Hard, G. 1973. Die Geographie. Eine wissenschaftstheoretische Einführung. Berlin, New York.

Harper, J. 1977. Population biology of plants. London.

Hengeveld, R. 1989. Dynamics of biological invasions. London, New York.

Higashi, M. & Burns, T.P. (eds.) 1991. Theoretical studies of ecosystems: the network perspective. Cambridge, New York.

Horn, H.S. 1976. Succession. In: May, R.M. (ed.): Theoretical ecology. Principles and Applications, Philadelphia, pp. 187–204.

Hubbell, S.P. & Foster, R.B. 1986. Biology, chance, and history and the structure of tropical rain forest tree communities. In: Diamond, J. & Case, T.J. (eds.): Community ecology. New York, pp. 314–329.

Jäger, E.J. 1988. Möglichkeiten und Prognose synanthroper Pflanzenausbreitungen. Flora 180: 101–131.

Kennedy, C.E.J. & Southwood, T.R.E. 1984. The number of species of insects associated with British trees: A re-analysis. Journal Animal. Ecol. 53.

Kikkawa, J. & Anderson, D.J. (eds.) 1986. Community ecology: pattern and process. Melbourne, Oxford, London, Edinburgh, Boston, Palo Alto (Blackwell Scientific Publ.).

Kikkawa, J. 1986. Complexity, diversity and stability. In: Kikkawa, J. & Anderson, D.J. (eds.) 1986: Community ecology: Pattern and process. Melbourne, Oxford, London, Edinburgh, Boston, Palo Alto.

Kostrowicki, A.S. 1979. Mechanisms stabilizing the structure of phytocoenoses subjected to an increasing impact of man management. Memorabilia Zool. 32: 25–36.

Kowarik, I. 1986. Ökosystemorientierte Gehölzartenwahl für Grünflächen. Das Gartenamt 35: 524–532.

Kunick, W. 1982. Zonierung des Stadtgebietes von Berlin-West. Ergebnisse floristischer Untersuchungen. Landschaftsentwicklung und Umweltforschung 14.

Kuznetzova, N.A. 1992. Structure of collembolan population as indicator of tree plantation state in urban areas. Paper presented at: II European Meeting of the Intecol and UNESCO-MAB International Network for Urban Ecology, Dec. 15–17, Warsaw.

Lawton, J.H. 1984. Non-competitive populations, non-convergent communities, and vacant niches: The herbivores of Bracken. In: Strong, D.R., Simberloff, D., Abele, L.G. & Thistle, A.B. (eds.) 1984: Ecological communities: Conceptual issues and the evidence. Princeton, New Jersey, pp. 67–99.

Leeuwen, C. van 1966. A relational theoretical approach to pattern and process in vegetation. Wentia 15.

Lohmeyer, W. & Sukopp, H. 1992. Agriophyten Mitteleuropas. Schriftenreihe für Vegetationskunde. 25: 7–185.

Margalef, R. 1968. Perspectives in ecological theory. Chicago.

Margalef, R. 1984. Simple facts about life and the environment not to forget in preparing schoolbooks for our grandchildren. In: Cooley, J.H. & Golley, F.B. (eds.) 1984: Trends in ecological research for the 1980s. NATO conference series I: Ecology, pp. 299–319.

McIntosh, R.P. 1985. The background of ecology. Cambridge.

Miles, J. 1987. Vegetation succession: Past and present perceptions. In: Gray, A.J., Crawley, M.J. & Edwards, P.J. (eds.) 1987: Colonization, succession and stability. Blackwell, Oxford: 1–29.

Newsome, E.A. & Noble, I.R. 1986. Ecological and physiological characters of invading species. In: Groves, R.H. & Burdon, J.J. (eds.) 1986: Ecology of biological invasions: An Australian perspective. Canberra, pp. 1–20.

Noble, I.R. 1989. Attributes of invaders and the invading process: terrestrial and vascular plants. In: Drake, J.A., Mooney, H.A., di Castri, F., Groves, R.H., Kruger, F.J., Rejmánek, M., Williamson, M. (eds.) 1989: Biological invasions: A global perspective. Chichester, New York, Brisbane, Toronto, Singapur, pp. 301–313.

Odum, E.P. 1969. The strategy of ecosystem development. Science 164: 262–270.

Orians, G.H. 1975. Diversity, stability and maturity in natural ecosystems. In: Dobben, W.H. van, & Lowe-McConnell, R.H. (eds.): Unifying concepts of ecology. Den Haag.

Patten, B.C. 1985. Energy cycling in the ecosystem. Ecol. Modelling 28: 1–71.

Patten, B.C. & Odum, E.P. 1981. The cybernetic nature of ecosystems. Am. Nat. 118: 886–895.

Pimm, S.L. 1989. Theories of predicting success and impact of introduced species. In: Drake, J.A., Mooney, H.A., di Castri, F., Groves, R.H., Kruger, F.J., Rejmánek, M., Williamson, M. (eds.) 1989: Biological invasions: A global perspective. Chichester, New York, Brisbane, Toronto, Singapur, pp. 351–388.

Price, P.W. 1984. Communities of specialists: vacant niches in ecological and evolutionary time. In: Strong, D.R., Simberloff, D., Abele, L.G. & Thistle, A.B. (eds.) 1984: Ecological communities: Conceptual issues and the evidence. Princeton, New Jersey, pp. 510–523.

Ravera, O. 1984. Considerations on some ecological principles. In: Cooley, J.H. & Golley, F.B. (eds.): Trends in ecological research for the 1980s. NATO Conference Series I: Ecology.

Reiter, H. 1885. Die Consolidation der Physiognomik als Versuch einer Oekologie der Gewächse. Graz.

Rejmánek, M. 1989. Invasibility of plant communities. In: Drake, J.A., Mooney, H.A., di Castri, F., Groves, R.H., Kruger, F.J., Rejmánek, M., Williamson, M. (eds.) 1989: Biological invasions: A global perspective. Chichester, New York, Brisbane, Toronto, Singapur, pp. 369–388.

Richardson, J.L. 1980. The organismic concept: Resilience of an embattled ecological concept. BioScience 30 (7): 465–471.

Roughgarden, J., May, R.M., Levin, S.A. (eds.) 1989. Perspectives in ecological theory. Princeton.

Rummel, J. & Roughgarden, J. 1983. Some differences between invasion-structured and coevolution-structured competitive communities. Oikos 41: 477–486.

Saarinen, E. (ed.) 1982. Conceptual issues in ecology. Dordrecht, Boston, London.

Sanders, H.L. 1969. Benthic marine diversity and the stability-time hypothesis. In: Woodwell, G.M. & Smith, H.H. (eds.): Diversity and stability in ecological systems (Brookhaven Symposia in Biology 22). Upton, New York, pp. 71–81.

Schoener, T.W. 1986a. Mechanistic approaches to community ecology: a new reductionism? Am. Zool. 26: 81–106.

Schoener, T.W. 1986b. Overview: Kinds of ecological communities – ecology becomes pluralistic. In: Diamond, J. & Case, T.J. (eds.) Community ecology. New York, pp. 467–479.

Schoener, T.W. 1986c. Resource partitioning. In: Kikkawa, J. & Anderson, D.J. (eds.) 1986: Community ecology: Pattern and process. Melbourne, Oxford, London, Edinburgh, Boston, Palo Alto, pp. 91–126.

Simberloff, D. 1986. Introduced insects: A biogeographic and systematic perspective. In: Mooney, H.A. & Drake, J A. (eds.): Ecology of biological invasions of North America and Hawaii. Ecological Studies 58: 3–26.

Simberloff, D. 1989. Which insect introductions succeed and which fail? In: Drake, J.A., Mooney, H.A., di Castri, F., Groves, R.H., Kruger, F.J., Rejmánek, M., Williamson, M. (eds.) 1989: Biological invasions: A global perspective. Chichester, New York, Brisbane, Toronto, Singapur, pp. 61–83.

Solbrig, O.T. 1991. Biodiversity. Scientific issues and collaborative research proposals. MAB Digest 9: 1–77.

Stöcker, G. 1979. Ökosystem – Begriff und Konzeption. Archiv für Naturschutz und Landschaftsforschung 19 (3): 157–176.

Strong, D.R., Simberloff, D., Abele, L.G. & Thistle, A.B. (eds.) 1984. Ecological communities: Conceptual issues and the evidence. Princeton, New Jersey.

Sukopp, H. 1972. Wandel von Flora und Vegetation unter dem Einfluß des Menschen. Ber. Landwirtsch. 50: 112–139.

Sukopp, H. 1973. Die Großstadt als Gegenstand ökologischer Forschung. Schrift. Ver. Verbreitung naturwiss. Kenntn. Wien, 113: 90–140.

Sukopp, H. 1983. Ökologische Charakteristik von Großstädten. In: Akademie für Raumforschung (ed.): Grundriß der Stadtplanung. Hannover, pp. 53–1.

Sukopp, H., Hejny, S. & Kowarik, I. (eds.) 1990. Urban ecology. Plants and plant communities in urban environments. The Hague (SPB Academic Publishing).

Sukopp, H. & Weiler, S. 1986. Biotopkartierung im besiedelten Bereich der Bundesrepublik Deutschland. Landschaft + Stadt 18: 25–37.

Sukopp, H. & Werner, P. 1987. Development of flora and fauna in urban areas. Nature and environment series No. 36 (Council of Europe), pp. 1–67.

Thellung, A. 1918-19. Zur Terminologie der Adventiv- und Ruderalfloristik. Allg. Bot. Zeitschr. 24/25 (9–12): 36–42.

Thomasius, H. 1988. Sukzession, Produktivität und Stabilität natürlicher und künstlicher Waldökosysteme. Archiv für Naturschutz und Landschaftsforschung 28 (1): 3–20.

Trepl, L. 1987. Geschichte der Ökologie. Vom 17. Jahrhundert bis zur Gegenwart. Zehn Vorlesungen. Frankfurt/M.

Trepl, L. 1990a. Research on the anthropogenic migration of plants and naturalization. Its history and current state of development. In: Sukopp, H., Hejny, S. & Kowarik I. (eds.): Urban ecology. Plants and plant communities in urban environments. SPB Academic Publishing bv, Den Haag, pp. 75–97.

Trepl, L. 1990b. Zum Problem der Resistenz von Pflanzengesellschaften gegen biologische Invasionen. Verh. Berl. Bot. Ver. 8: 195–230.

Trepl, L. 1992. Zur Vorgeschichte der Ökologie im 19. Jahrhundert. Verhandlungen der Gesellschaft für Ökologie XXI: 35–41.

Trepl, L. 1993. Biologische Invasionen als Modell für Probleme der Freisetzung gentechnisch veränderter Organismen – zur Frage der 'Resistenz' von Lebensgemeinschaften. In: Umweltbundesamt (ed.): Ermittlung und Bewertung des ökologischen Risikos im Umgang mit gentechnisch veränderten Organismen. Dokumentation eines Fachgespräches am 14. und 15. Oktober 1991. Berlin, pp. 147–160.

Trepl, I. 1994. Zur Rolle interspezifischer Konkurrenz bei der Einbürgerung von Pflanzenarten. Archiv für Naturschutz und Landschaftsforschung 33: 61–84.

Trepl, L. & Sukopp, H. 1993. Zur Bedeutung der Introduktion und Naturalisation von Pflanzen und Tieren für die Zukunft der Artenvielfalt. Bayerische Akademie der Wissenschaften (ed.): Rundgespräche der Kommission für Ökologie 'Dynamik von Flora und Fauna – Artenvielfalt und ihre Erhaltung', Verlag Pfeil, München, pp. 127–142.

Trojan, P. 1984. Ecosystem homeostasis. Warszawa.

Turcek, F.J. 1961. Ökologische Beziehungen der Vögel und Gehölze. Bratislava.

Ulanowicz, R.E. 1986. A phenomenological perspective of ecological development. Special Technical Publication 921: 73–81.

Ulanowicz, R.E. 1990. Aristotelean causalities in ecosystem development. Oikos 57: 42–48.

Westhoff, V. 1968. Die ausgeräumte Landschaft – biologische Verarmung und Bereicherung der Kulturlandschaften. In: Buchwald, K. & Engelhardt, W. (eds.): Handbuch für Landschaftspflege und Naturschutz 2, München, Wien, pp. 1–10.

Wiens, J.A. 1984. On understanding a non-equilibrium world: myth and reality in community patterns and processes. In: Strong, D.R., Simberloff, D., Abele, L.G. & Thistle, A.B. (eds.) 1984: Ecological communities: Conceptual issues and the evidence. Princeton, New Jersey, pp. 439–457.

Wilson, G.F. 1937. Insect pests of the genus Rhododendron. Proc. 7th Int. Congr. Entomol. 1938, 4: 2296–2323.

Woods, F.W. & Shanks, R. 1959. Natural replacement of chestnut by other species in the Great Smoky Mountains National Park. Ecology 40: 349–361.

Zwölfer, H. 1973. Possibilities and limitation in biological control of weeds. OEP/EPPO Bull. 3 (3): 19–30.

APPROACHES TO STUDYING SPONTANEOUS SETTLEMENT FLORA AND VEGETATION IN CENTRAL EUROPE: A REVIEW

PETR PYŠEK

Institute of Applied Ecology, University of Agriculture Prague CZ-281 63 Kostelec nad Černými lesy, Czech Republic

Abstract

Critical evaluation of methods currently used in the study of spontaneous plant cover in human settlements is presented. Flora and vegetation are discussed from the viewpoint of their (1) recording and description, (2) quantitative assessment, (3) relationships to the environment, and (4) dynamics. Studies on urban vegetation in central Europe are still mostly limited by the traditional phytosociological approach. Research in urban flora is considered to have brought more results of general validity. Further investigations should rely upon new attitudes and ask for general questions. However, reviews and reanalyses of previously published data can also yield results of general validity. Management of urban landscapes can profit considerably from the studies on plant cover. Closer international cooperation is, however, needed since there are still great differences in research efforts, methods and results obtained between central European countries.

1. Introduction: aims and definitions

Flora and vegetation in settlement habitats are recently receiving more attention, especially in central Europe; there is hardly any other region in the world that has been studied so extensively (Sukopp 1972, Bornkamm *et al.*, 1982, Kornaś 1983, Sukopp *et al.*, 1990; see Wittig 1991 for a detailed history of research in cities). This is partially due to their growing importance which is linked with ever increasing synanthropization of vegetation (Sukopp 1969, 1972, Kornaś 1983). The present boom of interest in settlement vegetation has several aspects: (1) It is now known that there is a specific flora and vegetation in cities representing a suitable object to be studied by plant ecologists and geographers. (2) The relationship of the public to spontaneous and cultivated urban flora and vegetation has changed; it is now generally accepted that it is a valuable part of urban environment, an opinion which was not common a few years ago. Moreover, (3) results of such studies are useful for practical purposes such as urban land management (Schulte *et al.*, 1986, Sukopp *et al.*, 1986, Sukopp & Weiler 1988, Rebele 1991).

The term 'urban vegetation' includes all types of both spontaneous and cultivated vegetation occurring in cities (Sukopp & Werner 1983); however, less is known about the latter. The present study thus considers only spontaneous vascular flora and vegetation; for lists of studies on the distribution of planted trees, lichens, mosses and fungi in urban environments see *e.g.*, Sukopp & Werner (1983) and for an updated review of results in this field see Wittig (1991). Areas with a total population exceeding 150,000 and with at least 1000 inhabitants per square km are usually considered urban agglomerations (Sukopp & Werner 1983). The present review is, however, extended to human settlements in general and therefore covers studies on flora and vegetation of small villages as well, since comparisons between settlements of different sizes can yield interesting results (Pyšek & Pyšek 1990, 1991b).

Flora and vegetation are treated separately in the following sections but 'plant cover' is

Urban Ecology as the Basis of Urban Planning, p. 23–39
edited by H. Sukopp, M. Numata and A. Huber
© 1995 SPB Academic Publishing bv, Amsterdam, The Netherlands

used as a general term to include both of them (Kornaś 1983). There is an extensive body of papers on plant cover in human settlements. Only the important references are mentioned in this review, with preference being given to papers which cover certain topics in detail. The list of references is therefore far from complete and more information may be obtained from the studies cited. Instead, this text is focused on critical evaluation of methods currently used in studies on plant cover of human settlements.

2. Recording flora and vegetation

2.1. Floristic lists and species numbers

Compiling floristic lists in human settlements started as long ago as the last century (Scholz 1960, Klotz 1987); the earliest investigations were concerned with introduction of aliens (e.g., Scheuermann 1928, see Wittig 1991). Nowadays, many data are availabe. Pyšek (1993) summarized species numbers reported for 56 central European cities from which 22 were located in Germany and 29 in Poland (for other summarizing studies see Krawiecowa & Rostanski 1976, Kunick 1982, Kowarik 1985, Pyšek 1989a, Klotz 1988, 1990). This list is, however, not considered complete.

The species number reported for a given city may vary considerably, not only due to environmental conditions but also according to the approaches of the respective authors (Pyšek 1989a, Brandes & Zacharias 1990). These can differ in the choice of study area, i.e., whether the fringe area between city and its surroundings is included or not (Haeupler 1974, Sukopp & Werner 1983). A taxonomic approach involved and considering or omitting particular chorological groups may further bias the resulting species number. It appears to be particularly important whether the species escaping from cultivation, garden weeds and ephemerophytes are recorded or not. Moreover, complicated terminology linked with immigration processes (Holub & Jirásek 1967, Schroeder 1969, Sudnik-Wójcikowska & Kozniewska 1988) can sometimes make the comparison of individual lists more difficult. It should be therefore always clearly stated which plant groups were excluded from the list (Sukopp & Weiler 1988). It is also necessary to consider the differences in the area studied; for example the study of Kunick (1974) in which 994 species were reported from Berlin, covered 18 km^2, whereas including the city area of 580 km^2 yielded 1432 species (Kowarik 1990a). The importance of research duration is demonstrated by the following example: investigations over several years on the flora of Warszawa (Sudnik-Wójcikowska 1987, 1988) recorded more than double (1416) the species number of 604 obtained in the 1960's. Some increase in the absolute species numbers reported for the analysed cities might be expected if more thorough and long-term investigations are carried out. However, in those cities where a detailed research has been conducted for a long time, the numbers seem to be near reality and further enrinchment of species lists would be mainly due to ephemeral occurrences of randomly introduced aliens or species escaped from cultivation. One should bear in mind that reported species numbers are usually derived by simply adding the new records to those of previous years, and are thus the cumulative number of species over the research period. This means that the number of species present at a given moment within the territory of the city would be somewhat lower. Nevertheless, these details are not expected to affect the general relationships between flora richness and settlement features.

City size, whether expressed in terms of population or area, is the environmental factor to which species number is most closely related (Klotz 1988, 1990, Pyšek 1989a, 1993, Brandes & Zacharias 1990). Habitat heterogeneity and increased possibilities of immigration of new species are the main causes of flora enrichment (Sukopp et al., 1979a, Sukopp & Werner 1983). Floristic richness of a given surrounding geographical area may also influence the number of urban species (Pyšek 1989a). The species number in European cities shows a log linear increase with the city size and approaches a maximum of about 1500 in cities with 1.5–2 million inhabitants (Pyšek 1989a, 1993, Klotz 1990). A total of 2061 species was recorded by Kunick (1982) in 9 large cities located on a longitudinal gradient. In villages, the effects of climate on species richness are more apparent than in cities (Pyšek 1993).

A higher species number in cities in comparison to the surrounding countryside was first pointed out by Walters (1970). Haeupler (1974), by dividing the countryside (Lower Saxony, Germany) into 5 × 5 km squares, found a higher species number in those squares containing a town. Pyšek (1992b) confirmed this pattern by considering more studies (Wittig & Durwen 1982, Kunick 1983, Kowarik 1985, Brandes 1987, Pyšek & Pyšek 1988a) but concluded that it is necessary to compare the given city with an area of surrounding landscape of approximately the same size. Unfortunately, this condition is not always kept. An alternative method is to document the changes by using transects running from the city centre to the adjacent landscape; it is then not necessary to compare complete cities with adjacent areas of equal size.

Kornaś (1983) pointed out that floristic data have been mostly collected without even the simplest quantitative methods, which he considered especially troublesome in attempts to assess historical changes. It is useful to characterize the occurrence of a species in a given settlement with some quantitative parameter. Mutual comparison of floristic lists containing such data usually provides more precise results and often reveals relationships that would otherwise be overlooked (Bornkamm 1987b, Pyšek & Pyšek 1988b, Kowarik & Seidling 1989).

Frequency, *i.e.*, the percentage of equal squares in which the species was recorded, can be used (Kunick 1974, Sudnik-Wójcikowska 1987); an alternative measure is the proportion of investigated localities in which the species occurred (Pyšek & Pyšek 1988a). When flora in a large number of villages is studied, the percentage of villages in which the species was found is a convenient measure of its commonness or rarity (Wittig 1984, Wittig & Wittig 1986, Pyšek & Pyšek 1988b, 1991b).

2.2. Description of vegetation and its quantitative assessment

Description of vegetation in central Europe is almost exclusively linked with the phytosociological approach (Mueller-Dombois & Ellenberg 1974). There was an extensive discussion on the merits of phytosociology during the last few years (*e.g.*, Feoli 1984, Herben 1986, Wiegleb 1986, Eliáš 1988, Krahulec & Lepš 1989, Moravec 1989, Klimeš 1989, Pyšek 1991). In general, the current opinion is often critical concerning mostly (1) the subjective choice of sampling plots, (2) sometimes untrustworthy or even obscure classification process, (3) the unconvincing concept of 'characteristic' species, (4) the overlooking of lower hierarchical levels and ignoring of underlying mechanisms, (5) the extensive body of special terminology and different understanding of terms (see Herben 1986, Wiegleb 1987, Krahulec & Lepš 1989 for details). This apparent subjectivity together with an insistence on treating phytosociological units as objective biological entities (see *e.g.*, Mucina 1982 cited by Eliáš 1988, Moravec 1989) has resulted in a deep misunderstanding between phytosociology and contemporary vegetation science (Herben 1986, Krahulec & Lepš 1989). The advantages of methods of numerical syntaxonomy (see Mucina & van der Maarel 1989 for review) appear to have been rather overestimated. Despite their usefulness (analysis of large data sets, brief presentation of results, relating vegetation features to the environment) they have failed in solving classification problems (Klimeš 1989).

General classification troubles are even more pronounced in studies of settlement vegetation because of spatial and temporal variability (Klimeš 1989, Pyšek 1991). This vegetation is composed mostly of species with wide ecological amplitudes and develops towards more uniform forms without recognizable characteristics. It is therefore increasingly more difficult to classify (Kopecký & Hejný 1978, Sukopp & Werner 1983). Relations of characteristic species to the units of phytosociological systems are very vague and classification of ruderal communities is mostly based on prevailing (so-called dominant) species (Pyšek 1991). Many vegetation types, even some of the commonest, are simply ignored due to classification problems (Klimeš 1989, Pyšek 1991).

The consequences of these problems are in some cases almost comical: Klimeš (1989) showed that two phytosociological systems covering the same area (southern Slovakia), compiled by different authors (Mucina 1982, Eliáš 1984, 1986) were completely unable to be compared because of each author's subjectivity and strong preference for units of their own creation. Such a decisive influence of a particular author's approach can be further seen in the relation between number of communities[1] recorded which may be expected to increase with the size of the area. However, the correlation found by Klimeš (1989) who plotted data from 30 studies was only at the border of significance. Similarly, Pyšek (1991) pointed to a conspicuous increase in the number of reported communities in both settlements and open landscape habitats during the last decade. There is no meaningful ecological explanation for such a trend and instead the gradual depauperation of settlement vegetation has been reported elsewhere (Brandes 1981, Pyšek 1983, Sukopp 1983, Kornaś 1990). Subjectivity of authors' approaches and resulting different understanding of basic phytosociological units are thus mainly involved; *e.g.*, Wittig (1973) gives 32 communities for Münster, whereas Gödde (1986) having used different classification methods recorded 110 communities in the same city.

Currently, ruderal phytosociology is mostly identified with syntaxonomy and it is frequently understood as being rather a means of classifying communities. This is reflected by the publishing of extensive surveys of phytosociological units (*e.g.*, Eliás 1984, 1986, Mucina & Maglocký 1985, Višňák 1986) without assessment of their ecology and dynamics. Many studies are of a purely descriptive nature and lack any attempt to reveal the relationships between vegetation and its environment. Description of environmental factors is often vague. Nowadays, this holds especially for Czech Republic, Slovakia and Poland. However, examples of phytosociological studies involving a more ecological approach do exist in these countries (*e.g.*, Kopecký 1980-84).

Attempts to cope with classification problems resulted in modifications of classification attitudes, such as the 'synsociological concept' used *e.g.*, by Kienast (1978, 1980), Hüllbusch (1978), Hard (1982) — see Klotz *et al.* (1984) for the list of references. Of these attempts, the so-called deductive method (Kopecký & Hejný 1974, 1978) may be considered the most promising. It has been used quite frequently (see Kopecký 1988 for review) and its strengths were demonstrated especially in the series of papers by Kopecký (1980-84, 1986). The method makes it possible to classify most of the stands found in the field; this is particularly important because those communities which can be considered as associations (*i.e.*, those having their association characteristic species) are diminishing (Pyšek 1992a). It is clearly seen when quantitative data are available: *e.g.*, in the factories of Prague such communities contributed only 10% to the total area covered by vegetation (Pyšek & Pyšek 1988c) and in the villages of the Bohemian Karst the value was 18% (Pyšek 1992a). Furthermore, the deductive method is much more able to record vegetation dynamics as exemplified by description of the gradual spread of native species to man-made habitats (so-called 'apophytization process') (Kopecký 1984b). The method allows the recognition of a large number of units (although this increase is not necessarily linked with its introduction, see Pyšek 1991, Kopecký 1990a), which may lead to the loss of clarity of the phytosociological system.

The final product of phytosociological research of a given area is therefore a survey of communities. This may, however, range from a simple list of units recorded in a single vil-

---

[1]Understood here as basic hytosociological units recognized by respective author, *e.g.*, associations and units of corresponding level.

lage to the extensive survey critically evaluating vegetation over a large area. The former case is nothing more than 'vegetation floristics' but the latter one is undoubtedly of great value (*e.g.*, Passarge 1964, Gutte 1972, Hejný *et al.*, 1979, Oberdorfer 1983, Kopecký & Hejný 1990). A comprehensive review on phytosociological research in the cities of former eastern Europe, was published by Mucina (1990), and other summarized information regarding this issue may be found in Klotz *et al.* (1984), Sukopp & Köstler (1986), Sowa & Olaczek (1987), Klotz (1987).

Concerning the quantitative assessment of vegetation, the number of communities in a given settlement was shown to be a rather unreliable character. It is less correlated with the city size than is the species number (Pyšek 1993). However, results gathered by the same author or by a group of people using a similar approach are expected to be more comparable. Pyšek (1993) gives numbers of communities for 39 European towns, of which 12 are in Czech and Slovak Republics, 9 in Germany and 18 in Poland, and for 85 Czech villages (Pyšek 1981, Pyšek & Pyšek 1985). Large sets of villages have been studied in Germany as well (Wittig & Wittig 1986, Dechent 1988, Brandes *et al.*, 1990).

To express the occurrence of a community in a given settlement, the same relative measures as for evaluation of individual species can be used (frequency, number of localities). However, phytosociological papers mostly express the quantity by terms such as 'common' or 'rare'. A method of estimating the area covered by an individual community has been thus proposed (Pyšek 1978, Pyšek & Pyšek 1987a). Carrying out this estimation directly in the field, it is possible to obtain quantitative data on the proportional contribution of each community to the total vegetation cover (*e.g.*, Pyšek 1978, Pyšek & Pyšek 1985, 1988c, Pyšek 1992a). Such data allow (1) more precise comparison between areas or settlements of different type and size (Pyšek & Pyšek 1990), (2) recording of vegetation dynamics over time (Pyšek & Pyšek 1987b), (3) calculating of vegetation diversity indices (Pyšek & Pyšek 1987a), and (4) using multivariate analysis in processing data on vegetation cover (Pyšek & Pyšek 1985).

3. Relationships between plant cover and its environment

Specific features of urban environment have been described with respect to climate (Miess 1979), soil (Sukopp *et al.*, 1979a) and in general (Horbert 1978, Laurie 1979, Sukopp *et al.*, 1980, Bornkamm *et al.*, 1982, Gilbert 1989, Wittig 1991, for summarizing of relevance to vegetation see Sukopp & Werner 1983). Ecological conditions of several cities have been described (see Sukopp *et al.*, 1979a for references).

3.1. Species level

Flora of a given area can be analysed with respect to various biological and ecological characteristics; a useful compilation of such traits concerning most species in the central European flora was published by Frank & Klotz (1990). Comparisons between cities (Saarisalo-Taubert 1963, Kunick 1982), between city and open landscape (Wittig & Durwen 1981, 1982, Pyšek 1992b), between cities and villages (Pyšek & Pyšek 1991b) and within a city (Kunick 1974, Sudnik-Wójcikowska 1987, 1988, Pyšek & Pyšek 1988a, Pyšek 1992b) represent a convenient method to analyse the impact of urbanization (Sukopp & Werner 1983).

Data on species origin and time of immigration are frequently used to analyse species lists (for review see Pyšek 1989b, for analysis Kowarik 1985b, 1988, 1990a). We are quite well informed about the invasion of aliens (review on both general principles and examples of case studies see in Kornaś 1983, classification in Holub & Jirásek 1967, Schroeder 1969). A complete species list with information on the time of origin and the degree of naturalization for aliens has been presented for Berlin (Böcker & Kowarik in Kowarik 1991b). A study of Kunick (1991) was focused upon spread of alien species escaping from cultivation.

Sorting out species into the classification categories may however cause difficulties, because we are often not able to distinguis the alien from natives among early man-accompanying plants (Kornas 1983). Moreover, the opinions on species origin may differ between local sources (compare Rothmaler 1986 with Zajac 1979, Opravil 1980).

The proportion of aliens is generally higher in large cities (Sukopp *et al.*, 1979a, 1981, Sukopp & Werner 1983, Pyšek 1989b, Pyšek & Pyšek 1991b) although some trends reported (Falinski 1971) seem to be rather simplistic (Pyšek 1989b). Nevertheless, they were frequently used as examples in later reviewing papers (Sukopp *et al.* 1979a, Sukopp & Werner 1983). Occurrence of aliens increases from outskirts to the city centre (Kunick 1974, Kowarik 1990). Of the species which prefer urban settlements, the majority appear to be of southern European origin (Saarisalo-Taubert 1963). Sukopp *et al.* (1979) pointed out that of the West Berlin aliens, 60% originated from areas warmer than central Europe. This may be quantified using indicator values for temperature (Ellenberg 1979): higher mean values and shifts in frequency distributions were recognized in alien species, especially neophytes, compared to the native ones in the Czech village vegetation (Pyšek 1989b). This seems to be valid not only for settlements but for the central European landscape in general (Kornaś 1983).

Sukopp & Werner (1983) concluded that most of the present-day neophytes spread best in cities and industrial areas whereas many archeophytes, having been introduced as weeds do better in rural areas. They considered the limitation of these species to human settlements to be more pronounced the further they were from their place of origin. The importance of climate selection in immigration processes has been emphasized (Kornaś 1983).

Life forms represent another frequently analysed characteristic; it has been repeatedly shown that the proprotion of therophytes is higher in large cities and city centers compared to their outskirts (Kunick 1974, Sukopp *et al.*, 1979a, Sukopp & Werner 1983, Kowarik 1985a, 1988, 1990a, Sudnik-Wójcikowska 1988, Pyšek & Pyšek 1988a, 1991b). Life strategies (Grime *et al.*, 1988), sociological behaviour (Ellenberg 1979, Hejný *et al.*, 1979, Rothmaler 1986), taxonomical groups or mode of dispersal are other characteristics that may be used to evaluate flora.

An insight into the ecological requirements of flora can be obtained by using indicator values (Ellenberg 1979, for a general discussion on their use see Mucina 1985, Klimeš 1987a, Kowarik & Seidling 1989). Frequency distribution of indicator values proved to be better than simply using their means (Kunick 1982, Pyšek 1989b). Wittig & Durwen (1981, 1982) compared cities and their rural surroundings and found that the urban flora required higher nitrogen and temperature and lower moisture. Similar results were obtained from a comparison of the industrial city of Plzeň with villages located in the same region (Pyšek & Pyšek 1991b). Kunick (1982) compared 9 European cities and was able to determine geographic and climatic trends in ecological demands of the floras.

Indices expressing flora synanthropization on the basis of various proportions of native and alien species were proposed by Polish authors (Kornaś 1977, Sowa & Warcholinska 1984). Some of these were dependent on the total number of species in the florula analysed (Pyšek 1989b). Based on more than 5000 vegetational relevés made in West Berlin, the hemeroby concept was used to construct spectra of hemeroby for each species (Kowarik 1990). This approach is particularly valuable relating a species response to the complex measure of human influence. Human impact consists of many partial environmental factors, some of which (stress, disturbance) cannot be directly measured. Wittig *et al.* (1985, also summarized in Wittig 1991) proposed a more intuitively based classification of species relationships to the urban environment with examples from German cities. The relation of individual species to habitat types was considered *e.g.*, by Kunick (1974), Sudnik-Wójcikowska (1987), Pyšek & Pyšek (1988a,b), Brandes *et al.* (1990) and many others.

Species rarity becomes increasingly relevant in the urban environment (Davis 1976, Sukopp *et al.*, 1978, Gemmell 1982, Sukopp & Kowarik 1986, Rebele 1988). At the end of the 1970's, 55% of the native flora of West Berlin was considered threatened (Sukopp *et al.*, 1981) and corresponding data to the loss of some species are available from other cities as well (see Sukopp *et al.*, 1979a). Areas of open space covered with vegetation are important for maintaining species diversity in the inner-urban areas (Sukopp & Werner 1983). The main principles to be considered in compiling red lists of endangered species were proposed by Kowarik (1991). It is especially important to pay attention to the whole spectrum of habitats, including those of heavily disturbed sites, and not only to those traditionally considered in nature conservation. Two main questions should be answered before any species, regardless of its status (*i.e.*, a native or an alien) is put on such a list, (1) Is the population established in the site?, and (2) Is the site endangered? (Kowarik 1991b). The principles of nature conservancy in central European cities were also discussed by Sukopp & Sukopp (1987).

Papers or books analysing adaptations of plant cover to urban environments and relating plant ecological investigations to other topics of urban ecological research have been frequently published in the last decade (Bornkamm *et al.*, 1982, Kowarik 1985a,b, 1990, Sukopp & Kowarik 1986, Gilbert 1989, Sukopp 1990, Wittig 1991).

3.2. Community level

To evaluate the ecology of a particular community, most studies use non-quantitative descriptions of soil conditions, temperature requirements and impact of anthropogeneous factors. This rough assessment is often enough to recognize those environmental factors that determine the occurrence of a community.

Direct measurements of ecological factors are rather rare in ruderal phytosociology (*e.g.*, Grosse-Brauckmann 1953, Grüll & Květ 1978). Because of considerable heterogeneity in substrata, many samples are necessary, so that measurements are frequently replaced by indicator values, those of Ellenberg (1979) being commonly used. The relation of a community to a given factor is then expressed by a mean value calculated for all species present in a given community (Tüllmann & Böttcher 1983, Pyšek 1992a, for discussion see Kowarik & Seidling 1989); semiquantitative data obtained by the relevé method can be included after simple transformation to the numerical scale (Ellenberg 1979). Nitrogen and moisture represent steep gradients in urban habitats and may be thus used for ranking communities according to their requirements (Pyšek 1992a).

In the urban environment, it is sometime more plausible to express community relationship to some complex measurement of human impact, rather than analysing single factors. Methods to express the intensity of human impact have been proposed (Olaczek sec. Sudnik-Wójcikowska 1988); theoretical concepts of the assessment of human impact on vegetation were reviewed by Kowarik (1991a). In such attempts, however, attention should be paid to avoid circular reasoning: vegetation feature (*e.g.*, community type or percentage of area covered by vegetation) is used to assess and classify the zones of different intensity of human impact and subsequently another characteristic of plant cover (*e.g.*, number of species) is related to these zones (Sudnik-Wójcikowska 1987). This may be overcome by describing environment exclusively by its own features (Pyšek 1992b) or by excluding indicator species from the assessment (Kowarik 1990).

Classification of habitat types was first proposed by Hejný using as an example a concrete city (1971a), more detailed and generally applicable studies appeared later (Sukopp & Werner 1983, Klotz 1986, Schulte *et al.*, 1986, Sukopp *et al.* 1986, Blume *et al.*, 1987). Because of different criteria, particular classifications are mostly applicable to given studies and are thus difficult to compare in detail. Hejný (1971a) distinguished 68 habitat types in Prague, whereas Pyšek (1978) only 21 in Plzeň , a difference which can be ascribed to the fineness of scales rather than to real differences in habitat heterogeneity between the cities. Distribution of communities with respect to habitat type was widely studied, sometimes using vegetation mapping (*e.g.*, Kienast 1978, Pyšek 1978, Tüllman & Böttcher 1983, Klotz 1986, Goldberg & Gutte 1988, Tlusták 1990, Chojnacki 1991 in cities, Pyšek & Rydlo 1984 in villages), so that rough generalizations are possible (Pyšek 1992b). Some attention has been paid to the vegetation of specific habitats, *e.g.*, railway sites (Brandes 1983, Jehlík 1986), cemeteries (Graf 1986, Pyšek 1988), road verges (Klimeš 1987b), factories (Rebele 1986, 1988, Pyšek & Pyšek 1988c). Sukopp & Werner (1983) divided West Berlin habitats into main zones of urban land use; they presented characteristics of climate and soil and analysed their consequences for plant vigour, species composition and migration possibilities within each zone. Another detailed study has been carried out in Warsaw by Chojnacki (1991) who mapped the vegetation within the whole city area. According to my knowledge, this map represents the first vegetation map of such a large city based on the basic phytosociological units. This approach made it possible to analyse spatial relationships between communities and habitat types (Chojnacki 1991).

Classification of depositional habitats has been rather unclear so far, because of diversity of substrata and complicated terminology (Gutte 1971a,b, Hejný 1971b). A simplified scheme based on (1) features of accumulated material, (2) its origin, and (3) type of accumulation process was proposed by Prach *et al.* (1994). Mucina (1982) published a broader classification of ruderal habitats covering not only urban environments but open landscape as well.

The comparison between cities and villages of vegetation distribution with respect to the site structure showed that in many communities, there was a preference for either town or village habitats (Pyšek & Pyšek 1990).

An analysis of a particular community carried out within a large geographical region can provide information on the sociological behaviour of the dominant species and changes in community composition on latitudinal/longitudinal gradients. Community response to climate changes can be evaluated (Mucina & Brandes 1985, Mucina 1989a). The problems of geographic, altitudinal and geological vicariance of synanthropic vegetation were reviewed by Mucina (1991).

3.3. Vegetation level

Surprisingly, there have been few attempts to analyse the ruderal vegetation of a certain area as a whole in quantitative terms. This is presumably caused by the lack of quantitative data on the composition of vegetation cover, which is necessary if some synthetic characteristics are to be calculated. Comparisons of different areas have been carried out mostly in terms of community presence/absence or using vague estimations (Hejný *et al.*, 1978, Hadač 1978).

Pyšek & Pyšek (1985) related features of village vegetation and changes in vegetation diversity to the altitude. It was possible to relate the character of ruderal vegetation to the climax vegetation type of the respective region. The comparison of settlements differing in size made it possible to quantify increase of vegetation diversity, expressed as Shannon index, with the city size (Pyšek & Pyšek 1990). The vegetation diversity in great cities shows a regular pattern which can be related to the urban space structure (Pyšek 1992b).

More general interpretations of the vegetation-environment-relationships can be also made using ordination techniques, as shown by Mucina and van Tongeren (1989) who analysed the coenocline of high-ranked syntaxa of ruderal vegetation.

4. Dynamic changes: comparisons in time

Unfortunately, there are few data recorded in the past which can be compared with the present (Kreh 1955, Scholz 1960, Sudnik-Wójcikowska 1987, Klotz 1987). In some cases even these data are not comparable because of unclear area delimitation (Prach *et al.*, 1994). Nevertheless, there is an example illustrating how useful such data are. Having compared floristic lists of Halle from 1848 and 1983, Klotz (1987) found the total number of species almost unchanged, but the floristic similarity between both lists was only 56.5%. The proportion of neophytes changed from 10 to 31% and indicator values for temperature, nitrogen, continentality and soil reaction increased, whereas that for moisture declined. Hence the same consequences of increasing synanthropization in space, shown by comparing flora of the city to its countryside (Wittig and Durwen 1981, 1982, Pyšek & Pyšek 1991b) also held for time (Klotz 1987).

Similarly, an increase in the number of neophytes in the flora of West Berlin during the last two centuries was related to the population explosion after the industrial revolution (Sukopp *et al.*, 1979a, Kowarik 1990). Sukopp (1973) estimated the proportion of species becoming extinct in some European cities between 1850 and 1950 and reported values between 4 and 16% of the total species number. Kowarik & Jirku (1988) reported on the changes in species composition of grasslands and meadows at the territory of ZOO Berlin between 1954-86.

A common approach to vegetation dynamics in human settlements is a phytosociological study at the community level. Research has been focused mostly on newly created deposits (see Pyšek & Pyšek 1991a, Prach *et al.*, 1994 for reviews). Studies in other habitats are rather rare (Krippelová 1972). Pyšek & Pyšek (1991a) summarized 17 studies, most of them using the method of repeating relevés in permanent plots over time (for review of permanent plots see Böttcher 1974). Data can be obtained by (1) following the changes in a site over time, or (2) comparing several currently existing stages of a different age. Combination of both methods is often used; provided that individual stands are followed for a sufficient time to allow overlap, quite a precise picture of the species/community sequence can be obtained. Kornaś (1990) pointed out three possible methods to document precisely temporal changes in vegetation: (1) repeating of phytosociological relevés in permanent plots, (2) collecting new representative sets of relevés within the area formerly studied and comparing this new relevé set with the corresponding old one, and (3) renewed mapping of the actual vegetation in the area formerly mapped.

Two main approaches can be distinguished in phytosociological studies on succession. The first one focuses upon individual communities and describes mutual transitions among them (*e.g.*, Pyšek 1977). The second approach is concerned with particular habitat types and makes it possible to compare successional seres among them (*e.g.*, Kreh 1935, Gutte 1971a,b, Holzner 1972, for references see Prach *et al.*, 1994). Initial stages of vegetation development on rubble waste sites were investigated after the war in numerous cities (Sukopp & Werner 1983). The results of phytosociological studies on succession are mostly presented in the form of syngenetical schemes (Pyšek 1977, Sukopp *et al.*, 1979a, Holzner 1972).

Although the phytosociological approach is not considered to have contributed to theoretical knowledge on succession (Prach *et al.*, 1994), it makes it possible to record main changes in vegetation such as species/community exchange, changes in species diversity, vegetation diversity and life form spectra, etc. Pyšek & Pyšek (1991a) expressed the changes in occurrence of each species in 46 permanent plots during a 6 year period of succession using frequency distribution of differences between initial and final values of the given species in Braun-Blanquet scale. This method allowed the characterization of the successional position of a species numerically and documented general trends, *e.g.*, increase in native species at the expense of aliens during succession.

A deeper insight into the mechanisms of ruderal succession was provided by Bornkamm (1984, 1986, 1987a). Soil type, starting time and nitrogen fertilization were used in experimental studies as variables affecting the course and rate of succession. It was not possible to find a constant series of dominant species exchange. If the process of succession is to be fully described, not only annual changes but also seasonal ones must be taken into account (Bornkamm 1987a).

Investigations of changes over time at the level of vegetation cover or landscape are often linked with diminishing ruderal communities, the decline of which has been mostly attributed to changes in land use and management (Brandes 1981, Pyšek 1983, Sukopp 1983, Kornaś 1990). Of 110 ruderal associations recorded in Czechoslovakia, over 45% are considered retreating (Prach *et al.*, 1994). Changes in contribution of individual communities to the vegetation cover were assessed quantitatively over the period of 15 years and a decrease in diversity of village vegetation was reported (Pyšek & Pyšek 1987b). There is a conspicuous retreat of communities considered typical of village sites, associated with the simultaneous increase of those preferring an urban environment (Pyšek & Pyšek 1990). Changes in agricultural management in south Bohemia were shown to affect the distribution of communities within the settlement area (Hejný 1973).

5. Conclusions: current state of research and future directions

'Ecosystems that have developed in urban conditions may be the prevailing ecosystems of the future.' (Sukopp *et al.*, 1979a). Unfortunately, much of the efforts devoted to studying these ecosystems so far have been concerned with pure phytosociology, repeatedly describing common vegetation types, without any ambition to get deeper under the cover of the issue. The situation is, however, different in particular central European countries. Among those involved most in intense settlement plant cover research, Czech Republic, Slovakia and Poland seem to be still limited by traditional approaches (although there are some exceptions). The field appears to be much more developed in Germany where new methods and approaches have been applied. The research seems to have been stimulated by some influential articles mapping the 'state of the art' at the turn of the 70's and 80's (Sukopp *et al.* 1979a, Sukopp & Werner 1983). In the contemprorary context, a similar starting point may be represented by the book edited by Sukopp *et al.* (1990) which covers both scientific and practical aspects of the field. Correspondingly, the book of Wittig (1991) is a useful summary of current knowledge and may serve as a link between traditional approaches and the recent development in urban ecology.

The subjectivity of phytosociological methods seems to have another general impact. This review indicates that there are more new approaches and methods applicable to the study of flora than of vegetation. The latter are more limited by traditional attitudes. Moreover, the results concerning flora have better general validity because they can be easily compared among settlements and regions. The main problem limiting the comparison of vegetation, *i.e.*, what it is we are working with and what we want thus to compare, has no relevance here. Faced with the contemporary progress in ecology, the role of phytosociology seems to be limited to that of a useful technique for describing vegetation rather than a progressive scientific method.

Research in urban ecology is undoubtedly of increasing practical importance (Sukopp 1990). Urban land management planning and nature conservancy can profit (Hard & Pirner 1985), especially from the method of habitat mapping (Sukopp *et al.*, 1979b, Schulte *et al.*, 1986, Sukopp & Werner 1987, Sukopp & Weiler 1988). Provided that the recommendations of the Working Group for Habitat Mapping are accepted by a wide range of researchers in different regions, results of general validity could be obtained by comparisons. As it has been widely applied only in Germany till now (see Sukopp and Weiler 1988 for survey), it is plausible to encourage use of the method in other central European countries.

Using synanthropic plants as bioindicators (Trepl 1983, Sukopp & Werner 1987) in monitoring the quality of urban environment represents another example of practical application. Furthermore, the use of urban vegetation research for health care was suggested; knowledge on the distribution of the main pollen producers can be used in preventing pollen allergies (Kopecký 1990b). A specific area in which the knowledge on ruderal flora and vegetation is being successfully used is the management of industrial wastelands (see Rebele 1991 for assessment and the outlook for the future). This habitat type can harbour highly diverse wildlife and is becoming increasingly relevant for nature conservancy, amenity and recreation (Gemmell 1982, Rebele 1988, 1991). Generally, considerable attention is being paid to the management of urban free space (see *e.g.*, Hüllbusch 1983, Hard 1984, Hard & Pirner 1985 for examples).

Further research of plant cover in human settlements should be of deeper scientific interest. Experimental methods can be successfully used in this type of environment as well (Bornkamm 1984, 1986, 1987a). Each particular level of study can provide specific results which are not recognizable at another scale (Krahulec & Lepš 1989, Krahulec 1990). Till now, the attention was concentrated mostly at community level. There this certainly much opportunity for studying relationships at landscape level (Prach *et al.*, 1994). Closer relating of plant cover (both spontaneous and planted) to animals, soil and climate in urban environments can yield more general conclusions (*e.g.*, Kowarik 1985a). Wider application of statistical methods, both in data analysis and designing research, is desirable to improve data interpretation.

Extreme ecological conditions in the urban environment provide an opportunity to study plant adaptations to stresses and its evolutionary aspects (*e.g.*, pollution, toxicity of substrata). Large areas of newly exposed land make it possible to study some problems of general ecological interest, *e.g.*, colonization processes and succession (Antonovics *et al.*, 1971, Bradshaw & McNeilly 1981, Rebele 1986, Cornelius 1988, 1990). Complex studies on autecology of alien species may be of great scientific value (Sukopp 1971, Dapper 1971, Zimmermann-Jaeger 1971, De Sante-Virzo 1971, Bornkamm 1971).

Generally speaking, new field methods, change of attitudes and more studies involved with general questions are needed. Close international cooperation may contribute substantially to the development of the field. There is a large body of information in those phytosociological studies carried out so far. This can be used for generalization by (1) application of statistical and computer methods (*e.g.*, Kowarik 1990), (2) careful reevaluation of the data (*e.g.*, Pyšek & Pyšek 1991a), or (3) reviewing and mutual comparing of large numbers of studies (Prach *et al.*, 1994, Pyšek 1992b).

'Modern cities are often deserts of brick, stones and concrete; plants can break this monotony...' (Woodell 1979). The more we know about them the better we can help them to do so.

Acknowledgments

My thanks are due to Herbert Sukopp, Berlin, for helpful comments and attention paid to the manuscript and to Roger L. Hall, Oxford, for improving my English.

References

Antonovics, J., Bradshaw, A.D. & Turner, R.G. 1971. Heavy metal tolerance in plants. Adv. Ecol. Res. 7: 1–85.
Blume, H.-P. *et al.* 1987. Stadtökologische Raumeinheiten. Umweltatlas, 2: 1–5.
Bornkamm, R. 1971. Beiträge zur Ökologie von Chenopodium botrys L. V. Gehalt an organischem Stickstoff, Nitrat und Asche. Verh. Bot. Ver. Prov. Brandenburg, 108: 57–73.

Bornkamm, R. 1984. Experimentell-ökologische Untersuchungen zur Sukzession von ruderalen Pflanzen-gesellschaften. II. Quantität und Qualität der Phytomasse. Flora 175: 45–74.

Bornkamm, R. 1986. Ruderal succession starting at different seasons. Acta Soc. Bot. Poloniae 55: 403–419.

Bornkamm, R. 1987a. Veränderungen der Phytomasse in den ersten zwei Jahren einer Sukzession auf unterschiedlichen Böden. Flora 179: 179–192.

Bornkamm, R. 1987b. Fragen der Auswertung und Bewertung floristischer Artenlisten. Mitt. der Biol. Bundesanstalt f. Land- u. Forstwirtschaft, Berlin-Dahlem, 234: 16–20.

Bornkamm, R., Lee, J.A. & Seaward, M.R.D. (eds.) 1982. Urban ecology. 2nd European ecological sympo-sium, Berlin. Blackwell, Oxford.

Böttcher, H. 1974. Bibliographie zum Problem der Sukzessionsforschung mit Hilfe von Dauerquadraten und der Vegetationskartierung. Exc. Bot., Stuttgart, Sect. B Sociologica, 141: 35–56.

Bradshaw, A.D. & McNeilly, T. 1981. Evolution and pollution. Edward Arnold, London.

Brandes, D. 1981. Gefährdete Ruderalgesellschaften in Niedersachsen und Möglichkeiten zu ihrer Erhaltung. Gött. Flor. Rundbr., Göttingen, 14: 90–98.

Brandes, D. 1983. Flora und Vegetation der Bahnhöfe Mitteleuropas. Phytocoenologia, Stuttgart, 11: 31–115.

Brandes, D. 1987. Verzeichnis der im Stadtgebiet von Braunschweig wildwachsenden und verwilderten Pflanzen. Braunschweig.

Brandes, D., Griese, D. & Köller, U. 1990. Die Flora der Dörfer unter besonderer Berücksichtigung von Niedersachsen. Braunschw. Naturkdl. Schr. 3: 569–593.

Brandes, D. & Zacharias, D. 1990. Korrelation zwischen Artenzahlen und Flächengrößen von isolierten Habitaten dargestellt an Kartierungsprojekten aus dem Bereich der Regionalstelle 10 B. Flor. Rundbr. 23: 141–149.

Chojnacki, J. 1991. Zroznicowanie przestrzenne roslinnosci Warszawy. Wydaw. Uniw. Warsz., Warszawa.

Cornelius, R. 1988. Plant strategies in relation to urban habitats. In: Zaliberová, M. et al. (ed.), Symposium Synanthropic flora and vegetation V, pp. 39–45, Veda, Bratislava.

Cornelius, R. 1990. The strategies of Solidago canadensis L. in relation to urban habitats. I.-III. Acta Oecol. 11: 19–34, 145–153, 301–310.

Dapper, H. 1971. Beiträge zur Ökologie von Chenopodium botrys L. II. Produktion an Ruderalstandorten. Verh. Bot. Ver. Prov. Brandenburg 108: 26–28.

Davis, B.N.K. 1976. Wildlife, urbanisation and industry. Biol. Conserv. 10: 249–291.

Dechent, H.-J. 1988. Wandel der Dorfflora – gezeigt am Beispiel einiger Dörfer Rheinhessens. KTBL-Schrift, Darmstad, 326: 1–162.

De Santo-Virzo, A. 1971. Beiträge zur Ökologie von Chenopodium botrys L. IV. Wasserhaushalt. Verh. Bot. Ver. Prov. Brandenburg 108: 37–55.

Eliáš, P. 1984, 1986. A survey of ruderal plant communities of Western Slovakia I., II. Feddes Repert., Berlin, 95: 251–276, 97: 197–221.

Eliáš, P. 1988. Inflácia syntaxónov vyššieho rangu teplomilnej ruderálnej vegetacie, skutočnosť ci konfúzia? Preslia, Praha, 60: 59–71.

Ellenberg, H. 1979. Zeigerwerte der Gefäßpflanzen Mitteleuropas. Scr. Geobot., Göttingen 9: 1–122.

Falinski, J.B. 1971. Synanthropization of plant cover. II. Synanthropic flora and vegetation of towns connected with their natural conditions, history and function. Mater. Zakl. Fitosocjol. Stos. UW, Warszawa-Bialowieza 27: 1–317.

Feoli, E. 1984. Some aspects of classification and ordination of vegetation in perspective. Studia Geobot., Trieste 4: 7–21.

Frank, D. & Klotz, S. 1990. Biologisch-ökologische Daten zur Flora der DDR. Halle.

Gemmell, R.P. 1982. The origin and botanical importance of industrial habitats. In: Bornkamm, R. et al., Lee, J.A. & Seaward, M.R.D. (eds.), Urban ecology. 2nd European ecological symposium, Berlin, pp. 33–39, Blackwell, Oxford.

Gilbert, O.L. 1989. Ecology of urban environment. Chapman & Hall, London.

Gödde, M. 1986. Vergleichende Untersuchung der Ruderalvegetation der Großstädte Düsseldorf, Essen und Münster. Düsseldorf.

Goldberg, A. & Gutte, P. 1988. Phytosoziologische Charakterisierung städtischer Flachennutzungsstrukturen, dargestellt an einem Transekt durch die Großstadt Leipzig. In: Zaliberová, M. (ed.), Symposium Synanthropic flora and vegetation V, pp. 59–66, Veda, Bratislava.

Graf, A. 1986. Flora und Vegetation der Friedhöfe in Berlin (West). Verh. Berliner Bot. Ver. 5: 1–210.

Grime, J.P., Hodgson, J.G. & Hunt, R. 1988. Comparative plant ecology. Unwin & Hyman, London.

Grosse-Brauckmann, G. 1953. Untersuchungen über die Ökologie, besonders den Wasserhaushalt von Ruderalgesellschaften. Vegetatio 4: 245–283.

Grüll, F. & Květ, J. 1978. Charakteristik der Bodentemperaturen in Ruderalzönosen der Stadt Brno. Preslia, Praha 50: 361–373.

Gutte, P. 1971a. Die Vegetation der Aschenhalde Rositz bei Altenburg. Abh. u. Ber. Naturkdl. Mus. 'Mauritianum' Altenburg 7: 7–16.

Gutte, P. 1971b. Die Wiederbegrünung städtischen Ödlandes, dargestellt am Beispiel Leipzigs. Herzynia, Leipzig, ser.n. 8: 58–81.

Gutte, P. 1972. Ruderalpflanzengesellschaften West- und Mittelsachsens. Feddes Repert., Berlin 83: 11–122.

Hadač, E. 1978. Ruderal vegetation of the Broumov basin. Folia Geobot. Phytotax., Praha 13: 129–163.

Haeupler, H. 1974. Statistische Auswertung von Punktrasterkarten der Gefäßpflanzenflora Süd-Niedersachsens. Scr. Geobot., Göttingen 8: 1–141.

Hard, G. 1982. Die spontane Vegetation der Wohn- und Gewerbequartiere von Osnabrück (I.). Osnabrück. Naturw. Mitt. 9: 151–203.

Hard, G. 1984. Spontane und angebaute Vegetation an der Peripherie der Stadt. In: Über Plannung. Eine Sammlung planungspolitischer Ansätze. GH Kassel, FB Stadtplannung u. Landschaftsplannung, p. 77–113.

Hard, G. & Pinter, J. Stadtvegetation und Freiraumplannung am Beispiel der Osnabrücker Kinderspielplätze. Osnabr. Stud. Geogr. 7: 1–84.

Hejný, S. 1971a. Metodologicky příspěvek k výzkumu synantropní květeny a vegetace velkoměsta (na příkladu Prahy). Zborn. predn. Zjazdu Slov. bot. spoloč., Tisovec 1970, 2: 545–567, Bratislava.

Hejný, S. 1971b. The characteristic features of vegetation of slag and flue dust substrates in Prague. In: Bioindicators of landscape deterioration, pp. 39–42, Praha.

Hejný, S. 1973. Beitrag zur Charakteristik der Veränderung der Ruderalgesellschaften in Südböhmen. Acta Bot. Acad. Sci. Hungaricae 19: 129–138.

Hejný, S. Husák, S. & Pyšek, A. 1979. Vergleich der Ruderalgesellschaften in erwählten Gesamtheiten südböhmischer und südmährischer Dörfer. Acta Bot. Slov. Acad. Sci. Slov., Bratislava, ser. A. 3: 271–281.

Hejný, S. et al. 1979. Přehled ruderálních rostlinných společenstev Československa. Rozpr. Čs. Akad. Věd, Praha, ser. math.-nat. 89: 2.1–100.

Herben, T. 1986 Problém využití fytocenologických znalostí v ČSSR – pokus o rozbor. Preslia, Praha 58: 223–229.

Holub, J. & Jirásek, V. 1967. Zur Vereinheitlichung der Terminologie in der Phytogeographie. Folia Geobot. Phytotax., Praha 2: 69–113.

Horbert, M. 1978. Klimatische und lufthygienischer Aspekte der Stadt- und Landschaftsplanung. Natur u. Heimat 38.

Holzner W. 1972. Einige Ruderalgesellschaften des oberen Murtales. Verh. Zool. Bot. Ges., Wien 112: 67–83.

Hüllbusch, K.H. 1978. Kartierung der Vegetation in Siedlungsgebieten. In: Tüxen, R. (ed.), Assoziationskomplexe, pp. 321–327, Vaduz.

Hüllbusch, K.H. 1983. Arbeitskreis: Biotopkartierung – Wissenschaft und Alibi. Jahrbuch f. Natursch. u. Landschaftspfl. 33: 143–145.

Jehlík, V. 1986. The vegetation of railways in northern Bohemia (eastern part). In: Vegetace ČSSR, Praha, ser. A 14: 1–366.

Kienast, D. 1978. Die spontane Vegetation der Stadt Kassel in Abhängigkeit von bau- und stadtstrukturellen Quartierstypen. Urbs et Regio 10: 1–414.

Kienast, D. 1980. Sigma-Gesellschaften der Stadt Kassel. Phytocoenologia, Stuttgart 7: 65–72.

Klimeš, L. 1987a. Použití tabelovaných indikačních hodnot v gradientové analýze vegetace. Preslia 59: 15–24.

Klimeš, L. 1987b. Succession in road bank vegetation. Folia Geobot. Phytotax., Praha 22: 435–440.

Klimeš, L. 1989. Příspěvek k ruderálním společenstvům Novosibirska (SSSR) a k obecným problémům syntaxonomie ruderální vegetace. Preslia, Praha 61: 259–277.

Klotz, S. 1986. Die Pflanzengemeinschaften des Ballungsraumes Halle – ihre Geschichte, Gefährdung und Bindung an die ökologischen Raumeinheiten der Stadt. Wiss. Z. Karl-Marx-Univ. Leipzig, ser. math.-natur. 35: 673–680.

Klotz, S. 1987. Floristische und vegetationskundliche Untersuchungen in Städten der DDR. Düsseldorf Geobot. Kolloq. 4: 61–69.

Klotz, S. 1988. Flora und Vegetation in der Stadt, ihre Spezifik und Indikationsfunktion. Landschaftsarchitektur 17: 104–107.

Klotz, S. 1990. Species/area and species/inhabitants relations in European cities. In: Sukopp, H., Hejný, S. & Kowarik, I. (eds.), Urban ecology, pp. 99–104, SPB Academic Publ., The Hague.

Klotz, S., Gutte, P. & Klausnitzer, B. 1984. Literaturübersicht, Charakterisierung und Gliederung urbaner Ökosysteme. Hercynia 21: 218–234.

Kopecký, K. 1980–1984. Die Ruderalpflanzengesellschaften im südwestlichen Teil von Praha (1)–(6). Preslia, Praha 52: 241–267; 53: 121–145; 54: 67–89; 54: 123–139; 55: 289–298; 56: 55–72.

Kopecký, K. 1984b. Der Apophytisierungsprozeß und die Apophytengesellschaften der Galio-Urticetea mit einigen Beispielen aus der südwestlichen Umgebung von Praha. Folia Geobot. Phytotax., Praha 19: 113–138.

Kopecký, K. 1986. Versuch einer Klassifizierung der ruderalen Agropyron repens- und Calamagrostis epigejos Gesellschaften unter Anwendung der deduktiven Methode. Folia Geobot Phytotax., Praha 21: 225–242.

Kopecký, K. 1988. Použití tzv. deduktivní metody syntaxonomické klasifikace ve fytocenologické literatuře. Preslia, Fraha 60: 177–184.

Kopecký, K. 1990a. K polemicé o syntaxonomických, syngenetických a synekologických aspektech deduktivní metody syntaxonomické klasifikace. Zpr. Čs. Bot. Společ., Praha 25: 3–13.

Kopecký, K. 1990b. Changes of vegetation and pollen respiratory tract allergies on Prague sample. In: Sukopp, H., Hejný, S. & Kowarik, I. (eds.), Urban ecology, pp. 267–271, SPB Academic. Publ., The Hague.

Kopecký, K. & Hejný, S. 1978. Die Anwendung einer deduktiven Methode syntaxonomischer Klassifikation bei der Bearbeitung der straßenbegleitenden Pflanzengesellschaften Nordostböhmens. Vegetatio, The Hague 36: 43–51.

Kopecký, K. & Hejný, S. 1990. Die stauden- und grasreichen Ruderalgesellschaften Böhmens unter Anwendung der deduktiven Methode syntaxonomischer Klassifizierung. Folia Geobot. Phytotax., Praha 25: 357–380.

Kornaš, J. 1977. Analiza flor synantropijnych. Wiadom. Bot., Warszawa 21: 85–91.

Kornaš, J. 1983. Man's impact on the flora and vegetation in Central Europe. In: Holzner, W. *et al.* (eds.), Man's impact on vegetation, p. 277–286, Junk, Hague.

Kornaš, J. 1990. Jak i dla czego gina nasze zespoly roślinne. Wiadom. Bot. 34: 7–16.

Kowarik, I. 1985a. Grundlagen der Stadtökologie und Forderungen nach ihrer Berücksichtigung bei der Stadtgestaltung am Beispiel Berlins. Schr.-Reihe DBV-Jugend 3: 22–39.

Kowarik, I. 1985b. Zum Begriff 'Wildpflanzen' und zu den Bedingungen und Auswirkungen der Einbürgerung hemerochorer Arten. Publ. Naturhist. Gen., Limburg 35(3-4.8-25).

Kowarik, I. 1988. Zum menschlichen Einfluß auf Flora und Vegetation. Theoretische Konzepte und ein Quantifizierungsansatz am Beispiel von Berlin (West) Landschaftsentw. u. Umweltforsch., Berlin 56: 1–280.

Kowarik, I. 1990. Some responses of flora and vegetation to urbanization in Central Europe. In: Sukopp, H. *et al.* (eds.), Urban ecology, pp. 45–74, SPB Academic Publ., The Hague.

Kowarik, I. 1991a. Unkraut oder Urwald? Natur der vierten Art auf dem Gleisdreieck. In: Bundesgartenschau 1995. pp 45–55, Berlin.

Kowarik, I. 1991b. Berücksichtigung anthropogener Standort- und Florenveränderungen bei der Aufstellung Roter Listen. In: Auhagen, A.R. *et al.* (eds.), Rote Listen der gefährdeten Pflanzen und Tiere in Berlin. Landschaftsent. u. Umweltforsch. 6: 25–56.

Kowarik, I. & Jirku, A. 1988. Rasen im Spannungsfeld zwischen Erholungsnutzung, Ökologie und Gartendenkmalpflege. Analyse von Nutzungskonflikten in Parkanlagen am Beispiel des Berliner Tiergartens. 1. Untersuchungskonzeption und Vegetationsanalysen. Gartenamt 37: 645–654.

Kowarik, I. & Seidling, W. 1989. Zeigerwertberechnungen nach Ellenberg – zu Problemen und Einschränkungen einer sinnvollen Methode. Landschaft u. Stadt 21: 132–143.

Krahulec, F. 1990. Introduction. In: Krahulec, F. *et al.* (eds.), Spatial processes in plant communities, pp. xi–x, Academia Praha/SPB Academic Publ., The Hague.

Krahulec, F. & Leps, J. 1989. Fytocenologie a soucasná veda o vegetaci. Preslia, Praha 61: 227–244.

Krawiecowa, A. & Rostanski, K. 1976. Zaleznosc flory synantropijnej wybranych miast polskich od ich warunkow przyrodniczych i rozwoju. Acta Univ. Wratislaw., Pr. Bot. 303/21,5–61.

Kreh, W. 1935. Pflanzensoziologische Untersuchungen auf Stuttgarter Auffüllplatzen. Jhr. Ver. Vaterl. Naturk. Wurttemberg. Schwabisch Hall 91: 59–120.

Kreh, W. 1955. Das Ergebnis der Vegetationsentwicklung auf dem Stuttgarter Trümmerschutt. Mitt. Flor.-Soz. Arb Gemeinsch., N.F. 5: 69–75.

Krippelová, T. 1972. Ruderálne spoločenstvá mesta Malaciek. Biol. Pr., Bratislava, 18/1,1–117.

Kunick, W. 1974. Veränderungen von Flora und Vegetation einer Großstadt, dargestellt am Beispiel von Berlin (West). Diss. Techn. Univ. Berlin.

Kunick, W. 1982. Comparison of the flora of some cities of the Central European lowlands. In: Bornkamm, R., Lee, J.A. & Seaward, M.R.D. (eds.), Urban ecology. 2nd European ecological symposium, Berlin, pp. 13–22, Blackwell, Oxford.

Kunick, W. 1983, Köln. Landschaftsökologische Grundlagen. T3, Biotopkartierung. Köln.

Kunick, W. 1991. Ausmaß und Bedeutung der Verwilderung von Gartenpflanzen. NAA-Berichte 4/1, 6–13.

Laurie, I.C. (ed.) 1979. Nature in cities. J. Wiley, Chichester.

Miess, M. 1979. The climate of cities. In: Laurie, I.C. (ed.), Nature in cities, pp. 91–114, J. Wiley, Chichester.

Moravec, J. 1989. Influences of the individualistic concept of vegetation on syntaxonomy. Vegetatio, Dordrecht 81: 29–39.

Mucina, L. 1982. Ku klasifikácii ruderálnych stanovíšť severozápadnej časti Podunajskej nížiny. Preslia, Praha 54: 349–367.

Mucina, L. 1985. Používať alebo nepoužívať Ellenbergove indikačné hodnoty? Biológia, 40: 511–516.

Mucina, L. 1989. Syntaxonomy of the Onopordum acanthium communities in temperate and continental Europe. Vegetatio, Dordrecht 81: 107–115.

Mucina, L. 1990. Urban vegetation research in European COMECON countries and Yugoslavia, a review. In: Sukopp, H., Hejný, S. & Kowarik, I. (eds.), Urban ecology, pp. 23–43, SPB Academic. Publ., The Hague.

Mucina, L. 1991. Variance and clinical variation in synanthropic vegetation. In: Nimis, P.L. & Crovello, T.J. (eds.), Quantitative approaches to phytogeography, pp. 263–276, Kluwer, The Hague.

Mucina, L. & Brandes, D. 1985. Communities of Berteroa incana in Europe and their geographical differentiation. Vegetatio, The Hague 59: 125–136.

Mucina, L. & Maglocký, S. (eds.) 1985. A list of vegetation units of Slovakia. Doc. Phytosoc., Camerino, N.S. 9: 175–220.

Mucina, L. & van der Maarel, E. 1989. Twenty years of numerical syntaxonomy. Vegetatio, Dordrecht 81: 1–15.

Mucina, L. & van Tongeren, O.F.R. 1989. A coenocline of the high-ranked syntaxa of ruderal vegetation. Vegetatio, Dordrecht 81: 117–125.

Mueller-Dombois, D. & Ellenberg, H. 1974. Aims and methods of vegetation ecology. J. Wiley, New York.

Oberdorfer, E. 1983. Süddeutsche Pflanzengesellschaften. 2 ed. Pflanzensoziologie, Jena 10: 1–455.

Opravil, E. 1980. Z historie synantropní vegetace 1–3. Živa, Praha 28(66): 4–5, 53–55, 88–90.

Passarge, H. 1964. Pflanzengesellschaften des Norddeutschen Flachlandes 1. Pflanzensoziologie, Jena 13: 1–324.

Pignatti, S. 1968. Die Inflation der höheren Pflanzensoziologischen Einheiten. In: Tüxen, R. (ed.), Pflanzensoziologische Systematik, pp. 85–97, The Hague.

Prach, K., Pyšek, P., Bartha, S. & Krahulec, F. 1994. Succession in man-made habitats. In: Mucina, L. (ed.), Synanthropic vegetation, Kluwer Publ. [in press].

Pyšek, A. 1977. Sukzession der Ruderalpflanzengesellschaften von Groß-Plzeň. Preslia, Praha 49: 161–179.

Pyšek, A. 1978. Ruderální vegetace Velké Plzně. Diss. Bot. Inst. Czechoslovak Acad. Sci., Průhonice.

Pyšek, A. 1981. Übersicht über die westböhmische Ruderalvegetation. Folia Mus. Rer. Natur. Bohem. Occid., Plzeň. ser. bot. 15: 1–24.

Pyšek, A. 1983. Gefährdete Ruderalpflanzengesellschaften Westböhmens. In: Zippelius, A. (ed.), Aus Liebe zur Natur, Bonn 3: 52–54.

Pyšek, A. & Pyšek, P. 1987a. Die Methode der Einheitsflächen beim Studium der Ruderalvegetation. Tuexenia, Göttingen 7: 479–485.

Pyšek, A. & Pyšek, P. 1987b. Quantitative Bewertung der Vegetationsdynamik in westböhmischen Siedlungsgebieten in den letzten 15 Jahren. In: Schubert, R. & Hilbig, W. (eds.), Erfassung und Bewertung anthropogener Vegetationsveränderungen 1, pp. 176–188, Halle/Saale.

Pyšek, A. & Pyšek, P. 1988a. Ruderální flóra Plzně. Sborn. Západočes. Muz., Plzeň, Přír. 68: 1–34.

Pyšek, A. & Pyšek, P. 1988b. Standörtliche Differenzierung der Flora der westböhmischen Dörfer. Folia Mus. Rer. Natur. Bohem. Occid., Plzeň, ser. bot. 28: 1–52.

Pyšek, P. 1988. Floristische- und Vegetationsverhältnisse des Zentralen Friedhofs in der Stadt Plzeň. Folia Mus. Rer. Natur. Bohem. Occid., Plzeň, ser. bot. 25: 1–46.

Pyšek, P. 1989a. On the richness of Central European urban flora. Preslia, Praha 61: 329–334.

Pyšek, P. 1989b. Archeofyty a neofyty v ruderální flóře některých sídlišť v Čechách. Preslia, Praha 61: 209–226.

Pyšek, P. 1991. Die Siedlungsvegetation des Böhmischen Karsts. 1. Syntaxonomie. Folia Geobot. Phytotax., Praha 26: 225–262.

Pyšek, P. 1992a. Die Siedlungsvegetation des Böhmischen Karsts. 2. Ökologische Charakteristik. Folia Geobot. Phytotax., Praha 27: 1–23.

Pyšek, P. 1992b. Settlement outskirts – may they be considered as ecotones? Ekológia (ČSFR), Bratislava 11: 273–286.

Pyšek, P. 1993. Factors affecting the diversity of flora and vegetation in central European settlements. Vegetatio, The Hague, 106: 89–100.

Pyšek, P. & Pyšek, A. 1985. Die Ausnutzung der Ruderalvegetation zur quantitativen Indikation von Standortverhältnissen mit Hilfe von Einheitsflächen (am Beispiel westböhmischer Siedlungen). Folia Mus. Rer. Natur. Bohem. Occid., Plzeň, ser. bot. 22: 1–35.

Pyšek, P. & Pyšek, A. 1988c. Die Vegetation der Betriebe des östlichen Teiles von Praha. 2. Vegetationsverhältnisse. Preslia, Praha 60: 349–365.

Pyšek, P. & Pyšek, A. 1990. Comparison of the vegetation and flora of the West Bohemian villages and towns. In: Sukopp, H., Hejný, S. & Kowarik, I. (eds.), Urban ecology, pp. 105–112, SPB Academic Publ., The Hague.

Pyšek, P. & Pyšek, A. 1991a. Succession in urban habitats: an analysis of phytosociological data. Preslia, Praha 63: 125–138.

Pyšek, P. & Pyšek, A. 1991b. Vergleich der dörflichen und städtischen Ruderalflora, dargestellt am Beispiel Westböhmens. Tuexenia, Göttingen 11: 121–134.

Pyšek, P. & Rydlo, J. 1984. Vegetace a flóra vybraných sídlišť v území mezi Kolínem a Poděbrady. Bohemia Centralis, Praha 13: 135–181.

Rebele, F. 1986. Die Ruderalvegetation der Industriegebiete von Berlin (West) und deren Immissionsbelastung. Landschaftsentw. und Umweltforsch., Berlin 43: 1–224.

Rebele, F. 1988. Ergebnisse floristischer Untersuchungen in den Industriegebieten von Berlin (West). Landschaft und Stadt 20: 49–66.

Rebele, F. 1991. Ecology on industrial wasteland. Symp. New nature on industrial sites, International Building Exhibition Emscher Park 1991, 17 pp. [ms.].

Rothmaler, W. et al. (eds.) 1976. Exkursionsflora für die Gebiete der DDR und der BRD. Berlin.

Saarisalo-Taubert, A. 1963. Die Flora in ihrer Beziehung zur Siedlung und Siedlungsgeschichte in den südfinnischen Städten Porvoo, Loviisa und Hamina. Ann. Bot. Soc. Vanamo 351: 1–90.

Scheuermann, R. 1928. Die Pflanzenwelt der Kehrichtplätze des rhein.-westf. Industriegebietes. Sitzungsber. Naturhist. Ver. Preuss. Rheinl. Westfalen 86: 256–342.

Scholz, H. 1960. Die Veränderungen in der Ruderalflora Berlins. Ein Beitrag zur jüngsten Florengeschichte. Willdenowia 2: 379–397.

Schulte, W., Sukopp, H., Voggenreiter, V. & Werner, P. 1986. Flächendeckende Biotopkartierung im besiedelten Bereich als Grundlage einer ökologisch bzw. am Naturschutz orientierten Plannung. Natur und Landschaft, Stuttgart 10: 371–389.

Sowa, R. & Olaczek, R. 1978. Stan badan szaty roślinnej miast polski. Wiad. Ekol. 24: 25–42.

Sowa, R. & Warcholinska, A.V. 1984. Flora synantropijna Sieradza i Zdunskej Woli. Acta Univ. Lodziensis, Fol. Bot 3: 151–207.

Sudnik-Wójcikowska, B. 1987. Dynamik der Warschauer Flora in den letzten 150 Jahren. Gleditschia, Berlin 15: 7–23.

Sudnik-Wójcikowska, B. 1988. Flora synanthropization and anthropopressure zones in a large urban agglomeration (exemplified by Warsaw). Flora, Jena 180: 481–496.

Sudnik-Wójcikowska, B. & Kozniewska, B. 1988. Slownik z zakresu synantropizacji szaty roslinnej. Warszawa.

Sukopp, H. 1969. Der Einfluß des Menschen auf die Vegetation. Vegetatio 17: 360–371.

Sukopp, H. 1971. Beiträge zur Ökologie von Chenopodium botrys L. I. Verbreitung und Vergesellschaftung. Verh. Bot. Ver. Prov. Brandenburg 108: 3–25.

Sukopp, H. 1972. Wandel von Flora und Vegetation in Mitteleuropa unter dem Einfluß des Menschen. Ber. Landw. 50: 112–139.

Sukopp, H. 1973. Die Großstadt als Gegenstand ökologischer Forschung. Schriften d. Vereins. z. Verbreitung naturwissensch. Kenntnisse in Wien 113: 90–140.

Sukopp, H. 1983. Die Bedeutung der Freilichtmuseen für den Arten- und Biotopschutz. In: Zippelius, A. (ed.), Aus Liebe zur Natur, Bonn 3: 34-42.

Sukopp, H. 1990. Urban ecology and its application in Europe. In: Sukopp, H., Blume, H.-P. & Kunick, W. 1979a. The soil, flora and vegetation of Berlins waste lands. In: Laurie, I.E. (ed.), Nature in cities, pp. 115–131, J. Wiley & Sons, Chichester.

Sukopp, H., Hejný, S. & Kowarik, I. (eds.) 1990. Urban ecology. SPB Academic. Publ., The Hague.

Sukopp, H. & Kowarik, I. 1986. Berücksichtigung von Neophyten in Roten Listen gefährdeter Arten. Schr. Reihe Vegetationsk., Bad Godesberg 18: 105–113.

Sukopp, H. & Köstler, H. 1986. Stand der Untersuchungen über dörfliche Flora und Vegetation in der Bundesrepublik Deutschland. Natur und Landschaft, Stuttgart, 7-8: 264–267.

Sukopp, H., Kunick, W. & Schneider, Ch. 1979b. Biotopkartierung in der Stadt. Natur u. Landschaft 54: 66–68.

Sukopp, H. & Sukopp, U. 1987. Leitlinien für den Naturschutz in Städten Zentraleuropas. In: Miyawaki, A. et al. (eds.), Vegetation ecology and creation of new environments, pp. 347–355, Tokyo Univ. Press.

Sukopp, H. Trautmann, W., Korneck, D. 1978. Auswertung der Roten Liste gefährdeter Farn- und Blütenpflanzen in der Bundesrepublik Deutschland für den Arten- und Biotopschutz. Schriftenreihe Vegetationskd. 12: 1–138.

Sukopp, H., Weiler, S. 1988. Biotope mapping and nature conservation strategies in urban areas of the Federal Republic of Germany. Lansc. Urban Plan. 15: 39–58.

Sukopp, H. & Werner, P. 1983. Urban environment and vegetation. In: Holzner, W., Werger, M.J.A., Ikusima, I. (eds.), Man's impact on vegetation, pp. 247–260, Junk Publ., The Hague.

Sukopp, H. & Werner, P. 1987. Development of flora and fauna in urban areas. European Committee for the Conservation of Nature and Natural Resources, Strassbourg.

Sukopp, H. et al. (1980). Contributions to urban ecology. Berlin (West). 2nd European Ecol. Symp., Excursionguide, Techn. Univ. Berlin.

Sukopp, H. et al. 1981. Liste der wildwachsenen Farn- und Blütenpflanzen von Berlin (West). Landesbeauftragter f. Natursch. Landschaftspfl. Berlin.

Sukopp, H. et al. 1986. Flächendeckende Biotopkartierung im besiedelten Bereich als Grundlage einer ökologisch bzw. am Naturschutz orientierten Planung. Natur u. Landschaft 61: 371–389.

Tlusták, V. 1990. Ruderální společenstva Olomouce. Diss. Bot. Inst. Czechoslovak Acad. Sci., Průhonice.

Trepl, L. 1983. Zum Gebrauch von Pflanzenarten als Indikatoren der Umweltdynamik. Sitzungsber. Ges. Naturforsch. Freunde zu Berlin 23: 151–171.

Tüllman, G. & Böttcher, H. 1983. Synanthropic vegetation and structure of urban subsystems. Coll. Phytosoc. Bailleuil 12: 481–523.

Višňák, R. 1986. Příspěvek k poznání antropogenní vegetace v severních Čechách, zvláště v měste Liberci. Preslia 58: 353–368.

Walters, S.M. 1970. The next twenty years. In: Perring, F. (ed.), The flora of changing Britain, pp. 136–141, Hampton,

Wiegleb, G. 1986. Grenzen und Möglichkeiten der Datenanalyse in der Pflanzensoziologie. Tuexenia, Göttingen 6: 365–377.

Wittig, R. 1973. Die ruderale Vegetation der Münsterschen Innenstadt. Natur u. Heimat, Heft 4: 100–110.

Wittig, R. 1984. Sterben die Dorfpflanzen aus? Der Gemeinderat 27 (6): 36–37.

Wittig, R. 1991. Ökologie der Großstadtflora. G. Fischer, Stuttgart.

Wittig, R., Diesing, D. & Gödde, M. 1985. Urbanophob – Urbanoneutral – Urbanophil. Das Verhalten der Arten gegenüber dem Lebensraum Stadt. Flora, Jena 177: 265–282.

Wittig, R. & Durwen, K.J. 1981. Das ökologische Zeigerwertspektrum der spontanen Flora von Großstädten im Vergleich zum Spektrum ihres Umlandes. Natur. u. Landsch. 56: 12–16.

Wittig, R. & Durwen, K.-J. 1982. Ecological indicator values spectra of spontaneous urban floras. In: Bornkamm, R., Lee, J.A. & Seaward, M.R.D. (eds.) 1982. Urban ecology. 2nd European ecological symposium, Berlin. Blackwell, Oxford.

Wittig, R. & Wittig, M. 1986. Spontane Vegetation in Westfalen. Decheniana, Bonn 139: 99–122.

Woodell, S. 1979. The flora of walls and pavings. In: Laurie, I.C. (ed.), Nature in cities, pp. 135–157, J. Wiley, Chichester.

Zajac, A. 1979. Pochodzenie archeofitow wystepujacych w Polsce. Rozpr. Habilit. Univ. Jagiel., Krakow 29: 1–213.

Zimmermann-Jaeger, S. 1971. Beiträge zur Ökologie von Chenopodium botrys L. III. Substanzproduktion und Wuchsfrom in Abhängigkeit von Beleuchtungsstärke, Feuchtigkeit und Substrat. Verh. Bot. Ver. Prov. Brandenburg 108: 29–36.

Cities

THE PLANT COVER OF ARCHAEOLOGICAL SITES IN CENTRAL ITALY*

ERIKA PIGNATTI[1], SANDRO PIGNATTI[2] and FERNANDO LUCCHESE[2]

[1]*Dipartimento di Biologia, Università di Trieste, Cas. Univ., 34127 Trieste, Italy;*
[2]*Dipartimento di Biologia Vegetale, Università di Roma "La Sapienza", Piazzale Aldo Moro 5, 00185 Roma, Italy*

Abstract

The plant cover and regeneration of natural and semi-natural vegetation types in archaeological areas with particular regard to historical sites in Central Italy are described as well as the different habitats on which they are growing. The grouping of communities on these man-made and controlled areas is analysed by the classical phytosociological method. The management of the plant cover and the importance of green surfaces within archaeological sites as a cultural heritage as well as areas of recreation and relaxation for visitors are discussed.

1. Introduction

The presence of vegetation in archaeological sites is closely related to climate, structure and material of artefacts and the type of management.

In humid climates natural or seminatural vegetation develops quite easily, invading empty spaces. Impressive examples are known from the humid tropics, such as the Maya's ruins in Yukatan, the Temples of Angkor in Cambodia, pioneer settlement of Jesuit colonisation in Misiones (Argentine). In very dry climatic conditions archaeological sites are devoid of any vegetation or buried under sand, as in Egypt.

Archaeological structures are not the most favourable substrate for vegetation but some plants from rocky habitats may colonise walls and stones. Only a few species are adapted to this very particular environment, above all the characteristic species of the class Parietarietea. Locally these species can become quite abundant. Other species occurring on archaeological sites may be considered more or less as casual invaders from other habitats, so that, in general, vegetation is richer in areas where ruins are surrounded by fertile soils and in the vicinity of natural vegetation.

Management can definitely influence the plant cover of archaeological sites: in some cases the presence of plants may be tolerated or even considered as ornamental, but in other cases plants are drastically eliminated. The question of whether an old wall is more beautiful being completely without any plant or with plants remains an open one. The presence of infrastructure (roads, parking areas etc.) is a further limit for the development of plant cover.

Little literature exists on the vegetation of archaeological sites. The study on vegetation of walls by Segal (1969) gives some hints but deals mainly with recent constructions. Oberdorfer (1968) published several contributions on vegetation of old walls in the mediterranean region. A recent survey of the class Parietarietea was carried out by Rivas Martinez (1982).

A lot of floristic information is available on some Roman monuments (Pignatti E. 1987a, 1987b). The earliest quotation on plants growing on ruins of the so-called "Villa of Pliny" near Rome were published by the pre-Linnéan naturalist Lancisi (1654–1720) at the beginning of the 18th century. The Flora of the Colosseum was repeatedly described in the 19th

* This investigation was carried out with grants from C.N.R. and MURST (40%).

Urban Ecology as the Basis of Urban Planning, p. 43–48
edited by H. Sukopp, M. Numata and A. Huber
© *1995 SPB Academic Publishing bv, Amsterdam, The Netherlands*

century (Fiorini Mazzanti 1875–78). The flora of other monuments in Italy and elsewhere has been studied (Oberdorfer 1969, Segal 1969).

2. Methods of investigation

Our investigations have been carried out in the area between Rome and Naples where an extremely rich archaeological heritage is present. They have also been developed during occasional visits in other areas within Italy (Northern part of Latium, Tuscany, Umbria, Puglia, Sicily) and abroad (Israel, China).

Vegetation has been studied mainly using the Braun-Blanquet approach (Westhoff & van der Maarel, 1972) *i.e.*, the phytosociological method. The associations living within the archaeological sites are evidently mostly man-made or a result of human activity but in general do not reveal major differences in comparison with other aspects of synanthropic vegetation. Sometimes the relevées taken may be considered as fragmentary because the surface area available was too small or the time for undisturbed development was too short. During our investigations in mediterranean Italy from Tuscany to Sardinia and Sicily nearly 300 relevées have been carried out within the last decade.

3. Flora of archaeological sites

The climatic conditions of Central Italy determining the biological and ecological characters of the flora, are annual mean temperatures about 14–16°C, rainfall about 650–850 mm with summer aridity lasting 2–3 months.

3.1. Flora in general

Some species groups appear well adapted to the particular environment and climatic conditions of Central Italy. Annuals are colonisers on walls and bricks where the soil stratum is extremely thin. These are species which produce a huge quantity of seeds, germinate rapidly and also for this reason are able to escape frequent management. Chamaephytes are abundant on rocky habitats, in crevices and on walls, and show thermophily. In shady and dark habitats where conditions are more humid, geophytes (mainly pteridophytes) may appear more frequently. Most species have large distribution ranges and the percentage of more or less cosmopolitan species is quite high. Many species are anemophilous and seeds have sufficient adaptation for dispersal by wind, animals, and man. Polyploids are prevalent. Many of these species have pioneer character.

The flora of archaeological sites is in general very rich. Thus single archaeological parks in Rome such as the Fori Imperiali, Domus Aurea or Terme di Caracalla, each have a flora of more than 300 species on a surface of a few hectars.

Most species are widespread but also relatively rare species can be present: *e.g.*, native orchids in the archaeological areas in the center of Rome and endemics like the rare *Micromeria microphylla* in Ostia Antica (Lucchese 1988).

3.2. Culture relicts

It can be assumed that on archaeological sites several species occur which have been cultivated frequently by the Romans or at least in earlier times. A few of them seem to have continued to grow by chance in the same habitat since then. *Laurus nobilis*, naturally growing along creeks on volcanic hills surrounding Rome, played an important role in Roman ceremonies and therefore it was practical to have it grow in Roman gardens. Presently *Laurus nobilis* is frequently cultivated around settlements and within gardens; it occurs in archaeological areas as an escape or dispersed by birds.

A few ornamental flowers may have been cultivated during the Roman Empire, which are no longer important in horticulture but still can be found on archaeological sites. This may be the case of the pantropical *Lippia nodiflora*, a small creeping chamaephyte not culti-vated in gardens now, or *Trachelium coeruleum*, an ornamental Campanulacea, growing now on old walls and even hanging down from Tito's Arch in the Fori Imperiali. Probably in-troduced in former times, this species is not known in Italy from natural habitats. Among widely distributed species in archaeological areas *Acanthus mollis* must be singled out. It is not clear whether this species has ever grown naturally in continental Italy. Nowadays the distribution of this western steno-mediterranean species can be considered as largely sec-ondary. The south-european – west-asiatic *Cercis siliquastrum* is indigenous in the calcareous mountains east of Rome. It has been cultivated in gardens and is now largely naturalized, also in archaeological areas. *Capparis spinosa* diffused along the coast is common in archaeo-logical areas but always grows on walls, from sea level to mountain areas.

Vitex agnus-castus, a shrub or small tree, indigenous in Southern Italy and the islands, was the symbol of virginity in Roman times and was later adopted by Christians as a symbol of the Lamb. It can be found quite often naturalized on archaeological sites. The same is the case with the southwest-asiatic ornamental *Punica granatum*.

Styrax officinalis which has its origin in the Middle East, occurs around Tivoli and in the Villa Adriana, Villa Mondragone in Frascati, on the Colli Albani, and in France around Avi-gnon and Marseille. An explanation for this uncommon distribution could be that this spe-cies was naturalized a long time ago, perhaps after it was cultivated by the Romans (Villa Adriana) and then escaped into the natural vegetation.

A still undescribed *Campanula* found first on the Palatino by B. Anzalone (verb. comm.) from the *C. fruticulosa* group and found later by one of us also within the Fori Imperiali, might have once been cultivated there. Now it is found locally on ruins of the Forum. In a similar way the now widely dispersed *Erysimum cheiri* once cultivated as an ornamental can be found on walls of many ruins, where it still plays an ornamental role (see Villa dei Gordani and other archaeological sites in Rome).

The endemic *Genista ephedroides* on (sometimes volcanic) rocks near the sea (Salerno), in Sicily and Sardinia, was found by us growing on the Palatino together with *Rhamnus alaternus*. It originally might have been planted there as an ornamental shrub. At which time this occurred cannot be dated exactly; the nearest wild growing populations are on the is-lands off the coast of Terracina, to which members of the imperial family were exiled in Roman times. This species has been only found on the Palatino within the Rome district. It can also be supposed that the showy *Vinca major* in the Fori Romani had been planted there a long time ago and has become established since then.

3.3. Neophytes

Since the discovery of America a lot of neophytes have been dispersed through Europe. About 450 species occur in the Flora of Italy (Pignatti, 1982), but only a few of them in ar-chaeological areas, for instance: *Setaria viridis*, *Amaranthus deflexus*, *A. lividus*, *A. retroflexus*, *Erigeron karvinskianus*, *Conyza albida*, *C. bonariensis*, *C. canadensis*, *Phytolacca americana*, *Aster squamatus*, *Datura stramonium*, *Ailanthus altissimus*, *Agave americana*, *Mirabilis jalapa*, *Gleditsia triacanthos*, *Robinia pseudoacacia*, *Dichondra repens*, *Parthenocissus quinquefolia*, *P. tricuspidata* and *Nicotiana glauca*. A relatively recent expansion had the now nearly cosmopolitan *Eleusine indica*.

In the metropolitan area of Rome where many archaeological sites are scattered among modern settlements, neophytes are frequently distributed in urbanized areas, mostly as ruderal elements and often covering wide surfaces. However they are rarely found within archaeological sites and if so, are never really frequent.

Amaranthus and *Setaria spec. div.* are frequent on waste places in Roman suburbs but are relatively rare in archaeological areas. Indigenous species compose 92% and more of the to-tal flora of the Palatino, Circo Massimo and Terme di Caracalla and 70–90% of the species growing in the historical centre (city) of Rome (Celesti & Nazzaro, 1991).

4. Plant communities on archaeological sites

Several associations occur in archaeological sites: they can be distributed over at least five main groups: vegetation on walls, on lawns, on sandy soils, on trampled sites and the regeneration of woody plant cover.

4.1. Vegetation on walls

The natural chasmophytic vegetation of this region belongs to the class Asplenietea but can hardly be observed in archaeological areas. Plant communities on walls belong to the class Parietarietea, probably a man-made vegetation. It consists prevalently of chasmophytes and is sometimes adapted to nitrate-rich soil. Dominant species are *Parietaria diffusa, Sonchus tenerrimus, Cymbalaria muralis* etc.

On shady and moist walls *Adiantum capillus veneris* is present in extended and compact populations; few other vascular plants can grow on this environment, but Bryophytes *(Eucladium)* and Cyanobacteria are very frequent.

In coastal environments a particular type of halophilous chasmophytes (Crithmo-Staticetea) can be observed. Significant species of this class are: *Crithmum maritimum, Limonium spec. div., Centaurea cineraria, Helichrysum litoreum, Matthiola incana, Capparis spinosa*: they develop on ancient walls near the sea (Terracina, Capri, Gaeta etc.). *Capparis spinosa* is also diffused in mainland areas, e.g., Fori Romani, Domus Aurea, Mura Aureliane), probably by bird dissemination.

Micromeria microphylla which was known in former times (Pignatti 1982) only for Puglia, Sicily, Malta and was considered endemic has recently been found on bricks in Ostia Antica. The appearance in the archaeological area of Ostia Antica can be explained by the source of material (marble or other) with which it seems to have been imported from elsewhere. Presently *M. microphylla* grows on and between bricks.

In very dry situations on top of walls or in their uppermost part xeric aspects with *Sedum sediforme, Sempervivum spec. div.* and others may develop.

4.2. Vegetation on lawns

Vegetation on lawns belongs to the class Thero-Brachypodietea. Several associations or fragments can appear. Species which can become dominant are the following: *Dasypyrum villosum, Vulpia ligustica, Trisetaria viridis, Hordeum murinum, Malva sylvestris, Brachypodium phoenicoides, Avena barbata* and different species of the genus *Trifolium* (*scabrum, repens, pratense, nigrescens* etc.); sometimes *Asphodelus microcarpus* invades such meadows. Most of these communities can be included in the Vulpio-Dasypyretum association (Fanelli, in press). Some of these communities are subjected to mowing or herbicid treatments and their composition may deviate largely from natural communities occurring under semi-natural conditions.

4.3. Vegetation on sandy soils

This is similar to the pioneer phase of the former vegetation, developing on sand which accumulates frequently in archaeological areas. Sometimes this material serves to protect parts of an area such as mosaics etc., sometimes it is of eolic origin. Its vegetation is mostly annual and shortlived and belongs to the class Thero-Brachypodietea, with *Brachypodium distachyum, Poa bulbosa, Scabiosa maritima, Catapodium rigidum, Capsella rubella* etc. as most frequent components.

4.4. Vegetation in trampled sites

Due to frequent disturbance in trampled sites such as pathways and roads and areas between pavements, a vegetation develops which is mostly formed by small species belonging to the Plantaginetea majoris, a worldwide distributed class. For the Rome area the association Lolio-Polygonetum arenastri was first described by Blasi & Pignatti (1982). Frequent species are *Lolium rigidum, Trifolium repens, Trifolium scabrum, Polycarpon tetraphyllum, Plantago lanceolata, Sagina apetala* etc.

4.5. Woody vegetation as a stage of succession

Sometimes even woody vegetation may develop within archaeological areas, starting a succession towards climax-like vegetation types. The succession may start with a *Rubus ulmifolius* scrub, continuing with *Ulmus minor, Euonymus europaeus, Hedera helix, Rosa canina, R. sempervirens, Prunus spinosa, Ficus carica*. A small evergreen treegroup may be formed by *Laurus nobilis*, which frequently functions as a starting point towards the regeneration of evergreen vegetation (Asplenio-Quercetum ilicis).

Often such small forest pioneers contribute greatly to the aesthetic charm of an archaeological site.

Sometimes it may be even possible that the natural vegetation develops again on top of an archaeological area, if time is sufficient and human interference low. This is the case of a regenerated Asplenio-Quercetum ilicis (climax vegetation in coastal mediterranean areas) on bricks and other remnants of old roman settlements a few hundred meters inside along the coastline of Castelporziano near Rome. Ancient documents indicate the presence of the roman village Vicus Augustanus Laurentinus in this vicinity, a clear proof that *Laurus nobilis* (presently widespread in this area) belongs to the natural vegetation. This is the only example known in Italy of spontaneous regeneration of a climax forest on a formerly populated area.

5. Urban significance

In Italy, as is generally the case in mediterranean countries, little space is given to green areas in the urban context and consequently many towns with a long history are presently composed of rather uniformly built blocks. The vegetation of archaeological sites, even if discontinuous and in most cases represented only by pioneer or fragmentary aspects, often is the only vegetation which can interrupt the continuity of buildings. Archaeological areas are efficiently protected and in most cases remain safe from the aggression of speculative constructions. The urban consequences are in some senses positive, in others negative.

A positive aspect is that archaeological areas have at least a portion covered by green surfaces and interrupt the polluting influence of traffic. In some cases they are included in parks which are necessary as recreation areas for the local population. Also tourists engaged in exhausting visits during the climatically uncomfortable summer can find refreshment and peace in such surroundings. In this sense the presence of plant cover and in particular the presence of trees is a welcome component of archaeological areas.

Negative effects on the urban environment can be caused by several species growing on walls which are agents of allergies: *Parietaria, Urtica, Artemisia* and in general grasses. This may represent a disturbance for visitors and people housing in the vicinity. Plants are also unwelcome when the roots are cracking old bricks and degrade some artifacts, so that many public administrations try to maintain archaeological sites free of wild growing species.

Regreening in archaeological areas is in general obtained by using the same species which are cultivated in gardens or along roadsides: *Eucalyptus, Myoporum, Agave, Opuntia,*

Geranium etc. This should be avoided as it is completely the wrong management. The use of species originating from other continents detracts from the cultural heritage of the monuments. In order to maintain archaeological areas in their pristine condition it seems better to give some space to spontaneous regreening with native vegetation. If necessary native species *(Quercus ilex, Pinus spec. div., Laurus nobilis, Myrtus communis, Nerium oleander, Helichrysum spec. div., Lonicera spec. div., Hedera helix, Narcissus, Hyacinthus, Tulipa, Iberis semperflorens, Lobularia maritima, Aubrietia spec. div., Campanula garganica agg.* etc.) can be introduced as ornaments within archaeological sites.

Archaeological artefacts cannot be managed as a museum and the pretension to maintain them free of vegetation is a form of perfectionism. In addition, the use of different types of "killers" (biocides, mechanical removal, destruction of roots by explosives) sharply contradicts the cultural message of these historic sites. Instead, a reasonable tolerance of natural vegetation may enhance the link between a humanistic and an ecological culture.

6. Conclusions

A first survey of plant grouping within archaeological areas in Italy shows that most communities have a pioneer character and deviate in some degree from the natural vegetation. The less a site is disturbed and the more time passes by, the better and more naturally the communities will develop. Even their pioneer state can be well documented by using the Braun-Blanquet method with phytosociological relevées. The coordination in higher taxa is possible; a variety of new combinations within the given communities can be observed. Man-made habitats and the possibility of regeneration have created an environment rich in species and of remarkable diversity.

References

Blasi, C. & Pignatti, S. 1984. La vegetazione degli ambienti calpestati della città di Roma. Annali di Bot./ Studi sul Territorio 2: 11–16.
Celesti, L. & Nazzaro, G. in press. Assetto urbanistico e sucessione nell' ambiente. Atti Congr. Ecol. Milano.
Fanelli, G. in press. La vegetazione a Dasypyrum villosum nel Lazio e nell' Italia tirrenica. Studi sul Territorio.
Fiorini Mazzanti, E. 1875–78. Florula del Colosseo. Atti Accad. Pont. Nuovi Lincei, 28–31.
Lancisi, G.M. 1714. Dissertazione de Plinianae Villae ruderibus atque Ostiensis litoralis incremento. Roma, pp. I–XXXII.
Lucchese, F. 1988. Segnalazioni floristiche italiane 546 – Micromeria microphylla. Inform. Bot. Ital. 20 (23).
Oberdorfer, E. 1969. Zur Soziologie der Cymbalario-Parietarietea, am Beispiel der Mauerteppich-Gesellschaften Italiens. Vegetatio 17: 208–213.
Pignatti, E. 1987a. Progetto di studio del popolamento vegetale in aree archaeologiche nella zona di Roma, MAB Project 11, Project Report 3: 77–79. Roma.
Pignatti, E. 1987b. Project Study of the Plant Cover in the Archaeological Areas of Rome – MAB Project 11, Project Report 3: 311–319. Roma.
Pignatti Wikus, E. & Visentin Niomi, M. 1993. Ostia Antica and its Vegetation, in Savoia Ubrizsy, A. (ed.) "Spontaneous vegetation in settlements". Braun-Blanquetia 3 (2).
Pignatti, S. 1982. Flora d'Italia, 3 vol. Edagricole. Bologna.
Rivas Martinez, S. 1980. Sinopsis de la vegetacion nitrofila rupestre (Parietarietea judaicae). Anal. Inst. Bot. Cavan. 35: 225–233.
Segal, S. 1969. Ecological notes on wall vegetation. The Hague.
Westhoff, V. & van der Maarel, E. 1973. The Braun-Blanquet approach. In: Whittaker, R.H. (ed.), Ordination and Classification of Vegetation. Handb. Veg. Sci. 5: 619–726.

THE FLORA OF OLD TOWN CENTRES IN EUROPE

DIETMAR BRANDES

Technische Universität Braunschweig, Universitätsbibliothek, Pockelsstr. 13, D-38106 Braunschweig, Germany

Abstract

The spontaneous floras of 66 old town centres have been mapped in different regions of Europe (Germany, France, Belgium, Austria, Switzerland, Italy, and Portugal). Similarity as well as geographical variability of the old town floras are studied. Our investigations show that the number of common species in old town centres of central and/or West Europe is high. Similar climatic conditions in old towns of the western part of the mediterranean area also lead to relatively uniform stocks of plant species. Differences between the floras of old cities and old villages are pointed out.

1. Introduction

In the last 3 decades there have been numerous papers concerned with the flora and vegetation of European cities (review: Sukopp 1990). Urban areas are very heterogeneous and contain a large number of different habitats, which are usually sharply separated: old town centres, young housing estates, railway sites, industrial sites, highways, cemeteries, villages, dumping sites, fields, urban forests.

This paper considers the old town centres, which differ from newer quarters in their long settlement and old buildings. One can assume that the floristic similarities between old town centres are high, as climatic and geographic differences are compensated – at least partly – by the similar and long-enduring use.

The botanical exploration of towns started with old town centres 140 years ago. In 1855 Deakin studied the flora of the Colosseum of Rome and found 420 taxa growing spontaneously upon its ruins. Jourdan (1866, 1867, 1872) analysed the flora of ancient walls in Algeria as well as in France. The systematic investigation of old town centres, however, did not start before 1980 (Aey 1990, Brandes 1982, 1985, 1991, Schulte 1989).

I tried to investigate as many old town centres as possible in different areas of Europe, using uniform methods to obtain comparable data. Our interest is focussed on the geographic variability of the flora, as well as on the question of which species are typical for old towns.

2. Methods

The floras of old town centres (within the historical fortifications) have been mapped in different seasons as completely as possible. To facilitate comparability, the data of the towns were combined regionally:
1.   Northern part of Lower Saxony (FRG): Emden, Leer, Lüneburg, Stade, Verden.
2.   Southeastern part of Lower Saxony (FRG): Brunswick (= Braunschweig), Goslar, Helmstedt, Hildesheim, Wolfenbüttel.

Urban Ecology as the Basis of Urban Planning, p. 49–58
edited by H. Sukopp, M. Numata and A. Huber
© *1995 SPB Academic Publishing bv, Amsterdam, The Netherlands*

Table 1. Frequency of vascular plant species in old town centres of different regions in Europe.

Region	1	2	3	4	5	6	7	8	9	10	11
Sisymbrium altissimum	III	IV	.	.	.	.	.	.	.	.	.
Rumex crispus	I	IV	II	IV	.	.	.	.	.	.	.
Heracleum mantegazzianum	IV	III	III	I	.	.	.	.	.	.	.
Helianthus annuus	I	I	II	IV	I	.	.	.	.	.	.
Lepidium ruderale	I	III	IV	I	IV	II	.	.	.	.	.
Oxalis europaea	I	IV	II	II	IV	IV	.	.	.	.	.
Acer platanoides	IV	V	V	IV	IV	I	II	.	.	.	.
Aegopodium podagraria	II	V	V	V	II	I	III	.	.	.	.
Calamagrostis epigejos	I	V	IV	II	II	.	I	.	.	.	.
Epilobium angustifolium	IV	IV	IV	II	.	I	III	.	.	.	.
Solidago canadensis	III	V	V	IV	V	.	I	.	.	.	.
Sorbus aucuparia	III	IV	II	I	.	.	III	.	.	.	.
Tanacetum vulgare	II	V	IV	II	II	.	I	.	.	.	.
Urtica urens	II	V	III	II	III	II	II	.	.	.	.
Bromus tectorum	II	I	.	.	IV	.	I	.	.	.	.
Impatiens glandulifera	III	.	II	IV	.	I	I	.	.	.	.
Acer pseudoplatanus	V	V	V	V	III	III	V	IV	.	.	.
Agrostis stolonifera	III	V	II	IV	.	I	III	III	.	.	.
Agropyron repens	V	IV	IV	III	V	.	IV	III	.	.	.
Atriplex patula	V	IV	III	IV	II	I	III	IV	.	.	.
Bromus hordeaceus ssp. hord.	IV	I	I	.	.	I	.	II	.	.	.
Cirsium arvense	V	V	V	V	V	II	V	II	.	.	.
Crepis capillaris	II	II	IV	II	.	.	I	IV	.	.	.
Dryopteris filix-mas	IV	IV	IV	I	II	V	IV	IV	.	.	.
Epilobium hirsutum	II	I	I	IV	.	.	V	IV	.	.	.
Geum urbanum	III	III	IV	V	I	I	I	IV	.	.	.
Lapsana communis	III	V	IV	V	V	IV	IV	IV	.	.	.
Matricaria discoidea	V	IV	IV	V	V	V	III	II	.	.	.
Medicago lupulina	II	II	III	IV·	IV	.	III	II	.	.	.
Poa nemoralis	III	IV	V	IV	I	V	III	IV	.	.	.
Poa pratensis	I	IV	III	IV	III	II	I	III	.	.	.
Poa trivialis	IV	.	I	IV	.	I	I	I	.	.	.
Poa compressa	III	V	III	IV	IV	II	V	I	.	.	.
Polygonum persicaria	II	II	II	III	II	.	IV	IV	.	.	.
Sonchus arvensis	I	II	I	IV	.	.	III	I	.	.	.
Sonchus asper	V	III	III	II	I	II	III	IV	.	.	.
Tripleurospermum inodorum	III	IV	IV	II	.	I	II	I	.	.	.
Tussilago farfara	II	V	IV	IV	III	.	III	I	.	.	.
Ulmus cf. campestris juv.	III	II	III	IV	.	.	II	III	.	.	.
Veronica arvensis	IV	II	I	II	II	V	I	II	.	.	.
Artemisia vulgaris	IV	V	V	IV	V	II	V	I	II	.	.
Asplenium ruta-muraria	III	V	V	V	V	V	V	II	II	.	.
Bellis perennis	IV	V	IV	II	V	III	III	IV	I	.	.
Betula pendula	V	V	V	V	V	V	V	II	II	.	.
Calystegia sepium	IV	IV	V	V	I	IV	III	V	II	.	.
Cerastium fontanum agg.	III	IV	III	IV	.	III	III	II	I	.	.
Chelidonium majus	IV	V	V	V	V	V	IV	IV	III	.	.
Clematis vitalba	III	III	V	III	.	III	V	II	I	.	.
Conyza canadensis	V	V	IV	V	V	V	V	III	V	.	.
Fraxinus excelsior juv.	V	V	V	V	I	I	V	IV	I	.	.
Galinsoga ciliata	II	III	V	IV	III	IV	III	.	V	.	.
Galinsoga parviflora	IV	IV	.	II	IV	.	I	.	II	.	.
Geranium pusillum	IV	I	II	II	III	I	III	II	I	.	.
Hordeum murinum	V	IV	III	I	V	III	V	II	III	.	.

Table 1. Continued.

Region	1	2	3	4	5	6	7	8	9	10	11
Lamium album	II	III	II	IV	.	II	I	.	I	.	.
Mycelis muralis	I	II	V	IV	III	V	V	.	I	.	.
Plantago lanceolata	III	IV	IV	V	V	I	III	IV	III	.	.
Prunella vulgaris	II	I	II	II	III	.	IV	III	II	.	.
Ranunculus repens	V	IV	IV	V	I	IV	IV	IV	I	.	.
Robinia pseudacacia juv.	II	III	I	II	III	I	IV	II	III	.	.
Rorippa sylvestris	V	II	IV	II	.	.	I	.	I	.	.
Rumex obtusifolius	V	V	V	IV	I	I	III	IV	II	.	.
Sagina procumbens	V	V	V	V	V	V	V	IV	V	.	.
Salix caprea	V	V	V	IV	IV	III	V	I	II	.	.
Sambucus nigra	V	V	V	V	V	V	V	V	I	.	.
Urtica dioica	V	V	V	V	V	V	V	IV	III	.	.
Viola odorata	III	V	III	II	IV	II	.	II	I	.	.
Bromus sterilis	II	III	III	I	IV	V	II	IV	.	I	.
Dactylis glomerata	III	V	V	V	V	II	III	V	I	II	.
Lolium perenne	V	V	V	V	V	IV	IV	V	III	I	.
Malva neglecta	II	IV	IV	V	IV	IV	III	II	I	II	.
Plantago major	V	V	V	V	V	V	V	V	V	V	.
Taraxacum officinale agg.	V	V	V	V	V	V	V	V	V	IV	.
Cymbalaria muralis	IV	V	V	V	IV	V	V	V	V	IV	V
Capsella bursa-pastoris	V	V	V	V	V	V	V	IV	II	I	I
Chenopodium album	IV	V	V	V	V	IV	V	IV	V	II	V
Convolvulus arvensis	II	IV	II	V	V	III	III	IV	I	I	II
Euphorbia peplus	III	IV	IV	IV	IV	IV	III	V	III	.	IV
Galium aparine	IV	II	II	III	II	IV	III	II	.	II	V
Hedera helix	V	V	IV	V	V	V	V	V	I	IV	II
Lactuca serriola	I	IV	V	III	I	V	III	II	.	I	?IV
Mercurialis annua	I	IV	.	I	V	IV	V	IV	I	.	V
Oxalis corniculata	II	.	I	.	III	I	II	II	V	V	V
Poa annua	V	V	V	V	V	V	V	V	V	IV	V
Polygonum aviculare agg.	V	V	V	V	V	IV	V	V	V	IV	IV
Sisymbrium officinale	V	V	V	IV	II	III	V	II	.	.	I
Senecio vulgaris	V	V	IV	V	V	V	V	V	III	III	V
Solanum nigrum	II	II	II	I	III	?	IV	V	II	IV	I
Sonchus oleraceus	V	V	V	V	V	V	V	IV	III	V	V
Stellaria media	V	V	V	V	V	V	V	V	V	III	V
Geranium robertianum	.	V	II	IV	.	V	II	IV	I	.	?V
Asplenium trichomanes	.	I	II	II	IV	III	III	IV	IV	III	.
Ailanthus altissima	.	I	.	I	III	.	III	I	V	.	.
Arrhenatherum elatius	.	II	III	II	IV	.	IV	III	I	.	.
Buddleja davidii	.	I	.	.	.	.	IV	II	II	.	.
Eragrostis minor	.	I	.	II	V	.	I	.	V	.	.
Trifolium pratense	.	III	III	IV	II	.	I	II	I	.	.
Corylus avellana	.	III	I	I	.	II	.	IV	.	.	.
Veronica persica	.	I	I	IV	.	.	.	IV	.	.	.
Festuca rubra agg.	.	III	II	IV	II	I	.	.	.	.	.
Lamium maculatum	.	II	.	IV	.	I	.	.	.	.	.
Ballota nigra ssp. nigra	.	IV	III	II	V	.	.	.	.	.	.
Potentilla anserina	.	.	II	IV	.	.	.	.	.	.	.
Rubus fruticosus agg.	.	.	II	I	.	III	III	V	.	.	.
Sedum reflexum	.	.	I	.	.	.	.	IV	.	.	.

Table 1. Continued.

Region	1	2	3	4	5	6	7	8	9	10	11
Parietaria judaica	.	.	I	I	.	I	III	V	V	V	V
Amaranthus retroflexus	.	.	.	I	IV	.	I	.	.	.	.
Digitaria sanguinalis	.	.	.	I	II	.	II	III	V	III	.
Sedum album	.	.	.	II	IV	V	I	II	I	.	I
Parthenocissus quinquefolia agg.	.	.	.	.	IV	I	.	.	.	.	.
Cynodon dactylon	.	.	.	.	IV	.	.	.	IV	IV	IV
Cheiranthus cheiri	.	.	.	.	.	III	III	V	.	III	.
Centranthus ruber	.	.	.	.	.	.	III	V	I	V	.
Polypodium vulgare	.	.	.	.	.	.	III	V	.	.	.
Amarantus deflexus	.	.	.	.	.	.	.	I	V	V	II
Coronopus didymus	.	.	.	.	.	.	.	II	.	I	V
Umbilicus rupestris	.	.	.	.	.	.	.	IV	.	III	V
Portulaca oleracea	.	.	.	.	.	.	.	.	V	II	I
Ficus carica	.	.	.	.	.	.	.	.	II	III	V
Conyza albida	.	.	.	.	.	.	.	.	.	IV	.
Hyoseris radiata	.	.	.	.	.	.	.	.	.	V	.
Lepidium graminifolium	.	.	.	.	.	.	.	.	.	IV	.
Bromus madritensis	.	.	.	.	.	.	.	.	.	I	V
Conyza bonariensis	.	.	.	.	.	.	.	.	.	II	V
Erodium malacoides	.	.	.	.	.	.	.	.	.	III	?V
Fumaria capreolata	.	.	.	.	.	.	.	.	.	II	V
Hyoscyamus albus	.	.	.	.	.	.	.	.	.	II	IV
Hordeum leporinum	.	.	.	.	.	.	.	.	.	V	III
Oxalis pes-caprae	.	.	.	.	.	.	.	.	.	II	V
Oryzopsis miliacea	.	.	.	.	.	.	.	.	.	IV	III
Polycarpon tetraphyllum	.	.	.	.	.	.	.	.	.	IV	III
Phagnalon saxatile	.	.	.	.	.	.	.	.	.	I	V
Urtica dubia	.	.	.	.	.	.	.	.	.	IV	V
Campanula erinus	.	.	.	.	.	.	.	.	.	.	IV
Centranthus calcitrapa	.	.	.	.	.	.	.	.	.	.	V
Lavatera cretica	.	.	.	.	.	.	.	.	.	.	V
Misopates orontium	.	.	.	.	.	.	.	.	.	.	V
Sagina apetala	.	.	.	.	.	.	.	.	.	.	V
Sonchus tenerrimus	.	.	.	.	.	.	.	.	.	.	V
Nicotiana glauca	.	.	.	.	.	.	.	.	.	.	V

3. Southern part of Lower Saxony (FRG): Einbeck, Göttingen, Hameln, Holzminden, Münden.

4. Southern part of Bavaria (FRG): Abensberg, Berching, Kelheim, Landsberg, Landshut, Munich (= München), Riedenburg.

5. Wachau (Lower Austria): Dürnstein, Krems, Langenlois, Melk, Stein, Weißenkirchen.

6. Alsace (France): Bergheim, Dambach-la-ville, Eguisheim, Kaysersberg, Ribeauvillé, Riquewihr.

7. Belgium and northern parts of France: Boulogne-sur-Mer, Bruges, Douai, Huy, Laon, Mons, Namur.

8. Brittany (France): Dinan, Guérande, La Trinité-Porhoet, Moncontour, Quintin, Uzel, Vannes, Vitré.

9. Insubrian region of the Alps (Switzerland and Italy): Bellinzona, Chiavenna, Ivrea, Laveno, Lugano, Luino.

10. Liguria (Italy): Albenga, Cervo, Finalborgo, San Remo, Taggia.

11. Algarve (Portugal): Albufeira, Faro, Lagos, Loulé, Silves, Tavira.

The frequency of the species is grouped into classes (*e.g.*, Brandes & Griese 1991): I: occurring in 1–20% of the towns; II: occurring in 21–40% of the towns; III: occurring in 41–60% of the towns; IV: occurring in 61–80% of the towns; V: occurring in 81–100% of the towns. Table 1 contains only species occurring with high frequency (IV or V) in at least one region.

3. The flora of old town centres

3.1. Central Europe

3.1.1. The flora

Walls and pavements
Table 1 (column 1–6) shows that about 90 species of vascular plants are widespread in the towns of Central Europe. The most important habitats in the crowded built-up old towns are walls and pavements. Common species typical for walls are *Asplenium ruta-muria, Asplenium trichomanes, Cymbalaria muralis, Dryopteris filix-mas* and *Hedera helix. Poa compressa, Bromus tectorum, Betula pendula* and *Sedum species* are growing on the wall top. If there are enough old walls in the town, the number of species can be rather high. Of special interest are old city walls with many species which have escaped from the gardens (Brandes 1992).

Directly in front of the wall base, *Conyza canadensis, Galinsoga ciliata, Galinsoga parviflora, Hordeum murinum, Lactuca serriola, Malva neglecta* and *Sisymbrium officinale* are to be found. At wall bases which are more shadowed, as well as beneath shrubs, *Chelidonium majus, Geum urbanum, Lapsana communis, Mycelis muralis, Sonchus oleraceus* and *Stellaria media* are growing. At shadowed and less trodden pavements we find young shrubs like *Acer pseudoplatanus, Acer platanoides, Betula pendula, Clematis vitalba, Fraxinus excelsior, Salix caprea* and *Sambucus nigra*. These species play an important role in succession on ruins of buildings. At wall bases with a southern aspect the thermophilous *Robinia pseudacacia* is often to be found. In the cracks of beaten pavements *Poa annua, Polygonum aviculare agg., Matricaria discoidea, Sagina procumbens, Plantago major* and *Lolium perenne* are common species.

Small gardens
Characteristic for the small gardens are *Aegopodium podagraria, Agropyron repens, Atriplex patula, Chenopodium album, Euphorbia peplus, Geranium pusillum, Galinsoga parviflora, Mercurialis annua, Oxalis europaea, Solanum nigrum* and others. In the medieval towns there were no lawns, those exist even nowadays only as small areas. Important species are: *Bellis perennis, Crepis capillaris, Lolium perenne, Prunella vulgaris*.

River embankments
The embankments of a river flowing through the centre of an old town are very rich in plant species, as the example of the river Oker in Brunswick shows (Grote & Brandes 1991). 311 different vascular plant species – almost one third of the spontaneous flora of the whole city – are present on the riverbanks. 64% of the species are indigenious, 10% are archaeophytes. 14.1% are naturalized aliens and 11.9% are ephemerophytes. On embankments in the town centre *Acer pseudoplatanus, Acer platanoides, Aesculus hippocastanum, Alnus glutinosa, Fraxinus excelsior, Robinia pseudacacia* and *Ulmus glabra* are the most common trees; the most frequent shrub is *Sambucus nigra*. Very obvious is a high proportion of climbing plants (*Hedera helix, Clematis vitalba, Bryonia dioica*).

Regional differences

Besides the great number of common species there are naturally regional differences: for example the neophyte *Sisymbrium altissimum* occurs only in the old towns of the northern part of Germany, while a number of species with complex nutritional requirements is declining. In the warm valley of the Danube in Lower Austria (column 5) the high frequency of *Amaranthus retroflexus, Cynodon dactylon, Eragrostis minor, Erigeron annuus* and *Parthenocissus quinquefolia* is noticable. This already indicates the fringe of the continental pannonian climate.

3.1.2. Life forms and ecological indicator value

In relation to their life forms the species are arranged as follows: Therophytes — 39.1%; Hemicryptophytes — 33.3%; Geophytes — 11.5%; Phanerophytes — 9.2%; Nanophanero-phytes — 3.4; Herbaceous chamaephytes — 3.4%.

An analysis of the ecological indicator values shows interesting results especially with respect to the factors temperature (T), water (F), and nitrogen (N):

(a) more than half the species are indicators of (fairly) warm conditions. With the exception of *Clematis vitalba* all warmth indicators (T=7) are neophytes or archaeophytes: *Bromus sterilis, Clematis vitalba, Cymbalaria muralis, Galinsoga ciliata, Hordeum murinum, Impatiens glandulifera, Lactuca serriola, Mercurialis perennis, Oxalis corniculata, Robinia pseudacacia, Solidago canadensis.*

Thus old towns — as for towns as a whole — are warmer habitats than the surrounding landscape. This applies, however, only to the temperate area of Europe and supposedly also to northern Europe.

(b) The old towns offer less dry places than often believed. Most of the species are moist-site indicators, mainly on soils of avarage dampness.

(c) Most of the more frequent species indicate a good nitrogen supply.

3.1.3. Differences between the flora of old towns and villages

What is the difference between the flora of old towns and villages? For Lower Saxony a direct comparison is possible, for villages have been investigated with the same methods as old towns (Brandes, Griese & Köller 1990):

(a) The main result is the large common number of species in both settlement types. Many of the so-called 'village plants' and 'town plants' are better to be declared as 'settlement indicators'.

(b) Only a few plants are characteristic of villages. The frequencies of *Arctium lappa, Arctium minus, Ballota nigra, Chenopodium bonus-henricus, Conium maculatum* and *Leonurus cardiaca* are higher in villages than in old towns, so that these species can be labelled as 'village plants'. Others included in this category, for example *Hyoscyamus niger, Marrubium vulgare* or *Nepeta cataria* are very rare in Lower Saxony and/or show no particular accumulation in villages. The species mentioned were all used for medical purposes; at least *Ballota nigra, Chenopodium bonus-henricus* and *Leonurus cardiaca* can be seen as cultural relicts.

(c) Species of the wall flora (*Cymbalaria muralis, Dryopteris filix-mas, Poa compressa, Poa nemoralis*) are more frequent in old towns than in villages. *Cymbalaria muralis* in our opinion is the most characteristic plant of old towns (and castles) in Europe. Also other warmth indicators as *Hordeum murinum, Galinsoga ciliata* and *Lactuca serriola* are common in old towns. The high frequency of *Calamagrostis epigejos, Mycelis muralis* and *Tussilago farfara* is noteworthy. There are also differences in the occurence of spontaneous woody plants: *Acer platanoides, Clematis vitalba* and *Hedera helix* are more frequent in old towns than in villages. Species of meadows, pastures and flooded places (Molinio-Arrhenatheretea, Agrostietalia

Table 2. Comparison between the floras of old town centres. (Number of species occurring in various old town centres which are also found in the old town centre of Brunswick.)

old town centre	number of common species	region	distance to Brunswick (average)
Wolfenbüttel	88	southeastern	30 km
Helmstedt	82	part of	
Goslar	70	Lower Saxony	
Hildesheim	66	(FRG)	
	∅ = 76.5		
Lüneburg	71	northern part	175 km
Verden	68	of Lower Saxony	
Stade	58	(FRG)	
Leer	56		
Emden	53		
	∅ = 61.2		
Munich (München)	72	southern part	410 km
Landshut	72	of Bavaria	
Riedenburg	69	(FRG)	
Kelheim	63		
Augsburg	60		
Abensberg	44		
Berching	43		
Landsberg	41		
	∅ = 58.0		
Bruges	71	Belgium and	515 km
Mons	64	northern part	
Douai	62	of France	
Namur	59		
Laon	53		
Boulogne-sur-Mer	49		
Huy	36		
	∅ = 56.3		
La Trinité-Porhoet	55	Brittany	1050 km
Moncontour	53	(France)	
Vitré	48		
Dinan	43		
Guérande	43		
Uzel	43		
Quintin	36		
Vannes	35		
	∅ = 44.5		
Bellinzona	41	Insubrian region	710 km
Luino	34	of the Alps	
Chiavenna	16	(Switzerland and	
Laveno	16	Italy)	
Ivrea	15		
Lugano	15		
	∅ = 22.8		
Mdina	11	Malta	1770 km
Tunis	1	Tunisia	1710 km

Table 3. Frequency of selected wall-dwelling species in towns of different regions in Europe.

Region	1	2	3	4	5	6	7	8	9	10	11
Hieracium sylvaticum	I	I	III	I	.	II	I	.	.	.	.
Corydalis lutea	I	III	I	II	.	I	III	.	.	.	.
Bromus tectorum	II	I	.	.	IV	.	I	.	.	.	.
Syringa vulgaris	I	II	I	I	II	.	II	II	.	.	.
Sedum acre	I	II	.	.	.	II	I	III	.	.	.
Dryopteris filix-mas	IV	IV	IV	II	II	V	IV	IV	.	.	.
Poa compressa	III	V	IV	IV	IV	II	IV	I	.	.	.
Asplenium ruta-muraria	III	V	V	V	V	V	V	II	II	.	.
Cymbalaria muralis	IV	V	V	V	IV	V	V	V	V	IV	V
Hedera helix	V	V	IV	V	V	V	V	V	I	IV	II
Cystoperis fragilis	.	II	II	I	.	.	I	.	.	.	.
Sedum reflexum	.	I	.	I	.	I	.	IV	.	.	.
Asplenium trichomanes	.	.	.	II	IV	III	III	IV	IV	III	.
Sedum album	.	.	.	II	IV	V	I	II	I	.	II
Phyllitis scolopendrium	.	.	.	.	.	I	I	II	.	.	.
Polypodium vulgare	.	.	.	.	.	.	III	V	.	.	.
Parietaria judaica	.	.	.	I	.	I	III	V	V	V	V
Antirrhinum majus	.	.	.	I	II	II	I	III	I	III	.
Cheiranthus cheiri	.	.	.	.	.	III	III	V	.	III	.
Centranthus ruber	.	.	.	.	.	.	III	V	I	V	.
Ficus carica	.	.	.	.	.	.	.	.	II	III	V
Sedum dasyphyllum	.	.	.	.	.	.	.	.	I	III	.
Erigeron karvinskianus	.	.	.	.	.	.	.	.	III	I	.
Adiantum capillus-veneris	.	.	.	.	.	.	.	.	.	III	.
Capparis spinosa	.	.	.	.	.	.	.	.	.	II	.
Ceterach officinarum	.	.	.	.	.	.	.	.	.	III	.
Hyoseris radiata	.	.	.	.	.	.	.	.	.	V	.
Veronica cymbalaria	.	.	.	.	.	.	.	.	.	III	.
Fumaria capreolata	.	.	.	.	.	.	.	.	.	II	V
Misopates orontium	.	.	.	.	.	.	.	.	.	I	V
Phagnalon saxatile	.	.	.	.	.	.	.	.	.	I	V
Umbilicus rupestris	.	.	.	.	.	.	.	.	.	III	V
Centranthus calcitrapa	.	.	.	.	.	.	.	.	.	.	V
Nicotiana glauca	.	.	.	.	.	.	.	.	.	.	V
Campanula erinus	.	.	.	.	.	.	.	.	.	.	IV

stoloniferae) however are of secondary importance in comparison with villages. For further discussions see Brandes & Griese (1991) and Pyšek & Pyšek (1990).

3.2. Western part of continental Europe (France and Belgium)

The old towns in Belgium and northern France (table 1, column 7) show a flora which is very similar to those of old towns in central Europe. There is also a high frequency of *Buddleja davidii* as well as the occurence of non-hardy wall plants (*Parietaria judaica, Centranthus ruber, Cheiranthus cheiri*). More significant are the differences between central Europe and Brittany (column 8): besides the above mentioned species especially *Umbilicus rupestris* and *Rubus fruticosus* agg. are highly frequent, whereas nitrophilous species like *Artemisia vulgaris, Lamium album* or *Mycelis muralis* are rare or even absent.

3.3. Southern Europe

Table 1 (column 9–11) shows the highly frequent species in old towns of the insubrian alps region. The basic components of the flora are definitely central European, even if many of nitrophilous and shade species are absent. The mild climate is reflected by the occurrence (with high frequency) of *Ailanthus altissima, Amaranthus deflexus, Cynodon dactylon, Digitaria sanguinalis, Eragrostis minor, Oxalis corniculata, Parietaria judaica* and *Portulaca oleracea*.

In the transition from submediterranean to mediterranean climate, old towns in Tuscany (Brandes 1985) and in Istria (Schulte 1989) had a relatively high number of species which are also common in central European old towns. The old towns in the mediterranean region are more densely built up, and a smaller percentage of the soil is uncovered in comparison to central Europe. The small number of species (highly frequent species at least) is noticeable. Spontaneous shrubs and trees, except *Ficus carica*, are not important (see Table 1, no. 10–11). Regionally *Ailanthus altissima, Nicotiana glauca* and/or *Rubus ulmifolius* are growing in old towns.

Highly frequent wall-dwelling species are *Cymbalaria muralis, Ficus carica, Hyoscyamus albus, Parietaria judaica* and *Umbilicus rupestris*. Regionally *Campanula erinus, Centranthus ruber, Hyoseris radiata, Phagnalon saxatile,* and *Sonchus tenerrimus* are common. Table 3 shows the great differences between the wall floras of central Europe and southern Europe: only *Cymbalaria muralis* and *Hedera helix* are common wall plants in all regions.

Important species in pavements are *Amaranthus deflexus, Aster squamatus* (regionally), *Cynodon dactylon, Euphorbia chamaesyce, Oxalis corniculata, Poa annua, Polygonum aviculare,* and *Polycarpon tetraphyllum*.

In densely built-up mediterranean old towns some tender leaf herbs, with surface area/weight ratios like those of shade plants, are able to grow, whereas they are absent from the surrounding garrigue. Our measurements showed that in summer time, noon temperatures in the towns can be a few degrees lower than in the surroundings. Similar climatic conditions lead to relatively uniform stocks of species in old towns in the mediterranean area. Despite the great distance between southern Portugal and Liguria (1560 km) the similarity of the flora in the old towns is very high.

3.4. Outlook on north Africa

The investigations started in Algeria (Jourdan 1866, 1867, 1872). Recently we only have investigated the kasba of Tunis, so it is not possible to give a general statement for northern Africa. In the kasba of Tunis we found spontaneous vegetation only on walls and – above all – on roofs. The most common species are *Hyoscyamus niger* and *Reseda alba*. Widespread are other minor mediterranean weeds such as *Conyza bonariensis, Lavatera cretica, Mercurialis annua, Ricinus communis, Sisymbrium irio,* and *Urtica dubia. Parietaria judaica* however seems to be quite seldom.

References

Aey, W. 1990. Historisch-ökologische Untersuchungen an Stadtökotopen Lübecks. Diss. TU Berlin. 229 S.
Brandes, D. 1982. Die synanthrope Vegetation der Stadt Wolfenbüttel. Braunschw. Naturk. Schr. 1: 419–443.
Brandes, D. 1985. Die spontane Vegetation toskanischer Städte. Tuexenia 5: 113–125.
Brandes, D. 1992. Flora und Vegetation von Stadtmauern. Tuexenia 12: 315–339.
Brandes, D. 1991. Die Ruderalvegetation der Altmark im Jahre 1990. Tuexenia 11: 109–120.
Brandes, D. & Griese, D. 1991. Siedlungs- und Ruderalvegetation von Niedersachsen. Braunschw. Geobotan. Arb. 1: 1–173.
Brandes, D. Griese, D. & Köller, U. 1990. Die Flora der Dörfer unter besonderer Berücksichtigung von Niedersachsen. Braunschw. Naturk. Schr. 3: 569–593.
Deakin, R. 1855. Flora of the Colosseum of Rome. London. VIII, 237 S.

Grote, S. & Brandes, D. 1991. Die Flora innerstädtischer Flußufer – dargestellt am Beispiel der Okerufer in Braunschweig. Braunschw. Naturk. Schr. 3: 905–926.

Jourdan, P. 1866. Flore murale de la ville de Tlemcen (Prov. d'Oran). Alger. 38 S.

Jourdan, P. 1867. Flore murale de la Chrétienne. Paris. 46 S.

Jourdan, P. (1872). Flore murale de la ville d'Alger. Alger.

Pyšek, P. & Pyšek, A. 1990. Comparison of the vegetation and flora of the west Bohemian villages and towns. In: H. Sukopp et al. (ed.), Urban ecology, pp. 105–112, The Hague.

Schulte, W. 1989. Zur Flora und Vegetation der Städte Rovinj und Krk (Jugoslawien). Tuexenia 9: 199–223.

Sukopp, H. 1990. Urban ecology and its application in Europe. In: H. Sukopp et al. (ed.), Urban ecology, pp. 1–22, The Hague.

AN ANALYSIS OF THE FLORA IN TIANJIN

HU DAN, WANG RUSONG and TANG TINGGUI
Research Center for Eco-Environmental Sciences, Academia Sinica, Beijing, P.R. China

Abstract

This paper deals with the flora in Tianjin city, including its vegetation pattern, species classification, species composition and distribution. The essential features of floristic succession under the influence of the urbanization process of Tianjin are then discussed.

1. The physical environment and its variation in Tianjin

Tianjin is situated in the northeastern part of the North China plain, facing the Bohai Bay. It ranges geographically from 38°33′57″ to 40°14′5″N and 116°42′5″ to 118°3′31″E, covering a total area of 11660 square kilometers and ranging in altitude from 0 to 1052 m above sea level. Its topography consists of mountainous regions, hilly land, plains (including marine-deposition plains and alluvial plains), low-lying lands, coastal zones, etc., with the plains comprising 95.4% of the total area.

Tianjin has a warm temperate continental climate with a typical seasonal wind. The principal features in its climate are low humidity in general, with more windy days and little precipitation in spring and winter and more precipitation in summer, when temperatures and humidity stay high. The average annual temperature (1981–1990) is between 11.1°C and 12.3°C, and the mean annual precipitation (1981–1990) ranges from 580 mm to 700 mm, 78% of which occurs in June and August. The global solar radiation averages 125.600 kcal/cm a year.

The types of soils in Tianjin are very diverse and include four main soil groups: saline soil, meadow soil, cinnamon soil and brunisolic soil. The soils of the mountainous area are derived from weathered rock, and the plain soils are formed and developed from Quaternary deposits. Alkali-saline soil easily develops in some low-lying lands of the plain area with its high salt concentration in groundwater and its high water table.

Since Tianjin city was established about 600 years ago, tremendous changes in the physical environment have taken place. The key agent for those changes has been the highly-intensified human activity, including land utility, forest-lumbering, migration of population towards the urban area, emission and accumulation of the wastes of the urban metabolism in the process of Tianjin's urbanization. Those have, on the one hand, exerted a great impact on the urban climate and soils (see Table 1), and therefore have disturbed or destroyed the original habitats of wild vegetation. For example, a large number of swamps, low-lying lands, natural ponds etc. in plains areas have disappeared, and they have been transformed into farmlands and other lands used for urban construction. On the other hand, the urban development in Tianjin has created all kinds of artificial urban environments such as urban highways or roads, parks, refuse dumps etc., which offer new, diversified habitats for the occurrence of more adapted species. This trend of variation in the physical environment has become more and more obvious with the urbanization of Tianjin.

2. The classification features of vegetation in Tianjin

Tianjin's zonal vegetation belongs to the warm temperate broadleaf deciduous forest annexed with the temperate coniferous forest. With its long history of agricultural exploita-

Urban Ecology as the Basis of Urban Planning, p. 59–69
edited by H. Sukopp, M. Numata and A. Huber
© *1995 SPB Academic Publishing bv, Amsterdam, The Netherlands*

Table 1. Average differences in some climatic factors between the urban area and suburbs in Tianjin

	Climate factors	Urban area compared with suburban district
Temperature	annual mean	0.4–1.2°C higher
	clear days	1.5–4°C higher
Wind speed	annual mean	5–20% more
Relative humidity	annual mean	3–9% more
Clouds	overcast	5–10% more
Precipitation	total	5–30% more
	lasting non-raining days	1–5% less
Pollution	main pollutants (SO_2, NO_x, CO)	10–25% more
	dust and other solid admixtures	15–30 times more

(Average value of 1985–1990 from the Meteorological Observatory of Tianjin).

tion, the majority of natural forests have been destroyed or have disappeared. There are only some small areas of original forests remaining, chiefly distributed in the mountainous region of Ji county, which, however, totals less than 7% of the area of that region. Some azonal plant species such as *Trifolium vulgare*, *Suaeda salsa*, *Chenopodium aristatum*, etc. develop rapidly instead of the original species in waterbodies, swamps, sandy lands and saline soils. The characteristics of vegetation distribution in Tianjin can be summarized as follows: (1) The horizontal zonality of its vegetation has been severely altered, but (2) there is a distinct vertical zonality of vegetation distribution; (3) the development of azonal plants such as halophytic meadow herbs are very exuberant in plain areas; (4) cultivated vegetation (including introduced species) comprises mainly crops, fruit forests and economic forests and includes maize, Chinese sorghum, soybean, peach, persimmon, Chinese chestnut, etc. The classification of the vegetation is shown in Table 2.

3. The characteristics of the flora in Tianjin

There exist 1049 species of vascular plants (including cultivated plants, subspecies and varieties) in Tianjin which respectively belong to 527 genera, 149 families, and consist of 3.87% of the total number of species in China (see Table 3) (Tang Tinggui et al., 1984). Of the species the majority belong to the families of Compositae, Leguminosae, Gramineae, Rosaceae, Liliaceae and Cyperaceae (see Table 4) (Tang Tinggui et al., 1984). Due to the influence of climatic and geological variation and the denudation of forest areas, the trees and shrubs have degraded gradually and the herbaceous plants have developed relatively robustly and have become dominant floristic components. The number of frequent wild weeds in Tianjin accounts for 160 species, 51 families (see Table 5) (Bai Yuhua et al., 1984).

Tianjin flora originated from the arctalpine flora of the Tertiary period, which chiefly consists of the elements of North China. There are complex floristic elements and many relict species such as *Koelreuteria paniculata* and *Broussinetia papyrifera* in this flora. Its plains floristic components usually include some colonizing species from the flora of the Asia arid steppe; mountain floristic components contain some species from the European Siberian flora. Some tropical parent-species are also distributed in this flora, and the adjacent floristic components often penetrate into it. Some representative species in this flora are the following: *Pinus tabulaeformis*, *Platyctadus orientalis*, *Quercus aliena*, *Q. variabilis*, *Q. dentata*, *Tilia*

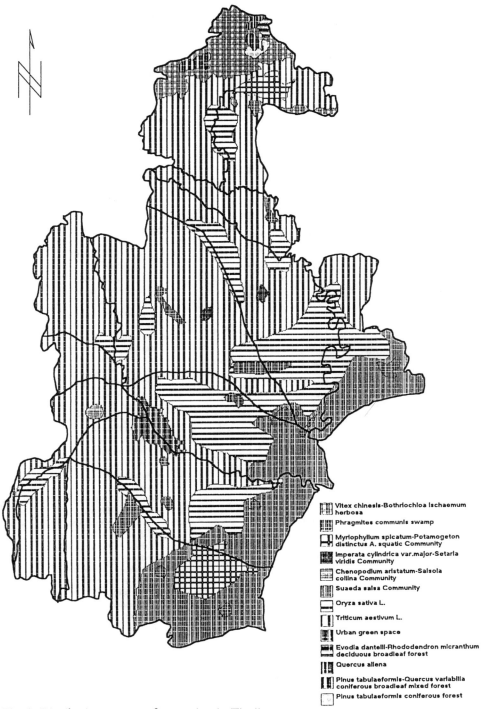

Vitex chinesis-Bothriochloa Ischaemum herbosa

Phragmites communis swamp

Myriophyllum spicatum-Potamogeton distinctus A. squatic Community

Imperata cylindrica var.major-Setaria viridis Community

Chenopodium aristatum-Salsola collina Community

Suaeda salsa Community

Oryza sativa L.

Triticum aestivum L.

Urban green space

Evodia dantelli-Rhododendron micranthum deciduous broadleaf forest

Quercus aliena

Pinus tabulaeformis-Quercus variabilia coniferous broadleaf mixed forest

Pinus tabulaeformis coniferous forest

Fig. 1. Distribution pattern of vegetation in Tianjin.

Table 2. Classification system of the major vegetation in Tianjin (Tang Tinggui *et al.*, 1984)

Type	Formation	Association
Coniferous forest	*Pinus tabulaeformis* forest	*Pinus tabulaeformis-Lespedeza floribunda* Community
	Platycladus orientalis forest	*Platycladus orientalis-Lespedeza floribunda* Community
Coniferous-broad-leaved mixed forest	*Pinus tabulaeformis*	*P. tabulaeformis + Q. variabilis-*
	Quercus variabilis, forest	*Indigofera kirilowii* Community
	P. tabulaeformis, Q. aliena forest	*P. tabulaeformis + Q. aliena-Lespedeza bicolor-Spodiopogon sibiricus* Community
Deciduous forest	*Quercus* spp. broadleaf forest	*Quercus aliena-Rhododendron micranthum-Carex lanceolata* Community
	deciduous broadleaf mixed forest	*Q.* variabilis-*Vitex chinensis* Community
		Evodia dantelli + Betula chinensis + Fraxinus rhynchophylla-Rhododendron micranthum Community
		Prunus armeniaca var. *ansu-Rhamnus parvifolia* Community
Herbosa	*Vitex chinensis* deciduous herbosa	*Vitex chinensis-Zizyphus jujuba-Bothriochloa ischaemum-Themeda japonica* Community
Meadow	meadow	*Imperata cylindrica* var. *major-Setaria viridis* Community
Halophytic vegetation	coastal halophytic meadow	*Suaeda salsa* Community
		Suaedasalsa-Aeluropus littoralis var. *sinensis* Community
Halophytic vegetation	meadow	*Suaeda salsa-Phragmites communis* Community
		Trifolium vulgare-Phragmites Community
Swamp vegetation	*Phragmites communis* swamp	*Trifolium vulgare-Suaeda salsa* Community
		Phragmites communis Community
Hydrophytic vegetation	submerged plant	*Myriophyllum spicatum* Community
	floating plant	*Myriophyllum-Ceratophyllum demersum-Hydrilla vertillata* Community
		Scirpus validus Community
		Scirpus planiculmis Community
Sand vegetation		*Chenopodium aristatum-Salsola collina* Community

Table 2. Cont.

Type	Formation	Association
Cultivated vegetation	rice, dry crops economic forest	single cropping of rice biannual wheat, maize, sorghum, millet, peanut, soybean, annual cotton
	fruits forest	Chinese chestnut, walnut forest, apple, pear, Persimmon, Chinese hawthorn forest, etc.

Table 3. Species numbers in the vascular flora of Tianjin (Tang Tinggui *et al.*, 1984)

Family		Genus		Species	
No. of families	% of total in China	No. of genera	% of total in China	No. of species	% of total in China
Pteridophyte 16	30.77	17	8.33	26	1.00
Gymnosperm 7	63.64	10	29.41	13	6.84
Angiosperm 126	43.30	570	19.39	1010	4.16
Total 149	42.09	597	18.22	1049	3.87

Table 4. The distribution features of the main families of floristic plants in Tianjin (Tang Tinggui *et al.*, 1984)

Number of species	% of total species	Lifetime	Distribution range in Tianjin
Compositae 107	11.61	He	mountainous, plain or coastal area
Leguminosae 65	7.04	Ph, Ch, He	mountain or plain
Gramineae 59	6.98	He	mountain or plain
Rosaceae 49	5.39	Ch, He, Ph	mountain or plain
Liliaceae 43	4.74	Ge	mountain or plain
Cyperaceae 22	2.20	Ge, He	plain
Labiatae 20	2.20	He, Ch	mountain or plain
Scrophulariaceae 19	2.08	Ph	mountain or plain
Ranunculaceae 18	1.98	He, Ge	mountain or plain
Umbelliferae 14	1.54	He	mountain or plain

He = Hemicryptophytes; Ch = Chamaephytes; Ph = Phanerophytes; Ge = Geophytes.

Table 5. A list of frequent wild weeds in Tianjin. All listed species are native (Bai Yuhua *et al.* 1984)

Family	Species
Moraceae	*Humulus scandens*
Polygonaceae	*Polygonum aviculare* L.
	P. bungeanum Turcz.
	P. sibiricum Laxim.
	P. lapathifolium L.
	P. lapathifolium var. *salicifolium* Sibth
	P. hydropiper L.
	P. amphibium L.
	Rumex dentatus L.
	R. patientia L.
Chenopodiaceae	*Salsola collina* Pall.
	Suaeda glauca Bunge
	S. salsa Kitag.
	Kochia scoparia (L.) Schrad.
	Chenopodium glaucum L.
	C. album L.
	C. serotinum L.
	Atriplex patens (Litv) Iljin
	A. centralasiatica Iljin
Amaranthaceae	*Amaranthus retroflexus* L.
	A. viridis L.
	A. ascendens Loisel.
Portulacaceae	*Portulaca oleracea* L.
Caryophyllaceae	*Vaccaria segetalis* (Neck.) Garcke
	Silene conoidea L.
Ceratophyllaceae	*Ceratophyllum demersum* L.
Ranunculaceae	*Ranunculus chinensis* Bge.
Cruciferae	*Rorippa globosa* (Turcz.) Thellung
	R. palustris (Leyss.) Bess.
	Capsella bursa-pastoris (L.) Med.
	Lepidium apetalum Willd.
	Lepidium latifolium L. var. *affine* C.A. Mey.
Rosaceae	*Potentilla chinensis* Ser.
	P. supina L.
Leguminosae	*Vicia amoena* Fisch.
	V. bungei Ohwi
	Lespedeza davurica (Laxm.) Schindl.
	Kummerowia striata Schindl.
	K. stipulacea (Maxim.) Makino
	Medicago lupulina L.
Oxalidaceae	*Oxalis corniculata* L.
Geraniaceae	*Erodium stephanianum* Willd.
Zygophyllaceae	*Tribulus terrestris* L.
Polygalaceae	*Polygala tenuifolia* Willd.
Euphorbiaceae	*Euphorbia lunulata* Bunge
	E. humifusa Willd.
	Acalypha australis L.
Malvaceae	*Abutilon theophrasti* Med.
	Hibiscus trionum L.
Violaceae	*Viola japonica* Langsd.
	V. prionantha Bge.
Haloragaceae	*Myriophyllum verticillatum* L.
	M. spicatum 1.
Umbelliferae	*Cnidium monnieri* (L.) Cusson
Primulaceae	*Androsace umbellata* (Lour.) Merr.
	Lysimachia pentapetala Duby
Plumbaginaceae	*Limonium bicolor* (Bunge) O. Kuntze
	L. sinensis (Girard) O. Kuntze
Apocynaceae	*Apocynum venetum* L.
Asclepiadaceae	*Metaplexis japonica* (Thunb.) Makino
	Cynanchum thesiodes (Freyn) K. schum.

Table 5. Cont.

Family	Species
	C. chinense R. Br.
Convolvulaceae	*Cuscuta chinensis* Lam.
	C. japonica Choisy
	Pharbitis purpurea (L.) Voigt
	P. nii (L.) Choisy
	Convolvulus arvensis L.
	Calystegia hederacea Wall.
	C. japonica Choisy
Boraginaceae	*Bothriospermum chinensis* (Turcz.) Bge.
	Messersmidia sibirica L. ssp
	angustior Kitag.
	Trigonotis peduncularis (Trev.) Benth.
	Lappula echinata Gilib.
Labiatae	*Lagopsis supina* (Steph.) Ik.-Gal.
	Leonurus heterophyllus Sweet
	L. sibiricus L.
	L. tataricus L.
	Lycopus lucidus Turcz.
	Mentha haplocalyx Briq.
Solanaceae	*Solanum nigrum* L.
	Datura stramonium L.
	Physalis alkekengi L. var. *franchetii* Makino
Scrophulariaceae	*Rehmannia glutinosa* Libosch.
	Mazus japonicus (Thunb.) D. Kuntz.
	Veronica anagallis-aquatica L.
Plantaginaceae	*Plantago asiatica* L.
	P. depressa Willd.
Rubiaceae	*Rubia cordifolia* L.
	Galium bungei Steud.
	G. verum L.
Valerianaceae	*Patrinia heterophylla* Bge.
	P. scabiosaefolia Fisch.
Compositae	*Xanthium sibiricum* Patrin.
	Carduus crispus L.
	Cephalanophlos segetum (Bunge) Kitam.
	C. setosum (Willd.) Kitam.
	Hemistepta lyrata Bunsg.
	Inula britannica var. *chinensis* Regel
	Erigeron canadensis L.
	Heteropappus altaicus (Willd.) Novopokr.
	Bidens bipinnata L.
	B. parviflora Willd.
	Siegesbeckia orientalis L.
	Eclipta prostrata L.
	Artemisia argyi Levl. et Vant.
	A. annua L.
	A. capillaris Thunb.
	Taraxacum mongolicum Hand.-Mazz.
	Sonchus oleraceus L.
	S. brachyotus DC.
	Ixeris denticulata Stebb.
	I. chinensis (Thunb.) Nakai.
Typhaceae	*Typha angustifolia* L.
Potamogetonaceae	*Potamogeton crispus* L.
	P. malainus Miq.
	P. natans L.
	P. pectinatus L.
	Zannichellia palustris L.
Najadaceae	*Najas minor* All.
	N. marina L.

Table 5. Con:.

Family	Species
Alismataceae	*Alisma orientale* Juzepez
	Sagittaria trifolia L.
Hydrocharitaceae	*Hydrocharis asiatica* Miq.
	Hydrilla verticallata (L.f.) Royle
	Vallisneria asiatica Miki
Gramineae	*Eleusinae indica* (L.) Gaertn.
	Chloris virgata Swartz.
	Phragmites communis Trin.
	Poa annua L.
	Eragrostis cilianensis Link
	E. poaeoides Beauv.
	Setaria viridis (L.) Beauv.
	S. lutescens (Weigel) F.T. Hubb
	Digitaria sanguinalis (L.) Scop.
	D. sanguinalis var. *ciliaris* Parl.
	Echinochloa colonum (L.) Link
	E. crus-galli (L.) Beauv.
	E. crus-galli var. *caudata* (Roshev) Kitag.
	Imperata cylindrica (L.) Beauv. var. *major* (Noes) C.E. Hubb.
	Hemarthria altissima Stapf
	Arthraxon hispidus (Thunb.) Makino
	Bothriochloa ischaemum Keng
	Puccinellia chinampoensis Ohwi
Cyperaceae	*Fimbristylis dichotoma* Vahl
	Scirpus planiculmis Fr. Schmidt
	S. validus Vahl.
	S. yagara Ohwi
	Juncellus serotinus C.B. Clarke
	Cyperus rotundus L.
	C. glomeratus L.
	C. fuscus L.
	C. difformis L.
	Pycreus globosus Reichb.
	P. sanguinolentus Ness
Araceae	*Pinellia ternata* Breit.
Lemnaceae	*Lemna minor* L.
	Spirodela polyrhiza Schleid
Commelinaceae	*Commelina communis* L.
Pontederiaceae	*Monochoria vaginalis* Presl
Juncaceae	*Juncus gracillimus* krecz.
Liliaceae	*Allium macrostemon* Bge.
Equisetaceae	*Equisetum arvense* L.
	E. ramosissimum Desf.
Marsilaceae	*Marsilea quadrilia* L.
Salviniaceae	*Salvinia natans* All.
Spirogyraceae	*Spirogyra* spp.
Characeae	*Chara foetida* A.Br.

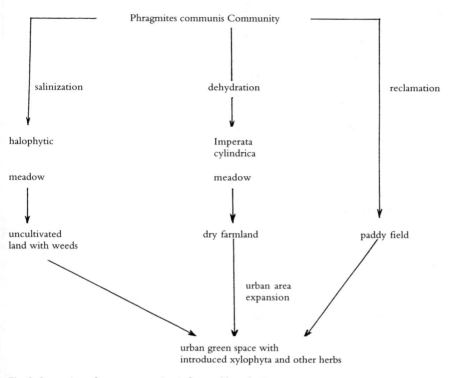

Fig. 2. Succession of swamp vegetation influenced by urbanization in Tianjin.

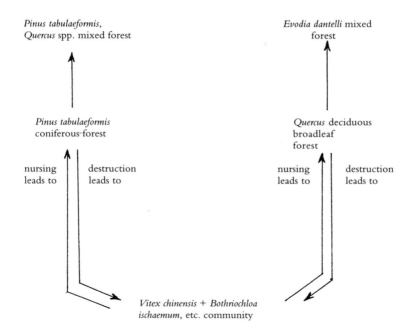

Fig. 3. Succession of natural vegetation disturbed by human economic activities in the mountainous region of Tianjin.

mongolica, T. mandshurica, Acer truncatum, Salix matsudana, Betula chinensis, Juglans mandshurica, Fraxinus rhynchophylla, Corylus heterophylla, Crataegus pannatifica, etc. Some tropical parent-species prevail in this area, they are: *Ailanthus altissima, Phellodendron amurense, Evodia denielli, Vitex chinensis, Zizyphus jujuba, Grewia biloba* var. *parviflora, Themeda japonica, Bothriochloa ischaemum, Arundinella hirta, Periploca sepium, Begonia sinensis, Actinidia arguta, Actinostemma racemosum* etc.

During the last four decades, a large number of plant species, chiefly woody plants, have been introduced from the subtropical zone and cultivated with success in the plain area. Some of them are *Platanus acerifolia, Pirmiana simplex, Ligustrum lucidum, Fraxinus velutina* var. *tomeyi,* other fruit trees and cultivated crops such as annual rice, biannual wheat, sorghum, etc. Of these plants, 393 species from 96 families have become naturalized. Thus the non-native components amount to 38% in the total number of species of the flora of Tianjin.

In the course of floristic succession of Tianjin influenced by its urbanization, these intro-duced and cultivated species such as *Robinia pseudoacacia, Amorpha fruticosa, Pirmiana simplex, Paulownia tomentosa, Fraxinus velutina* var. *tomeyi, Ligustrum lucidum, Pterocarya stenoptera,* etc. have replaced some original hydrophytes, helophytes, halophytes and psammophytes, espe-cially in urban areas and periurban areas. This has led to a decrease in species along the ur-ban-rural gradients (see Fig. 2). Meanwhile, in some areas of the mountain region, with the destruction and disturbance through local economic activities, some indigenous species such as *Pinus tabulaeformis, Tilia mongolica, Quercus* spp. have been supplanted by the competition of *Vitex chinensis, Zizyphus jujuba, Themeda japonica* and *Bothrichloa ischaemum* etc., which have greatly contributed to the development of *Vitex chinensis* shrubs with other herbs (see Fig. 3). These changes indicate more and more intensive impacts of local economic activi-ties on the floristic succession of vegetation in Tianjin.

4. Conclusion

The flora in Tianjin has changed during the process of its urban development, which has been demonstrated in its floristic composition, species number, distribution and floristic succession

The chief components of Tianjin's flora are from North China. Economic exploitation and urban expansion in Tianjin have disturbed or even altered the flora of original habitats, especially in the plains area, and obviously influenced the floristic composition. Alien plants have been introduced and some of these have naturalized.

It is very important for planners, natural scientists and municipal decision makers in Tianjin to monitor and trace the change of floristic composition and the occurrence of some adapted plant species in urban-specific micro-environments and to introduce some al-ien species and reintroduce original wild plants which tolerate the urban environment. Fur-thermore, they have to serve the conservation and regeneration of indigenous plant species and improve the urban physical environment of living. The urban expansion in Tianjin and the natural ecological succession have to be coordinated in order to ensure the best possible support of urban wildlife.

Acknowledgement

The authors wish to thank Professor H. Sukopp for his suggestive advises and review for this work. Acknowledgement is also given to Professor Yuhua Bai, Biology Department of Nankai University, and Fendi Zhang, Adjunct Professor of Normal University of Tianjin for offering background materials of the related researches.

References

Tang Tinggui et al. 1984. The vegetation of Tianjin. In: The vegetation of Tianjin. Edited by Tianjin Committee of Agricultural Zoning.

Zhang Fendi 1984. An approach of the geography of vegetation in Tianjin. In: The vegetation of Tianjin. Edited by Tianjin Committee of Agricultural Zoning.

Bai Yuhua et al. 1984. Tianjin frequency weeds analysis. In: The vegetation of Tianjin. Edited by Tianjin Committee of Agricultural Zoning.

Sukopp, H., Blume, H.P. & Kunick, W. 1979. The soil, flora and vegetation of Berlin's wastelands.

Kunick, W. 1982. Comparison of the flora of some cities of the central European lowlands. In: R. Bornkamm et al. (ed.), The Second European Ecological Symposium. Blackwell Scientific Publications, Oxford.

Jim, C.Y. 1987. The status and prospects of urban trees in Hong Kong. Landscape and Urban Planning, 14: 1–20.

ECOLOGICAL STUDIES ON URBAN LAWNS

GABRIELE BROLL and BEATE KEPLIN
Landscape Ecology Div., Department of Geography, University of Münster, Robert-Koch-Str. 26, D-48149 Münster, Germany

Abstract

The effects of different management practices on vegetation, fauna and soil of urban lawns were investigated. In the city of Dorsten (Germany) four suitable lawns were selected and divided into sample plots and then given to the following management practices: cutting several times a year, cutting twice a year and mulching twice a year. Before the treatments began, the soil of the sample areas was mapped and analysed. The development of the plant cover was controlled on permanent plots. Site factors, such as soil temperature, were continuously recorded. Changes in the composition and productivity of the vegetation also changed the microclimate, affecting the soil fauna as can be seen for example from the abundance of carabids and lumbricides. Alterations in the soil microbial site conditions are measured for example by substrate induced respiration.

Different ecological effects of the treatments are influenced by the specific soil conditions (*e.g.*, moisture, pH value) of urban lawns.

1. Introduction

At present a general trend from intensive to extensive management of urban lawns is obvious (Kunick 1983, Albertshauser 1985, Schmidt 1987). Intensive management by use of fertilizers or herbicides for example turned out to be unfavourable from the ecological point of view. This might cause a conflict between recreation and the management of a nature-like environment (Schulz & Jacob 1987, Kowarik & Jirku 1988, Bröring *et al.* 1989).

Thus, the question is what kind of extensive treatment can be recommended to the urban administration. There are many thorough studies on the effects of extensive management on grassland (Schiefer 1981, Schreiber 1985, Bakker 1989, Schwartze *et al.* 1989). Urban lawns however, are less investigated (UNESCO 1989, Sukopp & Werner 1987). Most of these studies are concerned with the vegetation (*e.g.*, Gutte 1984, Berg 1985, Fischer 1985, Müller 1988, Baudisch *et al.* 1989) or the epigaeic fauna (*e.g.*, Topp 1972, Czechowski 1980, Klausnitzer *et al.* 1980, Schaefer 1982, Müller 1986, Müller & Steinwarz 1988, 1990, Niedringhaus & Bröring 1988). In a few cases only the hemiedaphic soil fauna (Leuthold 1961, Weigmann & Stratil 1979, Kasprzak 1981, 1986, Niedballa *et al.* 1982, Sterzynska 1982) or the soil microbial activity (Nossag 1971, Weritz & Schröder 1988, 1990) of urban lawns are considered. The effects of different management practices are not taken into account, with the exception of a few projects (FLL 1988, Schulte *et al.* 1989).

Therefore this urban ecology project has the following objectives:
- comparison of the ecological site conditions of different urban lawns,
- investigation of the effects of extensive management practices on those sites, especially on the soil fauna and the decomposition rate, and
- at a later stage of the project, working out criteria for the application of ecologically reasonable management practices on comparable lawns.

The research area is located in Germany, at the northern rim of the Ruhr industrial zone. Within the urban district of Dorsten four study sites were selected. The study sites were divided into permanent plots (100 m^2 each) and then submitted to the following management practices:

Urban Ecology as the Basis of Urban Planning, p. 71–82
edited by H. Sukopp, M. Numata and A. Huber
© 1995 SPB Academic Publishing bv, Amsterdam, The Netherlands

1. cutting several times a year (grass crop not removed)
    = mulching several times a year (every three weeks)
2. cutting twice a year (grass crop removed) (June, September)
3. cutting twice a year (grass crop not removed)
    = mulching twice a year (June, September)

2. Methods

The soils were mapped and described according to AG Bodenkunde (1982), Blume (1987) and Umweltbundesamt (1989). The soil samples were analysed by standard methods (Schlichting & Blume 1966, Page et al. 1982). The following physical and chemical parameters were considered: texture, bulk density, water content, water availability, compaction, pH (CaCl$_2$), pH (H$_2$O), carbonate, organic carbon/total nitrogen (Analyzer NA 1500 CARLO ERBA), cation exchange capacity, conductivity and heavy metal content (Köster & Merkel 1982). Historical maps and air photos were interpreted for further information concerning the soil genesis. The soil microbial activity was measured by substrate induced respiration (Anderson & Domsch 1978), soil respiration (Jäggi 1976) and soil enzyme activity, especially dehydrogenase activity (Thalmann 1968).

The vegetation of the four urban lawns and their adjacent areas were mapped (Braun-Blanquet 1964). The composition and coverage of the vegetation are controlled on permanent plots (4 m × 4 m) (Schmidt et al. 1974, Wolf 1982). Ecological indicator values (Ellenberg 1979) were calculated without consideration of coverage, furthermore dry weight and nutrient content (N, P, K) of the phytomass were measured.

On one study site soil temperature was continuously recorded by a thermistor (Aanderaa) at different depths. Other site factors, such as relative humidity and air temperature at different heights above the soil surface were measured at intervals.

The soil fauna was investigated at two study sites only. Earthworms were sampled from the soil by electrical extraction (Thielemann 1986a) and determined by the glasstube-method (Thielemann 1986b) (keys: Wilcke 1968, Sims & Gerard 1985, nomenclature according to Easton 1983). The mean abundances were calculated from 5 samples (autumn and spring) and standardised (individuals/m^2). The weight of each individual (incl. gut contents) was measured and standardised (g/m^2). Thus, in this paper 'biomass' means total live weight.

To collect the soil mesofauna (springtails and mites) soil samples were taken at monthly intervals during two growing seasons. Each series consisted of 10 samples (sample rings, 200 cm^3, 8 cm height). The soil cores were extracted by using a Kempson bowl extractor (Kempson et al. 1963). From 11 samples the mean abundances were calculated and standardized (individuals/m^2). Carabids were sampled by barber traps (Barber 1931, Dunger & Fiedler 1989). Samples were taken during the first two weeks of each month; the traps were emptied daily.

3. Results

3.1. Soil

The soils of the investigated urban lawns were 'deposit soils', consisting of natural or technological matter, such as mining waste or rubble, covering Gleysols, such as a Humic Gleysol or a Spodo-Dystric Gleysol (Broll 1991b).

For the interpretation of the results of the soil (micro-) biological investigations some information on the specific characteristics of the top soil are shown (Table 1). There are im-

Table 1. Selected characteristics of the top soil (0–8 cm) at the different urban lawns.

Study site	pH (H$_2$O)	C$_{org}$[%]	N$_t$[%]	C/N	Texture
1	7.1	2.4	0.18	13.3	sand
2	5.8	2.5	0.20	12.5	loamy sand
3	5.4	1.5	0.18	13.9	silty sand
4	5.1	2.2	0.17	13.2	sand

portant differences between the soil moisture conditions of the urban lawns. The study sites 1 and 3 are relatively dry, whereas on the study sites 2 and 4 a relatively high soil moisture was measured.

In addition to the soil physical and chemical investigations, soil microbial activity was measured to assess the decomposition rate at the different study sites (Fig. 1). Final evidence of the effects of the different management practices cannot be given yet. However, differences in site conditions are already obvious. Since C/N ratio and soil texture, important factors for the microbial activity, are similar at the four study sites (Table 1), the pH value appears to be the controlling factor. Although the soil moisture conditions are better on study site 2 than on study site 1, the microbial activity is even lower.

3.2. Vegetation

The urban lawns consisted of grassland communities poor in species. The communities may be attributed to the Cynosurion (Broll 1991b). In most areas a more detailed differentiation of the Cynosurion into plant associations was impossible, because only a few differential species were represented. Only one study site could be attributed to the Lolio-Cynosuretum. Compared to normal Cynosurion-communities the percentage of herbs is relatively low.

In terms of the indicator values of the plant cover (Ellenberg 1979) the plots could be characterized as fresh to moist and poor in nitrogen. The soil acidity indicated by the plants was different on the study sites and thus corresponds to the measured pH values of the soil (Table 1). The phytomass yield was low at all plots (*ca.* 200 g/m^2).

3.3. Microclimate

Soil temperatures showed that the microclimate was modified by the different treatments (Keplin 1993). During the growing season the soil temperatures of the plots 'cutting twice a year' and 'mulching twice a year' were usually lower than those of the often cut lawn. The air humidity near the soil surface of the plot 'cutting twice a year' and under the mulch layer of the plot 'mulching twice a year' was higher in general than the humidity on the lawn 'cutting several times a year'. In most cases lower temperatures corresponded with higher soil moisture.

3.4. Fauna

At the selected study sites 6 lumbricid species were represented. However, striking differences were noted. Estimated abundances varied widely between study site 1 and study site 2, and were also different between the management practices (Table 2). The highest total population densities of each study site occurred on the plot 'cutting several times a year', while estimated abundances from samples 'cutting twice a year' closely correspond to those from the plot 'mulching twice a year'.

μg CO$_2$/g/h

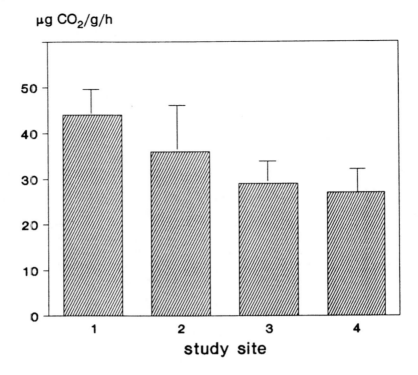

Fig. 1. Substrate induced respiration (μg CO$_2$/g/h) of the four study sites based on 12 samplings in 1990. Sampling depth 0–8 cm.
Comparison of study sites:
1/2: p < 0.05   2/3: p < 0.05
1/3: p < 0.01   2/4: p < 0.01
1/4: p < 0.01   3/4: n.s.

Table 2. Species diversity and percentages of lumbricides in dependence on the specific management practices.

Species	Study site 1			Study site 2		
	I %	II %	III %	I %	II %	III %
Lumbricus rubellus	1.1	2.3	7.0	11.7	10.8	11.1
L. castaneus	0.9	5.3	11.2	–	–	–
L. terrestris	0.9	–	1.6	0.8	–	–
Aporrectodea longa	1.7	3.5	2.7	–	2.7	–
A. caliginosa	14.0	21.1	21.9	11.7	10.8	11.0
Allolobophora chlorotica	0.3	–	0.5	–	–	–
Juvenile:						
L. spec.	35.8	46.2	25.1	31.7	43.2	25.9
Others	45.3	21.6	30.0	44.1	32.4	42.6
Total (%)	100	100	100	100	100	100
Individuals/m^2	558	273	299	192	59	86

management practices:
I   : cutting several times a year
II   : cutting twice a year
III   : mulching twice a year

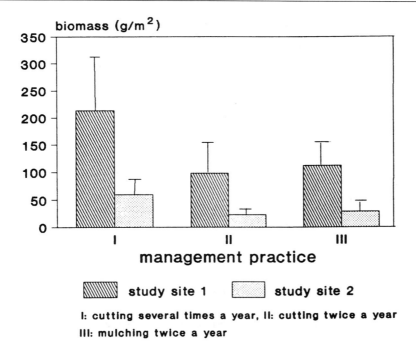

Fig. 2. Biomass (g/m²) of Lumbricidae based on 5 samplings in autumn 1989/90 and spring 1990 under the influence of different management practices.

Comparison of management practices:	study site 1:	I/II: p < 0.1	study site 2:	I/II: p< 0.05
		I/III: p < 0.1		I/III: p < 0.1
		II/III: n.s.		II/III: n.s.
Comparison of study sites:		1-I/2-I	: p < 0.01	
		1-II/2-II	: p < 0.05	
		1-III/2-III	: p < 0.01	

Estimated biomass (g/m²) for each management practice are shown in Fig. 2. Compared to the estimated abundances there are no differences in the rank order. Both abundance and biomass show significant correlations between the management practices 'cutting several times a year' and 'cutting or mulching twice a year'. However, there are no significant differences between the management practices 'cutting' and 'mulching' twice a year.

A total of 140,342 individuals of the mesofauna were extracted by the Kempson bowl extractor in 1989 and 1990 (springtails, 39.75%, mites 55.13% and other taxa 5.12%). Figure 3 shows the abundance (individuals/m²) at each plot and study site. Estimated population densities were lower on study site 1 than on study site 2. The differences between the management practices 'cutting several times a year' and 'cutting twice a year' are significant only on study site 1, whereas on study site 2 no significant differences exist. Compared to study site 1 the abundance is higher on the plots 'cutting several times a year' and 'cutting twice a year'.

Figure 4 illustrates the abundances of Collembola and Acarina on study site 1 and 2. In contrast to mites, the population density of springtails was nearly the same on all plots. The abundance of mites differs widely between the two study sites. Higher population densities

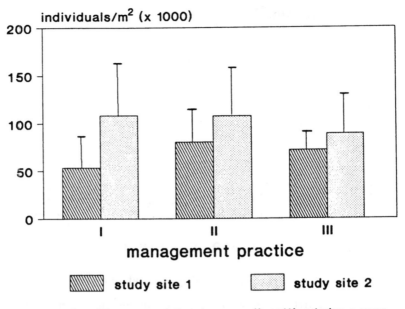

individuals/m^2 (x 1000)

management practice

▨▨▨ study site 1   ☐ study site 2

I: cutting several times a year, II: cutting twice a year
III: mulching twice a year

Fig. 3. Abundance (individuals/m^2) of total mesofauna based on 11 samplings in 1989/90 under the influence of different management practices. Sampling depth 0–8 cm.
Comparison of management practices: study site 1: I/II: p < 0.1   study site 2: all plots: n.s.
                                                         I/III: n.s.
                                                         II/III: n.s.
Comparison of study sites: 1-I/2-I: p < 0.01
                                                         1-II/2-II: n.s.
                                                         1-III/2-III: n.s.

were observed on the study site 2.

On both study sites 32 species of carabids were found, generally more species on study site 1 than on study site 2. On study site 1 the carabid activity abundance was the highest on the plot 'mulching twice a year', while on study site 2 the activity abundance was nearly the same on the plots 'cutting/mulching twice a year'. The management practice 'cutting several times a year' showed the lowest values (Keplin & Wanckel 1991).

4. Discussion

The mapped soils are typically 'Urbic Anthrosols' (FAO 1988) or 'Deposols' (Blume 1988, 1989). These soil types are common under urban lawns in many metropolitan areas (Blume & Sukopp 1976, Blume & Schlichting 1982, Siem et al. 1987). In general such areas are characterized as dry, compacted, nutrient rich, alkaline and contaminated with heavy metals for example (Blume & Runge 1975, Kunick 1987). That becomes evident in many cases, the present investigation however demonstrates that urban lawns may be quite different due to their specific ecological site conditions (Broll 1991b). Physical and chemical soil properties and thereby phytomass production, decomposition rates etc. vary considerably.

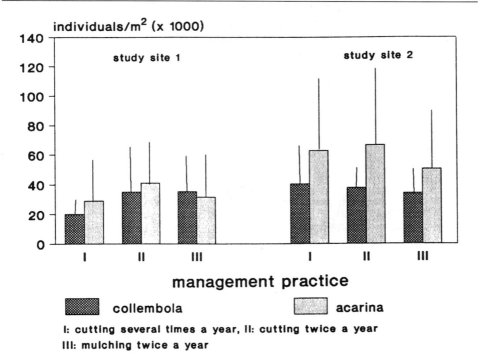

Fig. 4. Abundance (individuals/m²) of total Acarina and Collembola based on 11 samplings in 1989/90 under the influence of different management practices. Sampling depth 0–8 cm.
Comparison of management practices: all plots: n.s. except Collembola I/II: $p < 0.05$
Comparison of study sites: all plots: n.s.
except: Collembola   1-I/2-I: $p < 0.05$
                    Acarina   1-I/2-I: $p < 0.05$

These initial conditions play an important role with regard to the application of different management practices. Thus, a specific treatment may influence one urban lawn in a positive way, but cannot be recommended for another one.

The investigation of the soil microbial activity (Fig. 1) reflect above all the different soil chemical conditions, especially the pH value. This ecological factor dominates all other factors. Consequently the highest decomposition rate corresponds to a neutral soil reaction (Swift *et al.* 1979), although on study site 3, the microbial activity might have been reduced due to the relatively low humus content.

The decomposition rate measured at all investigated urban lawns is low compared to extensively managed grassland (Campino 1983, Iffert 1983, Broll 1989) and other urban open spaces (Runge 1975, Weritz & Schröder 1988, 1990). The soil microbial activity was probably not hampered by heavy metal contamination (Ohya *et al.* 1988, Weritz 1989, Weritz & Schröder 1989), because the heavy metal content in the top soil of the sites was very low.

Generally it seems difficult to classify the vegetation of the urban lawns taxonomically, because the alliance Cynosurion only refers to pastures. Most plant indicator species for grazing are missing because selection is only by cutting (Fischer 1985, Müller 1988, 1989). In case of intensive trampling a Lolio-Plantaginetum (Berg 1985) respectively a *Plantago-major–Trifolium-repens* association (Schulte *et al.* 1990) may also exist. In many cases lawns are derived from seed mixtures containing only grasses but no herbs (Hope 1978, Albertshauser 1985).

The management practice 'cutting several times a year' meant that the plant cover remained low during the whole growing season. The top soils warmed up considerably while the humidity near the soil surface was low. Consequently the soils were frequently affected by drought. On the lawns 'cutting twice a year' comparable microclimate conditions were only observed for a short while after cutting. Low soil temperatures, high humidity and high soil moisture occurred for the rest of the time because of the relatively tall plant cover (Wilmers 1985, Ellenberg et al. 1986, Oke 1987, Broll 1991a). On the plots 'mulching twice a year' the mulching layer prevents the soil from too intensive warming and from drought. Thus, this effect of mulching was more conspicuous on dry urban lawns than on moist sites. Mulching may lead to an accumulation of organic matter if accompanied for example by high soil acidity (Broll 1991b).

The different microclimates influence the soil fauna (e.g., Edwards & Lofty 1977, Bachelier 1978, Topp 1981, Dunger 1983, Lee 1985). The carabids in particular preferred those plots where the humidity is relatively high, due to the influence of a taller plant cover (Keplin & Wanckel 1991). The same humid conditions are to be found under a mulch layer (Steinwarz 1989).

The positive effect of the mulch layer was also observed in case of the mesofauna. The higher abundance of Collembola compared to that of Acarina (Fig. 4) indicates the effect of this management practice 'mulching twice a year' on study site 1. Evaporation declines while soil moisture increases. Consequently on that site Collembola were more numerous than Acarina. The same effect was observed by Höller-Land (1958). This is totally in accordance with the fact that in grassland soils the abundance of mites is generally higher than that of springtails (Persson & Lohm 1977, Topp 1981).

The mesofauna abundances (Fig. 4) were similar to those on grassland sites (Dunger 1983). They were much higher than those population densities reported from Munich (Bauchhenss 1986) and Warsaw (Pisarski et al. 1989) but lower than the abundances estimated by Persson & Lohm (1977) for grassland soils. Study site 2 showed higher densities than study site 1 because soil moisture was higher and soil temperature was lower. There were also differences in vertical distribution on both study sites (Keplin 1993).

Because of a lack of information about mesofauna on urban lawns it is difficult to compare these preliminary results to published data. There are a few investigations on soil mesofauna of urban lawns (Bankowska et al. 1984, Sterzynska 1987, Weigmann & Kratz 1987, Schulte et al. 1989), and collecting methods were also different (e.g., barber traps; Schulte et al. 1989).

The earthworm species (Table 2) are characteristic of grassland soils (Edwards & Lofty 1977, Lee 1985). However, they are also reported from urban lawns (Pilipiuk 1981, Bauchhenss 1982, Bankowska et al. 1984, Esser 1984, Schulte et al. 1989). Aporrectodea caliginosa, A. longa, Lumbricus castaneus and L. terrestris are common species (Nowak 1975). According to Pilipiuk (1981) these species with high environmental amplitude occur in almost all urban habitats. These species are able to colonize urban lawns due to the fact that in dry habitats (study site 1) they retreat to deeper soil layers. The lumbricid species diversity on study site 1 is similar to that observed on lawns in Bonn (Schulte et al. 1989). More species were found in Munich (Bauchhenss 1982, 1986, Esser 1984) and Warsaw (Pilipiuk 1981).

These lumbricid species are widely tolerant of soil pH. The relatively low pH value may be the reason that only a few species occur at study site 2. Compared to data from other investigations species diversity is poor in study site 2 (Bauchhenss 1982, 1986, Makeschin 1990).

The population densities differed widely between the study sites 1 and 2 and between the management practices, but they correspond to data from Bonn (Schulte et al. 1989), where abundances ranged from 91 to 244 individuals/m^2. A maximum biomass of

280 g/m^2 was estimated. On lawns in the botanical garden of Munich (Esser 1984) about 260 individuals/m^2 with a biomass of 146 g/m^2 were sampled. In the Nymphenburger Park in Munich Bauchhenss (1986) found 108 individuals/m^2 and measured a biomass of 117 g/m^2. The management practice 'cutting several times a year' show the highest population density (Table 2) and biomass (Fig. 2) both on study site 1 and 2. This may be explained by the fact that much and easily digestible food is always available (Lee 1985, Lavelle 1988). There was no significant difference between the management practices 'cutting' and 'mulching' twice a year, but the mulch layer seems to have a slightly positive effect on earthworm density and biomass (Table 2 and Fig. 2). In contrast to study site 2, the soil fauna on study site 1 is very likely to reflect an advanced succession stage (Pisarski *et al.* 1989).

From the present studies it has become evident that the physical and chemical soil conditions and thus the biological situation on urban lawns are more different than is generally expected. Consequently, the extensive management practices must be carried out closely related to the specific site conditions.

References

AG Bodenkunde 1982. Bodenkundliche Kartieranleitung. Hannover.

Albertshauser, E.M. 1985. Neue Grünflächen für die Stadt. Callway, München.

Anderson, J.P.E. & Domsch, K.H. 1978. A physiological method for the quantitative measurement of microbial biomass in soils. Soil Biol. Biochem. 10: 215–221.

Bachelier, G. 1978. La faune des sols. Son écologie et son action. O.R.S.T.O.M., Paris.

Bakker, J.P. 1989. Nature management by grazing and cutting. Geobotany 14.

Bankowska, R., Czechowski, W., Garbarczyk, H. & Trojan, P. 1984. Present and prognosticated fauna of the housing estate Bialoleka Dworska, Warsaw. Memorabilia Zoologica 40: 3–166.

Barber, H.S. 1931. Traps for cave-inhabiting insects. J Elisha Mitchel Soc. 46: 259–265.

Bauchhenss, J. 1982. Artenspektrum, Biomasse, Diversität und Umsatzleistungen von Lumbriciden (Regenwürmern) auf unterschiedlich bewirtschafteten Grünlandflächen verschiedener Standorte Bayerns. Bayer. Landw. Jahrb. 59: 119–125.

Bauchhenns, J. 1986. Die Bodenfauna landwirtschaftlich genutzter Flächen. Laufener Seminarbeiträge 6: 18–28.

Baudisch, F., Horstmann, C., Lützow, A., Letschert, U. & Gerhardt, A. 1989. Wege der Grünflächenpflege – eine vegetationskundliche Untersuchung der Grünflächen der Stadt Bielefeld. Verh. Ges. Ökol., Bd. XVIII (Essen 1988), 221–224.

Berg, E. 1985. Zur Vegetation öffentlicher Rasenflächen in Hannover. Landschaft und Stadt 17: 49–57.

Blume, H.-P. 1987. Bodenkartierung von städtischen Verdichtungsräumen. Die Heimat 9: 280–288.

Blume, H.-P. 1988. Zur Klassifikation der Böden städtischer Verdichtungsräume. Mitt. DBG 56: 323–326.

Blume, H.-P. 1989. Classification of soils in urban agglomerations. Catena 16: 269–275.

Blume, H.-P. & Runge, M. 1978. Genese und Ökologie innerstädtischer Böden aus Bauschutt. Z. Pflanzenernährung u. Bodenkunde 144: 181–196.

Blume, H.-P. & Schlichting, E. (eds.) 1982. Bodenkundliche Probleme städtischer Verdichtungsräume. Mitt. DBG 33: 1–280.

Blume, H.-P. & Sukopp, H. 1976. Ökologische Bedeutung anthropogener Bodenveränderungen. Schriftenreihe f. Vegetationskunde 10: 75–89.

Braun-Blanquet, J. 1964. Pflanzensoziologie. 3. Aufl. Wien, New York.

Bröring, U., Brux, H., Gebhardt, M., Heim, R., Niedringhaus, R. & Wiegleb, G. 1989. Grünanlagen zwischen Naturnähe und Erholungsfunktion – eine floristisch-faunistische Untersuchung. Verh. Ges. Ökol., Bd. XVII (Göttingen 1987), 689–694.

Broll, G. 1989. Die mikrobielle Aktivität der Böden einer Bracheversuchsfläche in Südwestdeutschland unter dem Einfluß verschiedener Landschaftspflegemaßnahmen. Arb. ber. Lehrstuhl Landschaftsökologie 10, Münster.

Broll, G. 1991a. Auswirkungen der Flächenstillegung auf den Abbau der organischen Substanz am Beispiel einer Grünlandbrache. Verh. Ges. Ökol., Bd. XIX/III (Osnabrück 1989), 105–114.

Broll, G. 1991b. Extensive Pflege städtischer Grünflachen. I. Böden, Vegetation und Mikroklima. Verh. Ges. Ökol., Bd. XX (Freising-Weihenstephan 1990), 451–458.

Campino, I. 1983. Die Mineralisation der organischen Substanz dreier verschiedener Grünlandböden. Kali-Briefe (Büntehof) 16(8): 471–497.

Czechowski, W. 1980. Influence of the manner of managing park areas and their situation on the formation of the communities of carabid beetles (Coleoptera, Carabidae). Fragmenta Faunistica 12: 199–219.

Dunger, W. 1983. Tiere im Boden. A. Ziemsen Verlag, Wittenberg.

Dunger, W. & Fiedler, H.J. (eds.) 1989. Methoden der Bodenbiologie. G. Fischer Verlag, Stuttgart.

Easton, E.G. 1983. A guide to the valid names of Lumbricidae (Oligochaeta). In: Satchell, J.E. (ed.), Earthworm ecology. From Darwin to vermiculture, pp. 475–487, Chapman and Hall, London.

Edwards, C.A. & Lofty, J.R. 1977. Biology of earthworms. Chapman and Hall, London.

Ellenberg, H. 1979. Zeigerwerte der Gefäßpflanzen Mitteleuropas. 2. Aufl. Scripta Geobotanica 9.

Ellenberg, H. Mayer, R. & Schauermann, J. (eds.) 1986. Ökosystemforschung. Ergebnisse des Sollingprojekts 1966–1986. E. Ulmer Verlag, Stuttgart.

Esser, J. 1984. Untersuchung zur Frage der Bestandsgefährdung des Igels (Erinaceus europaeus) in Bayern. Ber. ANL 8: 22–62.

Fischer, A. 1985. 'Ruderale Wiesen' – Ein Beitrag zur Kenntnis des Arrhenatherion-Verbandes. Tuexenia 5: 237–248.

FAO 1988. Soil map of the world, revised legend; world map, resources report 60. FAO-Rom.

Forschungsgesellschaft Landschaftsentwicklung Landschaftsbau (FLL) (ed.) 1988. Kurzfassung über das Forschungs- und Entwicklungsvorhaben 'Anlage naturnaher Grünflächen' untersucht in je einer Anlage in Essen, Hannover und Wiesbaden, Bonn.

Gutte, P. 1984. Die Vegetation Leipziger Rasenflächen. Gleditschia 11: 179–197.

Höller-Land, G. 1958. Der Einfluß des Grasmulchens auf die Kleinarthropoden des Bodens. Z. f. Acker- u. Pflanzenbau 105: 108–117.

Hope, F. 1983. Rasen. Anlage und Pflege von Zier-, Gebrauchs-, Sport- und Landschaftsrasen. Ulmer Verlag, Stuttgart.

Iffert, B. 1983. Nettoprimärproduktion und Umsatz der oberirdischen Pflanzenmasse einer nicht mehr genutzten Glatthaferwiese unter dem Einfluß der ungestörten Sukzession und des Mulchens. Diss. Univ. Gießen.

Jäggi, W. 1976. Die Bestimmung der CO_2-Bildung als Maß der bodenbiologischen Aktivität. Schweizerische Landwirtschaftliche Forschung 15: 371–380.

Kasprzak, K. 1981. Enchytraeids (Oligochaeta, Enchytraeidae) of Warsaw and Mazovia. Memorabilia Zoologica 34: 59–67.

Kasprzak, K. 1986. Structure of enchytraeid (Oligochaeta, Enchytraeidae) communities in urban areas of Warsaw. Memorabilia Zoologica 42: 71–80.

Kempson, D., Lloyd, M. & Ghelardi, R. 1963. A new extractor for woodland litter. Pedobiologia 3: 1–21.

Keplin, B. 1993. Untersuchungen zur Bodenfauna städtischer Grünflächen unter dem Einfluß verschiedener Pflegemaßnahmen. Diss. Univ. Münster.

Keplin, B. & Wanckel, W. 1991. Extensive Pflege städtischer Grünflächen. II. Untersuchungen zur Bodenbiologie. Verh. Ges. Ökol., Bd. XX (Freising-Weihenstephan 1990), 459–464.

Klausnitzer, B., Richter, K., Köberlein, F. 1980. Faunistische Untersuchungen der Bodenarthropoden zweier Leipziger Stadtparks unter besonderer Berücksichtigung der Carabidae und Staphylinidae. Wiss. Z. Karl-Marx-Univ. Leipzig 29: 583–597.

Köster, W. & Merkel, D. 1982. Beziehungen zwischen den Gehalten an Zn, Cd, Pb und Cu in Böden und Pflanzen bei unterschiedlichen Bodenuntersuchungsmethoden. Landwirt. Forsch. Sh. 39: 245–254.

Kowarik, I. & Jirku, A. 1988. Rasen im Spannungsfeld zwischen Erholung, Ökologie und Gartendenkmalpflege. Analyse von Nutzungskonflikten in Parkanlagen am Beispiel des Berliner Tiergartens. Teil 1: Untersuchungskonzeption und Vegetationsanalysen. Das Gartenamt 37: 645–654.

Kunick, W. 1983. Ökologische Bedeutung naturnäherer Gras- und Rasenflächen. Das Gartenamt 32: 26–29.

Kunick, W. 1987. Vegetation städtischer Biotope. In: Hohenheimer Arbeiten. Ökologische Probleme in Verdichtungsgebieten. Tagung über Umweltforschung an der Universität Hohenheim, Stuttgart 99–114.

Lavelle, P. 1988. Earthworm activities and the soil system. Biol. Fert. Soils 6: 237–251.

Lee, K.E. 1985. Earthworms. Their ecology and relationships with soils and land use. Academic Press, Sydney.

Leuthold, R. 1961. Vergleichende Untersuchungen der Tierwelt verschiedener Wiesenböden im oberbayerischen Raum, unter besonderer Berücksichtigung der Collembolen. Z. angew. Entom. 49: 1–50.

Makeschin, F. 1990. Die Regenwurmfauna forstlich und landwirtschaftlich genutzter Böden und deren Beeinflußung durch Düngung. Kali-Briefe (Büntehof) 20: 49–63.

Müller, H.-G. 1986. Zur Spinnenfauna einer Kulturrasenflächen in Mittelhessen. Dechcniana 139: 223–230.

Müller, N. 1988. Südbayerische Parkrasen – Soziologie und Dynamik bei unterschiedlicher Pflege. Dissertationes Botanicae, 123.

Müller, N. 1989. Zur Syntaxonomie der Parkrasen Deutschlands. Tuexenia 9: 293–301.

Müller, H. & Steinwarz, D. 1988. Auswirkungen unterschiedlicher Schnittvarianten auf die Arthropodenzönose einer urbanen Wiese. Natur und Landschaft 63: 335–339.

Müller, H. & Steinwarz, D. 1990. Grünflächenplanung und Pflegemanagement aus tierökologischer Sicht. Natur und Landschaft 65: 306–310.

Niedbala, W., Blaszak, C., Bloszyk, J., Kaliszewski, M. & Kazmierski, A. 1982. Soil mites (Acari) of Warsaw and Mazovia. Memorabilia Zoologica 36: 235–252.

Niedringhaus, R. & Bröring, U. 1988. Zur Zusammensetzung der Wanzen- und Zikadenfauna (Hemiptera: Heteroptera, Auchenorrhyncha) naturnaher Grünanlagen im Stadtgebiet von Bremen. Abh. Naturw. Verein Bremen 41/1: 17–28.

Nossag, J. 1971. Untersuchungen über die Präsenz und Aktivität von Mikroorganismen in den Straßenböden der Hamburger Innenstadt. Zbl. Bakt. Abt. II, 126: 313–342.

Nowak, E. 1975. Population density of earthworms and some elements of their production in several grassland environments. Ekologia Polska 23: 459–491.

Ohya, H., Fujiwara, S., Komai, Y. & Yamagucchi, M. 1988. Microbial biomass and activity in urban soils contaminated with Zn and Pb. Biol. Fert. Soils 6: 913.

Oke, T.R. 1987. Boundary layer climates. Methuen, Londen & New York.

Page, A.L., Miller, R.H. & Keeney, D.R. 1982. Methods of soil analysis. Agronomy 9, Madison.

Persson, T. & Lohm, U. 1977. Energetical significance of the Annelids and Arthropods in a swedish grassland soil. Ecol. Bull. (Stockholm) 23.

Pilipiuk, I. 1981. Earthworms (Oligochaeta, Lumbricidae) of Warsaw and Mazovia. Memorabilia Zoologica 34: 69–77.

Pisarski, B., Pilipiuk, I. & Sterzynska, M. 1989. Structural changes of communities of the soil fauna in an urban environment – the example of Warsaw. In: UNESCO (ed.), Report on MAB workshop 'International scientific workshop on soils and soils zoology in urban ecosystems as a basis for management and use of green/open spaces' in Berlin, 15.–19.9.1986, pp. 71–83, Bonn.

Runge, M. 1975. Westberliner Böden anthropogener Litho- oder Pedogenese. Diss. TU Berlin.

Schaefer, M. 1982. Studies on the arthropod fauna of green urban ecosystems. In: Bornkamm, R., Lee, J.A. and Seaward, M.R.D. (eds.), Urban ecology, pp. 65–73, Blackwell Scientific Publications, Oxford.

Schiefer, J. 1981. Bracheversuche in Baden-Württemberg. Beih. Veröff. Naturschutz Landschaftspflege, 22, Karlsruhe.

Schlichting, E. & Blume, H.-P. 1966. Bodenkundliches Praktikum. Verlag P. Parey, Hamburg.

Schmidt, H. 1987. 'Naturnähe' bei der Planung, Anlage und Pflege öffentlicher Grünflächen beim Gartenbauamt Karlsruhe. Das Gartenamt 36: 556–562.

Schmidt, W., Dierschke, H. & Ellenberg, H. 1974. Vorschläge zur vegetationskundlichen Untersuchung auf Dauerprobeflächen. Manuskript Göttingen.

Schreiber, K.-F. (ed.) 1985. Sukzession auf Grünlandbrachen. Münstersche Geographische Arbeiten, 20, Paderborn.

Schulte, W., Fründ, H.-Ch., Söntgen, M., Graefe, U., Ruszkowski, B. & Voggenreiter, V. 1989. Untersuchungen zur bodenökologischen Bedeutung von Freiflächen im Stadtbereich. Forschungsbericht im Auftrag des BMFT.

Schulte, W., Fründ, H.-Ch., Graefe, U., Ruszkowski, B., Söntgen, M. & Voggenreiter, V. 1990. Untersuchungen zur Biologie städtischer Böden. Natur und Landschaft 65: 491–496.

Schulz, H. & Jacob, H. 1987. Aufgaben und Eignung von Dauergrünland und Rasen in Verdichtungsgebieten. In: Hohenheimer Arbeiten. Ökologische Probleme in Verdichtungsgebieten. Tagung über Umweltforschung an der Universität Hohenheim, Stuttgart 115–128.

Schwartze, P., von Ruville-Jackelen, F., Vogel, A., Broll, G. & Schreiber, K.-F. 1989. Vegetationskundliche Differenzierung von Feuchtgrünland und dessen Beeinträchtigung durch Nutzungsänderung und Grundwasserabsenkung sowie Hinweise zu notwendigen Pflegemaßnahmen. Forschungsbericht im Auftrag des MURL NRW, Münster.

Siem, H.-K., Cordsen, E., Blume, H.-P. & Finnern, H. 1987. Klassifizierung von Böden anthropogener Lithogenese – vorgestellt am Beispiel von Böden im Stadtgebiet Kiel. Mitt. DBG. 55/II: 831–836.

Sims, R. & Gerard, B.M. 1985. Earthworms – Synopses of the British Fauna 31, London.

Steinwarz, D. 1989. Anlage naturnaher Grünflächen in Großstädten. Ökologische Untersuchungen an Käfern in Wiesbaden. Diss. Univ. Bonn.

Sterzynska, M. 1982. Springtails (Collembola) of Warsaw and Mazovia. Memorabilia Zoologica 36: 217–234.

Sterzynska, M. 1987. Structure of springtails (Collembola) communities in the urban green of Warsaw. Memorabilia Zoologica 42: 3–18.

Sukopp, H. & Werner, P. 1987. Development of flora and fauna in urban areas. Council of Europe, nature and environment series No. 36. Straßburg.

Swift, H.J., Heal, O.W. & Anderson, J.M. 1979. Decomposition in terrestrial ecosystems. Blackwell Scientific Publications, Oxford.

Thalmann, A. 1968. Zur Methodik der Bestimmung der Dehydrogenaseaktivität im Boden mittels Triphenyltetrazoliumchlorid (TTC). Landwirtsch. Forsch. 21: 249–258.

Thielemann, U. 1986a. Elektrischer Regenwurmfang mit der Oktett-Methode. Pedobiologia 29: 296–302.

Thielemann, U. 1986b. Glasröhrchen-Methode zur Lebendbestimmung von Regenwürmern. Pedobiologia 29: 341–343.

Topp, W. 1972. Die Besiedlung eines Stadtparks durch Käfer. Pedobiologia 12: 336–346.

Topp, W. 1981. Biologie der Bodenorganismen. UTB, Heidelberg.

Umweltbundesamt (ed.) 1989. Kartierung von Stadtböden. Empfehlung des AK Stadtböden der DBG für die bodenkundliche Kartieranleitung urban, gewerblich und industriell überformter Flächen (Stadtböden), Berlin.

UNESCO (ed.) 1989. Report on MAB workshop 'International scientific workshop on soils and soil zoology in urban ecosystems as a basis for management and use of green/open spaces' in Berlin, 15.–19.9.1986.

Weigmann, G. & Stratil, H. 1979. Bodenfauna im Tiergarten. In: Sukopp, H. (ed.), Ökologisches Gutachten über die Auswirkungen von Bau und Betrieb der BAB Berlin (West) auf den Großen Tiergarten, pp. 54–71, Berlin.

Weigmann, G. & Kratz, W. 1987. Oribatid mites in urban zones of West Berlin. Biol. Fert. Soils 3: 81–84.

Weritz, N. 1989. Untersuchungen zur Biologie städtischer Böden. 6. Mikroflora. Verh. Ges. Ökol., Bd. XVIII (Essen 1988), 211–213.

Weritz, N. & Schröder, D. 1988. Mikrobielle Aktivität in Stadtböden unterschiedlicher Nutzung. Mitt. DBG 56: 399–404.

Weritz, N. & Schröder, D. 1989. Mikrobielle Aktivitäten in Stadtböden und ihre Bewertung unter besonderer Berücksichtigung von Schwermetallbelastungen. Mitt. DBG 59/II, 1015–1020.

Weritz, N. & Schröder, D. 1990. Die Bewertung mikrobieller Aktivitäten in Stadtböden als Beitrag zum städtischen Bodenschutz. Mitt. DBG 61: 149–152.

Wilcke, D.E. 1968. Oligochaeta. In: Die Tierwelt Mitteleuropas. Quelle und Meyer, Leipzig.

Wilmers, F. 1985. Die Unterschiede im Temperaturregime verschiedener Bestände, dargestellt im Vergleich der Versuchsflächen Buche, Fichte, Wiese im Solling. VDI Berichte 560: 545–557.

Wolf, G. 1982. Minimalprogramm zur Entwicklung biologisch reichhaltiger Rasen im Siedlungsbereich. Rasen-Turf-Gazon 1: 8–9.

Villages

VEGETATION DYNAMICS OF MACCHIE AND THEIR DERIVATIVES UNDER THE INFLUENCE OF A SMALL SETTLEMENT NEAR ANTALYA (SW-TURKEY)

HARALD KEHL

Institut für Ökologie, Technische Universität Berlin, Rothenburgstr. 12, D-12165 Berlin, Germany

Abstract

The characteristic mosaic pattern of degraded Macchie near a rural settlement on the upper travertine terrace near Antalya (Turkey) is the result of various extensive agricultural influences. The variation, serial structure and interactions of characteristic species groups of Macchie derivates with forb fringes, heliophilous plants of extensive pastures and Macchie clearings, ruderal and segetal sites of the settlement are presented. Population diversity and ecological groups were determined by the direct gradient analysis. The seed bank was studied in germination experiments. These measures were taken to obtain more precise information about the potential species composition and the seasonal vegetation dynamics.

1. Introduction

The Mediterranean countries, which are among the oldest cultural areas on earth, possess a plant cover rich in species and formations, which are generally understood to result from degradation and human influence reaching back far into history.

However, according to the recent publication of Hempel (1981, 1983) human populations played a much less important role in the origins of present-day vegetation and the appearance of erosion. Human reduction of forest areas is assumed, but the crucial soil displacement is shown to have occurred in the subboreal to early Atlantic period.

It is generally agreed that relative to the vegetation of Central Europe (see Sukopp 1979), the Mediterranean vegetation is more original in its composition (Schwarz 1936, Braun-Blanquet 1936, Walter 1968, Schmidt 1969, Zohary 1973). Furthermore, many of its elements are felt to have high ecological resistance and ability to regenerate.

Remnants of Mediterranean shrub formations can often be identified in the immediate settlement area. Strongly devastated Macchie formations with mantle communities and forb fringes, which have been under high grazing pressure, are able to spread and regenerate rapidly if protected (Greuter 1975a, Amir & Sarig 1976, Godron *et al.* 1981). This raises the question of a systematic relationship between human influence and the real dynamics of semi-natural and anthropogenically influenced flora and vegetation.

This paper attempts to cast light on these questions, taking as an example the influence on the vegetation development of a small Turkish settlement on the south-west Anatolian coast near Antalya.

2. Situation and boundaries of the investigation area

The area investigated, at 30°34' longitude and 36°58' latitude, lies in a narrow Mediterranean coastal belt in South-West Anatolia. It is situated in the province (Villayet) of Antalya, some 15 km from the town of the same name.

Urban Ecology as the Basis of Urban Planning, p. 85–150
edited by H. Sukopp, M. Numata and A. Huber
© 1995 SPB Academic Publishing bv, Amsterdam, The Netherlands

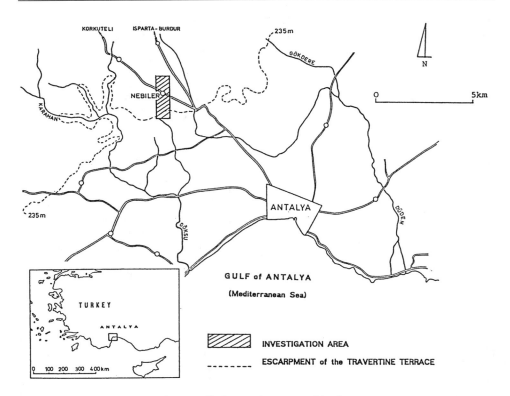

Fig. 1. The investigation area on the upper (2nd) travertine terrace of Antalya.

2.1. *Geological and topographical features*

Antalya lies at the edge of a series of steeply rising travertine terraces, bounded to the north-east and west by the high peaks of the Taurus Mountain chain. This part of the Eurasian fold belt changes its east-west orientation here, and to the west of Antalya divides into several mountain chains. The travertine terraces are delimited to the north-west by the 'Bey Daglari' mountains. This part of the Taurus chain, rising abruptly from the sea to a height of 3000 m and running north-south, also forms the western side of the Bay of Antalya.

Forming a barrier to the Anatolian Highlands, the south-western Taurus Chain thus encloses one of the few large bays on the Turkish south coast. Characterised by marked karst features, such as karren fields, karst plateaus, polje and swallow-holes (doline), the Taurus chain consists mainly of Mesozoic and Tertiary limestone, shale and ophiolite suites (Planhol 1956, Wippern 1962). Comparative geomorphological investigation of the physiographically uniform travertine terracing in front of the Taurus mountains (see Pfannenstiel 1952, 1953, Özbey 1960–61, Biju-Duval & Montadert 1977, Planhol 1956, Darkot & Erinc 1951) have established marked similarities to terracing and to wave-cut grooves and notches elsewhere on the Mediterranean coast. It is generally assumed that this is attributable to eustatic changes in sea level (see the comparisons in Jahn 1970: Fig. 8).

The Antalya Plain, covering an area of about 130 km² is one of the most expansive travertine terraces of the Mediterranean. Morphogenetically it consists of calcareous sinter deposits of acidic spring water from the Taurus mountains, forming layers of crystalline $CaCO_3$. High evaporation levels, and the fact that karst water is usually richer in CO_2 in Mediterranean areas (Sweeting 1972: 108) allow widespread deposition of travertine and tuff.

Plant fragments are often included in travertine, so that its structure is generally heterogeneous (see Steiner 1979: 30, Muranski 1938: 204, on the increased calcareous deposition due to plant fragments). Deposition processes can still frequently be observed at waterfalls on the steep coast near Antalya.

2.2. Climate

The Mediterranean south-west coast of Turkey, in the thermo-Mediterranean climate zone (UNESCO-FAO 1963: 33) is characterised by heavy winter precipitation and a very hot dry summer, due according to Zohari (1973: 31) to the southern exposure of the Taurus chain.

In the summer the coastal strip of Turkey lies in the range of the arid sub-tropics (*cf.* Walter 1968: 50, Christiansen-Weniger 1962: 229) and in the dry period experiences dry air masses and the influence of high-pressure zones. In the winter the cyclonic rains of the temperate zones dominate the whole of the Mediterranean coastal region of Turkey and lead to extremely high levels of precipitation.

The southern exposure of the slopes of the Taurus plays an important role in the distribution of rainfall. The mountains act as a barrier, protecting the coastal region from the influences of the highlands, while leading to increased precipitation in the hinterland of Antalya to the west, north and east, as humid air masses are held back in the hinterland of Antalya. Most of the humidity is deposited in the form of orographic rain (Meyer 1967, 1968: 39). The observation reported by Zech & Cepel (1972: 13) that the annual precipitation in the hinterland of Antalya has risen by about 50% (from an average of 1050 mm to approx. 1500 mm) (*cf.* Fig. 3) is of considerable significance for the area under investigation. Personal records (1979–1980) showed that the period free of rain was about 2 to 3 weeks shorter than in the vicinity of the measuring station of Antalya.

Although the continuous records over the last 50 years from the Antalya climate station cannot be transferred unreservedly to the area under investigation, which lies 15 km northwest and 270 m above sea level, the recorded data represent the climatic conditions over the coast region in general.

However, the mean temperatures only give a vague idea of the actual conditions. The highest measured temperature was 49.2°C in August 1979, apart from which Antalya experienced 86.8 tropical days (temperature during the day above 30°C), and 160.9 summer days (temperature during the day above 26°C) (Met. Bült. 1969). Frosts only occur occasionally in winter. However, due to the pressure gradient between a high-pressure region above the 1000 m higher Inner Anatolia and the Cyprus depression, a north-south flow over the borderhills (Taurus) can give rise to cold descending wind at the coast, with marked cold snaps and sudden drops of temperature below the freezing point.

The arid period lasts from April to October. It is marked by a drop in the monthly precipitation below the aridity index of 30 mm, Jahn (1970: 20) calculated after De Martonne (1927) and Lauer (1952: 15–98). The water budget, calculated using Thornthwaite's method (1948), shows a water deficit between June and October of 582 mm (Iufro 1975: 14). The mean annual relative air humidity of the coastal region is 64% and below 60% in the months June to September. A possible explanation could be the prevailing NW to N winds, which bring with them comparatively dry air from the highlands. Of particular importance for the Mediterranean vegetation is the high intensity of the insolation. From mid-March to approximately mid-October between 8 and 13 hours mean daily hours of

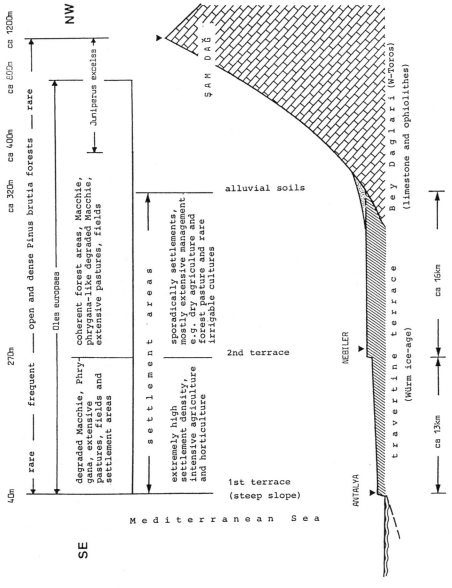

Fig. 2. Altitudinal profile of the travertine terrace and the 'SAM DAG' (Western Taurus) and location of the research area of Nebiler.

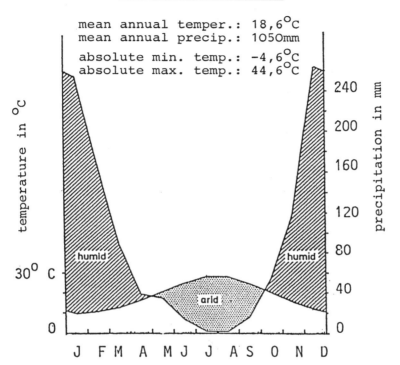

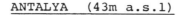

Fig. 3. Climate diagram of Antalya (after Walter & Lieth 1969).

sunshine were measured, and even in the winter the sun shines for an average of 5 hours per day (Met. Bült. Ankara 1962, 1967, Met. Stat. Antalya 1966).

2.3. Soils

The importance of insolation and climate for the pedogenesis of the area under investigation was emphasised by Christiansen-Weniger (1970: 36/37) after the climate formula of Köppen (1931). According to this the plain near Antalya belongs to the sub-tropical Csh-climate of the south-Anatolian coast, but is also given an additional 'r' (for rainy), since the mean annual precipitation exceeds 1000 mm. The Csa-climate otherwise typical for the Mediterranean coast is only found on the west coast of Turkey (Gansen 1972).
The parent rock has already been described (see also Darkot & Erinc 1961, Planhol 1956b, Poisson 1977). Pedological investigations in Turkey, including the area under investigation, have been carried out by Oakes & Arikök (1954, after Wilbrandt 1974). For the particular problems relating to agricultural soils in Turkey, reference is made to the comprehensive study of Christiansen-Weniger (1970). According to Oakes (1954: 57) the soils of the sinter terrace belong to the 'red prairie soils'. Following the morphological classification system of Schroeder (1978) and the description of the above-named soil type in North and Middle America (Gansen 1972: 224/225), for the specific area under investigation preference is given to the soil-type classification of Giesecke (1930, after Christiansen-

Weniger 1970: 103). The whole of the southern coastal strip is regarded as Mediterranean skeletal soils with Terra Rossa. These are climate-phytomorphic soils (Schroeder 1978: 105) of variable humidity of the sub-tropics, which frequently occur in the Mediterranean area as relict soils of Pleistocene variable climates (Klinge 1958). Recent Terra Rossa formations occurring on flat, well-drained limestone subsoils under extreme soil climates (heating, cooling, wetting and desiccation) could also be observed in the area under investigation. The destruction of protective vegetation by extensive agricultural activity leads to extreme soil climates and also to the loss of red soil, which is particularly susceptible to erosion.

Investigations of soil profiles and soil horizons were not carried out in connection with the phytosociological studies. In this context the work of Zech & Cepel (1972) is mentioned, who have investigated the 'Relationship between soil and relief properties and the growth of *Pinus brutia* in south Anatolia'. The test areas with the nos. 39 to 42 (Antalya-Kepezalti) of Zech & Cepel are located in a *Pinus brutia*-forest only a few kilometres away from Nebiler. In view of the homogeneity of the pedogenesis over travertine (Zech & Cepel 1972) the data can be regarded as representative of the study area outside the settlement, even though the humus layer and the A/B-horizon in the area of the Macchie are less deep. Thus the humus layer is 2 to 7 cm in depth under *Pinus brutia*, or the individual bush complex, but seldom more than 1 cm in clearings. The A/B-horizon is often broken by the parent rock, reaching a depth of 0 to 30 cm with a skeletal proportion of 30–50 vol %. Although, as already mentioned, travertine is a homogeneous parent rock with deep clefts and fissures filled with red soil, rooting to a depth of 120 cm is possible (Iufro 1975: 14). The soil profile descriptions of Zech & Cepel show an increase in hydrogenion concentrations with depth, as already described for Mediterranean red soils by Braun-Blanquet (1928, from Lundegardh 1949: 65). With an average pH-value of 6.65 in the A-horizon (0–10 cm) and 5.7 in the B-horizon (10–30 cm), the shallow Terra Rossa soils show a weak to moderate acidic reaction.

The relatively high humus layer of 2 to 7 cm under even sparse shrub complexes in the Macchie with unfavourable site conditions is understandable in view of the long periods of desiccation of the upper soil layers. Although the pH-values of the humus A-horizon are favourable for micro-organisms, the decomposition of litter is not controlled primarily by the acidity of the upper soil layers, as it is in the humid regions of central Europe, but by the length of the dry season (Zech & Cepel 1972: 36).

3. Phytosociological investigation of the dynamics of synanthropic formations in the Nebiler area

The area in the close vicinity of the village of Nebiler bears impressive witness to the various anthropozoogenous influences on the vegetation. Vegetation in Europe has long been known to change radially from the surrounding countryside to the centre of a settlement, reflecting the relationship between human influence (farming) and the floral composition of the vegetation.

Such a sequence of floral composition and typical formations could also be related to certain site factors in the Mediterranean area (*cf.* Oberdorfer 1965, Knapp 1971, Raus 1979a,b, Naveh & Whittaker 1979). The localised formations are generally the products of development series such as occur under natural conditions, but are in the vicinity of settlements due to a variety of activities.

In order to describe the dynamics of vegetation and the floral composition in the vicinity of this small Turkish settlement, and to allow phytosociological comparison with other results, primarily from the Aegean area, use is made of the dimensions proposed by Sukopp (1968, 1969) of intensity, extent and duration of influence. However, for at least two reasons this is only possible with some reservations in the area under investigation. Firstly, little attention is paid by plant sociologists to ecologically relevant site factors, and in particular to their variation over time, a fact pointed out by Walter & Breckle (1983: 125ff). Secondly, the causes of vegetation development in one area are frequently not transferable to another. Due to the scant information available about the history of the village, and conflicting statements about the current economic situation, official information from Antalya was compared with information from villagers and approximate values were determined.

The extent and intensity of human influence on vegetation doubtlessly varies in accordance with the socio-economic system and its environment. For example, in view of their extensive irrigation systems, a larger population can be assumed for the Greek-Roman period on the lower travertine terrace than in the early Middle Ages (Kündig-Steiner 1974). There has only really been an intensification of anthropozoogenic influence with the industrialisation of Antalya over the last 100 years and the development of the infrastructure on the Pamphylian plain, together with the rise in the numbers of sheep and especially of goats.

3.1. Socio-economic structure of Nebiler village

It is not clear when the Nebiler settlement was founded. Apart from the fact that old maps use various names for what was obviously the same settlement location, the placement on old maps often seems to be based on speculation, which is not unusual for smaller Turkish settlements. It is possible that the founding of Nebiler, in common with other small settlements in the poor region on the edge of the upper travertine terraces coincides with the decline of the Ottoman Empire, during which the population abandoned the more fertile areas to avoid the troubles (see Pazarkaya 1974: 348).

Although the human influence on the landscape cannot be quantified historically, it is not unreasonable to assume that the traditional social structure has been relatively continuous, since these have changed appreciably only in recent years in other, similar settlements.

The scattered structure of the village, and information from the villagers and the staff of the survey office of the province capital Antalya, give reason to suppose that the village is more than 300 years old. The present population numbers some 600 and is rising according to the mayor (muhtar), with only 279 entitled to vote, and thus older than 21 in 1980. Although there are no statistical records, the existing stock of old buildings, and the relatively small number of new buildings support the opinion expressed by villagers that the population has not suffered any wide variations. The village of Nebiler has some 25 small farmers' families whose livestock and land ensures an adequate income throughout the year.

The figures provided for land and livestock vary widely, and it is certain that villagers have little interest in clarification, at least as far as areas under cultivation are concerned. There has been no land registration, due among other things to the fact that views are divided on the exact distinction between forest and agricultural lands.

As a rule even small families have a garden, with some goats and sheep. Livestock of the village was said to comprise approximately 1500 goats, 3000 sheep, 150 cattle and 50 horses, mules and donkeys. There is an observable trend away from sheep and goats towards cattle.

In Nebiler dry agriculture is practised on uneven land in close proximity to the village. Fields often protrude into the Macchie (see Fig. 4). Animal husbandry provides the main source of income for the small farmers, in addition to which wheat and olives are produced solely for personal consumption.

Sowing is in November and the harvest follows in May. In addition to the few olive trees, there occasionally grow carobs (*Ceratonia siliqua*), figs (*Ficus carica*) and almonds (*Prunus amygdalus*). Dung is not used to fertilize the gardens or fields, but is sold to banana plantations or the market gardeners of Antalya.

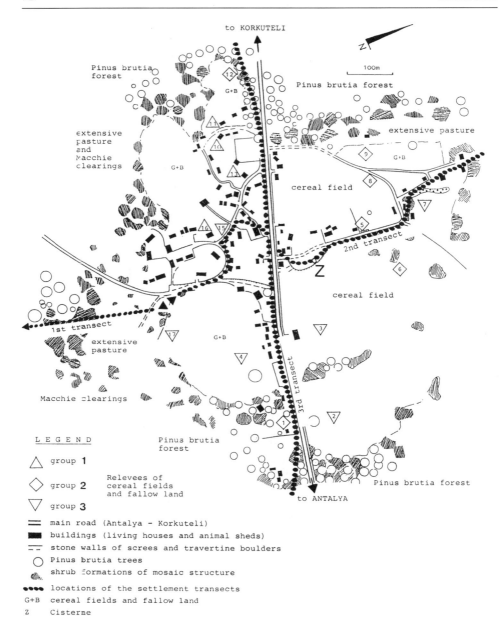

Fig. 4. The Nebiler settlement.

After the harvest in May, and before the onset of the dry season, which lasts until September, most of the villagers take their livestock, which have grazed on the extensive pastures (rough pasture, 'Trift') and the surrounding Macchie for the cooler parts of the year, and move to the summer pastures (Yayla) in the highlands near Korketuli. The village is virtually deserted throughout the summer; only a few old people and men with jobs in the town remain behind.

It should be noted that during field work in summer 1979 near Nebiler, other herds of goats were encountered in addition to those belonging to the village.

Current use of the Macchie and the local forest is primarily for foraging, and only secondarily as a source of fuel. Firewood is obtained mainly by coppicing the strawberry tree (*Arbutus andrachne*) and from the mock privet (*Phillyrea latifolia*) as well as from old pine trees some distance from the village. The situation has been eased considerably by recent guaranteed state deliveries of firewood from forestries.

It was not possible to establish whether the areas around Nebiler were also grazed on a regular basis by passing nomads, as mentioned by Jahn (1970) for the western upper terrace. Villagers said this was not the case. Nomads (Yuerueks) are said to have passed on the southern edge of the upper terrace until 1965, which is said not to have had adverse effects on the village's grazing. The absence of Yuerueks in recent years can be attributed to changes in animal husbandry. To meet the requirements of the Antalya market, Daglic sheep gained favour over goats (Jahn 1970: 36).

Asked about grazing behaviour, the villagers emphasised the difference between goats on the one hand and sheep and cattle on the other. In addition to grazing the herb layer, goats ate the spring shoots of almost all shrubs of the Macchie, including *Calicotome villosa* and *Sarcopoterium spinosum*. Exceptions are the toxic *Daphne sericea*, *D. gnidium* and *Myrtus communis*, and *Cistus* species. Sheep and cows, by contrast, restrict themselves to the herb layer, and thus to the range-type of vegetation (extensive pasture) and between the shrub complexes (Macchie clearings). From personal observation, however, it seems that sheep are not averse to the young shoots of *Phillyrea latifolia*, *Rhamnus oleoides* and even *Quercus coccifera*.

The radius of action of the grazers varies widely. The cattle, as well as asses and mules, are kept in the immediate vicinity of the village and tended by the children. Preferred areas are to the south between the Macchie and the village perimeter, and to a lesser extent the area to the north.

The vegetation to the west and south of the village on both sides of the high road consists of more or less continuous *Pinus brutia* forest, with sporadic to dense Macchie undergrowth to the east of the village perimeter. The picture to the north and south offers a sharp contrast, with no pines near the village. Typical vegetation of extensive pastures gives way to a highly sub-divided, Phrygana-like devastated Macchie vegetation, which gives way to *Pinus brutia* forest far outside the village.

The term Phrygana is used to characterise devastated, often cushion-shaped vegetation with character species of Macchie formations. 'True' Phrygana according to the definitions of Rauh (1975) or Quezel (1981) were not found in the research area.

Ruderal and segetal flora are concentrated in the village itself, and occur with gradually decreasing frequency in the extensive pastures. The depiction of these transitions of vegetation formations dependent on land-use, with their interactions and dynamics is intended to assist an inductive understanding of stages of degradation of evergreen sclerophyllous vegetation, while also providing a basis for comments on aspects of human influence.

3.2. Method of vegetation investigation

If a causal analysis of the intensity of land-use and the floristic composition of the synanthropic formations encountered exclusively in the area of investigation is to be made, it is essential to include syndynamic transitional stages in a survey of vegetation (*cf.* Moravec in Wagner 1972, Maarel 1976, Goodall 1963, 1973). This is supported by the observation of Raus (1979: 20) of a 'continually extensively used region' of East Thessalia, where disturbed vegetation covered disproportionately large areas compared with plant-sociologically balanced ones. Surveys of the diverse transitional stages of landscape elements determined by anthropozoogenous influence is particularly pertinent for ecological analysis (cf. Ellenberg in Brun-Hool 1966).

In terms of method, the distribution of species and the alteration of vegetation as a result of specific environmental influences can best be registered using the gradient analysis first applied by the Russian geo-botanist Ramensky (1926, 1930, 1932, cf. Sobolev & Utekhin 1982) and further developed by the American ecologist Whittaker (1967, 1973, 1982). This is based on the view that the vegetation of a landscape represents a complex and extended continuous population pattern which corresponds to the pattern of site gradients (Whittaker 1970: 56).

Plant societies, floristically classified by the Zurich-Montpellier school (Braun-Blanquet 1964, Tüxen 1956) in terms of characteristic and differential species, are seen by the Anglo-American school as overlapping integral units of vegetation perceived as a continuum (Goodall 1963). This continuum can, however, be disrupted by anthropogenic disturbances (Whittaker 1970), or can display boundary zones which correspond closely to the borders of the natural environment (Leeuwen 1965, 1966, 1970, Maarel 1976).

The direct gradient analysis requires a definable ecological parameter or a gradually changing ecological gradient. In our case it is assumed that there is a radial decrease in intensity of land-use from the centre of the settlement to the Phrygana and the Macchie (intensity gradient). While the degree of land-use cannot be measured directly, the distance from the notional centre of the village to the first sampling site some 1200 m from the village can be given and correlated with the individual sampling sites and their results. The sampling of the vegetation stands followed Ellenberg (1956), Braun-Blanquet (1964) and Knapp (1971).

Five layers were distinguished along the three transects (cf. Figs. 4, 5 and 6). The tree layer (I = > 3 m) was formed largely of *Pinus brutia*, the only species able to dominate clearly over the bush layer (II = 1–3 m, III = 0.5–1 m). The Macchie was subdivided to show the group of nano-phanerophytes, as well as areas in which potential macro-phanerophytes remain low. In layer III species already occur which are typical for the Phrygana, or are transitional to this formation. The herb layer is also subdivided (IV = 0.2–0.5 m; V = 0–0.2 m). The layer up to 20 cm is clearly dominated by thero- and hemicryptophytes of the extensive pastures or Macchie clearings, being also spatially distinct from the dwarf shrubs and ecotonic complexes of the Cistus-Micromeria associations of the Phrygana, consisting largely of chamaephytes (cf. Oberdorfer 1954a, Horvat et al. 1974 and Raus 1979a,b).

The dominance and the sociability were estimated in seven and five classes respectively after Braun-Blanquet (1964). The overlapping of the layers meant that the total sum of coverage was higher than the actual total coverage, which gives a good idea of the density of the vegetation.

The postulate of homogeneity for the classification in accordance with Braun-Blanquet (1964) cannot be realised completely in the gradient analysis, since the areas to be surveyed are to be evenly spaced along the environmental gradient. If the variation of populations and associations is to be registered in full, then the sampling areas cannot be placed preferentially in representative plant associations, since the method of exclusively homogeneous sampling areas is inappropriate for answering syndynamic questions (cf. Goodall 1963, 1973, Barkman 1968, Spatz 1975, Walter & Breckle 1983).

In order to register the entire complex of the Macchie, with residual *Pinus brutia* stands, the adjacent stages of degradation and its transition to ruderal and segetal vegetation, areas of 200 m² (20 × 10 m) generally 15 m apart from each other were examined. The 1st transect (cf. Figs. 4 and 5) was begun at the edge of the upper sinter terrace at 235 m above sea level some 1200 m SE of Nebiler, leading north-west to the margin of the settlement.

The choice of an area of 200 m² in the devastated Macchie was derived from the species number per area-graph after Braun-Blanquet (1964) (*cf.* Knapp 1971: 33). The herb layer was determined for two areas of 20 m² within the larger area. Within the settlement area (transects 2 and 3), sampling was necessarily restricted to smaller plots, but their spacing remained much the same.

In order to register the ruderal and segetal flora and their distribution, additional surveys were made outside the transects on and around the harvested arable fields. A valuable addition to the vegetation surveys in the settlement area (*cf.* Willems 1983) proved to be soil samples, from which information about the current seed bank could be obtained by germination tests, with indications of the seasonal (Oberdorfer 1954b) plant associations.

In the course of the survey a considerable number of plants were collected for determination with the *Flora of Turkey and the East Aegean Islands* (Davis 1965–1985).

3.3. Tabular classification of the vegetation

The emphasis on the dynamics of vegetation for the tabular classification of the vegetational mapping makes it necessary to organise the entries in the lists according to their position on the transect and to group the species corresponding to similar population densities. In order to be able to judge beyond the individuality of species in terms of their variation with grazing intensity (*cf.* Walter & Breckle 1983), the centres of distribution of character species group combinations, or in the syntaxonomic sense of associations or their fragments, the taxa found along the transects are assigned to groups of character species.

These groups are determined from a comparison of the phytosociological tables and from various group listings of the authors mentioned below. The tables, which are not intended to be a syntaxonomic classification, should only be understood as a deductive determination of groups with character species (abbreviated in the following text as CaS).

This approach makes it possible to portray stages of vegetation and to compare degrees of relationship of 'associations' directly.

Only sporadic floristic-sociological records of the coastal region of south-west Anatolia were available for comparison, so that for the synsystematic and subsequent syntaxonomic evaluation of the taxa found, in order to identify character species, investigations from elsewhere in the east Mediterranean had to be drawn on for comparison, in particular the work of Oberdorfer (1952a: North Aegean herb and dwarf shrub vegetation, 1956: Canary Islands), Raus (1979a,b: East Thessalia), Lavrentiades (1969: Rhodes), Dafis & Landolt (1975, 1976: Greece), Knapp (1965: Kephallinia), Horvat *et al.* (1974: Vegetation of SE-Europe) and for the ruderal and segetal vegetation Lohmeyer (1969, unpubl.), Lohmeyer & Trautmann (1970) and Oberdorfer (1954b).

Even if, as Raus (1979b: 20) says, 'heterotonic' tables which include transitional syndynamic states following the initially defined approach are not suited for syntaxonomic evaluations in the sense of Braun-Blanquet (*cf.* Tuexen 1972, 1974, Quezel 1981), they nevertheless allow delimitation between overlapping associations in those areas where species groups are withdrawing and others are entering (Whittaker 1973: 40, Maarel 1976: 420). The spatial dynamic aspect emphasised by the chosen means of presentation clearly shows the hierarchy of relationships of character species groups in the formation of coenoclines (Noy-Meir & Whittaker 1977) related to land-use gradients.

4. Evaluation of the vegetation relevees for the characterisation of sites and species combinations

4.1. General characteristics of the settlement area

The Macchie adjoining on the ruderal vegetation to the west, north and east of Nebiler (see Fig. 4), with stands of *Pinus brutia* which are continuous in some places, was only registered phytosociologically at its perimeter. The well-preserved *Pinus brutia* forest to the west of the village, along the road to Termessos and Korkuteli, only has slight shrub layers with isolated *Quercus coccifera* and *Phillyrea latifolia*. An habitual dwarf shrub layer is only developed along a narrow band around the settlement.

The *Pinus brutia* forest is relatively well-preserved because the state forest, with rather rigid controls against wood extraction, begins right outside the village (oral comm. Duezlercami). Undergrowth is only sporadic due to extraction by the villagers, and intense grazing, at least near the village. At some distance from the village the state forest has dense Macchie undergrowth.

A similar situation is encountered on either side of the road to Antalya, leaving the village to the east. However, there is thick undergrowth under a continuous *Pinus brutia* forest directly from the edge of the village. The villagers say that this area was privately owned until a few years ago, and grazing and wood-extraction were strictly controlled.

The periphery of the village to the north and south has an extensive pasture-type vegetation, with a mosaic of small shrub complexes intruding more frequently with increasing distance from the village. These complexes merge to form larger and larger units, with some individuals (*Quercus coccifera*, *Phillyrea latifolia* and *Pistacia terebinthus*) reaching heights of 2–4 m. At some distance from the village the first isolated *Pinus brutia* occur, and at a greater distance these form smaller continuous stands.

4.2. Distribution of character species and their groups along the 1st transect

Examining the graph of all species (Figs. 5 and 8), it is apparent that the southern part of the 1st transect shows an almost linear increase of species with decreasing remoteness from the village, and a sudden drop in the extensive pastures. If the species number is correlated with the running relevee number and the distance from the edge of the village (relevee no. 25), a coefficient of 0.91 is obtained, which represents a highly significant increase. The species diversity peaks at the periphery of the village (*cf.* Figs. 8 and 12), here the CaS of the ruderal, segetal, and range-communities overlap over a large band with the CaS of the Macchie (*Quercus coccifera* – *Pistacia terebinthus*) and the species of the extensive pastures.

The marked decline in the numbers of species between positions 20 and 25 coincides with the high dominance of only a few therophytes and a high abundance of species indicating degradation in the pronounced extensive pasture ranges, already a euhemerobic zone of the settlement periphery (*cf.* Fig. 5). The distribution of the determined CaS groups shows marked differences primarily between the CaS of the Macchie and Phrygana on the one hand, and on the other hand of the extensive pastures and the Macchie clearings, which are rich in therophytes. In contrast to the more-or-less constant numbers per relevee of phanerophytes and chamaephytes of the Macchie and the chamaephytes of the Phrygana, the proportions of therophytes and hemi-cryptophytes of the extensive pastures and Macchie clearings increase the nearer one comes to the village. Although the last-mentioned group is not completely absent from the village centre, it has only a very low cover.

The extensive pasture zone to the south of the village represents the real distribution boundary of the trampling and segetal vegetation, and with some reservations of the ruderal vegetation. It should be noted that some CaS of the *Hordeum leporinum* – *Chenopodium murale* association (e.g., *Hirschfeldia incana*, *Sisymbrium officinale* and *Crepis foetida*) stretch far into the boundary zone of the Macchie and Phrygana associations.

There is a marked difference in the proportional dominance of the characteristic groups. In particular the phanerophytes (*cf.* Table 1) of the Macchie, *Quercus coccifera*, *Phillyrea latifolia* and *Pistacia terebinthus*, as well as *Pinus brutia*, display high cover values from the start to the middle section of the transect, which then decline almost linearly to the edge of the village. Although the *Quercus coccifera* is well represented in all relevees, it becomes less and less frequent in the upper shrub stratum II (1–3 m), and grows in the extensive pastures in cushion shaped formations where it scarcely exceeds 1 m.

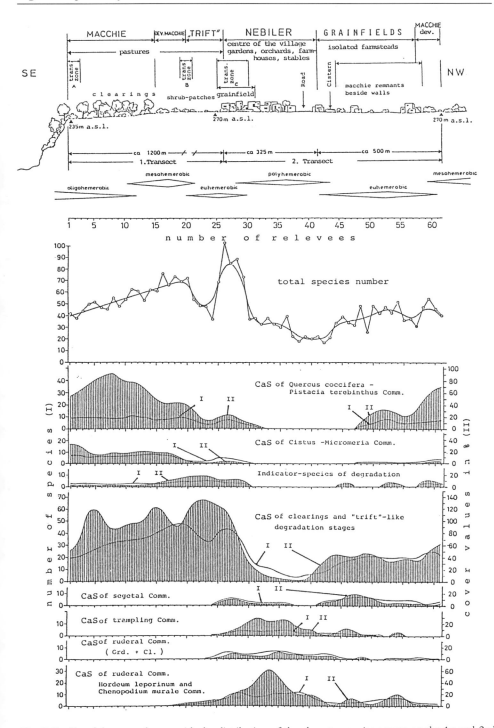

Fig. 5. Profile of the research area with the distribution of the character species groups on the 1st and 2nd transect.

Table 1. Relevees of the 1st transect from the escarpment of the travertine terrace to the extensive pastures of the settlement of Nebiler, arranged according to character species groups.

1979		27.	28.	30.	1.	3.	4.	6.	7.	7.	8.	8.	10.	10.	14.	15.	15.	17.	17.	19.	21.	21.	22.	22.	26.
		April			May																				
No. of relevee		1	2	3	4	5	6	7	8	9	10	11	12	13	14	15	16	17	18	19	20	21	22	23	24
Size of sample plots: 200m2																									
Altitude a.s.l. (m)		235	240	241	242	245	245	246	252	253	255	260	260	257	260	260	261	262	262	265	264	265	270	270	
Exposition		SE	SE	SE	SE	SE	-	SE	SE	SE	SE	NW	SE	NW	SE	SE	SE	NW	-	SE	SE	SE	SE	SE	SE
Inclination		35	20	10	10	15	-	10	20	10	10	15	20	15	9	20	5	5	-	5	10	10	5	10	10
I - Tree layer (Cover value)		8	-	9	6	10	-	-	12	-	8	-	9	9	-	30	5	5	20	5	-	-	-	-	-
II - (100-150cm) (%)		80	20	1	1	1	20	80	40	15	60	25	15	1	1	1	10	10	5	10	1	1	5	-	1
III - (50-150cm) (%)		2	2	30	10	25	2	30	30	5	25	5	25	25	10	10	10	20	5	10	10	15	25	20	10
IV - (20-50cm) (%)		30	2	30	15	80	10	20	20	15	15	15	15	25	25	35	25	25	40	60	25	15	80	90	15
V - (< 20cm) (%)		20	20	40	60	80	70	40	40	50	60	60	60	80	80	50	60	60	60	60	90	90	90	80	70
Number of species		42	38	44	50	52	47	46	55	48	62	62	61	62	76	61	69	72	69	54	49	49	37	69	

Character species of the Quercus coccif. - Pistacia tereb. Comm. (cf. ZOHARY 1973, LAVRENTIADES 1969, AKMAN et al. 1978, QUEZEL et al. 1978)

Species		I	II	III	IV	V
Pinus brutia	(i)					
Quercus coccifera	(i)					
Phillyrea latifolia	(i)					
Pistacia terebinthus						
Olea europaea var.	(i)					
Rhamnus oleoides	(i)					
Daphne gnidium						
Daphne sericea	(i)					
Calicotome villosa						

Code	Species
III	Crataegus monogyna
IV	Asparagus acutifolius
III	
IV	Rubia peregrina
IV	Osyris alba
III	Styrax officinalis

Character species of the Cistus - Micromeria - Comm. (cf. OBERDORFER 1954, RAUS 1979, HORVAT et al. 1974)

Code	Species
V	Fumana thymifolia
IV	Cistus creticus
IV	Micromeria myrtifolia
IV	Teucrium divaricatum
V	Teucrium polium
V	Satureja thymbra
IV	Cistus salviifolius
V	Tuberiaria guttata
V	Thymus revolutus

Indicator plants for extreme degradation

Code	Species
III	Euphorbia veneta var.
IV	Asphodelus microcarpus
IV	Urginea maritima
V	Andrachne telephioides

Character species of the extensive pastures and macchie openings rich in therophytes (cf. OBERDORFER 1954, BRAUN-BLANQUET 1964)
TB = Thero-Brachypodietea, -etalia, SG = seam communities, B = companions and accidental species

1st group (species with irregular distribution or more than one center of distribution)

Code	Species
V-SG	Geranium purpureum var.
V-TB	Salvia viridis
V-B	Urospermum picroides
V-TB	Trifolium stellatum
V-B	Plantago arenaria
V-B	Lagurus ovatus
IV-B	Cynosurus echinatus
V-TB	Onobrychis caput-galli
V-B	Legousia pentagonia
V-TB	Filago eriocephala
V-TB	Bromus intermedius
V-B	Plantago lagopus
V-B	Daucus guttatus
V-TB	Salvia horminum
V-B	Lophochloa phleoides

Table 1. Cont.

No. of relevee	1	2	3	4	5	6	7	8	9	10	11	12	13	14	15	16	17	18	19	20	21	22	23	24	25
2nd group (species with regular distribution ort more orientated to the extensive pasture)																									
V-B Psilurus incurvus	+	+	+	+	+	+	+	+	.	+	+	+	+	+	+	+	+	+	+	+	+	+	+	+	+
V-B Anthemis chia	1.1	+	1.2	2.4	3.3	2.3	1.2	+	.	1.2	+	1.2	2.2	2.2	1.2	+	1.2	+	+	2.3	1.2	2.2	2.2	2.2	+
V-B Plantago cretica	.	.	2.2	2.3	3.4	3.3	2.4	2.2	3.5	3.3	2.3	3.4	4.5	3.4	3.3	1.2	2.2	1.2	2.2	3.3	3.2	4.3	3.2	4.3	3.2
V-B Alyssum strigosum ssp.	1.2	.	1.2	1.2	1.2	+	+	1.2	+	+	1.2	r	+	+	+	1.2	+	r	r	+	+	+	+	+	1.2
V-TB Trifolium scabrum	.	.	+	+	2.2	+	1.2	1.2	+	+	1.1	1.2	r	+	1.1	+	+	r	+	+	+	+	+	+	+
V-B Trifolium campestre	+	+	1.3	+	1.1	1.1	r	+	+	+	3.4	r	r	+	1.1	1.1	+	r	+	+	+	r	+	r	+
V-B Valerianella vesicaria	.	r	1.1	+	1.1	1.1	+	+	2.1	+	+	1.1	+.1	1.1	1.1	1.1	+	.	+	+	+	+	r	1.1	+
V-TB Catapodium rigidum	.	r	+	2.2	1.2	1.2	r	1.2	1.2	1.2	1.2	+	+	+	1.1	+	r	r	+	r	r	+	+	1.1	1.2
V-TB Crucianella latifolia	.	.	+	1.2	+	+	1.1	+	+	.	+	+	.	.	.	+	r	+	.	.	r	+	+	+	+
V-TB Brachypodium distachyum	1.2	.	.	.	.	.	2.2	+	2.2	3.2	.	.	3.3	4.4	3.3	2.4	2.2	1.3	+	1.2	4.4	.	.	.	1.2
V-B Hymenocarpus circinatus	.	.	1.2	.	.	2.3	+	2.2	1.1	+	+	r	r	+	+	1.1	+	+	r	r	r	+	r	+	+
V-B Trifolium pauciflorum	.	.	2.2	.	+	+	1.2	2.2	+	1.2	+	+	+	1.2	1.2	1.1	+	1.2	+	+	+	+	+	+	+
V-B Trifolium purpureum var.	+	.	.	r	.	.	.	+	+	+	+	+	+	+	+	+	r	r	r	+	+	1.2	1.2	+	+
V-B Aegilops ovata	.	.	.	.	.	.	.	.	+	r	+	+	+	r	1.2	+	+	r	+	+	+	+	r	+	+
V-TB Hedynois rhagadioloides	.	.	.	.	.	.	+	.	+	.	.	+	+	+	+	+	r	+	r	+	+	r	r	r	.
3rd group (species mainly distributed in extensive pastures and fringes of shrub complexes)																									
IV-S Tordylium apulum	.	.	.	.	.	.	.	.	.	.	r	r	.	.	.	+	1.2	2.3	+	1.3	+	r	.	r	1.2
V-B Ornithopus compressus	.	.	.	.	.	.	.	.	.	.	.	.	.	.	r	r	.	r	1.2	+	+	+	+	+	r
V-TB Medicago coronata	.	.	.	.	.	.	.	+	.	.	+	.	+	.	+	+	.	r	r	r	r	+	r	.	r
V-TB Medicago minima	.	.	.	+	.	.	.	.	.	r	.	r	.	.	.	.	.	.	r	r	+	+	+	+	r
V-B Silene papillosa	.	.	.	.	r	.	.	.	.	.	.	.	.	.	r	r	r	r	r	+	+	.	+	+	.
V-B Crepis foetida ssp.	.	.	.	.	.	.	.	.	.	.	.	.	.	.	+	+	+	1.2	r	+	2.2	2.+	1.2	1.2	+
IV-S Scariola viminea	.	.	.	.	.	.	.	.	.	.	.	.	.	.	.	.	.	.	r	+	1.1	r	r	r	.
V-B Asteriscus aquaticus	.	.	.	.	.	.	.	.	.	.	.	.	.	.	.	+	+	+	+	r	2.3	1.2	1.2	1.2	+
V-TB Trigonella kotschyi	.	.	.	.	.	.	.	.	.	.	.	.	.	.	r	.	.	.	+	1.2	r	+	+	+	+
V-TB Medicago constricta	.	.	.	.	.	.	.	.	.	.	.	.	r	.	.	.	+	r	r	r	r	+	r	+	+
IV-B Verbascum leptocladum	.	.	.	.	.	.	.	.	.	.	.	.	.	.	.	.	.	r	.	r	.	+	1.2	2.3	+
V-B Phleum subulatum	.	.	.	.	.	.	.	.	.	.	.	.	.	.	.	.	+	+	+	+	2.3	1.2	r	r	+
V-TB Evax eriosphaera	.	.	.	.	.	.	.	.	.	.	.	.	.	.	.	.	.	r	r	r	2.3	4.5	2.3	3.4	2.4
V-B Centaurea solstitialis	.	.	.	.	.	.	.	.	.	.	.	.	.	.	.	.	+	+	+	+	+	1.2	+	+	r
IV-B Delphinium peregrinum	.	.	.	.	.	.	.	.	.	.	.	.	.	.	.	r	.	r	r	r	r	+	r	+	r
V-B Nigella arvensis	.	.	.	.	.	.	.	.	.	.	.	.	.	.	.	.	.	.	+	+	1.1	1.1	+	.	.
IV-S Tordylium aegaeum	.	.	+	.	.	.	.	.	.	.	.	.	.	.	.	.	r	r	+	r	1.1	+	.	+	+
V-B Consolida hellespontica	.	.	.	.	.	.	.	.	.	.	.	.	.	.	.	.	.	r	r	1.2	+	+	.	.	.
IV-B Hyparrhenia hirta	.	.	.	.	.	.	.	.	.	.	.	.	.	.	.	.	.	r	1.3	1.3	+	.	1.3	.	.
IV-S Anchusa undulata	.	.	.	.	.	.	.	.	.	.	.	.	.	.	.	.	r	+	+	1.2	+	+	1.2	1.2	.
IV-S Pterocephalus plumosus	.	.	.	.	.	.	.	.	.	.	.	.	.	.	.	.	.	+	+	1.2	r	+	+	+	.
IV-B Ononis pubescens	.	.	.	.	.	.	.	.	.	.	.	.	.	.	.	.	.	.	+	+	+	+	.	+	.
V-TB Atractylis cancellata	.	.	.	.	.	.	.	.	.	.	.	.	.	.	.	+	+	r	1.1	1.2	r	.	r	r	+
V-TB Linum strictum ssp.	.	.	.	.	.	.	.	.	.	.	.	1.2	.	.	.	.	.	r	1.2	r	.	+	.	+	+
IV-B Onosmo oreodoxum	.	.	.	.	.	.	.	.	.	.	r	.	.	.	1.3	1.3	2.3	2.3	1.2	1.3	+	+	+	+	+
IV-B Bupleurum sulphurum	+	.	.	.	.	.	.	.	.	.	.	.	.	+	1.2	1.2	1.2	1.2	+	1.2	+	.	.	.	.
IV-TB Xeranthemum annuum	.	.	.	.	.	.	.	.	.	.	.	.	.	+	1.2	.	.	.	.	.	.	.	.	.	.

Table 1. Cont.

4th group (species mainly distributed in the macchie)

IV-TB	Verbascum sinuatum
V-B	Cuscuta epithymum
IV-B	Dactylis hispanica
V-S	Lagoecia cuminoides
V-B	Asplenium ceterach
V-B	Galium setaceum
V-B	Sanguisorba minor
V-B	Sherardia arvensis
IV-B	Artedia squamata
V-TB	Euphorbia exigua
IV-S	Piptatherum coerulescens
IV-B	Scaligeria napiformis
V-TB	Echinaria capitata
IV-TB	Linum strictum
V-B	Trifolium globosum
V-B	Crepis zacintha
V-TB	Vaillantia muralis
V-B	Scorpiurus muricatus
V-B	Eryngium falcatum
V-B	Cheilanthes fragrans
V-B	Valerianella muricata
V-B	Trifolium echinatum
V-TB	Minuartia mediterranea
V-TB	Trifolium angustifolium
V-B	Trifolium lappaceum
V-B	Selaginella denticulata
V-B	Iberis taurica
V-B	Anthemis rosea ssp.

Additionally in one to three relevees:

Trifolium spumosum 4: +, 15: +; Plantago coronopus 6: +, 11: +; Gastridium phleoides 10:r, 14:r; Filago pyramidata 11: +, 25: +; Theligonum cynocrambe 10: +, 16: +; Euphorbia falcata 23:r, 24:r; Galium floribundum 24:2.2, 25: +; Linaria chalepensis 5:r, 11:r; Sideritis condensata 1:r, 20:r; Astragalus hamosus 16:r, 19:r; Coronilla scorpioides 13: +, 18: +; Medicago disciformis 16: +, 19: +; Physanthyllis tetraphylla 1:1.2, 16:r; Sedum rubens 3:1.2, 21:r; Echium plantagineum 24:1.2, 25: +; Trifolium glanduliferum 2: +, 3:r, 4: +; Muscari comosum 1:r, 2: +, 5:1.1; Antirrhinum orontium 2:r, 4:r, 16:r; Briza maxima 6:r, 9: +, 16:r; Lathyrus aphaca 12:r, 16:r, 23:r; Vicia pubescens 6:r; Althea hirsuta 17:r; Avena clauda 18: +; Falcaria vulgaris 19: +; Steptoramphus tuberosus 25:r; Rumex pulcher ssp. divaricatus 25:r; Hirschfeldia incana 25:r; Trigonella spruneriana var. spruneriana 4:r; Trigonella monspeliaca 3:1.1; Trigonella cariensis 16:r; Trifolium scutatum 16:r; Cynodon dactylon 24:r; Aegilops triuncialis 12: +; Anthemis cretica 3:r; Crepis diortica 25: +; Sisymbrium officinale 4: +; Polygonum arenastrum 2:r; Origanum onites 11: +; Medicago muricata 4: +; Geranium pusillum 3:r; Ophrys sphegodes ss. 2:r; Althea dissecta 18: +; Orobanche crenata 19:r; Lathyrus cicera 20:r; Medicago granatensis 21:r; Erodium cicutarium 24: +; Scabiosa reuteriana 25: +; Smilax aspera 12:r, 19:r, 25:r; Myrtus communis 20:2.3; Clematis cirrhosa 11:r; Cytinus hypocistus 13: +, 14: +; Sarcopoterium spinosum 8:r, 9: +; Thymbra spicata 16:r; Hippocrepis ciliata 11:r, 20:r, 21: +; Knautia integrifolia 22: +, 23: +, 25: +; Medicago rigidula 16:r, 18:r, 19:r.

The cover values of the CaS in the extensive pastures and the Macchie increase more or less in parallel with the rising number of species, showing only two notable divergences. Near the escarpment of the travertine terrace there is a massed occurrence of *Plantago arenaria*, *Plantago lagopus* and *Lophochloa phleoides* (see Fig. 5). This is due to the numerous sheep walks and small clearings attributable to the sporadic passage of the nomads along the edge of the terrace.

The marked drop of species diversity in the extensive pastures reflects the high dominance of *Evax eriosphaera* (*cf.* Fig. 9) and *Asteriscus aquaticus*, which occur only here, as well as *Plantago cretica* and *Pl. lagopus*, well represented in all relevees which form a thick carpet in some places. Adjacent clearings or free areas are frequently dominated by a single species. Although the character species of the Phrygana generally show an even distribution, declining only on the extensive pasture ranges, the cover values do increase somewhat near the edge of the escarpment, namely by *Cistus creticus*, *C. salviifolius* and *Thymus revolutus*.

Of the indicator species for degradation or severe over-grazing (*cf.* Walter 1968: 75, Knapp 1965: 138, Polunin 1977: 173), above all the two geophytes *Asphodelus microcarpus* and *Urginea maritima* should be mentioned, since they have their greatest distribution in the highly degraded Macchie of the 'mixed zone' and in the extensive pastures. *Euphorbia sibthorpii* has an increased dominance on the extensive pastures and the adjacent zones, but is also present sporadically over the entire area of investigation.

4.3. The centre of the settlement with broad mixed zones on the north-west edge of the village

Today the centre of the Nebiler settlement lies to the south of the Antalya/Korkuteli road, with only a few buildings and a large cistern on the northern side. The small gardens, surrounded by dry stone walls, are irregularly laid out and planted with intertilled crops during the winter season. Most of the single-story houses and sheds are on a north-south axis. With the exception of one large olive garden, some carob and almond trees, very occasionally *Rhus coriaria* are also found near dry stone walls. The arable fields around the village are only extensive in the north, where their outer edges reach in small bays into the surrounding Macchie.

On the fields themselves there are isolated bush-complexes of *Quercus coccifera* and *Phillyrea latifolia*, as well as some proud *Pinus brutia* on the eastern edge of the village. To the north the *Pistacia terebinthus* stand is harvested to provide fodder.

When considering the two transects through the settlement it should be borne in mind that the 2nd transect cuts across the fields on the southern edge of the village, so that small bush complexes growing against the stone walls are represented to a greater extent in the vegetation relevees (*cf.* Fig. 5, mixed zone C). Both in the eastern section of the 3rd transect (*cf.* Table 3) and in the northern area of the village, there has been sporadic settlement along the existing routes. In order to determine the floristic composition and distribution in these areas the transects were laid through the above mentioned settlement areas.

4.4. Species and group distribution of character species on the 2nd and 3rd transects

There are two focal points of the vegetational distribution of the 2nd transect, stretching through the inner settlement area and broad periphery with individual gardens and fields to the peripheral Macchie zone. The first of these is characterised by the occurrence of ruderal and segetal vegetation in the settlement itself, and the second by the re-occurrence of Macchie vegetation, including the CaS of the extensive pastures and Macchie clearings of the wide village periphery.

The CaS of the Macchie and Phrygana, which to the south-east are still well represented in the village, are absent here over a zone approx. 300 m wide. The CaS of the extensive pastures and Macchie clearings, rich in therophytes, are only represented by a few isolated

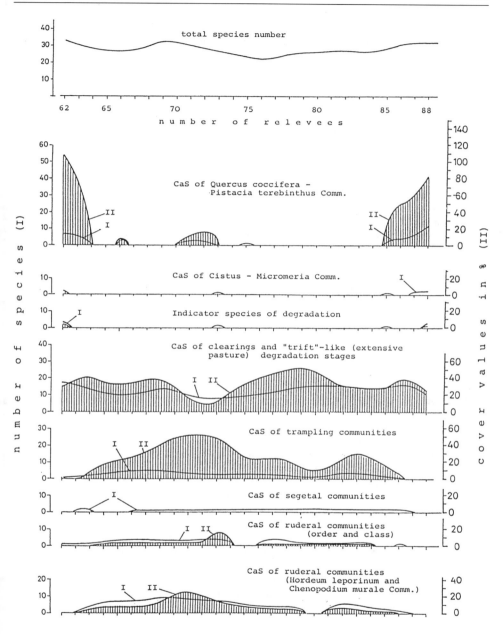

Fig. 6. Distribution of character species groups on the 3rd transect.

individuals. It is only around the widely spread buildings that almost the entire species' spectrum of the Macchie reoccur and the cover at the edge of the Macchie zone reaches the percentages of the terrace step. Of the CaS of the Phrygana, which occur together with the Macchie, only a few are present, mainly in the shade of the wall-bush complexes.

As already mentioned, the CaS of the extensive pastures are not completely absent even in the centre of the village (3rd transect, *cf.* Fig. 6), in particular *Poa bulbosa* and *Psilurus incurvus*. (Although these were not found in the dry spring of 1979, they were present in almost all soil samples taken from the relevant survey areas for seed bank investigation (*cf.* 4.6).)

To the north of the highroad around the cistern (see Fig. 4) the species of the extensive pastures increase rapidly, though without reaching the diversity and cover of the first transect. The vegetation of some of the open spaces of the settlement is determined above all by the endemic *Verbascum leptocladum* with its hairy white leaves. *Plantago lagopus* and *Pl. cretica* are also well represented along the waysides.

The CaS of the trampling communities, which frequently accompany the segetal, ruderal and Cistus-Micromeria communities (Braun-Blanquet *et al.* 1951: 128, Oberdorfer 1954: 91, Lohmeyer 1975: 135, Raus 1979: 54, Braun-Blanquet 1964: 498) show a similar distribution in the inner settlement area as the CaS of the ruderal communities. The species abundance varies only slightly, and the highest cover values occurred at the centre of the village. In contrast to the CaS of the trampling communities, the CaS of the ruderal communities intrude much further into the peripheral settlement zones where, together with the CaS of the extensive pasture and Macchie clearings, particularly large numbers of species occur. There is a marked difference here between the distribution of the CaS of the *Hordeum leporinum* (Hl) and the *Chenopodium murale* (Cm) communities (*cf.* Table 2). In the village centre and in the northern section around the building complexes, the CaS of the Hl community, which is well represented over the whole of the second transect, has higher abundance and dominance. In contrast, the CaS of the Cm community are clearly concentrated in the inner settlement area, where they establish particularly high dominance together with the CaS of the Hl community.

The distribution of the CaS of the segetal vegetation (field weeds) is dependent on the margins of the cornfields. Such species occurring primarily in fields, along the walls (*cf.* Fig. 11), show an increase in abundance between relevees 25–30 and 43–53, though with only low dominance.

On the 3rd transect, stretching from west to east, evidence of the peripheral village vegetation with abrupt transition to *Pinus brutia* forest is only provided at a few of the relevees. Although the abundance on the eastern settlement margin is much higher than it is to the west, due to the greater diversity of the Macchie undergrowth, the dominance of *Pinus brutia* and *Quercus coccifera* is almost identical. Relics of recurrent bush complexes with *Quercus coccifera*, *Ephedra fragilis* and *Asparagus acutifolius* between the edge of the fields and the dry stone walls can also be found in the village.

Only a few of the CaS of the Phrygana occur together with the CaS of the Macchie. As on the 2nd transect, on the 3rd transect *Teucrium polium* is the most common. *Cistus creticus* and *Fumana thymifolia* occur sporadically, solely on the western forest edge where the undergrowth is sparser.

The CaS of the extensive pastures and Macchie clearings have a very regular distribution. The slight decrease in the numbers of species in the inner settlement area is accompanied by a sharp decline in the dominance values.

Abundance and cover of the broad settlement margin are similar to those of the 2nd transect. In particular there are marked similarities between the northern section of the 2nd transect and the eastern section of the 3rd transect, with intermittent buildings along the paths or road. A somewhat higher cover and a slightly increased abundance at the very edge of the inner settlement area is a common feature of both transect sections. Although the characteristic species of the extensive pastures and their associations are represented almost throughout the transect, they do show considerably different abundance and above all cover values. Of all the species identified in this group, *Cynodon dactylon* has the highest cover values, and reaches about 60% with the other character species of the extensive pasture associations, which occur mainly in the village centre. The further slight increase in the eastern regions lies near a number of livestock sheds. In *P. brutia* stands with thick undergrowth the species of the extensive pasture association are absent, with one exception. *Cynodon dactylon* occurs even in stands with sparse undergrowth. The CaS of the segetal associations are represented by few taxa over the transect, and have very low cover values.

Abundance and cover values of the CaS of the ruderal associations are greatest in the central settlement area. The continually increasing numbers of species towards the centre of the village is similar to the 2nd transect with respect to the percentages of the CaS of the Hl- and Cm-associations. The CaS of the Hl-associations are represented relatively uniformly along the 3rd transect, whereas the CaS of the Cm-association are mainly encountered at the centre of the village. The highest cover values of both associations are at the very centre of the village, with a greater proportion of CaS of the Hl-association.

4.5. Vegetation of the harvested cereal fields and fallow lands

In the 16 relevees of harvested and fallow fields 43 species were registered (*cf.* Table 5 and Fig. 4). The CaS of the ruderal and segetal associations with their companions were most frequently represented, with 74%. The CaS of the extensive pasture associations were included in the group of segetal associations. With only 3 species they were only very sparsely represented.

Representing 26%, 11 species belong to the CaS of the extensive pastures and Macchie clearings (with companions) (*cf.* Table 4). The CaS of the ruderal and segetal associations demonstrate a preponderance of CaS of the ruderal associations, and this in turn of the CaS of the *Hordeum leporinum* association.

The summary of the vegetation relevees in Table 5 shows the formation of 2 or 3 relevee groups. There is a clear distinction between the virtually monotypic *Hypericum* group (group 3) with few companions and high cover of *Hypericum triquetrifolium*, and two groups dominated by the CaS of the ruderal and segetal associations (groups 1 and 2). In addition to a number of 'obligatory' and 'facultative' segetal species (*cf.* Zohary 1973: 648ff), above all *Chrozophora tinctoria* and *Thymelaea passerina*, it is only the second group with *Heliotropium hirsutissimum* and *Tribulus terrestris* that CaS of Chenopodietalia mediterranea Br.-Bl. (1931) 1936 or of Secalinetalia mediterranea occur with a high degree of regularity (*cf.* Oberdorfer 1954b and Zohary 1973).

Group 1 differs mainly from those mentioned by the absence of *Hypericum triquetrifolium* and only a sporadic presence of other segetal species, namely *Chrozophora tinctoria* and *Thymelaea passerina*, as well as the increased presence of the character species of the ruderal associations. Dominated by *Hypericum* spec., the third group is encountered mainly on deep unworked fields or shallow worked fields, as well as (with one exception) in the eastern reaches of the settlement.

On shallower unworked cornfields or fallows with consolidated upper soil horizons in the sparsely inhabited northern part of the settlement, the second CaS group of the ruderal and segetal associations was identified. Two exceptions are no. 8 and 9, which are shallow worked fields.

The first group of the vegetation relevees is concentrated mainly near larger building complexes, or in what is presumably the oldest settlement area. The soils are either deep, or shallow and worked. The latter is the case for no. 11, which lies not far from a flat rubbish heap and is dominated by *Hirschfeldia incana*. The distribution of the CaS of ruderal and segetal associations overlap to a large extent in groups 1 and 2. The character species of the ruderal association are linked more to the centre of the settlement, whereas the segetal species stretch across the middle sections out into the groups 1 and 2.

Table 2. Relevees of the 2nd transect from S to N, settlement-margin, –centre, –margin, arranged according to character species groups.

1979	26.	31.	01.	05.	05.	06.	06.	06.	06.	06.	08.	02.	02.	02.	02.	02.	02.	02.	02.	02.	06.	06.	06.	06.	06.	06.	06.	07.	07.	09.	09.	09.	10.	10.	11.	11.
	May		June																									July									
No. of relevee	26	27	28	29	30	31	32	33	34	35	36	37	38	39	40	41	42	43	44	45	46	47	48	49	50	51	52	53	54	55	56	57	58	59	60	61
Size of sample plot (m2)	50	50	50	50	50	25	10	16	10	10	10	18	20	20	20	10	10	30	30	20	15	17	30	20	18	20	50	30	30	20	30	30	40	40	40	40
Altitude a.s.l.: 270m																																				
Exposition: +/- plain																																				
Cover value in %	90	10	10	90	80	80	80	10	60	80	50	10	40	70	70	70	80	90	90	90	90	10	10	60	10	90	10	10	10	70	60	90	10	10	10	100
Number of species	10	85	89	73	37	38	33	33	30	40	22	18	22	17	21	31	39	34	32	48	26	42	47	42	51	36	37	31	47	54	45	40				

Character species of the Quercus coccifera - Pistacia tereb. Comm. (cf. ZOHARY 1973, LAVRENTIADES 1969, AKMAN et al. 1978, QUEZEL et al. 1978)

Species	26	27	28	29	30	31	32	33	34	35	36	37	38	39	40	41	42	43	44	45	46	47	48	49	50	51	52	53	54	55	56	57	58	59	60	61
Quercus coccifera	3.3	3.3	1.2	3.2																4.3			4.3		3.3	3.3	3.3	2.2	3.2		1.3	+	4.4	4.5	4.3	4.3
Rhamnus oleoides	2.2	+	+	+	+													r	r	r			r	r		r	r	+	+		+	2.2	r	2.2	+	1.2
Asparagus acutifolius	+	+	+	+	r	r												r	r				r	r	+	+	r	r	+		+		r		r	1.1
Pistacia terebinthus	r	r	r		r																			r	r	1.2	+	2.1			2.1	2.2	1.1	+	2.2	1.2
Daphne gnidium	+	1.2	r																							+	r	r			+			+	+	1.1
Ephedra fragilis			+	r	r	+	r		r																+			+			r				r	1.1
Rubia peregrina			+		r	r	+																		r			+			r	+				
Crataegus monogyna	+	r	+	r																1.2					+	+			+		r			r		1.1
Olea europaea var.	+	r	r																						+	3.1			+			+			+	
Phillyrea latifolia	r	r	r																							r										
Smilax aspera (incl. S. excelsa)	r			r							r														1.2				1.2						r	

Character species of the Cistus - Micromeria Comm. (cf. OBERDORFER 1954, RAUS 1979, HORVAT et al. 1974)

Species	26	27	28	29	30	31	32	33	34	35	36	37	38	39	40	41	42	43	44	45	46	47	48	49	50	51	52	53	54	55	56	57	58	59	60	61
Teucrium polium		r	r																		r	r		r						r				1.1	+	
Andrachne telephioides	+	+	+	+			r																		+						+	r		r		
Cistus creticus	+	+	r	r																+									r			+	+		r	
Fumana thymifolia	+	1.2																									r					+	+		+	
Micromeria myrtifolia	r							r																			1.2							r	r	

Indicator species of degradation

Species	26	27	28	29	30	31	32	33	34	35	36	37	38	39	40	41	42	43	44	45	46	47	48	49	50	51	52	53	54	55	56	57	58	59	60	61
Asphodelus microcarpus	+	2.2	2.2	3.2	+													r	1.2	3.3		1.2	3.3	+		+	2.3	1.2	1.2	r		4.4	1.3	2.3	3.3	+	1.1
Euphorbia sibthorbii	1.2	1.2	+	+																					1.2	1.2	+				r	+	+	1.1
Urginea maritima	r	+	1.1	r																	r					r			r				+	1.2		

Character species of extensive pastures ("Trift") and Macchie clearings (cf. OBERDORFER 1954, BRAUN-BLANQUET 1964)
TB = Thero-Brachypodietea -etalia, SG = species of seam comm., B = companions

Species		26	27	28	29	30	31	32	33	34	35	36	37	38	39	40	41	42	43	44	45	46	47	48	49	50	51	52	53	54	55	56	57	58	59	60	61
1 Poa bulbosa	B	+	+	+	+	+	+	+	+	+	+	+	+	+	+	+	+	+	+	+	+	+	+	+	+	+	+	+	+	+	+	+	+	+	+	+	+
1 Psilurus incurvus	B	+	+	+	+	+	+	+	+	+	+	r	+	+	+	+	+	+	+	+	+	+	+	+	r	+	+	+	+	r	+	+	r	+	+	r	+
Daucus guttatus	B	2.4	2.2	1.2	+	1.2	+	+	+		r				r		r		+		r	2.3		r	1.2	+		1.2	1.3		1.2	+	+
Verbascum leptocladum		3.2	1.2	1.2	r	1.2	2.3								1.2				2.3	+		2.3	3.3	1.2	1.2	1.2	1.3		+	2.3	2.2	1.2		r
Plantago lagopus	B	1.3	3.3	3.4	2.3										+				2.2	+	1.2		3.3	1.2	1.2	1.2		+	2.3	2.2	1.2		1.3	2.3
Catapodium rigidum	TB	1.3	1.3	+	+								1.2							1.2	+	2.3	3.3	+	1.2	1.3	1.2	1.3		1.2	2.3		1.3	+	1.3

Species	Form
Tordylium aegaeum	SG
Salvia horminum	TB
Trifolium scabrum	TB
Plantago cretica	B
Scabiosa reuteriana	SG
Phleum subulatum	TB
Medicago orbicularis	TB
Hedypnois rhagadioloides	TB
Medicago minima	TB
Trifolium purpureum var.	B
Trifolium campestre	B
Avena clauda	TB
Aegilops ovata	B
Oryzopsis miliacea	SG
6 Delphinium peregrinum	SG
Medicago disciformis	TB
7 Cichorium intybus	B
Scrophularia canina ssp.	SG
Crucianella latifolia	TB
Asteriscus aquaticus	B
Lagurus ovatus	B
Stipa bromoides	SG
Brachypodium distachyum	TB
Medicago rigidula	TB
Lagoecia cuminoides	SG
Evax eriosphaera	TB
Onobrychis caput-galli	TB
Silene discolor	SG
Trifolium spumosum	B
Allium callimischon	SG
Ornithopus compressus	SG
Phleum exaratum	TB
Bromus intermedius	TB
Trifolium resupinatum	B
Aegilops triuncialis	B
Legousia pentagonia	B
Trifolium stellatum	TB
Geranium purpureum var.	B
Pterocephalus plumosus	B
Silene kotschyi	SG
Silene papillosa	SG
Sideritis montana ssp.	SG
Melica magnolii	B
Astragalus hamosus	SG
Cynosurus echinatus	TB
Xeranthemum annuum	TB

Table 2. Cont.

No. of relevee		26	27	28	29	30	31	32	33	34	35	36	37	38	39	40	41	42	43	44	45	46	47	48	49	50	51	52	53	54	55	56	57	58	59	60	61
Species of trampling communities																																					
Cynodon dactylon				+		3.2	3.2		r	+	+	1.3	1.4		3.3	1.2		+			1.3	3.3	2.3		+	1.2	+		1.3	+							
Polygonum arenastrum		+		+		+		+		+	1.2	r	1.2	+	r		r	+																			
Matricaria camomilla			r		+		+		r	+	1.3	1.2	r	r		+																					
Polycarpon tetraphyllum		1.2		+	+	r	+	3.3	1.2	+	+																										
Plantago coronopus							1.2									+															1.3						
2 Telephium imperati																														+							
Herniaria hirsuta var.				+			r											r		r	+	r	+	+					+				r				
Poa infirma					1.3					1.3		+																			+						
Character species of segetal communities (KS = Secalinetea BR.-BL. 52, OS = Secalinetalia BR.-BL. (31)36 and Secal. medit. OBERD. 54)																																					
Hypericum triquetrifolium	OS		+	1.2		+	+	r		+		3.3							r	1.2	1.2	2.2	+	+	+	+	+	+	+	+	+	+	+			+	+
Filago pyramidata	OS		1.3	+	r	+		r												+	1.1	1.1	1.3		+	1.2	+		+	+	+	+				+	+
Papaver rhoeas	KS		+	r	+											1.1	+			r	r	r			+	1.2	r	r	r	+	+	r	r				
Anthemis arvensis	OS	2.3		+	1.3	1.2										+				r	+	+	+	+	+	+	r	+	r	r	r	+	+				
Nigella arvensis ssp.	OS											+			+					+	1.2	+	1.2	1.3	+	+	r	r	r	r	r	+					
Galium floribundum	KS		+							+	+											1.3	1.3			+	+	1.3	+	+	1.3						
Anthriscus caucalis	KS		+	r																																	
Thymelaea passerina	OS		r															r	r			+		r		r				r							
Rhagadiolus stellatus	OS		r				r																									r					
Matthiola longipetala ssp.	OS																	r				1.2	1.3	1.3	+												
Scandix pecten-veneris	OS		r																		r	+		+	r												
Character species of ruderal communities (KC = Chenopodietea BR.-BL. 52; OC = Chenopodietalia mediterranea BR.-BL. (31)36; OBERDORFER 54)																																					
Mercurialis annua	OC		+	+	1.2	1.3	1.2		r	1.2	1.2							r		r								+	1.2		r					r	
Lolium rigidum	KC		r	r		+		+					+							1.3						3.3										1.3	
Heliotropium hirsutissimum	OC		r	r										r																r			r	r	r		
Urospermum picroides	OC		+		r				+	+	r			+										+									+				
Euphorbia helioscopia	KC													r					+																		
Lactuca serriola	KC										+	+	r	1.2	+																						
Erodium cicutarium	OC		r						r		+	r	r	r	r			r		r		1.3															
Tribulus terrestris	OC								+	1.2	+	2.2																				+					
Sisymbrium altissimum	KC			r					+	+	+	r								r				r	r												
Rumex pulcher ssp.	OC												+						2.3									+									
Sinapsis arvensis	OC		+	1.3		+														r									r								r
Chenopodium album	KC		+	2.2							+	+		+	+							r															

Character species of Hordeum leporinum (Hl) and Chenopodium murale (Cm) Communities (cf. BRAUN-BLANQUET 1952, OBERDORFER 1954)

Species	Type	Cover/abundance values
Hirschfeldia incana	Hl	+ 2.3 2.2 + + · · · r 1.3 + · · · r + 1.1 3.3 1.2 + + · · r 1.3 + 2.3 2.3 · · +
Crepis foetida ssp.	Hl	+ r r + + · · · r + + · · + · 1.2 · · · r + · + 1.3 + · · r r
Sisymbrium officinale	Hl	1.2 2.3 2.3 1.2 1.3 4.3 1.2 1.2 + 1.2 · · r + · · · · r · 1.2 1.2 1.2 2.2 + · · ·
Hordeum leporinum	Hl	· · + 1.2 1.2 2.2 4.3 3.3 1.2 2.2 2.3 r · + · · · · · · · · 1.3 + · · +
Echium plantagineum	Hl	r r r + 1.2 · · 3.3 r r r r · · · · · · · · · + + · · ·
Malva nicaeensis	Hl	+ 1.3 + r + 1.2 4.3 1.2 1.2 + · r r · · · · · + + · · · · · ·
Arum italicum	Cm	+ + · + · · · + · · r · · · · r + + · · · · · · · r ·
Marrubium vulgare	Cm	r 1.2 + 2.2 r · 1.2 · · · r + + · · · · · · · · · + r + · ·
Plumbago europaea	Cm	1.2 r · + · · + 1.2 2.2 2.3 · · · · · · · · · · · r · · · ·
Brassica napus	Cm	+ + · · + 1.2 + r · · + + · · · · · · · · · · · · ·
Chenopodium murale	Cm	+ + · + + r r r · · · · · r · · · · · · · + · ·
4 Verbascum undulatum	Cm	r r · · r r r + + · · · · · · · · · · · · · r · ·
Chenopodium opulifolium	Cm	r · r · r + + 1.2 · · · · · · · · · · · · · · + · ·
5 Antirrhinum orontium	Cm	r + r + · · + r + · · · · · · · · · · · · · ·
Nonea pulla	Hl	· · · · r · · · · · r r r r · · · · · · · · r ·
Althaea dissecta	Hl	r r r r · · r · · r · · · · · · · · · · · r · ·
Malva pusilla	Hl	· · · · · + + + r · · · r · · · · · · · · · ·
Salvia verbenaca	Hl	· + · · r + r · · · · · · · · · · · · · + · ·
Chenopodium vulvaria	Cm	· · · · · 1.3 + · · · · · · · · · · · · + · ·
Bromus madritensis	Hl	· · · · · · · r · r r + + · · · · · · · · ·
Carthamus lanatus	Hl	· · · · · · · · · · · · · · · · · · r · + · r
Plantago lanceolata	Cm	+ + · + · · · + · · · · · · · · · · · · 1.2 · ·

Additionally in one to three relevees;

Ajuga chamaepitys ssp. chia 54:+; Peucedanum ehryseum 52:+; Roemeria hybrida ssp. hybrida 35:r; Aristolochia maurorum 26:+, 29;r; Bupleurum subovatum 26r; Solanum nigrum 41:r, 54:r; Picnomon acarna 52:r; Streptoramphus tuberosus 26:r, 27:r; Aegilops caudata 31:+; Haplophyllum theseoides 26:+; Piptatherum coerulescens 26:+; Medicago turbinata 26:r; Stachys cretica 26:r; Aira carophyllea 26:r; Blarum tenuifolium 36:r; Bupleurum croceum 36:r; Crepis micrantha 36:r, 48:+; Erodium hoefftianum 36:r; Trigonella carica 26:1.2; Muscari comosum 26:+; Lolium rigidum var rottboIlioides 30:+, 48:+; Valerianella vesicaria 26:r; Filago eriocephala 26:1.2; Briza maxima 26:r; Trifolium scutatum 26:r; Crepis diorttica 27:+; Lathyrus cicera 27:r; Sanguisorba minor ssp. 28:r; Trifolium 56:r; Lycopersicon esculentum 28:r; Torilis trinadiata 28:r, 54:+; Medicago granatensis 29:r; Hippocrepis ciliata 32:r; Ornithopus sativus ssp. sativus 31:r; Astragalus suberosus 31:+; Trifolium angustifolium 59:+; Sidertis condenstata 59:+; Medicago coronata 47:+; Galium floribundum 58:r; Delphinium virgatum 52:r; Silene cappadocica 41:r; Osyris alba 50:+, 52:r, 56:r; Daphne sericea 56:r; Teucrium divaricatum 26:r; Hymenocarpus circinatus (B) 26:+, 27:r, 30:+; Trifolium pauciflorum (TB) 26:r, 27:r, 29:r; Medicago polymorpha (TB) 31:r, 32:1.3, 33:r; Salvia viridis (TB) 26:r, 27:r, 29:r; Chondrilla juncea (TB) 51:1.2, 52:+, 53:+; Lathyrus aphaca (SG) 26:r, 48:r, 60:+; Scariola viminea (SG) 58:r, 59:+, 61:r; Knautia integrifolia (SG) 45:r, 54:+, 59:+; Valerinella viscaria (B)46:r, 50:r, 60:r; Consolida hellespontica (B) 48:r, 50:r, 60:r; Anthemis chia (B) 26:1.3, 27:+, 28:r; Alyssum strigosum ssp. (B) 26:+, 27:+, 28:+; Lophochloa phleoides (B) 26:+, 27:1.2, 28:+; Erodium malacoides (B) 26:r, 27:r, 28:r; Hypericum nummeralia (B) 26:r, 27:+, 29:r; Silene vulgaris (SG) 26:+, 44:r, 52:r; Torilis nodosa (OC) 32:+, 35:r, 36:r; Euphorbia peplus (OC) 35:r, 37:r, 38:+; Calendula arvensis (KC) 36:r, 46:r; Urtica urens (OC) 28:r, 35:r; Euphorbia falcata (OC) 26:+, 56:r; Peganum harmala (OC) 41:r; Amaranthus albus (Cm) 39:1.3, 40:+, 54:+.

Remarks:

1: Poa bulbosa and Psilurus incurvus was absent (respectively withered) in 1979, but was very frequent in early springtime of 1980 (settlement area and extensive pastures)

2: According to POLUNIN (1980: 2209) Telephium imperati is a character species of stony extensive pastures

4-7: These species are also companions of the ruderal and segetal communities

Table 3. Relevees of the 3rd transect from W to E, settlement-margin, –centre, –margin, arranged according to character species groups.

1979 June	62	63	64	65	66	67	68	70	71	72	73	74	75	76	77	78	79	80	81	82	83	84	85	86	87	88
(type)	14	13	13	13	13	13	12	12	12	12	12	14	14	17	17	17	17	17	17	17	21	21	21	21	22	22
Size of sample plot (m2)	200	200	150	40	20	10	10	10	10	10	10	10	30	20	20	30	20	30	10	10	10	10	10	100	150	200
Altitude a.s.l.: 270m																										
Exposition: +/- plain																										
Cover value in %	100	100	80	60	70	80	80	60	90	100	80	80	100	80	40	80	70	80	60	70	40	80	100	100	90	100
Number of species	43	28	22	30	24	30	36	39	22	28	24	32	24	16	27	29	22	23	31	21	26	29	27	37	28	30

Character species of the Quercus coccif. - Pistacia tereb. Comm. (cf. ZOHARY 1973, LAVRENTIADES 1969, AKMAN et al. 1978, QUEZEL et al. 1978)

	62	63	64	65	66	67	68	70	71	72	73	74	75	76	77	78	79	80	81	82	83	84	85	86	87	88
Pinus brutia	5.4	4.3	.	.	.	.	.	.	.	.	.	.	.	.	.	.	.	.	.	.	5.4	3.1	3.1	.	.	5.3
Quercus coccifera	3.3	3.3	r	.	1.2	+	.	.	.	.	.	.	+	.	.	.	.	.	.	.	3.3	2.3	2.3	+	r	3.3
Asparagus acutifolius	+	+	.	+	+	.	.	.	.	.	.	.	.	.	.	.	.	.	.	.	+	.	.	.	r	+
Ephedra fragilis	+	r	.	+	r	.	r	+	.	.	.	.	.	.	.	.	.	.	.	.	.	.	1.2	.	.	+
Rhamnus oleoides	+	+	.	r	.	.	.	r	.	.	.	.	.	.	.	.	.	.	.	.	.	.	1.2	.	.	+
Pistacia terebinthus	r	r	.	r	.	.	.	.	.	.	.	.	.	.	.	.	.	.	.	.	.	r	r	.	.	+
Daphne gnidium	+	+	.	.	.	.	.	.	.	.	.	.	.	.	.	.	.	.	.	.	+	.	.	.	.	+
Crataegus monogyna	+	+	.	.	.	.	.	.	.	.	.	.	.	.	.	.	.	.	.	.	.	.	.	.	.	+
Osyris alba	.	+	.	.	.	r	.	r	.	.	.	.	.	.	.	.	.	.	.	.	.	.	.	.	+	r

Character species of the Cistus - Micromeria Comm. (cf. OBERDORFER 1954, RAUS 1979, HORVAT et al. 1974)

	62	63	64	65	66	67	68	70	71	72	73	74	75	76	77	78	79	80	81	82	83	84	85	86	87	88
Teucrium polium	1.1	r	+	.	.	.	.	.	.	.	.	.	.	.	.	.	r	.	.	.	.	r	.	.	r	+
Cistus creticus	+	.	.	.	.	.	.	.	.	.	.	.	.	.	.	.	.	.	.	.	.	.	.	.	.	.
Fumana thymifolia	+	.	.	.	.	.	.	.	.	.	.	.	.	.	.	.	.	.	.	.	.	.	.	.	.	.
Thymbra spicata	.	.	.	.	.	.	.	.	.	.	.	.	.	.	.	.	.	.	.	.	.	.	r	.	.	.

Indicator species of degradation

	62	63	64	65	66	67	68	70	71	72	73	74	75	76	77	78	79	80	81	82	83	84	85	86	87	88
Asphodelus microcarpus	+	.	.	.	.	.	.	.	.	.	.	.	.	.	.	.	.	.	.	.	.	+	.	.	.	1.2
Euphorbia sibthorpii	.	.	.	.	.	.	.	.	.	.	.	.	.	.	.	.	.	.	.	1.2	.	.	.	.	.	+
Urginea maritima	1.1	.	.	.	.	.	.	.	.	.	.	.	.	.	.	.	.	.	.	.	.	.	.	.	.	.

Character species of extensive pastures ("Trift") and Macchie clearings (cf. OBERDORFER 1954, BRAUN-BLANQUET 1964)

TB = Thero-Brachypodietea, -etalia, SG = species of seam communities, B = companions

		62	63	64	65	66	67	68	70	71	72	73	74	75	76	77	78	79	80	81	82	83	84	85	86	87	88
Poa bulbosa	B	+	+	+	+	+	+	+	+	+	+	+	+	+	+	+	+	+	+	+	+	+	+	+	+	+	+
Psilurus incurvus	B	+	+	+	+	+	+	+	+	+	r	+	+	+	+	r	+	+	+	+	r	+	r	+	+	+	+
Scabiosa reuteriana	SG	r	.	1.2	r	+	+	r	+	1.2	1.2	+	+	r	+	+	+	1.2	1.2	+	1.2	+	r	+	+	r	r
Verbascum leptocladum		.	.	3.3	2.2	2.3	4.3	2.2	3.3	.	.	1.2	r	4.3	2.2	3.2	4.4	2.2	.	2.2	.	2.2	1.2	3.3	.	.	.
Daucus guttatus	B	r	3.3	.	r	.	+	2.2	1.2	.	+	.	1.2	1.2	1.2	1.2	2.2	+	+	+	.	1.2	+	+	.	.	.
Aegilops ovata	B	+	2.3	+	.	.	.	+	.	.	.	r	.	+	+	+	1.2	.	1.2	r	r	1.2	1.2	.	r	r	.
Plantago lagopus	B	.	+	.	.	.	.	+	.	.	.	+	.	+	+	+	+	.	+	+	+	+	+	+	.	+	.
Trifolium scabrum	TB	+	.	.	.	r	.	r	.	.	.	+	.	+	+	r	r	+	r	+	+	+	+	r	r	4.4	.
Hedypnois rhagadioloides. ssp.	TB	.	+	.	.	.	.	.	.	.	.	.	.	.	.	.	.	.	.	.	+	.	+	1.2	+	+	.

Species	Group
Aegilops triuncialis	B
Plantago cretica	B
Catapodium rigidum	TB
Trifolium purpureum var.	TB
Salvia horminum	TB
Phleum exaratum	TB
Avena clauda	TB
Chondrilla juncea	TB
Medicago orbicularis	TB
Medicago rigidula	TB
Medicago minima	TB
Medicago litoralis	TB
Trifolium resupinatum	B
Cichorium intybus	SG
Tordylium aegaeum	SG
Onobrychis caput-galli	TG
Lophochloa phleoides	B
Asteriscus aquaticus	B
Trifolium campestre	B
Brachypodium distachyum	TB
Crucianella latifolia	TB
Astragalus hamosus	TB

Species of trampling communities

Cynodon dactylon
Polygonum arenastrum
Polycarpon tetraphyllum
Plantago coronopus
Telephium imperati
Herniaria hirsuta var.
Matricaria chamomilla

Character species of segetal communities (KS = Secalinetea BR.-BL. 52, OS = Secalinetalia BR.-BL. (31)36, and Secal. medit.

Species	Group
Anthemis arvensis	OS
Filago pyramidata	OS
Hypericum triquetrifolium	OS
Papaver rhoeas	KS

Character species of ruderal communities (KC = Chenopodietea BR.-BL. 52, OC = Chenopodietalia mediterranea BR.-BL. (31)36, OBERD. 54)

Species	Group
Tribulus terrestris	OC
Heliotropium hirsutissimum	KC
Mercurialis annua	KC
Euphorbia peplus	OC
Lactuca serriola	KC
Lolium rigidum	KC

Table 3. Cont.

No. of relevee		62	63	64	65	66	67	68	69	70	71	72	73	74	75	76	77	78	79	80	81	82	83	84	85	86	87	88
Rumex pulcher ssp.	OC	.	.	.	.	.	.	.	r	.	.	+	+	+	.	.	.	.	.	.	.	.	.	.	.	.	.	.
Amaranthus albus	OC	.	.	.	+	+	.	.	.	.	.	.	.	.	.	.	.	.	.	.	.	.	.	.	.	.	.	.
Euphorbia helioscopia	KC	.	.	.	.	.	.	.	.	.	.	.	.	.	.	+	r	.	.	.	.	.	.	.	.	.	.	.
Chenopodium album	KC	.	.	.	+	.	.	.	.	.	.	+	.	.	.	.	.	.	.	.	.	.	.	.	.	.	.	.
Sisymbrium altissimum	KC	.	.	.	.	.	.	.	.	.	r	.	.	r	.	.	.	.	.	.	.	.	.	.	.	.	.	.

Character species of Hordeum leporinum (HI) and Chenopodium murale (Cm) communities (cf. BR.-BL. 52, OBERDORFER 54)

No. of relevee		62	63	64	65	66	67	68	69	70	71	72	73	74	75	76	77	78	79	80	81	82	83	84	85	86	87	88
Hordeum leporinum	HI	.	2.3	.	+	.	+	1.2	r	+	3.3	+	1.3	1.2	2.2	1.2	2.2	+	+	+	r	r	+	+	.	.	.	.
Echium plantagineum	HI	.	.	.	r	r	r	1.3	r	r	.	+	+	+	+	.	r	+	1.1	.	1.2	+	r	r	1.3	.	.	.
Nonea pulla	HI	.	.	.	r	r	r	r	r	r	.	.	r	r	.	.	r	.	.	.	.	+	+	.	r	r	r	.
Crepis foetida ssp.	HI	.	.	+	r	r	r	r	r	+	2.2	+	.	.	+	.	.	r	.	+	+	+	+	+	.	r	.	.
Hirschfeldia incana	HI	.	.	+	+	.	.	.	r	1.1	.	+	.	.	.	.	.	.	.	+	+	+	.	.	r	.	.	.
Sisymbrium officinale	HI	.	.	.	.	.	r	r	r	+	.	+	+	+	.	.	.	.	r	.	.	.	.	.	.	.	.	.
Malva nicaeensis	HI	.	.	.	.	.	r	r	r	+	+	+	.	r	r	r	.	.	.	.	.	.	.	.	.	.	.	.
Plumbago europaea	Cm	.	.	.	r	+	.	+	+	+	.	1.2	1.3	.	.	.	.	.	.	.	.	.	.	.	.	r	.	.
Verbascum undulatum	Cm	.	.	.	r	.	r	+	r	r	.	+	+	.	.	.	.	.	.	.	r	.	.	.	.	.	.	.
Arum italicum	Cm	.	.	.	.	.	.	.	.	.	r	.	.	.	.	.	.	.	.	.	.	.	.	.	.	.	.	.
Carthamus lanatus	HI	.	.	.	.	.	.	.	.	.	.	.	.	.	.	.	.	.	.	.	r	+	+	.	.	.	.	.
Althea dissecta	HI	.	.	.	.	.	.	.	.	.	.	.	.	.	.	.	.	.	.	.	r	r	.	r	.	.	r	+
Chenopodium murale	Cm	.	.	r	.	.	.	.	.	.	r	.	.	.	.	.	.	.	.	.	.	.	.	.	.	.	.	.

Additionally in one to three relevees:

Trifolium spumosum 62:r, 63:r; Legousia pentagonia 64:1.3; Medicago granatensis 70:1.3; Lophochloa obtusiflora 70:1.3; Medicago orbicularis 62:+, 70:+; Vaillantia muralis 74:+, 78:+; Trifolium pauciflorum 62:r, 78:1.2; Knautia integrifolia 73:+; Geranium purpureum var. purpureum 66:+, 73:+; Trifolium physodes 78:2.2; Eryngium creticum 62:+; Lens ervoides 62:+; Ornithopus sativus ssp. sativus 62:r; Trifolium angustifolium 62:1.2; Scrophularia xanthoglossa 64:+; Scrophularia canina ssp. bicolor 73:r, 75:r; Ranunculus muricatus 75:r; Ononis viscosa 62:r; Trifolium scutatum 62:+; Hymenocarpus circinatus 62:+; Trigonella kotschii 62:+; Sideritis montana ssp. montana 64:r; Lagurus ovatus 65:r; Galium tricornutum 65:r; Medicago circinata 66:r, 72:+; Galium divaricatum 69:+; Alyssum strigosum ssp. strigosum 68:r; Trifolium angustifolium 88:+; Lathyrus aphaca var. modestus 88:r; Dactylis hispanica 88:r; Sanguisorba minor 88:r; Antirrhinum orontium 87:r; Ajuga chamaepitys ssp. chia 87:+; Thymelaea passerina 87:+; Crepis zacintha 86:r; Ornithopus compressus 86:r; Oryzopsis miliacea 85:+; Lolium rigidum var. rottbollioides 85:r; Silene cappadocica 84:r; Erodium cicutarium 83:r; Crepis micrantha 74:+; Matthiola longipetala ssp. bicornis 79:r; Verbena officinalis 71:r; Rubia peregrina 87:+, 88:r; Phillyrea latifolia 88:r; Daphne sericea 88:+; Ruscus aculeatus 88:+; Bromus intermedius 64:r, 69:+, 80:r; Evax eriosphaera 63:1.3, 64:1.3, 80:1.2; Phleum subulatum 70:1.2, 84:r, 87:r; Torilis nodosa 73:+; Crepis diortica 73:r, 75:+, 77:r; Neslia paniculata 73:r, 74:r; Marrubium vulgare 69:r, 70:+.

Remarks:

Poa bulbosa and Psilurus incurvus was absent (respectively withered) in 1979, but was very frequent in early springtime of 1980

Table 4. Components of character species groups of ploughed field and fallow land.

CaS of extensive pastures + Macchie clearings (rich in therophytes) TB = Thero-Brachypodietea, -etalia, EC = ecotonic communities, C = companions

TB	Chondrilla juncea	C	Verbascum leptocladum
EC	Knautia integrifolia	C	Sideritis montana ssp remota
TB	Salvia viridis	C	Ononis spinosa
TB	Verbascum sinuatum	C	Consolida hellespontica
		C	Delphinium peregrinum
		C	Nigella arvensis ssp. glauca
		C	Bunium ferulaceum

CaS of trampling comm. = T   CaSof segetal comm. = S

		S	Filago pyramidata	*
T	Herniaria hirsuta var.	S	Raphanus raphanistrum	
		S	Chrozophora tinctoria	
		S	Hypericum triquetrifolium	*
		S	Ajuga chamaepitys	*
		S	Papaver rhoeas	
*	according to *ZOHARY (1973)*	S	Thymelaea passerina	*
	facultative segetal flora	S	Scandix pecten-veneris	*

CaS of ruderal comm. = OC (cf. Chenopodietalia mediterranea BR.-BL. (1931) 1936, OBERDORFER 1954)

OC	Amaranthus albus	OC	Rumex pulcher ssp. divaricatus
OC/S	Heliotropium hirsutissimum	OC	Peganum harmala

CaS of Hordeum leporinum- (Hl) and Chenopodium murale- (Cm) comm.

Hl	Echium plantagineum	Cm	Chenopodium opulifolium
Hl	Nonea pulla	Cm	Marrubium vulgare
Hl	Hirschfeldia incana	Cm	Antirrhinum orontium
Hl	Sisymbrium officinale		
Hl	Lolium rigidum		
Hl/S	Tribulus terrestris		

Companions of the ruderal and segetal communities, E = margins of cushion-like shrub complexes

E	Silene vulgaris		Rhagadiolus stellatus
E	Pterocephalus plumosus	E	Scabiosa reuteriana
	Salvia dichroantha		Althea dissecta
	Scrophularia cannina ssp. bicolor		Verbena officinalis

For comparison, two further vegetation relevees are provided from the periphery of the central open space in the village which borders on a dry stone wall (*cf.* Table 5.1).

The vegetation mapped at the old centre of the settlement near the wall between the open space and the harvested cornfield is dominated by *Hirschfeldia incana*, a widely spread CaS along paths and edges of fields during summer in the Eastern Mediterranean (Oberdorfer 1954b, Zohary 1973). The relict vegetation of the Macchie is severely devastated (*cf.* 4.4), but nevertheless extends with some species of the extensive pastures and Macchie clearings into the centre of the village.

4.6. Seed bank investigations

In order to complete the vegetation records, soil samples were taken from the transects 1, 2 and 3 to identify seeds of plants which had already completed their life cycle in the comparatively long dry period of 1979 (*cf.* Schneider & Kehl 1987).

Table 5. Vegetation relevees of harvested cereal fields and fallow land.

Date: July 14, 1979   Size of sampling plots: 25m2   Altitude: 270m a.s.l.   Exposition: +/- plain
No. of relevee   16 10 11   13   5 12 1   8   9   6   2   4 17 15   7   3
Cover value   30 20 80   80   20 10 30 15 30 10 60 40 30 25 60 60
Number of species   4 11 10   11   11 10 10   8   5   4   5   4   2   2   6   3
Soils:
profound (t), ameliorated   f   t   f   t   f   f   t   f   t   f   t   t   f   t   f   f
medium (f), uncultivated (b   b   b   b   u   u   u   b   u   u   u   b   b   u   u
Cereal field (G), fallow la   G   G   G   G   B   B   G   G   G   B   G   G   G   G   G   B
Type of soil   Terra rossa on Travertine   Kind of soil: sandy loam

	group 1	group 2	group 3		

Character species of ruderal comm. (KC = Chenopodietea BR.-BL. 52, OC = Chenopodietalia mediterranea BR.-BL. (31) 36, cf. OBERD. 1954; HI = Hordeum leporinum and Cm = Chenopodium murale Comm., cf. BR.-BL. 52, OBERD. 1954, ZOHARY 1973)

Species	group 1	group 2	group 3	code	symbol
Amaranthus albus	. . . +.2	r.1	. . . . . .	OC	(b/f)
Marrubium vulgare	. . . (+.2)	. . . . . .	. . . . . .	Cm	(f)
Salvia dichroantha	. . . +.1	. . . . . .	. . . . . .	BRS	(b)
Antirrhinum orontium	. . r.1 .	. . . . . .	. . . . . .	Cm	(b/f)
Sisymbrium officinale	. . +. .	. . . . . .	. . . . . .	HI	(f/v)
Hirschfeldia incana	. +. 4. r.1	. . . . . .	. . . . . .	HI	(f/v)
Echium plantagineum	. +. . (+.2)	. . . . . .	. . . . . .	HI	(f/v)
Nonea pulla	+.1 . . .	r.1	. r.1	HI	(b/f)
Scrophularia canina ssp.	3.3 1. . .	. . . . . .	. . . . . r.1	BRS	(b/f)

Character species of segetal comm. = S, (cf. BR.-BL. 1936, OBERD. 1954, ZOHARY 1973)

Species	group 1	group 2	group 3	code	symbol
Heliotropium hirsutissimu	. . 1. 4.3	1. +. . 2. 2. .	. . . . . .	S(OC)	(b)
Tribulus terrestris	. . . 1.3	r.1 +. r.1 . 2. .	. . . . . .	S(HI)	(b/f)
Chrozophora tinctoria	. . . +.1	r.1 +. +. +. +. r.1	. . . . . .	S	(b/f)
Thymelaea passerina	. +. . .	2. r.1 2. +. r.1 2.	. . . . . .	S(F)	(f)
Ajuga chamaepitys ssp. c	. r.2 . .	+. . 1. +. . .	. . . . . .	S(F)	(b)
Cynodon dactylon	. r.1 +. .	. +. +. r.1 . .	+.	T	(b/f)
Verbascum leptocladum	+.2 r.1 +. r.1	. +. +. . . .	. . . . . .	BTB	(b/f)
Salvia virids	(1.2 . . .	+. . +. . . .	1.	BT	(b)
Delphinium peregrinum	. . +. +.2	+. . r.1 . . .	. . . . . .	BTB	(b)
Herniaria hirsuta	. . . .	+. +. +. +. . .	+.	T	(b/f)
Polygonum arenastrum	. . +. .	. r.1	. r.1	T	(f)
Sideritis montana ssp.	+.1 . . .	1. . . . r.1 .	. . . . . .	BTB	(b)
Papaver rhoeas	. . r.1 .	. . . . . .	. . . . . r.1	S	(b/f)
Filago pyramidata	. . . .	. +.	1. . 1. . . .	S(F)	(tw/v)
Ononis spinosa	. . . .	. . . +. . .	. . . . 1. .	BTB	(b/f)
Pterocephalus plumosus	. . . .	. . . 1. . .	. . . . 1. .	BRS	(v)
Scandix pecten veneris	. . . .	. . . . . .	. . . . +. +.	S(F)	(v)
Hypericum triquetrifolium	. . . .	r.1 . . . r.1	4. 3. 3. 3. 4. 4.	S(F)	(b)

Additionally in one to three relevees:

Rumex pulcher ssp. divar. 4:(2.4) OC(f/v); Peganum harmala 13:(r.1) OC(b); Lolium rigidum ?bs HI(f); Chenopodium opulifolium 9:r.1 Cm(b/f); Raphanus raphinastrum 13:(3.1) S(b/f); Scabiosa reuteriana 10 BRS(b/f); Althea dissecta 12:r.1 BRS(f); Rhagadiolus stellatus 7:r.1 BRS(f); Silene vulgaris 7: r.1 BRS(f); Consolida hellespontica 10:r.1 BTB(b); Nigella arvensis 10:r.1 BTB(b/f); Bunium ferulaceum 7:1.2 BTB(f); Chondrilla juncea 3:r.1 BT(b); Verbascum sinuatum 11:r.1 BT(Ros); Knautia integrifolia 10:r.1 BTB(b/f).

Additional abbreviations:

BRS = companions of ruderal and segetal comm.; T = character species of trampling comm.; BT = character species of extensive pastures and Macchie; BTB = companions of BT-species; (b) = flowering; (f) = fruiting; (v) = withered; (Ros) = rosette; tw = partly; F = according to ZOHARY (1973:648ff) a species of facultative segetal comm.

Table 5.1. Typical vegetation near dry stone walls in the centre of the village.

			A open space/dry wall/field edge	B
HI	Hirschfeldia incana	(f/v)	3.3	4.3
F/M	Plumbago europaea	(tw/b)	1.3	1.2
S(F)	Hypericum triquetrifolium	(b)	+.2	(r.1)
S(OC)	Centaurea solstitialis	(b)	+.2	
OC	Arum italicum	(f)	+.2	(r.1)
BRS	Pterocephalus plumosus	(b/f)	+.2	
OC	Peganum harmala	(b)	r.1	
BTB	Alyssum strigosum	(f/v)	+.2	
OC	Marrubium vulgare	(f)		+.2
BTB	Delphinium peregrinum	(b)		r.1
BRS	Verbena officinalis	(b)		r.1
HI	Echium plantagineum	(b)		r.1
TB	Verbascum sinuatum	(R)		+.1
Mac	Quercus coccifera	(dev)	1.3	(+.1)
Mac	Rhamnus oleoides	(dev)	r.1	
Mac	Asparagus acutifolius	(dev)	+.2	

Date : July 14, 1979,
Size of sample plots: 25m2
Soils: shallow, in parts covered with travertine rocks

Abbreviations:
Character species of the Hordeum leporinum- (HI), medit. ruderal- (OC), medit. segetal- (S) and Macchie (Mac) - communities; S(F) = facultative segetal-flora, BRS = companions of the ruderal- and segetal - communities, BTB = companions of the Thero-Brachypodieta, TB = character species of the Thero-Brachypodietea, F/M = often in rock crevices and on dry stone walls, (R) = rosette, (b) = flowering, (f) = in fruit, (v) = withered, (tw) = in part, (dev) = devastated.

Ten random samples (10 × 10 × 10 cm) were taken for each relevee, these were mixed and a representative soil sample of about 1 kg taken. Before sampling all loose surface debris were brushed away, to ensure that only the non-transient seed bank was registered. Of the 40 soil samples collected, 6 were from the 1st transect, 20 from the 2nd, and 14 from the 3rd.

In investigations over 1½ years, 1714 seeds germinated, of which 1469 seedlings could be identified. 81% of all seedlings germinated during the first vegetation period. Stand thicknesses varied widely, with extreme values from 839 seeds/m^2 of investigation area up to 35720 seeds/m^2.

A comparison of the spectrum of species recorded in the spring and summer of 1979 with those identified in the seed bank reveals considerable differences. Of the 83 species in the seed bank, 35 (42%) were new (*cf.* Table 6). When attributed to the CaS groups (*cf.* Table 7) the largest proportion belongs to the group of the extensive pastures and Macchie clearings (47% = 39 species). This group increases at the margin of the settlement, far exceeding the species of the ruderal and segetal associations. Of particular importance are the extensive pasture species *Sagina apetala*, which germinated very frequently in the soil samples of the pasture area, and *Gagea bohemica* as a CaS of the extensive pastures, neither of which was found during the vegetation survey.

The CaS of the segetal associations and their accompanying species are very scarce inside the village. At the edges of the settlement and on the extensive pastures they are only represented sporadically. Nearly half of all seedlings were *Veronica arvensis*, which shows a uniform pattern of distribution through the entire 2nd transect.

The species of the trampling association also have a uniform distribution restricted to the settlement. In addition to the 8 CaS already registered in the vegetation survey, *Erophila*

Table 6. List cf 35 species found only in the seed bank listed according to flowering period (after Scheider & Kehl 1987).

Names accord. to FLORA OF TURKEY (1965–85)	Flowering period	Life-form	CaS-group
Capsella rubella	1–12	A–B	R
Erophila verna	2–3	A	T/eP
Trifolium tomentosum	2–4	A	eP
Asterolinon linum-stellatum	2–5	A	eP
Arenaria leptoclados	2–6	A–B	eP
Galium murale	3–4	A	eP
Geranium molle	3–4	A	S
Cardamine hirsuta	3–4	A	R
Gagaea bohemica	3–5	G	eP
Valantia hispida	3–5	A	eP
Fumaria parviflora	3–5	A	R
Hedypnois cretica	3–5	A	eP
Cerastium semidecandrum	3–5	A	T
Cerastium glomeratum	3–6	A	eP
Veronica arvensis	3–6	A	S
Eremopoa persica	3–6	A	eP
Sideritis curvidens	3–6	A	eP
Crepis sancta	3–7	A	eP
Senecio vulgaris	3–8	A–B	R
Euphorbia taurinensis	3–8	A	eP
Malva parviflora	4	A	S/R
Stellaria media	4–6	A	R
Trigonella spicata	4–6	A	S
Papaver dubium	4–6	A	S
Torilis leptophylla	4–7	A	R
Cnicus benedictus	4–7	A	S
Velezia quadridentata	5	A	eP
Parietaria lusitanica	5–6	A	R
Amaranthus retroflexus	5–7	A	R
Sagina apetala	5–8	A	eP
Velezia rigida	5–8	A	eP
Consolida orientalis	5–8	A	S
Anagalis arvensis	5–10	A	S
Chenopodium botrys	7–10	A	R
Portulaca oleracea	7–11	A	R

Key: A = annual, B = biennial, G = geophyte, R = ruderal, S = segetal, eP = extensive pastures and Macchie clearings, T = trampling areas.

verna and *Cerastium semidecandrum* are also found, the former with a high population density. Attention is also drawn to the high germination numbers of *Polycarpon tetraphyllum* in the extensive pastures and settlement areas and to *Matricaria chamomilla* at the centre of the village.

In the inner settlement area the species of the ruderal association form the second largest group with 23 species (30%), but with relatively few seedlings. A characteristic of the centre of the settlement is the frequency of *Amaranthus albus*, *Sisymbrium officinale* and *Lolium rigidum*.

Table 7. Seedbank populations of 26 soil samples from two transects (relevee nos. 20–25 and 26–60) arranged according to constancy and species groups of extensive pastures, ruderal- and segetal-associations.

Nos. of selected relevees	*	20	21	22	23	24	25	26	27	28	29	31	33	35	37	38	39	41	44	45	49	50	52	53	55	59	60
species of extensive pasture communities																											
Psilurus incurvus		2	15	1	1	2	.	2	2	.	1	2	4	.	.	.	1	4	2	1	.	.	1	.	2	.	3
Sagina apetala	*	1	5	25	.	1	6	2	4	1	1	.	.	.	1	.	2	1	.	3	.	.	2	.	.	1	6
Lophlochloa phleoides		4	1	6	1	1	.	4	1	.	.	2	.	.	1	.	.	1	1	.	.	1	2	.	1	.	1
Galium murale	*	.	6	1	.	3	.	1	3	.	2	.	3	.	.	.	5	.	.	2	.	1	1	.	.	.	.
Arenaria leptoclades	*	.	1	2	3	.	.	2	1	.	2	1	1	.	.	.	.	.	.	.	.	.	.	.	.	.	.
Gagea bohemica	*	20	3	2	17	.	.	1	1	.	.	1	.	.	.	.	.	3	2	.	.	2	.	.	.	.	.
Poa bulbosa		.	1	.	.	3	1	.	.	.	.	.	11	.	.	.	.	19	1	.	4	.	1	3	2	.	.
Trigonella monspeliaca		.	1	2	.	.	.	1	1	.	.	.	.	.	.	.	.	.	.	.	1	.	.	.	.	.	1
Plantago lagopus		.	1	2	.	.	.	3	1	.	.	.	.	.	.	.	.	.	.	.	.	.	.	.	.	.	.
Crepis foetida		.	.	.	1	.	.	.	1	.	.	.	2	.	1	.	.	.	.	.	.	.	.	.	2	.	.
Phleum subulatum		.	.	.	.	.	.	.	.	.	.	.	.	.	.	.	.	1	1	.	.	.	.	.	.	.	.
Filago eriocephala		.	1	1	1	.	.	.	.	.	.	.	.	.	.	.	.	.	.	.	.	.	1	.	.	.	.
Cerastium glomeratum	*	.	.	.	.	.	.	.	.	.	.	.	.	.	.	.	.	.	.	.	.	.	2	2	.	.	.
Vaillantia hispida	*	.	.	.	1	.	.	.	.	.	.	.	.	.	.	.	.	.	.	.	.	.	.	.	.	.	.
Asterolinon linum-stell.	*	.	1	.	1	.	.	.	.	5	.	.	.	.	.	.	.	.	.	.	.	.	.	.	.	.	.
Verbascum leptocladum		.	.	.	1	.	.	.	.	.	.	.	.	.	.	.	.	1	.	.	.	.	2	2	.	.	.
Species per soil sample		7	13	9	7	7	2	8	10	2	4	4	5	3	3	0	4	3	6	8	0	6	7	2	5	4	5
Number of seedlings		30	38	42	25	15	3	20	17	2	5	7	23	3	4	0	10	6	27	13	0	10	11	3	9	6	12
species of segetal communities																											
Veronica arvensis	*	.	1	.	.	.	2	3	.	1	.	5	.	1	.	.	7	3	2	1	.	2	.	.	.	.	.
Anthemis arvensis		1	.	2	.	.	.	.	1	.	.	1	.	2	1	.	1	1	.	1	.	.	.	.	.	.	1
Filago pyramidata		.	.	1	.	.	.	.	.	.	.	.	.	.	.	.	.	.	.	.	.	.	.	.	.	.	.
Papaver rhoeas		.	.	.	.	.	.	.	.	.	1	.	.	.	.	.	.	.	.	.	5	.	.	.	.	.	.
Species per soil sample		1	1	1	0	1	0	3	1	3	1	2	2	1	1	1	2	1	2	2	1	3	4	0	0	0	0
Number of seedlings		1	1	2	0	1	0	4	3	6	1	2	6	1	1	2	8	3	3	2	1	7	5	0	0	0	0
species of trampling communities																											
Polycarpon tetraphyllum		4	.	3	3	1	.	.	.	3	6	6	14	6	24	8	11	.	30	1	2	3	6	1	5	.	15
Herniaria hirsuta		.	1	.	.	.	.	.	.	.	8	1	.	.	.	.	1	9	1	2	.	.	1	.	.	3	1
Matricaria chamomilla		.	1	.	.	.	.	.	.	4	19	2	7	4	.	.	7	.	.	1	.	.	.	.	.	.	1
Poa infirma		.	.	.	.	.	.	.	.	17	15	5	.	8	.	.	.	.	2	.	.	3	2	.	.	.	.
Erophila verna	*	.	1	.	8	.	.	.	.	.	1	.	.	.	.	.	.	.	2	.	.	6	1	1	.	.	.
Species per soil sample		2	2	2	1	1	0	0	0	3	5	4	2	1	4	1	3	1	3	2	2	3	5	2	1	1	3
Number of seedlings		5	2	11	3	1	0	0	0	24	49	14	21	6	37	8	19	9	33	3	3	12	10	2	5	3	17
species of ruderal communities																											
Amaranthus albus		.	2	.	.	.	.	2	1	1	10	3	2	.	7	.	1	.	.	.	5	.	1	.	.	1	1
Capsella rubella	*	.	.	.	.	.	.	.	1	.	1	2	1	3	.	.	1	1	.	.	.	.	.	.	.	.	1
Verbascum undulatum		.	.	.	.	.	.	.	.	3	.	3	2	.	.	1	.	.	.	.	.	1	.	1	.	.	.
Sisymbrium officinale		.	.	.	.	.	.	10	1	.	.	1	.	3	10	1	1	.	.	.	.	1	.	.	.	.	.
Stellaria media	*	.	.	2	.	.	.	.	.	.	.	2	.	1	10	.	1	.	.	.	.	1	.	.	.	.	1
Parietaria lusitanica	*	.	.	.	1	.	.	.	.	2	.	.	4	.	.	.	1	.	.	.	.	3	.	.	1	.	.
Lolium rigidum		.	.	.	.	.	.	.	.	.	5	3	2	1	3	.	.	.	.	.	.	2	.	.	.	.	.
Mercurialis annua		.	.	.	.	.	.	.	.	.	3	.	.	1	.	1	.	1	.	.	.	1	.	.	.	.	1
Hirschfeldia incana		.	.	.	.	.	.	.	2	.	.	.	.	.	.	.	.	.	.	.	.	1	.	.	.	.	.
Heliotropium hirsutissimum		.	.	.	.	.	.	.	.	.	.	.	.	.	.	2	.	2	.	.	.	.	.	2	3	.	3
Erodium cicutarium		.	.	.	1	.	.	.	.	.	1	1	.	.	.	.	.	.	.	.	.	1	.	.	.	.	.
Euphorbia peplus		.	.	.	.	.	.	.	.	.	.	3	.	1	.	.	.	.	.	.	.	.	.	.	.	.	.
Antirrhinum orontium		.	.	.	.	.	.	.	.	.	.	.	.	.	1	.	.	.	.	.	1	.	1	.	.	.	.
Senecio vulgaris	*	.	.	.	.	.	.	.	.	.	.	1	.	.	.	.	.	1	.	.	.	1	1	.	.	.	.
Species per soil sample		1	2	1	1	1	0	1	2	5	3	8	8	9	8	8	7	4	0	1	3	3	9	1	2	1	4
Number of seedlings		1	5	2	1	1	0	10	3	6	4	24	16	15	30	14	6	4	0	1	7	3	12	2	4	2	8

Additionally in one to three relvees (incl. 3rd transect = T3), marked (*) species are present only in the seed bank):

Lamium purpureum 31:1, 33:1, T3:2; Alyssum strigosum 60:1, T3:3; Crepis micrantha 59:1, T3:1; (*)Velezia quadridentata 20:1, T3:2; (*)Chenopodium botrys 39:1, T3:1; Medicago disciformis 31:1, T3:1; Medicago coronata 20:1, T3:1; (*)Cnicus benedictus 50:1, 52:1; Urtica urens 29:1, 41:1; (*)Fumaria parviflora 29:1, T3:1; (*)Geranium molle 31:1, T3:1; (*)Anagallis arvensis 26:1, T3:1; Medicago orbicularis T3:2; Crucianella latifolia T3:2; Urospermum picroides 35:1, T3:1; Nigella arvensis 82:1, T3:1; Trifolium campestre 24:1, 44:1; Euphorbia helioscopia 35:1, 37:2; Marrubium vulgare 33:2, 38:1; Catapodium rigidum 52:1, T3:1; Silene papillosa 21:1; Linaria chalepensis T3:3; Plantago coronopus T3:1; Tuberiaria guttata 45:1; Tordylium apulum 35:1; Anthemis chia 21:1; Legousia pentagonia 20:1; (*)Trigonella spicata 49:1; (*)Eremopoa persica 55:1; (*)Hedypnois cretica 41:1; (*)Crepis sancta T3:1; (*)Cerastium semidecandrum 52:1; (*)Velezia rigida T3:1; (*)Malva parviflora 28:4; (*)Cardamine hirsuta 20:1; (*)Euphorbia taurinensis T3:1; (*)Trifolium tomentosum T3:1; (*)Papaver dubium 38:1; (*)Consolida orientalis 52:1; (*)Sideritis curvidens 45:2; (*)Amaranthus retroflexus 49:1; (*)Portulaca oleracea 38:1; Chenopodium murale 37:1; (*)Torilis leptophylla 33:3, 35:1.

5. Discussion of results

5.1. *Species diversity and grazing pressure on the 1st transect in the Macchie around the settlement*

The first transect passes through a highly structured phytocoenosis, whose diversity of species and associations increases almost linearly with the increase of extensive cultivation.

A further human influence on the diversity is apparent in the extensive pasture type of vegetation, where the extreme grazing has negative effects on the numbers of species (*cf.* Schuster 1979, after Pfadenhauer 1976).

The continuous change of the floristic and structural features of the vegetation, which can be regarded as a degradation sequence, is the result of an extensive, pre-industrial mode of production, which for grazing had the desirable effect of increasing biomass production. The average level of influence which allows a maximum of communities (Schuster 1979: 383) is realized in the region of the devastated Macchie with a high proportion of extensive pasture species, which could theoretically extend right to the edge of the village, as an extrapolation of the diversity graph shows (*cf.* Fig. 8).

Field experiments on typical Phrygana with *Quercus coccifera* in Southern France, comparing the dynamics of vegetation and the effects of use, showed a considerable increase in biomass production as a result of moderate use (Poissonet *et al.* 1978, Fay *et al.* 1979, Godron *et al.* 1981). However, the measure of the average use appropriate to achieve the highest possible diversity and biomass production is dependent on the specific vegetation of the production landscape. Thus Whittaker (1979), and Naveh & Whittaker (1979) report the differing effects of grazing pressure on the Mediterranean vegetation in Israel and the USA. An increased level of grazing on Israelian Batha led over a wide range to increased species diversity (*cf.* Fig. 7), whereas comparable levels in the USA decreased the diversity.

In addition to the reasons noted in the introduction (chapter 1) to the regenerative capacity of Mediterranean vegetation, Naveh (1975: 206), Naveh & Whittaker (1979) and Houerou (1981) see the historical development there of species which are adapted to grazing as a major difference to the USA. An additional factor, especially in the eastern Mediterranean is the heterogeneous topography with considerable differences in altitude, offering a wide range of differing habitats. Many of the species occurring in the Macchie and the extensive pastures are thus almost pre-adapted and form a large reservoir of potential invaders for the new sites created by grazing (*cf.* Heyn 1971: 191).

The complex pattern of species density demonstrated well on the first transect shows intermediary distribution curves for many species (*cf.* Fig. 9), which indicates an overlapping and differentiation of ecological niches (*cf.* Whittaker 1982). The steady succession of emerging and disappearing species with an overall increase in the number of species shows the individuality of the species and the existence of a slowly changing ecological factor, in this case the intensity of land use. With Sobolev & Utekin (1982: 76) and Walter & Breckle (1983: 127) it must further be concluded that the individual species show no sociological links to one another, but only characterise an ecologically defined site. As Whittaker (1982: 34) comments: 'Species can be assigned to ecological groups by similarity of distribution, but the limits of such groupings are essentially arbitrary.'

It is especially important for the evaluation of population patterns that the edaphic and topographic conditions were originally almost homogeneous, and that trampled and shallow-soil sites developed only as a consequence of grazing and wood-cutting. The following section analyses the agricultural use and ecology of the individual sites.

5.2. *Character species group density of formation types and associations, with variation graphs for some species*

A comparison of the CaS groups of the *Quercus cocciferea-Pistacia terebinthus* association, the *Cistus-Micromeria* association and the therophyte rich extensive pastures and Macchie clear-

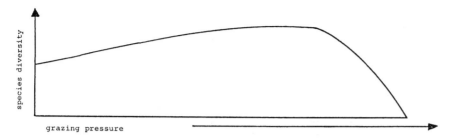

Fig. 7. Evolution of a flora under grazing: Hypothetical curve and a trend surface for the relationship of plant species diversity to grazing pressure (after Naveh & Whittaker 1979: 183).

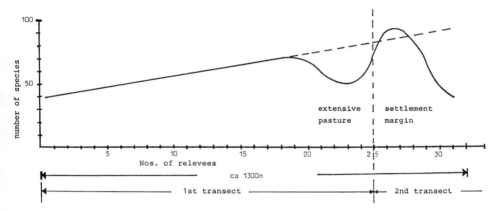

Fig. 8. Distribution of plant species diversity on the 1st and in part 2nd transect.

ings with degradation indicators on the first transect (*cf.* Fig. 5) shows that the species spectrum of the Macchie and Phrygana groups stay nearly the same until about relevee no. 18. The CaS of the extensive pastures, on the other hand, increase continuously, as to a lesser degree do the degradation indicators. However, the situation is completely different in terms of cover. The Macchie species have their highest density (almost 100%) between nos. 5–10, falling steadily to below 30% at the edge of the extensive pastures. The values are also lower at the travertine escarpment, where patches of extensive pastures occur.

These differences can be traced back to the changing stand structures and physiognomy of the CaS group of the Macchie. The mixed zone A (*cf.* Fig. 5) with only a rudimentary system of paths (*cf.* 4.3) has a slightly patchy shrub vegetation in which some CaS of the Macchie are missing, and others such as *Quercus coccifera* and *Phillyrea latifolia* are only found in the upper shrub layers. The well developed, but non–continuous layering of stands, with isolated *Pinus brutia* in the tree layer and *Quercus coccifera* and *Phillyrea latifolia* in the upper shrub layer, offers good opportunities in small clearings and along infrequently used paths for pasture species and small Phrygana shrubs which require light. Much denser vegetation borders on this zone to the north. All characteristic Macchie species are to be found in the upper and lower shrub layers (II and III) and in the upper herb layer (IV) with high cover values. *Pistacia terebinthus* and *Olea europaea* var. have their highest population densities here.

The continually decreasing cover values for the Macchie character species with relevee 8 is due firstly to the habitual change of the Macchie elements caused by grazing and secondly to the total disappearance of *Phillyrea latifolia*, which is still well represented in the

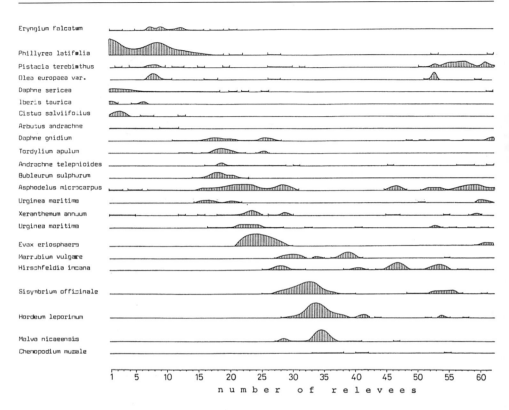

Fig. 9. Distribution of some plant species populations and their dominance along the grazing pressure gradient on the 1st and 2nd transect.

middle section. *Quercus coccifera* only reaches the shrub layer sporadically in isolated bush complexes, and has its highest cover value between nos. 16 and 25 in the upper herb layer (IV), where it frequently only forms an ankle-high cushion. The variation curves of some CaS of the Macchie (*cf*. Fig. 9) prove their varying ability to counter grazing pressure: *Phillyrea latifolia*, a class and order CaS of Quercetea (-etalia) ilicis. (Br.-Bl. *et al.* 1951, Horvat *et al.* 1974), is represented with a high frequency, with the exception of relevee no. 17, but from the start of the transect to relevee no. 9 shows remarkable growth (*cf*. Fig. 9). If the vegetation curve of *Phillyrea latifolia* is compared with the distribution of *Daphne gnidium*, according to Raus (1979: 37) a good indicator of the degree of use, then it is noticeable that their overlap is considerably between nos. 11 and 17 (*cf*. Table 1 and Fig. 9).

The light requiring (heliophyte) *Daphne gnidium*, which is not bitten by grazing animals, occurs regularly along the margins of extensive pastures, marking the transfer from patchy bush formations to isolated mosaic complexes. The transfer area is also marked by *Asphodelus microcarpus* with increasing cover and *Andrachne telephioides* (*cf*. Table 1). The latter species is a frequent companion of the *Cistus-Micromeria* community (Raus 1979), which is still found at ruderal locations (Polunin 1977).

Returning to the distribution of *Phillyrea latifolia* it can be assumed that this species only partially intrudes into the degradation stadium named *Daphne gnidium*-phase by Raus (1979) (*cf*. Table 3 in Raus 1979: 38/39). It has little ability to regenerate under heavy grazing pressure. If this declines then *Phillyrea latifolia*, just as *Quercus coccifera* can form thick shrub cushions (see relevees nos. 3–10). The deciduous *Pistacia terebinthus*, *Olea europaea* var. and the sporadically occurring *Arbutus andrachne* have similar distribution concentrations to *Phillyrea latifolia*.

It is also noticeable that in this section young *Pinus brutia* are more common, and are also found in all layers of the relatively continuous Macchie. However, it should be noted that there are always smaller clearings around or near old trees of *Pinus brutia* where the young plants establish themselves.

Of the CaS of the Macchie the *Quercus coccifera* has the highest population density along the transect. The species, which only forms taller shrubs in the first two relevees, changes its habitus, but its growth and substance production only decrease slightly at the margin of the settlement. Due to its considerable ability to regenerate (*cf.* Wraber 1952: 268, Markgraf 1958: 163ff, Knapp 1965: 62, Godron *et al.* 1981: 326ff, and others) the undemanding *Q. coccifera* still provides a good source of grazing even in extremely dry summers, when almost all other therophytes have succumbed. It is only gradually displaced by heavy grazing and then only occurs in the extensive pasture area as an ankle-high cushion.

Near the escarpment of the travertine terrace *Quercus coccifera* has a very different appearance. In the first two relevees the low shrub form is missing; the same applies for *Phillyrea*. This is because of the different impacts of the two important forms of land use, grazing and wood pollarding, on the Macchie vegetation. As emphasised by Greuter (1975: 126) the population density and physiognomy of various character species of this vegetation type react differently to these forms of use.

Grazing occurs up to the edge of the travertine escarpment, increasing towards the edge of the settlement. In the case of wood extraction by coppicing, however, two directions of extraction can be identified, one going from the village, and the other from the path system of the mixed zone A. Wood is taken from established bush complexes as long poles. The bushes regenerate by pole growth, remaining as individual plants growing up to 2–3 m. This applies to *Quercus coccifera*, *Phillyrea latifolia*, *Pistacia terebinthus* and *Olea europea* var., of which the latter three have their highest population density in relevee no. 8.

The coppicing and grazing from the mixed zone A is relatively weaker than from the settlement margin, as can be concluded from the absence of bitten *Quercus coccifera* bushes in the relevees nos. 1 and 2, as well as the presence in relevee no. 3 in the lower shrub layer of *Phillyrea latifolia*. In contrast to *Quercus coccifera*, *Phillyrea latifolia* reacts more sensitively to increased grazing pressure and disappears from the lower shrub and upper herb layer.

Pistacia terebinthus and in particular *Arbutus andrachne*, which are only sporadically found with pole shoots, suffer particular destruction from grazing and, in the latter case also from firewood collection.

If this CaS group is examined only in economic terms, an optimum biomass production in relation to intensity of land-use, then this optimum occurs between the relevees nos. 5 and 10. *Pinus brutia* occurs only infrequently, and in its shade there are on the whole few species with high biomass production. The diversity on the above mentioned section of the transect, however, lies some 20% above the first relevee. Therophytes make up the largest proportion, but contribute only to a few percent to the biomass production. The phanerophytes, which are more able to withstand competition, but whose ability to regenerate in this section is countered by the intensity of land use, would quickly close all clearings if anthropozoogenous influence were to cease. This would be accompanied by a decline in biomass production (*cf.* the experiments of Poissonet *et al.* 1978, Fay *et al.* 1979 and Godron *et al.* 1981). The regeneration and biomass production of CaS of the Macchie is then decisively influenced by the intensity of the intervention, which was pointed out at an early date by Adamovic (1929: 33).

In the interspecific competition, with the absence of anthropozoogenous influence, the much larger numbers of smaller species would lose out to the few CaS of the Macchie with very high biomass production (*cf.* also Bornkamm 1961 and Walter & Breckle 1983).

5.3. Character species distribution of the Phrygana community, the indicators of extreme degradation and the character species of the extensive pastures and Macchie clearings

The syndynamically closely related species of Macchie degradation are discussed here together, since they overlap in their succession (*cf.* Knapp 1971, Raus 1979, Naveh & Whittaker 1979). The character species of the *Cistus-Micromeria* association are determined mainly with reference to the investigations of Oberdorfer (1954a).

In the Oleo-Ceratonion zone of the North Aegean, Oberdorfer (1954a) has grouped all Phrygana formations of the *Quercus coccifera* area in the class and order Cisto-Micromerietea (-etalia). The comparison of tables by Oberdorfer (1954a), Horvat *et al.* (1974) and Raus (1979a,b) with the findings at Nebiler showed that the first transect contained a large proportion of the order and class CaS of these communities.

Micromeria myrtifolia, a vicarious species of *M. juliana*, has its focus of distribution in the south-eastern Mediterranean area of Asia Minor (Rechinger 1950: 83) and has a high presence in almost all relevees in the Macchie. Together with *Cistus creticus, Fumana tymifolia* var., *Teucrium divaricatum, Teucrium polium, Thymus revolutus* and others, it settles clearings or the borders of shrub complexes.

Although the CaS of the Phrygana only have low abundances and lower population densities in the total species spectrum, they are a good indicator for the degradation stage of the vegetation in the area under investigation (*cf.* Fig. 5 and Table 8).

Together with the cropped, frequently cushion-like *Quercus coccifera* between relevees nos. 15 and 20, there are already signs of a devastated Macchie, as is described by Knapp (1965) for Kephallinia in Greece. However, important components of the Phrygana he describes are either absent in the area under investigation, or are only sparsely represented. *Sarcopoterium spinosum* and *Calicotome villosa*, both well protected against grazing and important elements of the true Phrygana (Rauh 1975, Quezel 1981), are only marginally involved in the structure of the vegetation. This section on the transect is emphasised because of the habitual similarity of the above-mentioned highly devastated Macchie to the Phrygana-like formation (*cf.* Fig. 5).

Only minor differences can be observed in the distribution of the CaS of the Phrygana, with one exception. Whereas *Fumana thymifolia* var. and *Teucrium polium* are still encountered frequently in the zone of extensive pastures, the occurrence of *Cistus salviifolius* is restricted to the mixed zone A at the beginning of the transect.

This species, described by Rübel (1930: 98–100) as undemanding and mainly occurring in the east-Mediterranean area, is characteristic on Crete of the transition from the Macchie to the Phrygana. In this context it should be noted that Oberdorfer (1954: 93) sees *Cistus salviifolius* as a character species of the Cistion orientale alliance (Oberdorfer 1954), sociologically closely related to the Phrygana community. In contrast to the *Cistus-Micromeria* communities, which settles mainly on degraded red earth soils, Cistion orientale prefers deeper soils with a higher humus content in the upper strata. In terms of development history, Cistion orientale is closely related to the bush communities of Quercion ilicis.

The above mentioned observations of Oberdorfer are in good agreement with my own findings. In mixed zone A the soils are less burdened, deeper, and have a comparatively marked accumulation of debris, particularly around the cleared shrub formations, as was found by Zech & Cepel (1972) in the vicinity of *Pinus brutia* stands (*cf.* 2.3). It is noticeable that in the zone occupied by *Cistus salviifolius, Micromeria myrtifolia* occurs only sporadically, which can be seen as an indicator that the mixed zone A is most distant from the Phrygana in the degradation series.

Near the area of the extensive pastures at the edge of the settlement the main group of the CaS cf the Phrygana between relevees nos. 14 and 19 gradually drops out. This transition is characterised on the one hand by the higher population density of the *Daphne gnidium* already mentioned, and on the other hand by the increased occurrence of the indi-

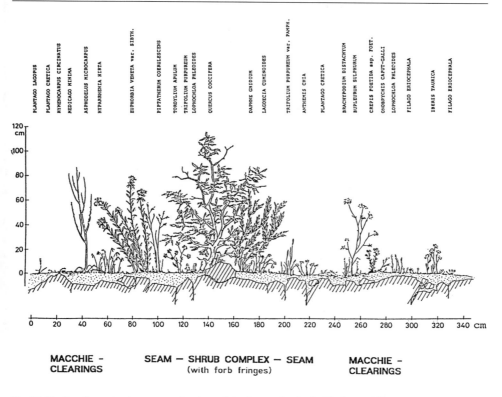

MACCHIE –
CLEARINGS

SEAM – SHRUB COMPLEX – SEAM
(with forb fringes)

MACCHIE –
CLEARINGS

Fig. 10. Profile of an extensive pasture, border and shrub complex in the Daphne gnidium stage.

cators for extreme degradation. The penultimate stage of Macchie destruction is reached directly at the edge of the settlement with the highest population density and cover on eroded, stony and very shallow soil of the extensive pastures.

Already between nos. 19 and 21 the mosaic-like interlocking shrub complexes of mainly *Quercus coccifera, Rhamnus oleoides* and *Daphne gnidium* have completely broken up, leaving only isolated, heavily disturbed *Quercus coccifera* bushes with ecotonic vegetation (*cf.* Fig. 10).

In the shallow-soil pasture zone there is a drop in species diversity, accompanied by a jump in the cover values for a few species. Due to the extreme grazing pressure and the associated soil erosion, conditions have been altered decisively, favouring some dwarf therophytes. The ground was covered with a thick carpet of *Evax eriosphaera*, only growing a few centimetres high and already withered at the time of the investigation, together with *Asteriscus aquaticus*, which had also faded. *Plantago cretica* and *Pl. lagopus* also had high cover values.

A few ruderal and segetal species, which intrude on the extensive pastures from the inner settlement area, and others which are frequently encountered on nutrient-rich sites or along paths, such as *Centaurea solstitialis* (*cf.* Horvat *et al.* 1974: 128) suggest that the soil on the pastures, though shallow, has in fact a high level of nutrients. This would not be surprising, since cows and donkeys frequently graze there.

In the seed bank the geophyte *Gagea bohemica* was also frequently encountered between nos. 20 and 25 (*cf.* Table 7), as a geo-element of the steppes (Horvat *et al.* 1974: 68), as well as *Sagina apetala* as CaS of Thero-Brachypodietea (Oberdorfer 1954a: 90) and the steppes element *Erophila verna* (Horvat *ibid.*: 327).

Therophyte stands, which in the east Mediterranean area often mediate to the *Cistus-Micromeria* communities at the margins of settlements, are combined by Oberdorfer (1954a: 89) in the alliance Romulion because of their species combination. However, the assignation of the extensive pasture area investigated to this alliance is uncertain, since the important genus *Romulea* is completely absent. Whether this is an eastern form with *Gagea bohemica* and *Evax eriosphera*, or rather a *Poa bulbosa-Plantago lagopus* community, can only be answered with additional material for comparison.

There can, however, be no doubt that the entire therophyte vegetation of the extensive pastures and the Macchie clearings can be classified as Thero-Brachypodietea (annual calciferous ext. pasture). Whereas in the North Aegean Oberdorfer (*ibid.*) only found 50% of the characteristic species of the *Th.-Br.* known from the west Mediterranean in dominances which determine the association, around Nebiler there were only 50% of those species named by Oberdorfer. An important CaS of this class, *Brachypodium distachyum* is represented in almost all relevees of the transect with high cover values, with the exception of the mixed zone A and the extensive pastures.

The distribution pattern of the therophytes along the transect allows four ecologically-defined groups to be distinguished, which at the same time demonstrate the gradient of land-use.

In addition to the first group (*cf.* Table 1) which avoids the denser Macchie and has two distribution focal points, a second group can be recognised, whose species regularly settle with few exceptions in the mixed zone A and the extensive pastures, with a high cover value between the settlement and layer step borders. The first two relevees in the mixed zone A are poorer in therophytes. For the species in the first group the higher levels of shade in the denser Macchie are obviously a limiting factor for distribution, as are the layer step border zone, rich in chamaephytes with more humus in the upper soil levels. Almost all clearings of the bush formations and mosaics of shrub complexes are occupied by species of the second group, which with *Psilurus incurvus, Anthemis chia* and *Plantago cretica* are also an essential part of the species spectrum of the shallow-soiled extensive pastures.

The heavily grazed and eroded extensive pasture zone is occupied by the third group with *Evax eriosphaera, Gagea bohemica* (*cf.* Table 7) and *Astericus aquaticus*. It is not possible to say whether *Gagea bohemica* can be regarded as an indicator of the penultimate stage of Macchie destruction in view of the lack of information about its occurrence on the southern transect section. On the other hand *Evax eriosphaera*, an east Anatolian vicariant (Rechinger 1959: 86) of the western *E. pygmaea*, occurring on stony pastures and dry places (*cf.* Polunin 1980: 448), can serve as CaS of the pasture areas exposed to intense land-use. An observation by Braun-Blanquet (1964: 408) is also instructive in this context, namely that the CaS of the Thero-Brachypodion, to which the west Mediterranean *Evax pygmaea* belongs, have a high resistance against extreme soil temperatures. It can be assumed that on the extensive pasture area the virtual absence of a shading shrub layer means that the highest soil temperatures are reached there.

In the heavily devastated Macchie with open mosaics of shrub complexes, the third group of the extensive pasture species is neighboured by a further species group of clearings and borders. This group accompanies the *Daphne gnidium* stage with *Hyparrhenia hirta, Xeranthemum annuum, Bupleurum sulphurum* and *Tordylium apulum* (Raus 1979: 37). The latter two groups populate the main distribution area of the CaS for extreme degradation and together characterise the last stage of destruction of Macchie around Nebiler. The species groups indicating the *Daphne gnidium* stage are mainly followed by species occurring in the Macchie, with intermediate distribution patterns of their populations.

Table 8. Structural and floristic changes on the 1st transect.

		←— Escarpment	1st transect		settlement margin —————→
CONTINUOUS CHANGE OF ECOLOGICAL PARAMETERS FROM THE PLATEAU EDGE TO THE SETTLEMENT	INCREASE	grazing pressure - clearing - nutrient content and supply - openings with radiation stress desiccation of the topsoil - trampling stress - danger of erosion - different ecological niches			
	DECREASE	top-soil depth - shady sites - biomass production - detritus layer and accumulation stability of soil surface conditions			
BIOMASS PRODUCTION		medium	high	medium	low
TOP-SOIL DEPTH		profound	medium	low	extrem low
THICKNESS OF DETRITUS LAYER cm		3 - 7	2 - 4	1 - 3	< 1
PHASES OF MACCHIE DEGRADATION		Cistus salviifolius stage	Quercus coccifera - Pistacia terebinthus stage	Daphne gnidium stage	Evax eriosphaera - Plantago spp. stage
FLORA AND VEGETATION	FORMATIONS	shrub formation with clearings and isolated Pinus brutia - stands		mosaic - like patches of bushes and cushion shaped thickets / single chamaephytes and phanerophytes	
	LAYERING IN MTR >3	groups of trees	single trees	strongly devasted shrubs	
	LAYERING IN MTR 1 - 3	Phillyrea latifolia with Quercus coccifera		extensive pastures (Trift)	
	LAYERING IN MTR 0,5 - 1	Pistacia terebinthus Arbutus andrachne Olea europaea var.			
	LAYERING IN MTR 0,2 - 0,5			mainly Quercus coccifera patches	
	CHARACTER - SPECIES	Cistus salviifolius	Pistacia terebinthus Arbutus andrachne	Daphne gnidium	Evax eriosphaera
	DISTRIBUTION OF GROUPS	character - species group of Cistus - Micromeria Comm.		high cover values of degradation indicators	
		character - species of clearings and marginal strips			"trift" - species

5.4. Summary of results for the 1st transect

Although, as emphasised in 6.1, species diversity and character species group distribution overlap considerably, it is possible to prove marked focal points in the distribution. However, distinct boundaries between the species groups, which in their combination may well characterise communities in the Braun-Blanquet sense of the term, do not occur, with one exception. In the sense of the definition of Westhoff & Leeuwen (1966) and Leeuwen (1970) the extensive pastures can be distinguished from the rest of the transect as a concentration boundary area (Limes convergens) with a pronounced compaction of the upper soil layer, relatively low species diversity, and a high population density of one species. The gradual transitions with soft dispersion boundaries (Limes divergens) of the CaS groups and individual populations, which can also be observed at the shrub-border-pasture complex, is a feature of the Macchie vegetation of the first transect.

The observations recorded by Schwarz (1936: 324) on the north-west Mediterranean coast of Turkey, and by Oberdorfer (1954a: 89) in the North Aegean, that the usually impassable bush stands of the Macchie takes on a mosaic pattern near settlements or their lines of access, and that between the individual shrub complexes the open soil is covered with therophytic vegetation, or species of the Phrygana, also applies to the Nebiler area. The formation of a true Phrygana, with stand formations of thorny dwarf shrubs (Rauh 1975, Quezel 1981), or species characterised by seasonal dimorphism (*cf.* Orshan 1964, Margaris & Vokou 1982), could not be established in the area under investigation. It was, however, possible to establish degeneration stages of Macchie with marked layer formation, in the lower shrub layer of which some typical representatives of the *Cistus-Micromeria* community have migrated.

The suspicion expressed by Turrill (1937), Regel (1943), Zohary (1973) and also Walter (1956), that Macchie at higher levels from which *Pinus brutia* was extracted would not be able to regenerate to a forest, except after bush fires (Walter 1973: 129, 1975: 77), cannot be confirmed by my observations made around Nebiler at an average of 250 m above sea level. Even very sparse *Pinus brutia* stands with a well developed and thick shrub layer on a weakly developed topsoil show a high proportion of seedlings and young plants.

5.5. Character species distribution of the trampling, ruderal and segetal communities in the settlement area and their syntaxonomic evaluation

A comparison of phytosociological studies shows markedly different syntaxonomic weighting of individual ruderal and segetal species, which can be explained firstly as in Oberdorfer (1954b: 385) in terms of the different focal points of distribution (*cf.* also Kojic 1976) and secondly the lack of adequate phytosociological studies in the east Mediterranean. Thus the valid character species selected for comparison, with narrow sociological ties in north and central Europe, prove to have a wide ecological amplitude in the Mediterranean, spreading here into the extensive pastures and Macchie areas of the settlement margin, as already reported by Schwarz (1936) (compare also Fig. 12). The main cause of this is that many CaS of ruderal or segetal habitats in north and central Europe are archaeophytes, which settle there with close ties to cultivated plants (*cf.* Wilmanns 1973, Ahti & Haemet Ahti 1971), whereas in the Mediterranean they have their natural distribution (Schmidt 1969, Zohary 1971, 1973). These widely spread species therefore only are of limited use to characterise specific plant communities. Thus *e.g.*, Zohary (1973: 502) points out that the natural distribution of many so-called segetal species extends to the degraded Macchie, as well as establishes itself on sites virtually without anthropogenous influence.

Furthermore, it is generally difficult to draw a clear distinction between CaS of Secalinetea and Chenopodietea. In contrast to Oberdorfer (1954b: 381), who found barely any overlap, Zohary (1973: 636ff) notes a broad overlap of the two communities, which could be confirmed in this investigation. Above all on the harvested fields there is close intermeshing of ruderal and segetal species (*cf.* Table 5). The co-existence of ruderal, segetal, trampling, extensive pasture and Macchie species (*cf.* Fig. 11) on dry stone walls between fields and along paths was observed by Schwarz (1936: 381) in West Anatolia. A systematic registration of segetal communities seemed to him to be impossible, as did any generalisation, since 'if at one place certain species seem to be mutually exclusive, the same species may cover the ground elsewhere in harmony, and colourful profusion' (Schwarz 1936: 318). Even though it definitely is possible to recognise focal points with clear mass development in the area under investigation and the species cannot be said to have no diagnostic value, in contradiction to Schwarz's view, his comment does illustrate the fluid borders of the so-called weed communities with those of the *Quercus coccifera* communities in the margins of the settlements.

5.6. Cornfields and fallow fields

A tabular comparison of the species belonging to the Order Secalinetalia mediterranea and various communities according to Zohary (1973: 636ff), with those belonging to the Order Chenopodietalia mediterranea according to Oberdorfer (1954: 386ff) and various communities shows a wide agreement in the CaS composition. Thus Oberdorfer (1954b: 385) orders the Heliotropeto-Chrozophoretum Oberdorfer 54 of the Balkan peninsula to the

Diplotaxidion Br.-Bl. 36 and thus to the Mediterranean 'intertilled cropweeds' community. The naming CaS *Heliotropium hirsutissimum* and *Chrozophora tinctoria*, as well as *Hypericum triquetrifolium* (*H. crispum*) occur very regularly in the vegetation relevees of harvested fields and fallow land (*cf.* Table 5, group 2 and 3). For Zohary (1973: 636) the above mentioned taxa are, however, typical CaS of the class Secalinetea orientalia, which is found in the summer on harvested fields over wide areas around the Mediterranean.

The last-named species is also classed by Oberdorfer (1954: Table 6) as order CaS of the Chenopodietalia mediterranea Br.-Bl. (31) 36. The species spectrum of group 2 (*cf.* Table 5) also includes *Thymelaea passerina* and *Ajuga chamaepitys* subsp., whose membership to the 'culm crop-weed' communities is also disputed (*cf.* Braun-Blanquet *et al.* 1951: 48, Oberdorfer 1954b: Table 1, Horvat *et al.* 1974: 315). The virtually isolated occurrence of *Hypericum triquetrifolium* in the outer margin areas of the fields has been remarked on in chapter 5.8. This normally perennial species (Zohary 1966: 223, Davis 1965–85, Polunin 1980: 336) completes its entire vegetation cycle in one vegetation period in the area under investigation, like summer-annual plants. *Hypericum triquetrifolium* is spread throughout to the Cyrenaica in North Africa (*cf.* Rikli 1946: 991), settling on open stony sites of degraded Macchie, and is frequently a companion of the *Sarcopoterium* communities.

In the east Mediterranean this species, also found on harvested fields and fallow lands, must instead be included in the facultative segetal flora as in Zohary (1973: 649ff). This group includes species which have their natural distribution in the 'primary plant communities', but are able to settle cultivated areas during secondary expansion. It also includes *Ajuga chamaepitys* subsp. *chia* and *Thymelaea passerina*, which in the Danube Basin of Vojvodina (*cf.* Horvat *et al.* 1974: 315) can be a CaS of Secalinion orientalis assoc. (*cf.* also Braun-Blanquet *et al.* 1951: 47). Further species are *Scandix pecten-veneris* and *Filago pyramidata*, the latter being a frequent companion of the Cisto-Micromerietalia Oberdorfer 1954 (*cf.* Raus 1979: 68 and Table 1 of this paper), in which Braun-Blanquet *et al.* (1951: 48) sees an alliance character species of the Secalinion mediterranea. Zohary (1973: 649), on the other hand, includes *Filago pyramidata* in the group of the 'Post-Segetals', which forms the initial stage for succession series on abandoned fields together with *e.g.*, *Plantago cretica*, *Trigoella monspeliaca*, *Delphinium peregrinum*, *Consolida hellespontica* etc. (*cf.* Table 5).

In summary, the vegetation surveys of the harvested cornfields and fallow in the settlement area of Nebiler produced only a small proportion of really obligatory segetal flora. According to Zohary (1973), only two important CaS of the 'culm crop weeds' (non-irrigated winter and summer crops) are well represented in group 2. Although there are similarities to the Heliotropeto-Chrozophoretum of Oberdorfer (1954) the assignation to the Diplotaxidion seems problematical, at least for the south-eastern Mediterranean. On the one hand the titular *Diplotaxis* species are absent, as Oberdorfer (*ibid.*: 385) emphasised, and on the other hand all the named CaS of this community occur mainly on summer stubble fields, shallow fallow land, and some of them even frequently on rocky sites as companions of the Phrygana (Zohary 1966: 223, 1973: 634ff, 1971, Raus 1979: 60, Polunin & Huxley 1976: 178, Polunin 1980: 336, Horvat *et al.* 1974: 119).

In this context, attention is again drawn to the mass development of *Hypericum triquetrifolium*. A clear correlation between higher population density and site conditions could not be established. The majority of the relevees of this group are in the outer eastern margin area of the fields, so that it can be assumed that in particular nos. 2, 4, 7 and 17 lie in areas which have not long been used agriculturally, but this criterion no longer applies to the nos. 3 and 15.

Only long-term observations over several years on the same fields could establish whether the population density is due solely to the diaspora supply of differing farming or fertilizing methods, or to edaphic conditions.

The relevees from the more central settlement areas combined in group 1, with a high proportion of CaS of the ruderal community, are essentially intermediate to the road- and fieldside plant communities of the 2nd transect (*cf.* Table 2). The relevee no. 13 with high cover values of *Heliotropium hirsutissimum* and the presence of *Amaranthus albus*, *Marrubium vulgare*, *Hirschfeldia incana*, *Chrozophora tinctoria* and *Tribulus terrestris* points to the segetal group 3, the additional occurrence of ruderal species also produces certain similarities with Heliotropeto-Chrozophoretum Oberdorfer 1954. Alliance CaS of the Diplotaxidion however are completely absent.

Whereas no. 15 has *Hypericum triquetrifolium* as dominant species, no. 16, only a few metres away has *Scrophularia canina* subsp. *bicolor* which grows directly next to buildings, on extremely shallow, poorly worked soil. This perennial *Scrophularia*, frequently encountered on rocky sites (*cf.* Rikli 1946: 540, Polunin 1977: 312, 1980: 540), and which also occurs as a companion of the *Picnomon acarna* community along paths (Oberdorfer 1954b: Table 20), characterises a situation at the edge of fields where adequate and sufficient working is hardly possible.

The relevees nos. 10 and 11 lead over to the CaS combination of communities growing at the foot of walls, on field and path sides. *Hirschfeldia incana*, which is particularly well represented here, spreads out into the adjacent fields, but it has its highest population densities on the less-frequented edges of fields, paths and around buildings. At the same time there is an increase in the proportion of species which find their way from the nearby extensive pastures and Macchie along the pathways into the centre of the settlement (*cf.* the vegetation relevees of the periphery of the central village open space in chapter 4.5).

5.7. Centre of the settlement and waysides

Oberdorfer (1954b) reports an observation on the seasonal rhythm of the communities of the ruderal vegetation in the Balkans which is very important for their syntaxonomic assessment in the Nebiler settlement. According to this the surveys from the end of May to the beginning of July would only have registered a small section of the sequence of ruderal communities. Seed bank investigations (*cf.* 4.6) showed that of 84 species determined there less than 50% (35) had not been determined in the survey in Spring 1979.

In the group of ruderal species (*cf.* Table 6) there were 11 new species in the seedbank, of which only five CaS of the Mediterranean 'intertilling crop weeds' germinated more than three times in the soil samples, none of which according to Oberdorfer (1954b: 395) led the characteristic ruderal communities established by him for the early spring on the Balkan peninsula. Thus neither *Sisymbrium orientale* nor *S. irio* could be determined in the seed bank. On the other hand there were many seedlings of *Amaranthus albus*, found irregularly in the vegetation surveys, and of *Sisymbrium officinale*, which in particular was already found frequently in the central settlement area. The high population density of *Sisymbrium officinale* deserves particular attention, since according to Oberdorfer (1954b: 382) in addition to *Lactuca serriola* as typical CaS of the Euro-Siberian Ruderetea, *Sisymbrium officinale* already belongs to the rare species of the southern Balkan. In the area under investigation this species clearly marks considerably eutrophied sites in the centre and to the north of the settlements (*cf.* Table 2) where the concentration of dwellings and sheds gives rise to an accumulation of dung and kitchen waste at waysides and near houses. If one studies the array of species, and the proportion of nitrophile species, important differences become apparent.

Between nos. 51 and 56 a *Hirschfeldia incana-Hordeum leporinum*-wayside community forms, with a high proportion of accessory pasture and segetal species, but few of the CaS of *Chenopodium murale* communities restricted to sites rich in nitrogen. At the foot of walls a character species, *Arum italicum*, is somewhat more frequently represented, and only the relevee no. 54, with the sporadic occurrence of *Chenopodium murale*, *Chenopodium opulifolium* and *Marrubium vulgare* can be linked to nitrogen enrichment indicating *Chenopodium* communites of the centre of the settlement.

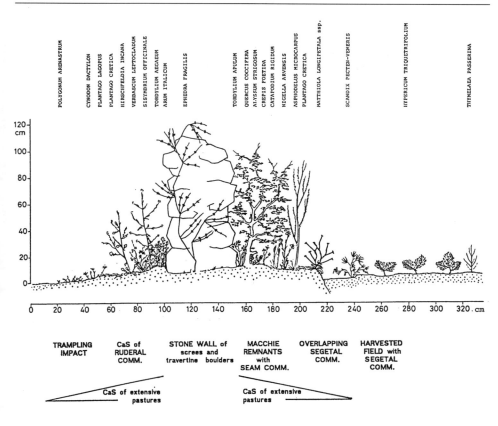

Fig. 11. Profile of a wayside, dry stone wall and field border.

A comparison with the table of wayside communities in the Balkans drawn up by Oberdorfer (1954: 394) shows overlapping with the *Hordeum leporinum* assoc. described along roads outside the settlement, in which *Hirschfeldia incana* plays a dominant role in the early summer. The same also applies for the *Bromus-Hirschfeldia* community recorded by Lohmeyer (1975: 122) on Gran Canaria (Bromo-Hirschfeldietum Lohmeyer 75) or for the *Hirschfeldia incana-Hordeum murinum* community on moderately nitrogen-rich sites outside the settlements from Oberdorfer (1965: 64) from Teneriffa and Gomera. A similar situation has also been observed by Lohmeyer on Crete (1985, pers. comm.). Although in the *Malva nicaensis-Hirschfeldia incana* communities described by Zohary (1973: 646) the *Sisymbrium* species are completely absent (in surveys of the winter aspect), they show a close relationship to my relevees. This is particularly the case for nos. 26 to 32 of the southern settlement margin, even though this is a marked mixed zone of Macchie, extensive pasture, segetal and ruderal communities.

Hirschfeldia incana, well represented over the settlement area as a whole, is completely absent from the actual centre of the settlement (see Table 2). More nitrophilous species occur such as *Chenopodium murale*, *Chenopodium opulifolium* (rare), *Chenopodium vulvaria*, *Marrubium vulgare*, *Brassica napus*, *Mercurialis annua*, *Euphorbia helioscopia*, *Erodium cicutarium*, *Amaranthus albus*, *Stellaria media* and *Lolium rigidum* var., which in their combination clearly show in the vegetation of the central settlement area the alliance Chenopodion muralis Br.-Bl. 1936 of less-frequented ruderal places.

From a floristic-ecological point of view the CaS spectrum of the central settlement area are intermediate to the closely related Euro-Siberian alliance Sisymbrion officinalis Tuexen, Lohmeyer and Preising 50 of the warmer East-European, nitrogen-rich ruderal sites. The Euro-Siberian alliance, with a more predominantly summer life-cycle and a higher proportion of short-lived species (Oberdorfer 1954b: 395, Horvat *et al.* 1974: 410) extends into the margins of the settlement, in contrast to the Chenopodion muralis alliance, which lasts from spring to late-summer.

As Oberdorfer (1954b) observed on the Balkan peninsula, and Lohmeyer (1985, pers. comm.) on Crete, the CaS of the alliance Chenopodion muralis in Nebiler are tied closely to the actual centre of the settlement, though without any precise border to neighbouring CaS groups. For example the well-developed *Mercurialis annua* community, on 'dry sites, poor in fine soil' (see Oberdorfer 1954: 390, Table 13) spreads far into the *Hirschfeldia-Hordeum* community of the settlement margins. However, with its CaS *Mercuralis annua*, *Calendula arvensis* and *Antirrhinum orontium* this community settles the base of walls and pathways, with soils rich in fine soil, humus and frequently covered with travertine rocks, but is also found in the shadow of loose stone walls next to the CaS of the Macchie and the extensive pastures. This society of the 'Steinschutthalden' as Oberdorfer (*ibid.*) called it, is doubtlessly restricted to nitrogen-rich ruderal sites, but already forms a transition to the communities dominated by *Hirschfeldia incana*.

A CaS group limited solely to the centre of the settlement could not be found, but an area was identified which was characterised by the presence of *Chenopodium murale* and by the almost total absence of *Hirschfeldia incana*, and which can be regarded as the real core area of the Chenopodion muralis alliance. Only here is it possible to recognise slight tendencies to the Chenopodion muralis Br.-Bl. (1931) 36, although the most important CaS of this association are sparsely represented. The reason for the weak formation of this association could be that, according to Oberdorfer (1954b: 395), the main development of this ruderal community only occurs in late summer or early autumn. Another factor could be the lower levels of nutrients, and more extreme dryness than for example on the Balkan peninsula. The seed bank investigations do not support the possibility of the seasonal low development of the Chenopodion muralis (*cf.* also 5.9), since it provides no significant augmentation of the spectrum of CaS. It can therefore be assumed that the relatively low levels of eutrophication as a function of the density and extent of the settlement are the reason why Chenopodion muralis did not develop fully.

The wayside community reaching nearly to the heart of the settlement, with *Hirschfeldia incana*, *Crepis foetida* subsp., *Hordeum leporinum*, *Sisymbrium officinalis* and occasionally also *Malva nicaeensis* could be attributed to the Hordeion murini Br.-Bl. 31 alliance, or to Bromo-Hirschfeldion Lohm. 75.

Hirschfeldia incana and *Hordeum leporinum*, major components of the wayside communities, and determinants of the aspect in spring, had already died back during the survey in June/July 1979 due to the very hot and dry conditions. Only *Malva nicaeensis* and *Echium plantagineum* were still flowering.

As already stated, *Hirschfeldia incana* characterises the nitrogen-rich sites outside settlements, but can also extend along the waysides into the heart of a settlement, where it is replaced by *Chenopodium murale*. The CaS of the alliance of Hordeion murini, *Hordeum leporinum* has a much wider distribution, and can frequently be found with a high presence as CaS of the Chenopodion muralis (*cf.* Oberdorfer 1954b, Horvat *et al.* 1974, Lohmeyer 1975, Lohmeyer & Trautmann 1970) and beyond the wayside communities near the settlement is also a good character species of the Onopordion illyrici (Chenopodietalia mediterranea) succeeding the Mediterranean therophytes.

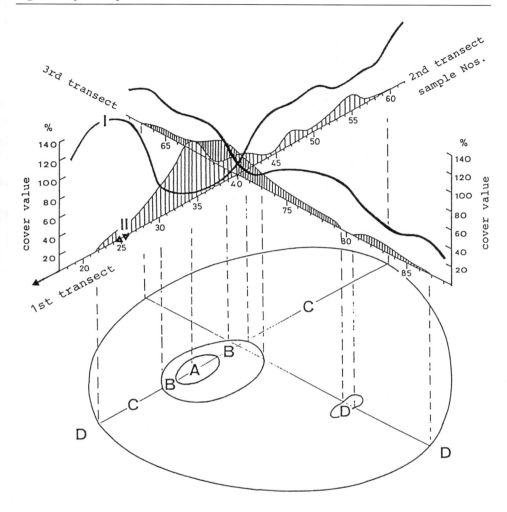

I = Characteristic species of Macchie clearings and extensive
    pastures ("Trift")

II = Characteristic species of Hordeum leporinum - (Hirschfeldia
     incana) and Chenopodium murale Communities (ruderal comm.)

A = Centre of settlement with highest eutrophication, dominance
    of the Chenopodium murale Comm., greatest decline of the
    CaS group of Macchie clearings and extensive pastures

B = Mixed zone of CaS of the ruderal communities and the CaS of
    Macchie clearings and pastures

C = Main distribution zone of the wayside communities
    (e.g. Hirschfeldia incana, Hordeum leporinum) of slightly
    decreased hemerobic sites, high abundance and diversity of
    the CaS group of Macchie clearings and extensive pastures

D = Settlement margin without CaS of the ruderal communities and
    transition belt to the pattern structure of degraded Macchie

Fig. 12. Dominance and plant species diversity of character species on the eutrophy gradient on the 2nd and
3rd transect of the settlement area of Nebiler.

In view of the extent to which *Hordeum leporinum* extends into adjacent communities or CaS groups of the settlements and settlement margins of the eastern Mediterranean, and following the observation made by Lohmeyer on Crete (1985, pers. comm.), the alliance of wayside communities at the settlement margins shall be named after *Hirschfeldia incana*. In this Hirschfeldion alliance, which corresponds to the Bromo-Hirschfeldion Lohm. 75 on Gran Canaria or the Hordeion Br.-Bl. (31) 47, a *Malva nicaeensis-Hirschfeldia incana* community can be determined in the southern part of the 2nd transect and in the western middle section of the 3rd transect, as has been described by Zohary (1973: 645) and is widely distributed on calcareous wayside sites in Syria.

In addition to *Hirschfeldia incana* (which determines the early summer aspect), *Malva nicaeensis*, *Lolium rigidum*, *Avena barbata*, *Urospermum picroides* and *Cynodon dactylon*, according to Zohary (ibid.) *Hordeum murinum* (?) is also represented as a CaS (on the distribution of *H. murinum* and *H. leporinum* see also Faruqi 1980). The vicariant of *Malva parviflora*, *M. nicaeensis*, mediates in its distribution in the settlement centre with the Chenopodion muralis, where the relevees 36 and 37 show similarities to the Chenopodio-Malvetum parviflorae of Lohmeyer & Trautmann (1970: 221) for La Palma. Although already occurring together with many CaS of the Macchie and extensive pastures at walls and the edges of fields in the 2nd transect, there are signs in the northern section between nos. 52 and 56 of a *Hirschfeldia incana-Hordeum leporinum* association. The species spectrum recorded, with only a few characteristic nitrophilous species corresponds to the *Hirschfeldia incana-Hordeum murinum* community described by Oberdorfer (1965) for Teneriffa or the association Hordeetum leporini Br.-Bl. 36 proposed by Braun-Blanquet (1936) for the western Mediterranean.

A close inter-weaving with communities remote from the settlement, or with their CaS groups can be observed on the southern margin of the settlement. CaS of all the groups determined settle on a small area, and only the extensive pasture and trampling species make use of the more compacted and frequented space between wall and path (see Fig. 11).

There is a flowing transition from the trampling community with *Cynodon dactylon*, *Polygonum arenastrum*, *Matricaria chamomilla*, *Polycarpon tetraphyllum* and *Plantago coronopus* (see Table 2) to the narrow zone of extensive pasture species and wall foot communities with *Hirschfeldia* or *Chenopodium murale*. The CaS of the extensive pastures and Macchie clearings mediate as accessory species between both communities, but can also occupy the entire area between the ways and limiting walls as *Poa bulbosa-Plantago lagopus* assoc., if the trampling and wall foot communities retreat.

Polygonum arenastrum, an east Mediterranean vicariant of *P. aviculare*, occurring in close accompaniment with *Malva nicaeensis*, *Mercurialis annua* and *Euphorbia helioscopia* (*cf.* Table 2, nos. 33–36, and Zohary 1973: 646) characterises nitrogen-rich sites in the settlement, and is attached to the *Chenopodium murale*-wayside community. Similar to *Polygonum aviculare* in Central Europe (*cf.* Bornkamm & Meyer 1977), *Polygonum arenastrum* occupies more polyhemerobic than euhemerobic sites in the area under investigation (*cf.* Sukopp 1972, Blume & Sukopp 1976, Bornkamm 1980). The character species of the extensive pastures are only represented very sporadically outside the central settlement area. Only *Cynodon dactylon* occurs regularly on waysides over almost all the 2nd and 3rd transect. After Oberdorfer (1954b) it can no longer be used as a characteristic Mediterranean species of the trampling community, since it is widespread around the Mediterranean on dry ground and as a companion of nitrophilous communities as well as therophyte flora (*cf.* also Lohmeyer 1975: 134. Raus 1979: 54).

Without *Cynodon dactylon* and *Telephium imperati* (see note to Table 2) the CaS group of the trampling communities are closely restricted to the heavily trodden and eutrophied settlement core. It must also be emphasised that *Polycarpon tetraphyllum* after Lohmeyer (1975: 135) does occur mainly in nitrophilous trampling communities, but that it is frequently a companion of the stony extensive pastures and therophyte stands (Braun-Blanquet *et al.* 1951: 218, Oberdorfer 1954: 91) as well as accessory to the segetal communities (Zohary

1973: 638). The exceptionally high numbers of seedlings of *Polycarpon tetraphyllum* (*cf.* Table 7) in the soil samples of the extensive pasture area suggests that this species is also widely spread on the clearings of the Macchie in the spring.

5.8. Characteristic sites of species of extensive pastures and Macchie remnants on the 2nd and 3rd transects

The extent to which CaS of the extensive pastures and Macchie reach along waysides far into the Nebiler settlement (*cf.* Fig. 5 and Table 2) confirms the wide ecological amplitude of natural vegetation in the area under investigation.

Since the vegetational surveys of Table 2 recorded hardly any Macchie species (but see chapter 5.6 and 5.8), it should be emphasised that even in the very centre of the settlement Macchie remnants, mainly of *Quercus coccifera* are to be found in the corners between houses and sheds and near walls on the field side.

The lianas *Ephedra fragilis* and *Asparagus acutifolius* also occur sporadically throughout the village at or on dry stone walls (field side).

Even species which are only found in the Macchie in a very devastated state, such as *Quercus coccifera* and *Pistacia terebinthus* were found in the village in some cases as tall trees (*cf.* the observations of Schwarz 1936). Thus in the northern section of the 2nd transect there is a larger stand of *Pistacia terebinthus* which is coppiced, and a little way away a 7 m high *Quercus coccifera* tree with dense, hairy-white foliage.

There are clear differences in the site distribution of the Macchie remnants from the periphery to the centre of the settlement. At the outer margin, shrub complexes are spread around the cornfields in a mosaic pattern (*cf.* Figs. 4, 10 and 11) generally characterising piles of stones collected from the field, but the nearer they are to the centre of the settlement the more they are confined to the loose walls around the fields (*cf.* Fig. 11). The species which are most resilient and best able to expand remain pressed up against the walls. The Macchie species originally encountered on both sides of the enclosing walls disappear from the waysides near the village centre, and can only be found sporadically on the field-side of the walls.

The bush complexes of the Macchie remnants also display zoning (*cf.* Fig. 11). Thus the wayside polyhemerobic, trodden and compacted soils are included in a narrow zone of CaS of the trampling communities. This is followed by the heliophyte extensive pasture species in a well developed species spectrum in a more euhemerobic zone, which can reach to the foot of walls or can mediate to bush complexes with the CaS of the border communities.

Scabiosa reuteriana, *Geranium purpureum* var. and *Tordylium aegaeum* are as frequently represented here as outside the settlement. Beneath the bushes themselves are almost all the shade-requiring plants which are recorded together with the shrub complexes of the devastated Macchie. Species spectrum and soil situation here show the transition from euhemerobic to mesohemerobic conditions, as exists in mixed zone B (*cf.* Fig. 10) between extensive pastures and heavily devastated Macchie.

In the shrub and bush complexes of the fields and walls we find repeated on a small scale the hemerobic zoning which occurs on a larger scale for the settlement situation (*cf.* Fig. 5 and the following subsection). The rare untrodden sites, isolated and thus largely undisturbed in the settlement centre are almost as rich in species as complexes with similar habitats in the Macchie. Missing on the whole are the species of the fourth group (see Table 1) which have their centre of distribution in the Macchie or partially also in the border area of the vegetation patches (*cf.* third group of Table 1). Furthermore, only 50% of the species of the *Cistus-Micromeria* communities determined in the Macchie are also represented in the settlement area.

Relative to the area and the proportion of CaS of Macchie, Phrygana (*Cistus-Micromeria* communities) and the extensive pastures the overall species spectrum in the core of the settlement declines rapidly and is dominated by the CaS of the ruderal and segetal communities.

5.9. Evaluation of the vegetation landscape in zones of land-use intensity and hemerobic stages

The importance attached in Chapter 4 to the dimensions proposed by Sukopp (1968/69) of intensity, extent and duration of anthropozoogenous influence for the alteration to ecosystems, is taken into account by the classification of the area under investigation in terms of grades of hemeroby (*cf.* Fig. 5).

In the research area there are essentially two forms of land-use and intensities, which are ordered in zones corresponding to the land-use gradients. The heart of the settlement with some buildings, piles of rubble, waste heaps and small garden allotments is the centre of highest eutrophication with the most intensive use, and characterised by the dominance of the CaS of the *Chenopodium murale* communities (*cf.* Fig. 12, zones A+B). Although durable weed communities are mostly encountered here (*cf.* Blume & Sukopp 1976), the inner settlement area must be classified polyhemerobic, if only because built-up areas, the pathway system with its intermittent trampling communities and the high proportion of hemerochores.

Even if the degree of naturalisation of the ruderal and segetal hemerochores cannot be further evaluated because of the lack of comparative investigations, it could nevertheless be proved that many of the segetal species only occur facultatively, and occur naturally in the original vegetation of the East-Mediterranean.

At its margins, with the adjacent farm land and grazing areas (of extensive pastures) the polyhemerobic settlement centre goes over to an euhemerobic zone (*cf.* Fig. 12, zone C), which is separated by the two major forms of use, dry farming (intensive) and grazing (extensive). The proportion of extensive pasture and Macchie species in the vegetation increase considerably, and the ruderal and segetal species in the mixed zone B (*cf.* Fig. 5) disappear completely in the transition from the eu- to meso-hemerobic zones. Using the distinction between α- and β-euhemerobic stages made by Blume & Sukopp (1976), then the cornfields belong to the α-euhemerobic zone and the well-developed extensive pastures to the β-euhemerobic zone. Ruderal communities are completely absent from the latter zone.

The β-euhemerobic zone is essentially characterised by the high grazing pressure and trampling, which have led to a depletion of species and a negative selection of species in terms of grazing potential. The typical indicator plant for this stage of hemeroby, at least under the pertaining habitat conditions is *Evax eriosphaera*, which occurs massively (*cf.* also Tables 1 and 8). Anthropozoogenous influences almost completely govern the ecosystem of the extensive pastures, so that it is culturally determined as an α-euhemerobic zone.

The structure and floristic composition of the vegetation in the meso-hemerobic zone are largely determined by human activities. Mosaics of bush complexes with *Daphne gnidium* and a high proportion of thero- and hemikryptophytes settling the clearings (*cf.* Tables 1 and 8) indicate the intensity of use. Though the floristic composition of the vegetation in terms of phanerophytes and chamaephytes is not very different from the present-day potential natural vegetation or from the climax plant community, the high level of species indicating degradation and the structural state of the devastated Macchie offer a good measurement criteria for the degree of hemeroby of this vegetation zone, characterised by *Daphne gnidium*.

The mesohemerobic zone, largely determined by cultivation, is succeeded by relatively natural vegetation, which is very close to the presumed natural potential vegetation. The floral composition differs only slightly from the Macchie to be expected under *Pinus brutia* forest. However, there are clear signs throughout this zone of anthropozoogenous influence from grazing and wood-cutting. Although there can only rarely have been any homogeneous vegetation without human influence around Nebiler, the high proportion of indicator species for an extreme stage of degradation and character species of the *Cistus-Micromeria* community are a good indicator of 'cultivation influence'.

5.10. *The importance of the seed bank investigations*

In view of the fact that vegetation surveys were conducted in the late spring in a year when this period was unusually hot and dry, it was essential to gain information about the species in the floral spectrum which may already have died.

From observation of Oberdorfer (1954) and Simonis (1954) about changes to the species spectrum in the course of a vegetation period, together with the investigations by Major & Pyott (1966) and Thompson & Grime (1979) of density and frequency of seed banks of grass and herb communities it seemed advisable to take soil samples for seed bank investigations.

Oberdorfer (1954b) had determined seasonal plant communities on the Balkan peninsula, but the germination tests carried out over a period of 1½ years failed to establish such communities for the area under investigation.

Although an average of 7178 seedlings/m² were found, additional information regarding the dominance of well known species was not found and it was not possible to recognise any really new species combination (*cf.* Table 7). Of the species occurring in the seed bank (*cf.* Table 6) more than 90% belong to the therophytes, and nearly half of these to the CaS of the extensive pastures and Macchie clearings. Among the CaS of the latter group those with the largest numbers of seedlings are mainly species which flower between February and May.

Even though it has not been clarified whether the seeds with the greater tendency to germinate came from the preceding vegetation period (*cf.* Thompson & Grime 1979), it is questionable whether such germination rates would be as high under natural conditions.

Continuous water supply and the absence of any of the disturbance experienced by the extensive pasture species throughout the winter, represent fundamental changes to the conditions under which the seed-bank annuals are competing. The investigations of Simonis (1954) established a close dependence of the large populations in plant communities with many therophytes (Brachypodietum ramosi and *Barbula gracilis-Onobrychis caput galli* assoc.) on the water supply and the resultant ability to compete.

Since, according to Simonis (*ibid.*) a marked decline of annuals tending to mass development at the onset of the dry period can be seen as a measure of vitality and competitive ability, then firstly the growth period of these species (*e.g., Sagina apetala, Galium murale, Arenaria leptoclados, Psilurus incurvus, Veronica arvensis, Capsella rubella* and *Stellaria media*) must be at the start of the year when precipitation is plentiful, and they must also be capable of establishing a permanent seed bank (Schneider & Kehl 1987). Once more it has to be pointed out that before the samples were taken the surface debris was removed (see 4.6) to exclude temporary seed banks, so that all seeds collected must have already been in the soil, or at least just under the surface.

Returning to the mass development of some species, observations from Spring 1980 must also be taken into consideration. The much cooler and wetter April and May meant that many plants started flowering much later. Even eroded areas, completely free of vegetation in 1979, were densely covered in 1980, with *Plantago cretica* or *Pl. lagopus* frequently dominating. Above all *Psilurus incurvus*, found in the seed bank and easily overlooked on the ground, and also *Poa bulbosa* showed a regular distribution in the Macchie clearings, extensive pastures and wayside areas of the settlement. *Sagina apetala, Galium murale, Arenaria leptoclada* and *Gagea bohemica*, frequent in the seed bank investigations, were not found, but in the extensive pastures the circum-Mediterranean geophyte *Ornithogalum umbellatum* was frequent, though not determined in the vegetation survey in early 1979.

Although in the present investigation the species spectra for the 1st and 3rd transects were not changed significantly by the germination tests, these have highlighted many questions of vegetation dynamics. Of the some 10% new species only 2% occurred in more than 5 of the 40 soil samples between relevees nos. 20 and 88. Many species with high population densities in the vegetation surveys could not be determined by the seed-bank investigations. In particular *Cynodon dactylon*, *Hordeum leporinum* and the frequent *Plantago* species, *Pl. cretica* and *Pl. lagopus* or *Evax eriosphaera* would have been expected as seedlings. Whether seeds of these species only belong to the temporary seed bank, or were removed with the surface debris, or merely failed to germinate under the test conditions is unclear. Interestingly, *Poa bulbosa* only grew from bulbs, and no germination from seeds could be determined (*cf.* Sukopp & Scholz 1968).

The floral-geographic assignment of the most common species in the seed bank shows a remarkable similarity of potential distribution. *Gagea bohemica* and *Erophila verna* are elements of pontic steppes of the dry continental climate (Horvat *et al.* 1974); *Sagina apetala* is a middle European geoelement according to Walter & Straka (1970, from Horvath *et al.* ibid.); *Psilurus incurvus* occurs in the sub-Mediterranean areas of the Macedonian steppe (Horvath *et al.*, ibid.), and *Capsella rubella* with *Polycarpon tetraphyllum* are widely distributed in north Mediterranean and middle European plant communities. *Veronica arvensis* also belongs to the middle and south European geoelements. The only purely east Mediterranean species found in the seed bank was *Verbascum leptocladum*, an endemic of the Pamphylian plain (Huber-Morath, correspondence).

In summary, the ability to germinate can be established for sub-Mediterranean, south European and Pontic steppes annual floral elements. However, this statement does not take account of the temporary seed bank, which was not registered, so that important information about the potential species spectrum is missing.

When establishing the seed bank as part of the vegetation, the aspects to be taken into account include the dormancy, the necessary resting periods, germination conditions and quantitative seed production of various populations as survival strategies.

6. Conclusion

After a decline in the intensity of land-use (grazing, coppicing, etc.) around the small settlement of Nebiler it can be assumed that there would be a development to a *Pinus brutia* forest, from which the more heliophile species would disappear step-by-step. The current vegetation, with a degradation sequence corresponding to the impact of the intensity of land-use (*cf.* Table 8) must therefore be seen as the result of a continual influence over space and time (*cf.* 3.1). The occurrence of characteristic species of the *Cistus-Micromeria* communities can function as indicator species for the stages of degradation and the different ability of the described phanerophytes (*Pinus brutia* and Macchie elements) to regenerate, to withstand or to re-establish under grazing pressure, coppicing, etc.

Synecologically the vegetation is in a state of equilibrium, or in an artificial steady state between anthropogenous influence and regeneration potential which would otherwise lead to the formation of a forest (*cf.* Schwarz 1936: 417, Regel 1943: 83, Oberdorfer 1970: 277, Walter 1973: 129, Zohary 1973: 502, Specht 1981: 259).

The high level of species diversity in the degraded margins of the Macchie is a result of the numerous variety of habitats, often covering small areas which have often arisen with the development of mosaic of shrub complexes. This did not lead necessarily to an increase in the biomass suitable for grazing use, since the migration of ecologically more resistant species to extreme habitats such as *Evax erisophaera* to the extensive pastures, was accompanied by a process of negative selection (Zohary 1973: 652, Radke 1976: 411). Extreme xerophytes, avoided by livestock, could spread much more, and had a corresponding advantage over competition (*cf.* Greuter 1975: 162/190, Walter 1956: 271). This is basically true for all those indicator species of an extreme stage of degradation which together with *Daphne gnidium* characterise a species group combination. This also includes *Verbascum leptocladum*, which only infrequently shows bite marks. In order to assess the species spectrum and the high species diversity in relationship to biomass production relevant for grazing, it is necessary to conduct thorough investigations of grazing behaviour, also considering seasonal development of vegetation. Relevant work on the nutritional value of Mediterranean therophyte and chamaephytes and their selection under grazing pressure was not found in the literature.

The concept of hemeroby, introduced by Jallas (1956) and augmented and extended by Sukopp (1969, 1972) and Blume & Sukopp (1976) as a term for the totality of direct and indirect human intervention in and influence on the ecosystem, *i.e.*, as a site factor, can well be used to classify the retrogressive site and vegetation development.

On the other hand the criteria developed for the classification of hemeroby in central and northern Europe cannot be transferred directly to the area under investigation, since the relationship of the extent and the significance of vegetation changes to the intensity and duration of anthropogenic influence depends upon the habitat in question and its vegetation (*cf.* Ellenberg 1954 in Sukopp 1972: 113). As frequently emphasised, a decisive factor for assessing the degree of hemeroby in the area under investigation is the robust nature and regenerative capacity of many Mediterranean species and the more original floral composition of the vegetation. Thus modified assessment criteria are required for determining the changes to the species stand due to neophytes (*cf.* Sukopp *ibid.*) *i.e.*, to plant migration under human influence, and for deducing the significance of the proportion of therophytes in the spectrum of life forms, as well as the significance of soil forming and changing processes at anthropogenously influenced sites.

Acknowledgements

I wish to thank Prof. Dr. H. Sukopp and Dr. W. Lohmeyer for their advise and helpful discussions. I am very grateful to P.H. Davis, I. Hedge, V. Matthews and D.F. Chamberlain for their cooperation and allowance to work in the Herbarium of the Royal Botanic Garden, Edinburgh. I owe many thanks for determination and revision to A.R. Smith, Kew (Euphorbiaceae), A. Huber-Morath, Basel (*Verbascum leptocladum*), H. Demiriz, Istanbul (*Delphinium* spec., *Consolida* spec.), H. Runemark, Lund (*Tordylium* spec., *Bupleurum* spec.), F. Ehrendorfer, Wien (Rubiaceae), H. Scholz, Berlin (Graminae), H.-W. Lack, Berlin (Compositae) and Y. Akman, Ankara. I thank the colleagues of the Forestry Research Institute in Antalya for their cooperation and the Deutscher Akademischer Austauschdienst (DAAD) for the grant which made this investigation possible.

7. List of species

(names and families in brackets [ ] according to Davis 1965–1985)

Amaranthaceae
Amaranthus albus L.
Amaranthus retroflexus L.

Anacardiaceae
Pistacia terebinthus L.
Rhus coriaria L.

Araceae
Arum italicum Mill.
Biarum tenuifolium (L.) Schott

Aristolochiaceae
Aristolochia maurorum L.

Boraginaceae
Echium plantagineum L.
Heliotropium hirsutissimum Grauer
Nonnea pulla (L.) DC
Onosma oreodoxum Boiss.

Campanulaceae
Legousia pentagonia (L.) Thell.

Caryophyllaceae
Arenaria leptoclados (Reichb.) Guss.
Cerastium glomeratum Thuill.
Cerastium semidecandrum L.
Herniaria hirsuta L. var. *hirsuta*
  [*cf.* Illecebracaceae]
Petrorhagia velutina (Guss.) Ball et Heywood
Polycarpon tetraphyllum (L.) L.
Sagina apetala Ard.
Sagina saginoides (L.) Karsten
Silene cappadocica Boiss. et Heldr.
Silene discolor Sibth. et Sm.
Silene kotschyi Boiss.
Siline papillosa Boiss.
Silene vulgaris (Mnch.) Garcker
Stellaria media (L.) Vill.
Telephium imperati L.
Velezia quadritentata Sibt. et Sun.
Velezia rigida L.

Chenopodiaceae
Chenopodium album L.
Chenopodium botrys L.
Chenopodium murale L.
Chenopodium opulifolium Schrad.
Chenopodium vulvaria L.

Cistaceae
Cistus creticus L.
Cistus salviifolius L.
Fumana thymifolia (L.) Verlot. var. *thymifolia*
Tuberaria guttata (L.) Fourr. var. *guttata*

Compositae (Asteraceae)
Anthemis arvensis L.
Anthemis chia L.

Anthemis cretica L.
Anthemis rosea Sm. subsp. *carnea* (Boiss.) Grierson
Asteriscus aquaticus (L.) Less
Atractylis cancellata L.
Calendula arvensis L.
Carthamus lanatus L.
Centaurea solstitialis L.
Cnicus benedictus L.
Evax eriosphaera Boiss. et Heldr.
Filago eriocephala Guss.
Filago pyramidata L.
Matricaria chamomilla L.
Picnomon acarna (L.) Cass.
Senecio vulgaris L.
Xeranthemum annuum L.

Compositae (Cichoriaceae)
Chondrilla juncea L.
Cichorium intybus L.
Crepis dioritica Schott et Ky.
Crepis foetida L. subsp. *communata* (Spreng.) Babcock
Crepis foetida L. subsp. *foetida*
Crepis micrantha Czer.
Crepis sancta (L.) Babcock
Crepis zacintha (L.) Babcock
Hedypnois rhagadioloides (L.) Willd.
      [*Hedypnois cretica* (L.) Dum.-Cours.]
Lactuca serriola L.
Rhagadiolus stellatus (L.) Gärtn.
Scariola viminea (L.) F.W. Schmidt
Steptoramphus tuberosus (Jacq.) Grossh.
Urospermum picroides (L.) F.W. Schmidt

Crassulaceae
Sedum rubens L.

Cruciferae
Alyssum strigosum Banks et Sol. subsp. *strigosum*
Brassica napus L.
Capsella rubella Reuter
Cardamine hirsuta L.
Erophila verna (L.) Chevall.
Hirschfeldia incana (L.) Lag.-Foss.
Iberis taurica DC
Matthiola longipetala (Vent.) DC ssp. *bicornis* (Sib. et Sm.) P.W.B.
Neslia paniculata (L.) Desv.
Raphanus raphanistrum L.
Sinapis arvensis L.
Sisymbrium altissimum L.
Sisymbrium officinale (L.) Scop.

Cuscutaceae
Cuscuta epithymum (L.) L.

Dipsacaceae
Knautia integrifolia (L.) Bert.
Knautia integrifolia (L.) Bert. var. *bidens* (Sm) Borbas
Pterocephalus plumosus (L.) Coulter
Scabiosa reuteriana Boiss.

Ephedraceae
Ephedra fragilis Desf.
  [*Ephedra campylopoda* C.A. Meyer]

Ericaceae
Arbutus ardrachne L.

Euphorbiaceae
Andrachne telephioides L.
Chrozophora tinctoria (L.) Rafin.
Euphorbia exigua L.
Euphorbia falcata L.
Euphorbia helioscopia L.
Euphorbia kotschyana Fenzl
Euphorbia peplis L.
Euphorbia peplus L. var. *peplus*
Euphorbia veneta Willd. var. *sibthorpii* (Boiss.) Hayek
  [*Euphorbia characias* L. subsp. *wulfenii* (Hoppe) A.R. Smith]
Euphorbia taurinensis All.
Mercurialis annua L.

Fagaceae
Quercus ccccifera L.
Quercus infectoria Oliv. subsp. *boisseri* (Reut.) Schwarz

Geraniaceae
Erodium ccutarium (L.) L'Hér.
Erodium hoefftianum C.A. Meyer
Erodium malacoides (L.) l'Hér.
Geranium molle L.
Geranium purpureum Vill.
Geranium pusillum L.

Graminae (determined by H. Scholz)
Aegilops caudata L.
  [*Aegilops markgrafii* (Greuter) Hammer]
Aegilops geniculata Roth.
Aegilops ovata L.
Aegilops triuncialis L.
Aira caryophyllea L.
Avena clauda Dur.
Brachypodium distachyon (L.) P.B.
  [*Trachynia distachya* (L.) Link]

Brachypodium sylvaticum (Huds.) P.B. subsp. glaucovirens Murb.
Briza maxima L.
Bromus intermedius Guss.
Bromus madritensis L.
Catapodium rigidum (L.) C.E. Hubb.
Cynodon dactylon (L.) Pers.
Cynosurus echinatus L.
Dactylis hispanica Roth.
   [*Dactylis glomerata* L. subsp. *hispanica* (Roth.) Nyman]
Echinaria capitata (L.) Desf.
Eremopoa attalica H. Scholz
Eremopoa persica (Trin.) Roshev.
Gastridium phleoides (Nees et Mey.) C.E. Hubb.
Hordeum leporinum Link.
   [*Hordeum murinum* L. var. *leporinum*]
Hyparrhenia hirta (L.) Stapf.
Lagurus ovatus L.
Lolium rigidum Gaud. var. *rottbollioides* Heldr.
Lophochloa obtusiflora (Boiss.) Gontsch.
   [*Rostraria obtusiflora* (Boiss.) Holub]
Lophochloa phleoides (Vill.) Reichenb.
   [absent in Flora of Turkey]
Melica magnolii Gr. et Godr.
   [*Melica ciliata* L. subsp. *magnolii* (Gren. et Godr.) Husnot]
Oryzopsis miliacea (L.) Bentham et Hooker
   [*Piptatherum miliaceum* (L.) Cosson subsp. *miliaceum*]
Phleum exaratum Hochst.
Phleum subulatum (Savi) A. et Gr.
Piptatherum coerulescens (Desf.) P. Beauv.
Poa bulbosa L.
Poa infirma H.B.K.
Psilurus incurvus (Gouan) Schinz. et Thell.
Stipa bromoides (L.) Dörfler

Hypericaceae
   [*cf. Guttiferae*]
Hypericum triquetrifolium Turra

Labiatae
Ajuga chamaepitys (L.) Schreb. subsp. *chia* (Schreber) Arcangeli
Lamium purpureum L.
Marrubium vulgare L.
Micromeria myrtifolia Boiss. et Hohen.
Origanum onites L.
Phlomis grandiflora H.S. Thompson
Phlomis lycia D. Don.
Salvia dichroantha Stapf
Salvia horminum L.
   [*Salvia viridis* L. var. *horminum* (L.) Batt. et Trab.]
Salvia verbenaca L.
Salvia viridis L.
Satureja thymbra L.

Sideritis condensata Boiss. et Heldr.
Sideritis curvidens Stapf
Sideritis montana L. subsp. *remota* (d'Urf.) P.W.B.
Stachys cretica L.
Teucrium chamaedrys L. subsp. *lydium* O. Schw.
Teucrium divaricatum Sieber
Teucrium polium L.
Thymbra spicata L.
Thymus revolutus Celak.

Leguminosae (Caesalpiniaceae)
Ceratonia siliqua L.

Leguminosae (Fabaceae)
Astragalus hamosus L.
Astragalus suberosus Banks et Sol. subsp.
Biserrula pelecinus L.
Calicotome villosa (Poiret) Link
Coronilla scorpiodes (L.) Koch
Hippocrepis ciliata Willd.
Hymenocarpus circinnatus (L.) Savi.
Lathyrus aphaca L. var. *modestus* P.H. Davis
Lathyrus cicera L.
Lens ervoiaes (Brign.) Grande
Medicago circinnata L.
    [ident. with *Hymenocarpus circinnatus* (L.) Savi]
Medicago constricta Durieu
Medicago coronata (L.) Bart.
Medicago disciformis DC
Medicago granadensis Willd.
Medicago littoralis Rohde var. *littoralis*
Medicago minima (L.) Grufbg.
Medicago muricata Benth.
    [*Medicago doliata* Carmign. var. *muricata* (Benth.) Heyn]
Medicago orbicularis (L.) Bartal.
Medicago polymorpha L.
Medicago rigidula (L.) All. var.
Medicago turbinata (L.) All. var. *chiotica* Urb.
Onobrychis caput-galli (L.) Lam.
Ononis pubescens L.
Ononis spinosa L.
Onosis viscosa L.
Ornithopus compressus L.
Ornithopus sativus Brot. subsp. *sativus*
Physanthyllis tetraphylla (L.) Boiss.
    [*Anthyllis tetraphylla* L.]
Scorpiurus muricatus L.
Trifolium angustifolium L.
Trifolium campestre Schreb.
Trifolium echinatum M.B.
Trifolium glanduliferum Boiss.
Trifolium globosum L.

Trifolium lappaceum L.
Trifolium pamphylicum Boiss. et Heldr.
 [*Tr. purpureum* Lois. var. *pamphylicum* (Boiss. et Heldr.) Zoh.]
Trifolium pauciflorum d'Urf.
Trifolium physodes Stev. var. *physodes*
Trifolium resupinatum L. var. *resupinatum*
Trifolium scabrum L.
Trifolium scutatum Boiss.
Trifolium spumosum L.
Trifolium stellatum L.
Trifolium tomentosum L.
Trigonella caerulea (L.) Ser.
 [found in the seedbank]
Trigonella carica Hub.-Mor.
Trigonella cariensis Boiss.
Trigonella kotschyi Fenzl
Trigonella monspeliaca L.
Trigonella spicata Sibth. et Sm.
Vicia pubescens (DC) Link.

Liliaceae
Allium callimischon Link subsp.
Asparagus acutifolius L.
Asphodelus microcarpus Salz. et Viv.
 [*Asphodelus aestivus* Brot.]
Gagea bohemica (Zauschner) Schultes et Schultes fil.
Muscari comosum (L.) Mill.
Ornithogalum umbellatum L.
Ruscus aculeatus L.
Smilax aspera L.
Smilax excelsa L.
Urginea maritima (L.) Baker

Linaceae
Linum strictum L.
Linum strictum L. subsp. *corymbulosum* (Reichb.) Rouy
 [*Linum corymbulosum* Reichb.]

Malvaceae
Althea dissecta Baker
 [*Alcea dissecta* (Baker) Zoh.]
Althea hirsuta L.
Malva nicaeensis All.
Malva parviflora L.
Malva pusilla Sm.
Malva sylvestris L.

Myrtaceae
Myrtus communis L.

Oleaceae
Fraxinus angustifolia Vahl subsp. *angustifolia*

Jasminum fruticans L.
Olea europæa L. var. *oleaster* (Hoffmanns. et Link) DC
  [*Olea eurcpaea* L. var. *sylvestris* (Miller) Lehr.]
Phillyrea latifolia L.

Orchidaceae
Ophrys sphegodes Miller subsp.

Orobanchaceae
Orobanche crenata Forsskål.

Papaveraceae
Fumaria parviflora Lam.
Papaver dubium L.
Papaver rhoeas L.
Roemeria hybrida (L.) DC subsp. *hybrida*

Pinaceae
Pinus brutia Te.

Plantaginaceae
Plantago arenaria W. et K.
  [*Plantago scabra* Moench]
Plantago coronopus L.
Plantago cretica L.
Plantago lagopus L.
Plantago lanceolata L.

Plumbaginaceae
Plumbago europaea L.

Polygonaceae
Polygonum arenastrum Bor.
Rumex pulcher L. subsp. *divaricatus* (L.) Arc.
  [*Rumex pulcher* L.]

Polypodiaceae
Asplenium ceterach L.
  [*Ceterach officinarum* DC]
Cheilanthes pteridioides (Reichb.) C. Chr.
  [*Cheilanthes fragrans* (L. fil.) Sw.]

Portulacaceae
Portulaca oleracea L.

Primulaceae
Anagallis arvensis L.
Anagallis foemina Mill.
Asterolinon linum-stellatum (L.) Duby
  [*Lysimachia linum-stellatum* L.]

Rafflesiaceae
Cytinus hypocistis (L.) L.

Ranunculaceae
Clematis cirrhosa L.
Consolida hellespontica (Boiss.) Chater
Consolida orientalis (Gay) Schrödinger
Delphinium peregrinum L.
Delphinium virgatum Poiret
Nigella arvensis L. subsp. *glauca* (Boiss.) Terracc.
Ranunculus muricatus L.

Rhamnaceae
Rhamnus oleoides L.

Rosaceae
Crataegus monogyna L. subsp.
Sanguisorba minor Scop. subsp. *muricata* (Spach) Briq.
Sarcopoterium spinosum (L.) Spach

Rubiaceae
Crucianella latifolia L.
Galium divaricatum Pourr. ex Lam.
Galium floribundum Sm.
Galium murale (L.) All.
Galium tenuissimum Bieb.
Galium tricornutum Dandy
Rubia peregrina L.
Sherardia arvensis L.
Valantia hispida L.
Valantia muralis L.

Rutaceae
Haplophyllum thesioides (Fisch.) G. Don.

Santalaceae
Osyris alba L.

Scrophulariaceae
Antirrhinum orontium L.
  [*Misopates orontium* (L.) Raffin.]
Linaria chalepensis (L.) Mill. var.
Scrophularia canina L. subsp. *bicolor* (Sibth. et Sm.) W. Greuter
Scrophularia peregrina L.
Scrophularia xanthoglossa Boiss.
Verbascum leptocladum Boiss. et Heldr.
Verbascum sinuatum L.
Verbascum undulatum Lam.
Veronica arvensis L.

Selaginellaceae
Selaginella denticulata (L.) Link

Solanaceae
Lycopersicon esculentum Miller
Solanum nigrum L.

Styracaceae
Styrax officinalis L.

Thymeleaceae
Daphne gnidium L.
Daphne sericea Vahl.
Thymelaea passerina (L.) Coss. et Germ.

Umbelliferae
Anthriscus caucalis M.B.
Artedia squamata L.
Bunium ferulaceum Sm.
Bupleurum croceum Fenzl
Bupleurum subovatum Link. ex Spreng.
  [*Bupleurum intermedium* Poiret]
Bupleurum sulphureum Boiss. et Bal.
Daucus guttatus Sm.
Eryngium creticum Lam.
Eryngium falcatum Delar.
Falcaria vulgaris Bernh.
Lagoecia cuminoides L.
Peucedanum chryseum (Boiss. et Heldr.) Chamberlain
Scaligeria napiformis (Sprengel) Grande
Scandix pecten-veneris L.
Tordylium aegaeum Run.
Tordylium apulum L.
Torilis leptophylla (L.) Reichenb.
Torilis nodosa (L.) Gärtn.
Torilis triradiata Boiss. et Heldr.

Urticaceae
Parietaria lusitanica L.
Urtica urens L.

Valerianaceae
Valerianella muricata (Stev.) W. Baxt.
Valerianella orientalis (Schlecht.) Boiss. et Bal.
Valerianella vesicaria (L.) Moench

Verbenaceae
Verbene officinalis L.

Zygophyllaceae
Peganum harmala L.
Tribulus terrestris L.

References

Adamovic, L. 1929. Die Pflanzenwelt der Adrialänder. Gustav Fischer Verlag, Jena.
Ahti, T. & Hämit-Ahti, L. 1971. Hemerophilous flora of the Kuusamo district, northeast Finland, and the adjacent part of its origin. Ann. Bot. Fennici 8: 1–91.
Amir, S. & Sarig, G. 1976. Planning the multiple use of maqui land. Center for Urban and Regional Studies,

Technion Institute for Research and Development. Technion – Israel, Institute of Technology, Haifa, Working papers, curs. wp, 68.

Barkman, J.J. 1968. Das synsystematische Problem der Mikrogesellschaften innerhalb der Biozönosen. In: Tüxen, R. (ed.), Pflanzensoziologische Systematik, pp. 21–53, Ber. Int. Symp. Stolzenau/Weser (1964).

Biju-Duval, B. & Montadert, L. 1977. Structure and evolution of the Mediterranean Sea basin. Initial Rep. DSDP, XXXXII, Washington.

Blume, H.P. & Sukopp, H. 1976. Ökologische Bedeutung anthropogener Bodenveränderungen. Schr. Reihe Vegetationskunde 10: 74–89.

Bornkamm, R. 1980. Hemerobie und Landschaftsplanung. Landschaft und Stadt 12(2): 49–55.

Bornkamm, R. 1961. Zur quantitativen Bestimmung von Konkurrenzkraft und Wettbewerbsspannung. Ber. Dtsch. Bot. Gesellschaft 74: 75–83.

Bornkamm, R. & Meyer, G. 1977. Ökologische Untersuchungen an Pflanzengemeinschaften unterschiedlicher Trittbelastung mit Hilfe der Gradientenanalyse. Mitt. flor.-soz. Arbeitsgemeinschaft N.F. 19/20: 225–240.

Braun-Blanquet, J. 1964. Pflanzensoziologie. (3. Auflage) Springer Verlag, Wien-New York.

Braun-Blanquet, J. 1936. La Chênaie d'Yeuse méditerranéenne (Quercion ilicic). Comm. S.I.G.M.A. 45.

Brun-Hool, J. 1966. Ackerunkraut-Fragmentgesellschaften. In: Tüxen, R. (ed.), Anthropogene Vegetation, pp. 38–50, Ber. Int. Symp. Stolzenau/Weser (1961).

Christiansen-Weniger, F. 1970. Ackerbauformen im Mittelmeerraum und Nahen Osten, dargestellt am Beispiel der Türkei. DLG-Verlag, Frankfurt/Main.

Christiansen-Weniger, F. 1962. Vordringliche Probleme der türkischen Landwirtschaft. Zeitschrift f. Kulturaustausch, Jg. 12, Heft 2–3.

Dafis, S. & Landolt, E. (eds.) 1976. Mazedonien, Thessalien-Epirus, Attika, Peloponnes. Einzelne Pflanzengesellschaften, Systematik einzelner Pflanzengruppen, botanische Literatur über Griechenland. Veröff. Geobot. Inst. der ETH Zürich, Stiftung Rübel, Heft 56.

Dafis, S. & Landolt, E. (eds.) 1975. Zur Vegetation und Flora von Griechenland. Ergebnisse der 15. Internationalen Pflanzengeographischen Excursion (IPE) durch Griechenland 1971 und Ägäische Inseln 1975. Veröff. Geobot. Inst. der ETH Zürich, Stiftung Rübel, Heft 55.

Darkot, B. & Erinc, E. 1951. Aksu batisinda Antalya traverten taracalari (Terrasses de travertin d'Antalya à l'W de l'Aksu). Istanbul Univ. Cografya Enst. derg. I(2): 56–65.

Davis, P.H. (ed.) 1965–1985. Flora of Turkey and the East Aegean Islands. University Press, Edinburgh.

Ellenberg, H. 1956. Aufgaben und Methoden der Vegetationskunde. In: Walter, H. (ed.), Einführung in die Phytologie, IV (1). Verlag E. Ulmer, Stuttgart.

Faruqi, S.A. 1980. Studies on Libyan grasses VI. An annotated catalogue and key to the species. Willdenowia 10: 171–225.

Fay, F., Long, G. & Trabaud, L. 1979. Evolution de la masse végétale en milieu de Garrigue soumise à diverses interventions humaines. In: Tüxen, R. & Sommer (eds.), Gesellschaftsentwicklung (Syndynamik), pp. 125–131, Ber. Int. Symp. Rinteln (1967).

Ganssen, R. 1972. Bodengeographie (2. Aufl.). Verlag K.F. Köhler, Stuttgart.

Ganssen, R. 1968. Trockengebiete, Böden, Bodennutzung, Bodenkultivierung, Bodengefährdung. Mannheim.

Godron, M., Guillerm, J.L., Poissonet, P., Thiault & Trabaut, L. 1981. Dynamics and management of vegetation. In: di Castri Goodall, W. & Specht, R.L. (eds.), Mediterranean-type shrublands. Ecosystems of the World, Vol. 11, Chapter 19.

Goodall, W. 1973. Sample similarity and species correlation. In: Whittaker, R.H. (ed.), Handbook of vegetation science, Vol. 5, pp. 104–156, Dr. W. Junk Publ., The Hague.

Goodall, W. 1963. The continuum and the individualistic association. Vegetatio 11: 297–316.

Greuter, W. 1975a. Die Insel Kreta – Eine geobotanische Skizze. Veröff. Geobot. Inst. ETH Zürich, Stiftung Rübel, Heft 55: 141–197.

Greuter, W. 1975b. Historical phytogeography of the southern half of the Aegean area. In: Problems of Balkan flora and vegetation, Chapter 1, pp. 17–21, Proceedings of the 1st Intern. Symp. of Balkan Flora and Vegetation, Varna, June 7–14, 1973.

Hempel, L. 1983. Klimaveränderungen im Mittelmeerraum – Ansätze und Ergebnisse geowissenschaftlicher Forschungen. Universitas, Jg. 38: 873–885.

Hempel, L. 1981. Mensch und/oder Klima – Neue physiogeographische Beobachtungen über das Lebens- und Landwirtschaftsbild Griechenlands seit der Eiszeit. Hellenika, Jahrbuch 1981, 61–67.

Heyn, C.C. 1971. Biosystematic approaches to the solution of taxonomic problems in Israel. In: Davis, P.H., Harper & Hedge, n. (eds.), Plant life of south-west Asia, pp. 181–193, Bot. Soc., Edinburgh.

Horvat, I., Glavac, V. & Ellenberg, H. 1974. Vegetation Südosteuropas. Gustav Fischer Verlag, Stuttgart.

Houerou, H.N. Le 1981. Impact of man and his animals on Mediterranean vegetation. In: di Castri Goodall, W. & Specht, R.L. (eds.), Mediterranean-type shrublands, Ecosystems of the World, Vol. 11, Chapter 25.

IUFRO. 1975. Waldbau und Umwelt, Waldverjüngung, bzw. Naturverjüngung. Abt. 1, Exkursions-Gruppe A, 24.–28. Sept. 1975, Türkei.

Jahn, G. 1970. Studien zur Höhengliederung einer südwestanatolischen Gebirgslandschaft. Giessener Geograph. Schr., Heft 18.

Kehl, H. 1985. Zur mediterranen Flora und Vegetation der SW-Türkei und Problematik der Vegetationsentwicklung am Beispiel einer küstennahen Siedlung bei Antalya. Diss. an der Technischen Universität Berlin.

Klinge, H. 1958. Eine Stellungnahme zur Altersfrage von Terra-Rossa-Vorkommen, under Berücksichtigung der Iberischen Halbinsel, der Balearischen Inseln und Marokkos. Zeitschr. für Pflanzenernährung, Düngung und Bodenkunde 81: 56–63.

Knapp, R. 1971. Einführung in die Pflanzensoziologie. Verlag E. Ulmer, Stuttgart.

Knapp, R. 1965. Die Vegetation von Kephallinia, Griechenland. Verlag Otto Koeltz, Königstein.

Köppen, W. 1931. Grundriß der Klimakunde. Leipzig-Berlin.

Kojic, M. 1976. Über die syntaxonomische Gliederung segetaler Pflanzengesellschaften vom ökologischen und ökophysiologischen Standpunkt. Ber. Dtsch. Bot. Ges. 89: 392–399.

Kündig-Steiner, W. 1974. Die Türkei – Raum und Mensch, Kultur und Wirtschaft in Gegenwart und Vergangenheit. Horst Erdmann Verlag, Tübingen-Basel.

Lauer, W. 1952. Humide and aride Jahreszeiten in Afrika und Südamerika und ihre Beziehung zu den Vegetationsgürteln. Bonner Geograph. Abh. 9: 15–98.

Lavrentiades, G.J. 1969. Studies on the flora and vegetation of the Ormos Archangelou in Rhodos Island. Vegetatio 19: 309–329.

Leeuwen, C.G. van 1979. Raum-Zeitliche Beziehungen in der Vegetation. In: Tüxen, R. (ed.), Gesellschaftsmorphologie, pp. 63–68, Ber. Int. Symp. Rinteln (1966).

Leeuwen, C.G. van 1966. A relation theoretical approach to pattern and process in vegetation. Wentia 15: 25–46.

Leeuwen, C.G. van 1965. Het verband tussen natuurlijke en anthropogene landschapsvormen, bezien vanuit de betrekkingen in grensmilieus. Gorteria 2: 93–105.

Lohmeyer, W. 1975. Über einige nitrophile Unkrautgesellschaften der Insel Gran Canaria. Schr. Reihe f. Vegetationskunde, Heft 8: 111–180.

Lohmeyer, W. & Trautmann, W. 1970. Zur Kenntnis der Vegetation der kanarischen Insel La Palma. Schr. Reihe f. Vegetationskunde 5: 209–236.

Lundegardh, H. 1949. Klima und Boden in ihrer Wirkung auf das Pflanzenleben. Verlag von Gustav Fischer, Jena.

Maarel, E. van der 1976. On the establishment of plant community boundaries. Ber. Deutsch. Bot. Ges. 89: 415–443.

Major, J. & Pyott, W.T. 1966. Buried viable seeds in two California bunchgrass sites and their bearing on the definition of flora. Vegetatio 13: 253–282.

Margaris, N.S. & Vokou, D. 1982. Structural and physiological features of woody plants in phryganic ecosystems related to adaptive ecosystems. Ecologia mediterranea, Tome VIII, Fascicule 1/2: 449–459.

Markgraf, F. 1958. Waldstufen im Westtaurus. Veröff. Geobot. Inst. ETH Zürich, Stift. Rübel, Heft 33: 154–164.

Martonne, E. de 1962. Traité de géographie phytique. Paris.

Meteoroloji Bülteni, Ankara 1962, 1967.

Meteoroloji Report, Antalya 1966.

Meyer, F.H. 1967/68. Baum- und Strauchvegetation Anatoliens. Mitt. der Deutschen Dendrologischen Gesell. 63: 38–53.

Naveh, Z. 1975. Degradation and rehabilitation of Mediterranean landscapes. (Neotechnological degradation of Mediterranean landscapes and their restoration with drought resistant plants.) Landscapes Planning 2: 133–146.

Naveh, Z. & Whittaker, R.H. 1979. Structural and floristic diversity of shrublands and woodlands in northern Israel and other Mediterranean areas. Vegetatio 41: 171–190.

Noy-Meir, I. & Whittaker, R.H. 1977. Continuous multivariate methods in community analysis, some problems and developments. Vegetatio 33: 79–88.

Oakes, H. 1954. The soils of Turkey. Ankara.

Oberdorfer, E. 1954a. Nordaegaeische Kraut- und Zwergstrauchfluren im Vergleich mit den entsprechenden Vegetationseinheiten des westlichen Mittelmeergebietes. Vegetatio 5/6: 88–96.

Oberdorfer, E. 1954b. Über Unkrautgesellschaften der Balkanhalbinsel. Vegetatio 4: 379–411.

Oberdorfer, E. 1965. Pflanzensoziologische Studien auf Teneriffa und Gomera (kanarische Inseln). Beitr. naturk. Forsch. S-W-Deutschl. 24: 47–104.

Orshan, G. 1964. Seasonal dimorphism of desert and Mediterranean chamaephytes and its significance as a factor in their water economy. In: Ruttel, n. & Whitehead, n. (eds.), The water relations in plants. Blackwell, Edinburgh.

Özbey, S. 1960/61. Antalya area lithostratigraphic section. Geologic map of the Antalya area. Rapport of the Turkish GULF-OIL-Company.

Pazarkaya, Y. 1974. Die osmanische Geschichte. In: Kündig-Steiner, W. (ed.), Die Türkei, pp. 335–355, Horst Erdmann Verlag, Tübingen-Basel.

Pfannenstiel, M. 1952. Das Quartär in der Levante. 1 – Die Küste Syriens. Akad. d. Wissensch. u. d. Lit., Abh. der math. Klasse, 7.

Pfannenstiel, M. 1953. Die pleistozänen, klimatisch bedingten Spiegelschwankungen des Mittelmeeres und des Schwarzen Meeres. Zeitschr. Dtsch. Geol. Ges., Band 105.

Planhol, X. de 1956. Contribution à l'étude géomorphologique du Taurus occidental et des plaines bordières. Rev. Géogr. Alpine 54(4): 1–86.

Poisson, A. 1977. Recherches Géologiques dans les Taurides Occidentales (Turquie). Orsay No. d'Ordre 1902, Thèse presentée à l'Université de Paris-Sud (Centre d'Orsay) pour obtenir le grade de Docteur en Sciences.

Poissonet, P., Romane, F., Thiault, M. & Trabaud, L. 1978. Evolution d'une Garrigue de Quercus coccifera L. soumise à divers traitements: quelques résultats des cinq premières annéees. Vegetatio 38: 135–142.

Polunin, O. 1977. Pflanzen Europas. BLV Verlagsgesellschaft, München.

Polunin, O. 1980. Flowers of Greece and the Balkans – A field guide. University Press, Oxford.

Quezel, P. 1981. Floristic composition and phytosociological structure of sclerophyllous matorral around the Mediterranean. In: di Castri, Goodall, W. & Specht, R.L. (eds.), Mediterranean-type shrublands. Ecosystems of the World, Vol. 11, Chapter 6.

Radke, G.J. 1976. Ökologische Grenzen zwischen Pflanzengesellschaften als Ausdruck einer hierarchischen Ordnung der Landschaftsfaktoren für eine optimale Dokumentation der Landschaftsökologie, dargestellt an den natürlichen Gegebenheiten des mitteleuropäischen Gebirgsraumes. Ber. Dtsch. Bot. Ges. 89: 401–414.

Ramensky, L.G. 1926. Die Grundgesetzmäßigkeiten im Aufbau der Vegetationsdecke. Bot. Zbl., N.F. 7: 453–455.

Ramensky, L.G. 1930. Zur Methodik der vergleichenden Bearbeitung und Ordnung von Pflanzenlisten und anderen Objekten, die durch mehrere, verschiedenartig wirkende Faktoren bestimmt werden. Beitr. Biol. Pfl. 18: 269–304.

Ramensky, L.G. 1932. Die Projektionsaufnahme und Beschreibung der Pflanzendecke. Handb. Biol. Arb. Meth. 11(6): 137–190.

Rauh, W. 1975. Morphologische Beobachtungen an Dornsträuchern des Mediterrangebietes. Colloq. C.N.R.S. 235: 261–271.

Raus, T. 1979a. Die Vegetation Ostthessaliens (Griechenland), I. Vegetationszonen und Höhenstufen. Bot. Jahrb. Syst. 100(4): 564–604.

Raus, T. 1979b. Die Vegetation Ostthessaliens (Griechenland), II. Quercetea ilicic und Cisto-Micromerietea. Bot. Jahrb. Syst. 101(1): 17–82.

Rechinger, K.H. 1950. Grundzüge der Pflanzenverbreitung in der Aegaeis. Vegetatio 2: 55–119, 239–308, 365–386.

Regel, C. 1943. Pflanzengeographische Studien aus Griechenland und Westanatolien. Bot. Jahrb. 73.

Rikli, M. 1943–1948. Das Pflanzenkleid der Mittelmeerländer. (3 Vol.), Verlag Hans Huber, Bern.

Rübel, E. 1930. Pflanzengesellschaften der Erde. Verlag Hans Huber, Bern.

Schmidt, J. 1969. Vegetationsgeographie auf ökologisch-soziologischer Grundlage. G. Teubner Verlagsgesellschaft, Leipzig.

Schneider, U. & Kehl, H. 1987. Samenbank und Vegetationsaufnahmen ostmediterraner Therophytenfluren im Vergleich. Flora 179: 345–354.

Schroeder, D. 1978. Bodenkunde in Stichworten. Verlag Ferdinand Hirt, Kiel.

Schuster, H.-J. Analyse und Bewertung von Pflanzengesellschaften im nördlichen Frankenjura – Ein Beitrag zum Problem der Quantifizierung unterschiedlich anthropogen beeinflußter Ökosysteme. Diss. an der Technischen Universität, Berlin.

Schwarz, O. 1936. Die Vegetationsverhältnisse Westanatoliens. Bot. Jahrb. 67: 297–436.

Simonis, W. 1954. Beobachtungen zur Ökologie einiger Therophyten in zwei mediterranen Pflanzengesellschaften. Vegetatio 5/6: 553–561.

Sobolev, L.N. & Utekhin, V.D. 1982. Russian (Ramensky) approaches to community systematization. In: Whittaker, R.H. (ed.), Ordination of plant communities, Dr. W. Junk Publ., The Hague-Boston-London.

Spatz, G. 1975. Die direkte Gradienten-Analyse in der Vegetationskunde. Angew. Bot. 49: 209–221.

Specht, R.L. 1981. Primary production in mediterranean climate ecosystems regenerating after fire. In: di Castri, Goodall, W. & Specht, R.L. (eds.), Mediterranean-type shrublands. Ecosystems of the World, Vol. 11, Chapter 11.

Steiner, W. 1979. Der Travertin von Ehringsdorf und seine Fossilien. Die Neue Brehm Bücherei, Band 522.

Sukopp, H. 1968. Der Einfluß des Menschen auf die Vegetation und zur Terminologie anthropogener Vegetationstypen. In: Tüxen, R. (ed.), Pflanzensoziologie und Landschaftsökologie. Ber. Int. Symp. Stolzenau/Weser (1963), 65–74.

Sukopp, H. 1969. Der Einfluß des Menschen auf die Vegetation. Vegetatio 17: 360–371.

Sukopp, H. 1972. Wandel von Flora und Vegetation in Mitteleuropa unter dem Einfluß des Menschen. Ber. über Landwirtschaft Bd. 50, Heft 1: 112–139.

Sukopp, H. & Scholz, H. 1968. Poa bulbosa L. ein Archäophyt der Flora Mitteleuropas. Flora, Abt. B, Bd. 157: 494–526.

Sweeting, M.M. 1972. Karst landforms. Mac Millan Press, London.

Thompson, K. & Grime, 1979. Seasonal variation in the seed banks of herbaceous species in ten contrasting habitats. J. Ecol. 67: 893–921.

Thornwaite, C.-W. 1948. An approach towards a rational classification of climate. Geogr. Rev. 38: 55–94.

Turrill, W.B. 1937. On the flora of the Nearer East. Kew Bull. 79.

Tüxen, R. 1956. Die heutige potentielle natürliche Vegetation als Gegenstand der Vegetationskartierung. Angew. Pflanzensoziologie (Stolzenau) 13: 5–42.

UNESCO-FAO 1963. Bioclimatic map of the Mediterranean zone – explanatory notes. Arid Zone Research, XXI.

Wagner, H. 1972. Zur Methodik der Erstellung und Auswertung von Vegetationstabellen. In: Tüxen, R. (ed.), Grundfragen und Methoden der Pflanzensoziologie, pp. 225–237, Ber. Int. Symp. Rinteln (1970).

Walter, H. 1956. Die heutige ökologische Problemstellung und der Wettbewerb mediterraner Hartlaubvegetation und den sommergrünen Laubwäldern. Ber. Dtsch. Bot. Ges. 69: 263–273.

Walter, H. 1968. Die Vegetation der Erde (Band 2). VEB Gustav Fischer Verlag, Jena.

Walter, H. 1973. Vegetationszonen und Klima. Verlag Eugen Ulmer (UTB 14), Stuttgart.

Walter, H. 1975. Betrachtungen zur Höhenstufenfolge im Mediterrangebiet (insbesondere in Griechenland) mit dem Wettbewerbsfaktor. In: Dafis, S. & Landolt, E. (eds.), Zur Vegetation und Flora von Griechenland, Heft 55: 72–83.

Walter, H. & Breckle, S.-W. 1983. Ökologie der Erde – Ökologische Grundlagen in globaler Sicht (Band 1, UTB, Grosse Reihe). Gustav Fischer Verlag, Stuttgart.

Walter, H. & Straka, H. 1970. Arealkunde – Floristisch historische Geobotanik – Einführung in die Phytologie (Band 3, Teil 2). Verlag Eugen Ulmer, Stuttgart.

Walter, H. & Lieth, H. 1960. Klimadiagramm – Weltatlas. VEB Gustav Fischer Verlag, Jena.

Westhoff, V. & van Leeuwen, C.G. 1966. Ökologische und systematische Beziehungen zwischen natürlichen und anthropogenen Vegetationen. In: Tüxen, R. (ed.), Anthropogene Vegetation, pp. 156–172, Ber. Int. Symp. Stolzenau/Weser (1961).

Whittaker, R.H. 1967. Gradient analysis of vegetation. Biol. Rev. 42: 207–264.

Whittaker, R.H. 1970. The population structure of vegetation. In: Tüxen, R. (ed.), Gesellschaftsmorphologie, pp. 39–62, Ber. Int. Symp. Rinteln (1966).

Whittaker, R.H. 1973. Handbook of vegetation science (Vol. 5). Dr. W. Junk Publ., The Hague.

Whittaker, R.H. 1982. Ordination of plant communities. Dr. W. Junk Publ., The Hague-Boston-London.

Wilbrandt, H 1974. Landwirtschaft. In: Kündig-Steiner, W. (ed.), Die Türkei, pp. 475–541, Horst Erdmann Verlag, Tübingen-Basel.

Willems, J.H. 1983. The seed bank as a part of the vegetation. Acta Bot. Neerl. 32: 243.

Wilmanns, O. 1973. Ökologische Pflanzensoziologie (UTB 269). Verlag Quelle und Meyer, Heidelberg.

Wippern, J. 1962. Die Bauxite des Taurus und ihre tektonische Stellung. Bull. Min. Res. Expl. Inst. (Turkey) 58: 47–70.

Wraber, M. 1952. Zum Wasserhaushalt von Quercus coccifera. Vegetatio 3: 266–278.

Zech, W. & Cepel, N. 1972. Beziehungen zwischen Boden- und Reliefeigenschaften und der Wuchsleistung von Pinus brutia Beständen in Südanatolien. Istanbul Universitesi, Orman Fakultesi, Yayinlari, No. 1753, Yayin No 191.

Zohary, M. (ed.) 1966. Flora Palaestina, Vol. 1 (text). The Israel Academy of Sciences and Humanities, Jerusalem.

Zohary, D. 1971. Origin of south-west cereals: wheats, barley, oats and rye. In: Davis, Harper, & Hedge, (eds.), Plant life of south-west Asia, pp. 235–263, Bot. Soc., Edinburgh.

Zohary, M. 1973. Geobotanical foundations of the Middle East, 2 Vol. Gustav Fischer Verlag, Stuttgart.

FLORA AND VEGETATION OF VARIOUS TYPES OF SETTLEMENTS IN THE CZECH REPUBLIC: A CONCISE COMPARISON

ANTONÍN PYŠEK[1] AND SLAVOMIL HEJNÝ[2]
[1] Husova 342, CZ-439 82 Vroutek, Czech Republic;
[2] Botanical Institute, Academy of Sciences of Czech Republic, CZ-252 43 Průhonice, Czech Republic

Abstract

In the present study basic units of human settlement as found in Czech Republic are characterized. Their structural hierarchy is explained from the viewpoint of quantitative floristics and phytosociology.

1. Introduction

Much attention has been paid to settlement flora and vegetation during the last 80 years (Sukopp 1982, Sukopp & Werner 1983, Hale 1987, Kowarik 1988, Sudnik-Wójcikowska 1988). Various types of settlements ranging from villages to urban centres, including great industrial cities, have been studied. History and development of settlement ecology have been only partly described (Hejný 1971, Sukopp et al., 1990). Although some attempts were made (see Pyšek, this volume, for a review) a complex phytosociological synthesis is still missing, partly due to the absence of sufficient data from various regions. This paper summarizes some results of research in this field.

2. Methods and definition of terms

Data used for analyses come from central European settlement units located in western, southern and northern districts of the Czech republic.

The term settlement unit is used for a spatial and socioeconomical unit (Hejný 1973). The smallest unit is represented by a lonely house, inhabited only seasonally and surrounded by natural rather than cultivated landscape. It 'grows in' with rural or forest landscape.

A recreation settlement is a group of very small houses, recently being used mainly for leisure activities; seasonal inhabitants prevail over those permanently present. It is usually in close contact with the rural landscape.

The village is basically formed only by agricultural and forestry activities. It is a pocket-size town, having, however, its own characteristic and specific life milieu (Wittig 1990). The type of the surrounding landscape determines the structure of plant and animal life within the settlement. Rural settlements are surrounded by rural landscape.

In the area studied, a typical large village has an administrative management centre, a school, and a church; there are more inhabitants employed in agriculture than in services and industry. Small villages usually lack these attributes, possessing only structures associated with agricultural and forestry activities.

In general, a town is characterized by industrial and handicraft production accompanied by a certain degree of pollution. The biotopes are more or less transformed into 'lurotopes' (the term for polluted biotopes introduced by Wischarenko & Tolokontzew 1988). The ru-

Urban Ecology as the Basis of Urban Planning, p. 151–160
edited by H. Sukopp, M. Numata and A. Huber

ral town differs from an industrial one in a less intense transformation of rural ecosystems into urban ecosystems and the closer contact with the agricultural landscape that is not so distant as in the case of an industrial town. Furthermore, the impact of pollution is usually bigger in the industrial town.

In a very large town (city) the human influence decreases from the centre to the periphery (Sukopp *et al.*, 1982) and the connection between town and landscape is disturbed through lurotopes at the periphery. The city in contrast with the town has a greater habitat diversity and also a more intense concentration of species and communities on a limited area.

In the present paper, the term plant community is used in the following senses:

1. In connection with the name of an alliance it stands for the whole complex of communities classified within this alliance, without their precise identification.
2. In connection with the name of a species, it represents a vegetation unit in which only one species is dominating and other species have lower importance values.

Names of plant associations follow Hejný *et al.* (1979).

3. Hierarchy and analysis of settlement units

Basic characteristics of the settlement units investigated are summarized in Table 1. Information about the numbers of plant species and communities are given in Tables 2 and 3. In the text, settlement features and a brief description of habitats available to plants are given in the first paragraph, being followed by the vegetation characteristics in the second one.

3.1. Basic settlement units

Several different types of basic settlement units are characterized in this section: lonely house, cabin, abandoned mill, and recreation settlement.

3.1.1. Chaloupky lonely house (1)

1. At this lonely house with two permanent residents the characteristic ecotopes of anthropogeneous origin are trampled sites, small dung-heaps (with excrements of goats, rabbits and hens), rubbish-heaps and a small garden.

2. Only Agropyro repentis-Aegopodietum podagrariae, Lolio-Plantaginetum majoris and, on small-scale disturbed habitats, Poo-Tussilaginetum farfarae are represented among associations. There are only 32 different species to be found.

3.1.2. Sudoměř cabin (2)

1. This 17 year-old cabin is situated between the riverbank and an old orchard that has been converted into a complex of rural vegetation (Carduetum crispi) and alluvial meadows (Sanguisorbo-Deschampsietum caespitosae). It is now used as a field research station of the Botanical Institute of the Czech Academy of Sciences and is only temporarily inhabited (February–November).

2. The number of associations is slightly higher due to the persisting existence of the orchard and the proximity to vast meadows in the surroundings. The following associations are present: Agrostietum stoloniferae, Carduetum crispi (both restricted only to small areas), Poetum trivialis, Aegopodio-Urticetum (the latter two occurring on large areas). The species number is high (74). The flora is enriched by apophytes and neophytes arriving along the Otava river with imported organic substrate from Průhonice and from river deposits.

Table 1. Basic data characteristics of the settlements investigated. Settlement numbers correspond to those used in the text and Tables 2 and 3. The abbreviations used for reconstructed natural vegetation are as follows: P – Piceetum, AP – Alno-Padion, Q – Quercion robori-petraeae, SC – Stellario-Carpinetum, C – Carpinion betuli. As district roads are termed those serving as a connection between district cities (*i.e.*, district centres).

Settlement Type	Chaloupky lonely house 1	Sudoměř cabin 2	Sudoměř old mill 3	Lužnice field station 4	Božejovice recreation 5
Location	5 km SW of Nejdek	1 km N of Sudoměř	1 km N of Sudoměř	2 km N of Lužnice village	on Tvrzský fishpond
District	Sokolov W Bohemia	Strakonice S Bohemia	Strakonice S Bohemia	J. Hradec S Bohemia	Písek S Bohemia
Inhabitants (seasonal/permanent)	0/2	2-4/0	0 (see text)	0/irregular	4/0
Geology	gneiss alluvial	quarternary sediments	quarternary sediments	quarternary sediments	granite sediments
Altitude (m a.s.l.)	810	380	380	385	400
Natural vegetation	AP	AP	AP	AP,Q	AP
Number of buildings	1	1	1-3	3	1
Roads	rural	rural	rural	district	rural
Water courses	mountain brook	Otava river	Otava river	Lužnice river	brook from fishponds

Table 1. Cont.

	Měděnice little village 6	Úloh little village 7	Vroutek large village 8	Sušice country town 9	Chomutov industrial town 10	Plzeň large town 11
	5 km N of Protivín Písek S Bohemia	14 km S of Klatovy Klatovy W Bohemia	7 km SW of Podbořany Louny N Bohemia	20 km SE of Klatovy Klatovy W Bohemia	district town Chomutov NW Bohemia	regional centre Plzeň W Bohemia
	20/30	11/79	1,600	8,000	45,000	171,000
	gneiss granite	gneiss alluvial sediments	clay sediments alluvial sediments	gneiss limestones	gneiss loess	clay shales carbon
	440	500	360	485	342	350
	SC,AP	AP,Q	AP,Q,C	AP,Q	AP,C,Q	AP,Q,C
	6	24	416	518	3,642	14,000
	rural	district	district, railway	district, railway	motorway railway	motorway railway
	brook from fishpond	Drnový brook	Podhora brook	Otava river	Chomutovka river	Úhlava, Úslava, Radbuza, Mže rivers

Table 2. Occurrence of communities in the settlements investigated. See Table 1 for information on settlement numbers

Community	1	2	3	4	5	6	7	8	9	10	11	Total
	Settlement number											
1 Agropyro repentis – Aegopodietum podagrariae	+	+	+	+	+	+	+	+	+	+	+	11
2 Agropyro repentis – Aegopodietum chaerophylletosum aurei									+			1
3 Agropyro – Convolvuletum						+				+	+	3
4 Agrostietum stoloniferae		+	+	+								3
5 com. Arrhenatherion elatioris											+	1
6 Atriplicetum nitentis								+		+	+	3
7 Balloto – Chenopodietum boni henrici							+	+	+	+	+	5
8 Balloto – Leonuretum cardiacae								+			+	2
9 com. Balloto – Sambucion											+	1
10 Balloto – Urticetum			+									1
11 Bromo – Hordeetum murini								+		+	+	3
12 com. Calamagrostis epigejos										+	+	2
13 Campanulo rotundifoliae – Dianthetum deltoidis						+						1
14 Cardario – Agropyretum										+	+	2
15 Carduetum crispi		+	+									2
16 Chaerophylletum aromatici											+	1
17 Chaerophylletum aurei							+	+			+	3
18 Chenopodietum albi – viridis										+		1
19 Chenopodietum glauco – rubri							+	+	+	+	+	5
20 Chenopodietum stricti								+	+		+	3
21 Chenopodietum vulvariae								+				1
22 Cenopodietum boni henrici							+	+		+		3
23 Com. Digitaria sanguinalis											+	1
24 Echio – Melilotetum								+	+	+	+	4
25 Eragrostio – Polygonetum avicularis											+	1
26 Erigeronto – Lactucetum									+	+	+	3
27 Festuco – Alopecuretum				+								1
28 Lolio – Plantaginetum	+	+	+	+	+	+	+	+	+	+	+	11
29 Malvetum neglectae						+	+	+		+	+	5
30 Onopordetum acanthii								+				1
31 com. Onopordum acanthium											+	1
32 Phalaridetum arundinaceae			+									1
33 Plantagini – Polygonetum avicularis								+	+	+	+	4
34 Poetum angustifoliae						+						1
35 Poetum annuae		+										1
36 Poetum trivialis		+		+								2
37 Polygono – Bidentetum							+	+			+	3
38 Potentillo argenteae – Artemisietum absinthii								+		+		2
39 Poo – Tussilaginetum farfarae	+								+	+	+	4
40 Potentilletum anserinae							+	+	+	+	+	5
41 com. Puccinellia distans											+	1
42 Sagino – Bryetum						+					+	2
43 Sambucetum nigrae			+		+						+	2
44 com. Sambuco – Salicion											+	1
45 Sisymbrietum loeselii										+	+	2

Table 2. Cont.

Community	Settlement number											Total
	1	2	3	4	5	6	7	8	9	10	11	
46 Sisymbrietum sophiae								+				1
47 Sisymbrio – Atriplicetum oblongifoliae											+	1
48 com. Solidago canadensis											+	1
49 Tanaceto – Artemisietum vulgaris						+		+	+	+	+	5
50 Tanaceto – Artemisietum/com. Arrhenatherion										+		1
51 Trifolio – Festucetum rubrae						+						1
Total number of communities in the settlement	3	6	7	5	4	8	9	20	12	21	32	

Table 3. Comparison of the number of species and associations in the settlement units investigated. Sources [1]Pyšek 1973b, [2]Pyšek 1973a, [3]Pyšek 1972, [4]Pyšek 1975, [5]Pyšek 1978, [6]Pyšek & Pyšek 1988

Name (no)	Type of settlement	Number of species	Number of associations
Chaloupky (1)	lonely house	32	3
Sudoměř (2)	cabin	74	6
Sudoměř (3)	mill	61	7
Lužnice (4)	lonely house (field station)	116	5
Božejovice (5)	stronghold (recreation cottage)	151	4
Měděnice (6)	recreation settlement[1]	170	6
Úloh (7)	small village[1]	142	10
Vroutek (8)	large village[2]	231	20
Sušice (9)	country town[3]	232	11
Chomutov (10)	industrial town[4]	318	19
Plzeň (11)	large town[5,6]	548	24

3.1.3. Sudoměř mill (3)

1. This settlement is more than 200 hundred years old. In the past there had been a working mill, a bakery and a farm with about 20 permanent residents. After 1950 the mill has not been working; from 1976 on it has been without permanent inhabitants and since 1989 it has been abandoned, *i.e.*, without seasonal inhabitants as well.

2. The number of species and associations is similar to that found in the neighbouring settlement (Sudoměř cabin). The difference in the composition of the vegetation cover is caused by the fact that at the mill the original synanthropic associations are diminishing and remain only as fragments (Hejný 1994), being slowly absorbed by edificators of seminatural associations (Carduetum crispi, Sambucetum nigrae).

3.1.4. Lužnice biological station (4)

1. Originally there was a lonely house, a farm of defence, with a square ground plan, founded in the 19th century and transformed into the field biological station of the Botanical Institute in the 1970s. The station is situated about 300 m from the Lužnice river bank. There are several small gardens and orchards with meadows; in the past, a small pond was located in this part of the locality. In the northern part, the station is bordered by shrubs.

Although the dung heap does not exist anymore, the station has retained the character of a lonely house surrounded by vast meadows.

2. The number of associations reflects given conditions; the high number of species (116) indicates the change from a lonely house to a biological station. Only five developed associations were recorded: Agrostietum tenuis, Festuco-Alopecuretum (both in the gardens, large-scale stands), Lolio-Plantaginetum majoris (large-scale, instead of the dung heap), Poetum trivialis (small-scale stands), Aegopodio-Urticetum (large areas, margins of shrubs).

3.1.5. Božejovice stronghold (5)

1. A lonely house, built in the Middle Ages as a water stronghold of the Tvrzský pond, is now being used for leisure activities. Only a few visitors are coming from April to November.

2. The small number of associations, forming mostly large stands, is typical of this locality (Poetum angustifoliae, Sambucetum nigrae, Lolio-Plantaginetum majoris, Aegopodio-Urticetum dioicae, Agropyro repentis-Aegopodietum podagrariae). Due to a characteristic microrelief, little anthropogeneous pressure and long lasting isolation, the diversity of associations is not remarkable. On the other hand, the species growing in gardens (57) and grasslands (68), representing together two thirds of the total species number recorded (151), contribute to the higher species diversity (151 species, *i.e.*, five times the number of the other lonely house, Chaloupky). The contrast between the small number of associations and high number of species can be the consequence of this settlement having been developing continuously from the 15th century. The archaeophytes originally present (*Cynoglossum officinale*, *Hyoscyamus niger*) were accompanied more recently by ergasiophytes (*Galega officinalis*, *Achillea macrophylla*).

3.1.6. Měděnice (6)

1. A typical recreation settlement; the number of permanent inhabitants has rapidly decreased, and the number of visitors increased. This settlement belongs to the 'fishpond villages' (not fisher-villages in the sense of Wittig 1990) which are not rare, especially in the South Bohemian region.

2. The associations are not numerous; among those six recorded, Trifolio-Festucetum rubrae, and Campanulo rotundifoliae-Dianthetum deltoidis belong to the seminatural vegetation, and Sagino-Bryetum, sparse in house yards, will disappear when the keeping of hens is ceased. The species typical of agrophytocoenoses are practically missing due to the change of the settlement character from an agricultural to the recreational one. The species richness (170) results from the combination of meadow, forest and wetland species at the locality.

3.2. Small village – Úloh (7)

1. The category of a small village is exemplified by Úloh, sitting at the foothills of the Šumava Mountains. The majority of biotopes are wet. Inversions of temperature are typical of the Drnový potok brook valley.

2. Ruderal vegetation is characterized by Agropyro repentis-Aegopodietum podagrariae, Potentilletum anserinae and Chaerophylletum aurei; Balloto-Chenopodietum, Chenopodietum glauco-rubri, Urtico-Malvetum neglectae and Tanaceto-Artemisietum vulgaris are rather rare. Communities of the alliance Aegopodion podagrariae occur most frequently, followed by Agropyro-Rumicion crispi, Polygonion avicularis, and Bidention tripartiti (Pyšek 1973b). The low species number (142) corresponds to the low diversity of available habitats.

3.3. Large village – Vroutek (8)

1. Considerable habitat heterogeneity, resulting from both agricultural and industrial activities, is a feature typical of this village. In addition to farms, there is a small factory located at the village periphery. The village lies in a warm and very arid climatic district. This is reflected by the enrichment of the plant cover from the adjacent thermophilous vegetation.

2. Among 20 associations distinguished (Pyšek 1973a), the following are considered the most characteristic: Tanaceto-Artemisietum vulgaris, Agropyro repentis-Aegopodietum podagrariae, Lolio-Plantaginetum majoris, Balloto-Leonuretum cardiacae, Plantagini-Polygonetum avicularis. The associations occurring most frequently belong mainly to the Arction lappae, Aegopodion podagrariae and Sisymbrion officinalis alliances. Remarkable habitat heterogeneity results in the high species number (231).

3.4. Country town – Sušice (9)

1. The town of Sušice is situated along the Otava river at the foot of the Šumava Mountains, surrounded by inundation forests, bushy hills and cultural landscape. The inhabitants are employed mainly in industry (a large match factory) and services. Being a point of entrance to the mountain area, the town is strongly affected by tourism. Various biotope types are present on the territory of the town, ranging from wet to dry and from basic to acid.

2. Communities of Arction lappae, Polygonion avicularis and Sisymbrion loeselii are the most frequent, namely Tanaceto-Artemisietum, Lolio-Plantaginetum majoris, Agropyro repentis-Aegopodietum podagrariae and Balloto nigrae-Chenopodietum boni-henrici. Totally, 11 associations were distinguished (Pyšek 1972).

3.5. Industrial town – Chomutov (10)

1. A medium-sized industrial town is represented by Chomutov, a regional northwestern Bohemian centre with 45,000 inhabitants employed mainly in various branches of industry, mining and services. The town is situated in a moderately warm climatic district and surrounded mostly by spontaneous birch-sallow woods occurring on reclaimed soil heaps. Furthermore, forests of the Ore Mountains foothills together with fields are the main components of adjacent landscape. Chomutov is an important crossing of roads and railways.

2. The most important alliances are Convolvulo-Agropyrion, Arrhenatherion elatioris, Polygonion avicularis and Sisymbrion officinalis. Altogether 19 associations and 3 communities (see Table 2 for a complete list) were distinguished, belonging to 13 alliances (Pyšek 1975).

3.6. Large town – Plzeň (11)

1. Vegetation and flora of a large Bohemian town are exemplified by Plzeň which lies at the confluence of four rivers in a moderate climatic area. During the research period (1967–1974, Pyšek 1978) the town had 171,000 inhabitants. The town of Plzen possesses all attributes of a large industrial city, thus providing a variety of habitats to spontaneous flora (see Pyšek & Pyšek 1988) and vegetation (Pyšek 1978). It is an important traffic centre.

2. Altogether 24 associations and 8 communities were reported (Table 2), classified into 16 alliances (Pyšek 1978) among which Polygonion avicularis, Sisymbrion officinalis, Convolvulo-Agropyrion and Arction lappae were the most important with respect to the area covered (see Pyšek 1978 for data, and Pyšek & Pyšek 1990 for a detailed quantitative comparison of the vegetation of Plzeň with that of Chomutov). In total, 548 species were found in ruderal habitats at the territory of Plzeň (Pyšek & Pyšek 1988) which number corresponds to those expected for central European towns of the respective size (Pyšek 1993).

4. Conclusions

Settlement units of different types (Table 1) were selected in northwestern and southern Bohemia for assessing the differences in plant cover (Tables 2 & 3). Of the settlements investigated, all but one (the Chaloupky lonely house, 810 m) lie at lower altitudes (350–500 m a.s.l.). More attention was paid to the basic settlement units (lonely house, recreation cottage, cabin, inhabited mill, research field station). The following conclusions may be drawn:

a) Low vegetation and species diversity is a general feature of basic settlement units. However, the composition of the plant cover depends on the combination of various factors.

b) The lowest diversity of plant species and communities was found in the mountain lonely house (no. 1 – 32 species/3 associations recorded), being followed by the cabin (no. 2 – 74/8). In other types of basic settlement units the flora richness is enhanced by the presence of immigrant species; this is the case with the field research station (no. 4 – 116/8). The low species number and the relatively high number of associations found in the abandoned mill (no. 3 – 61/7) is a consequence of the presence of transitional communities, with succession proceeding from the typical settlement ruderal vegetation to less disturbed marginal communities. This spontaneous development was possible because of the abandonment of the site in the 1970s.

c) The analysis of basic settlement units has shown that further investigations are needed to obtain deeper insight in both their genesis and functional transformation (recreation establishment, biological station, etc.) as well as the effect of these processes on the vegetation cover.

d) The recreation settlement (no. 6 – 170/6) and the small village (no. 7 – 142/7) show comparable species and vegetation diversity. In this respect, both of them are more similar to the basic settlement units than to hierarchical units of higher level.

e) The large village (no. 8) and country town (no. 9) do not differ in the number of species (231 and 232, respectively). To explain the differences in the number of syntaxa (20 and 11, respectively) further investigation based on more data is needed.

f) The number of associations recorded in the industrial town of Chomutov (no. 10 – 19 associations) was similar to that reported for the large town of Plzeň (no. 11 – 24). The species numbers, however, have shown a strong dependence on the city size (*cf.* Pyšek 1993).

Acknowledgments

Our thanks go to Herbert Sukopp, Berlin, and Petr Pyšek, Kostelec, for their comments on the manuscript and to the latter for improving the English.

References

Hale, M. 1987. Urban ecology: a problem of definition? J. Biol. Educat. 21: 14–16.

Hejný, S. 1971. Metodologický příspěvek k výzkumu synantropní kveteny a vegetace velkoměsta (na příkladu Prahy). In: Magic, D. (ed.), Zborník prednášok zo zjazdu SBS Tisovec, Bratislava, p. 545–567.

Hejný, S. 1973. Beitrag zur Charakteristik der Veränderung der Ruderalgesellschaften in Südböhmen. Acta Bot. Acad. Sci. Hungaricae 19 (4): 129–138.

Hejný, S. 1994. Problémy synantropní botaniky na příkladu sídel. Zpr. Čs. Bot. Spolec., Praha [in print].

Hejný, S. *et al.* 1979. Přehled ruderálních rostlinných společenstev Československa. Rozpr. Čs. Akad. Věd., ser. math.-nat., Praha, 89 (2): 1–100.

Kowarik, I. 1988. Zum menschlichen Einfluß auf Flora und Vegetation. Landschaftsentwicklung u. Umweltforschung 56.

Pyšek, A. 1972. Ein Beitrag zur Kenntnis der Ruderalvegetation der Stadt Sušice. Folia Mus. Rer. Natur. Bohem. Occid., Plzeň, ser. bot., 6: 1–37.

Pyšek, A. 1973a. Přehled ruderálních společenstev obce Vroutku v okrese Louny. Severočes. Přír., Litoměřice, 4: 1–35.

Pyšek, A. 1973b. Ruderální vegetace obce úloh v okrese Klatovy. Zpr. Muz. Západočes. Kraje-Přír., Plzeň, 15: 7–18.

Pyšek, A. 1975. Základní charakteristika ruderální vegetace Chomutova. Severočes. Přír., Litoměřice, 6: 1–69.

Pyšek, A. 1978. Ruderální vegetace Velké Plzně. Dis. Bot. Inst. Czechoslovak Acad. Sci., Průhonice.

Pyšek, A. & Pyšek, P. 1988. Ruderální flóra Plzně. Sborn. Západočes. Muz., Plzeň-Přír., 68: 1–34.

Pyšek, P. 1994. Approaches to studying spontaneous settlement flora and vegetation in central Europe: a review. In: Sukopp H., Urban ecology as a basis for landscape planning, pp. 23–42, SPB Academic Publ., The Hague.

Pyšek, P. 1993. Factors affecting diversity of flora and vegetation in central European settlements. Vegetatio 106: 89–100

Pyšek, P. & Pyšek, A. 1990. Comparison of the vegetation and flora of the West Bohemian villages and towns. In: Sukopp, H., Hejný, S. & Kowarik, I. (eds.), Urban ecology, SPB Academic Publ., pp. 105–112.

Sudnik-Wójcikowska, B. 1988. Flora synantropization and anthropopressure zones in a large urban agglomeration (exemplified by Warsaw). Flora, Jena, 180: 259–265.

Sukopp, H. et al. 1982. Freiräume im zentralen Bereich Berlins. Landschaftsplan. Gutachten, Bd. 2, Berlin.

Sukopp, H., Hejný, S. & Kowarik, I. (eds.) 1990. Urban ecology. Plants and plant communities in urban environments. SPB Academic Publ., The Hague.

Sukopp, H. & Werner, P. 1983. Urban environments and vegetation. In: Holzner, W., Werger, M.J.A. & Ikusima, I. (eds.), Man's impact on vegetation, pp. 247–260.

Wischarenko, V.S. & Tolokontzew, N.A. (eds.) 1988. Surrounding environment of a big city. Social-economic aspects. Nauka, Leningrad [in Russian].

Wittig, R. 1990. Dorfbiotope u. Dorfbiozönosen. Courrier Forsch. Inst. Senekenberg, Frankfurt, 126: 133–140.

Green spaces

HABITAT CONSERVATION AND DEVELOPMENT IN THE CITY OF DÜSSELDORF (GERMANY)

MICHAEL GÖDDE[1], NORBERT RICHARZ and BIRGIT WALTER[2]
[1] Dept. of Environmental Protection, Town of Bremerhaven, P.O. Box 210360, D-27524 Bremerhaven, Germany; [2] Dept. of Parks, Cemeteries and Forests, Town of Düsseldorf, P.O. Box 1120, D-40001, Düsseldorf, Germany

Abstract

The habitat mapping as a basis for a special landscape plan (Grünordnungsplan) in the city of Düsseldorf is discussed by showing the distribution of vascular plants, butterflies, grasshoppers, land snails and woodlice in the habitats. Furthermore the distribution of a woody plant community in a part of the city and the planning of habitat network in this area are explained. Other important goals of the habitat conservation and development

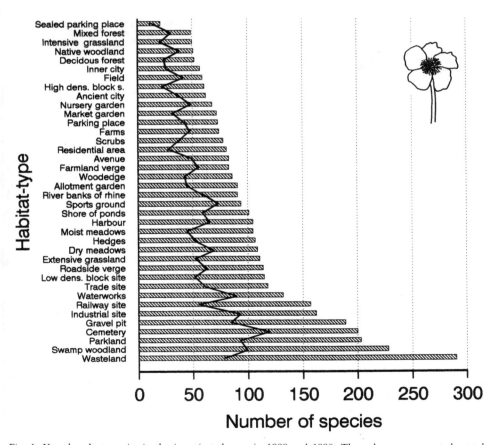

Fig. 1. Vascular plant species in the investigated areas in 1989 and 1990. The columns represent the total number of vascular plants within a special kind of habitat. The line shows the middle number of species found in each habitat type.

Urban Ecology as the Basis of Urban Planning, p. 163–171
edited by H. Sukopp, M. Numata and A. Huber
© 1995 SPB Academic Publishing bv, Amsterdam, The Netherlands

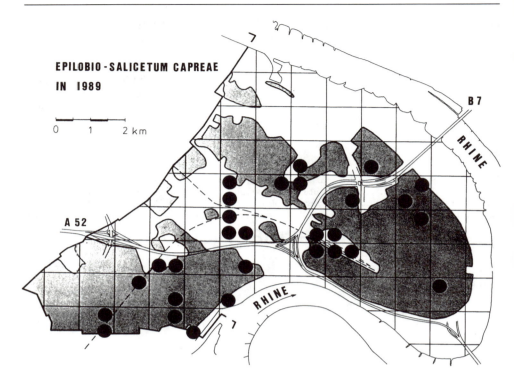

Fig. 2. Distribution of Epilobio-Salicetum capreae in the western part of Düsseldorf in 1989.

habitats. Furthermore the distribution of a woody plant community in a part of the city and the planning of habitat network in this area are explained. Other important goals of the habitat conservation and development in Düsseldorf are the setting up of urban wildlife circuits for the public, concepts of regular biomonitoring and information for the planning authorities.

A plan, which aims at the conservation and development of urban wildlife must be based on the inventory of the ecological situation. Different strategies of area protection, modification of land-use forms, extensive care of parklands or rehabilitation of water courses are necessary. To work out which object of management and conservation is to be set up, habitat mapping in the town is the first step (Gilbert 1989, Sukopp & Weiler 1988). A previous mapping in Düsseldorf (Northrhine-Westphalia, FRG) was done ten years ago (Wittig & Schreiber 1983) in selected areas. The mapping in 1989 and 1990 is being undertaken to investigate all habitats. As the area of Düsseldorf is very large and the financial resources are limited the inventory of the species had to be done in similar sites, each representing a special habitat type. Therefore the town is divided into approximately 75 types of habitats such as cemeteries, inner city, intensive grassland, parkland, parking places etc. The selection of the types had been done prior to the fieldwork by evaluation of aerial photos. In detail there are the following steps:
1. habitat types of the whole town (scale 1:5,000);
2. vegetational types of the whole town (scale 1:10,000) (Baader et al., 1990);
3. habitat mapping of a minimum of two sites of each type (1:5,000);
4. description and discussion of the fieldwork results;

Butterflies

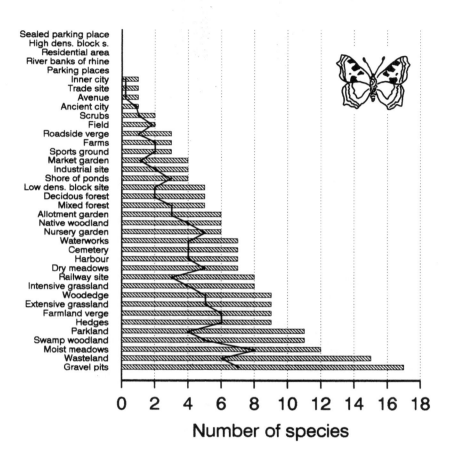

Fig. 3. Butterflies in the investigation areas in 1989 and 1990. The columns represent the total number of butterfly species living within a special kind of habitat. The line shows the middle number of species found in each habitat type.

5. list of sites and their importance, *e.g.*, for environmental impact assessment and town planning;
6. setting up of urban wildlife circuits (Schulte 1987) and habitat network planning (Roweck *et al.*, 1987);
7. conception of regular biomonitoring;
8. basic information for local planning authorities;
9. information for the public.

The public as well as the specialists should be able to follow the evaluation of the different types and the decision-making process. Furthermore all participants including the politicians should be able to judge the consequences of the destruction of special sites.

In each of the habitat types, flora, vegetation and some animal groups had been investigated (Gödde *et al.*, 1992). In total there are more than 550 vascular plants (Fig. 1) and

Grasshoppers

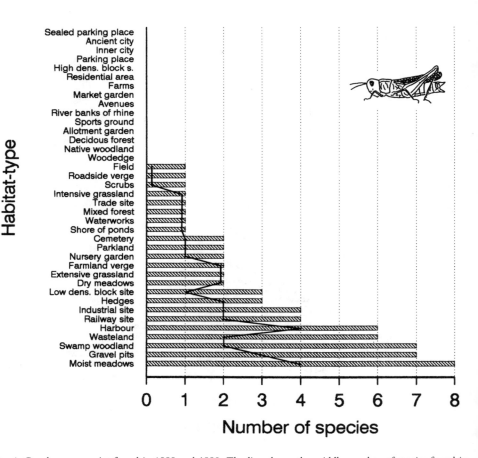

Fig. 4. Grasshopper species found in 1989 and 1990. The line shows the middle number of species found in each habitat type.

nearly 140 plant communities (Gödde 1986). Figure 2 shows the distribution of a shrub community (Epilobio-Salicetum capreae) with dominance of goat willow (*Salix caprea*) and birch (*Betula pendula*) in the western part of the town (Diesing & Gödde 1989). A large proportion of the flora were the neophytes (61 species). For example, the South African ragwort (*Senecio inaequidens*) is expanding rather quickly in most of the habitats in Düsseldorf. Also, because Düsseldorf is situated on the river Rhine, many riverians were found, such as *Rumex thyrsiflorus*, *Xanthium strumarium* and *Inula britannica*. In a former mapping (Haeupler & Schönfelder 1988) nearly one thousand plant species were found in the whole town between 1945 and 1981.

The total sum of the butterfly species (Blab & Kudrna 1982) found in 1989 and 1990 was 21 (Fig. 3). Most of them had been noted in wasteland, extensive cultivated grassland and old gravel pits (Petersen 1984). Also a lot of species could be found in extensive culti-

Landsnails

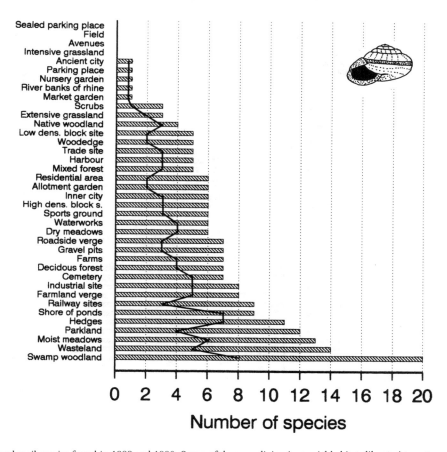

Fig. 5. Land snail species found in 1989 and 1990. Some of them are living in special habitats like moist waste-land or riverbanks. The greatest numbers of species could be collected in swamp woodland. The line shows the middle number of species found in each habitat type.

vated parts of parklands and in the relicts of swamp woodlands. The moth species were investigated only to a small extent, because only the individuals being disturbed were noted. Nearly at all sites the small tortoise shell (*Aglais urticae*), the small and the green veined white (*Artogeia rapae* and *A. napi*) could be recognized. Only in high grown grassland were the small copper (*Lycaena phlaeas*), the meadow brown (*Maniola jurtina*) and the small heath (*Coenonympha pamphilus*) to be seen.

In the two years of investigation 14 grasshopper species (Ingrisch 1980) were found (Fig. 4). One of them, the long-winged cone-head (*Conocephalus discolor*), a species with long antennae was frequently recorded. Although this species was entered formerly in the red data book (Lölf 1986), it is obviously expanding. High numbers of species could be found on moist extensive grassland, in swamp woodland and under temperate conditions in old gravel pits. Atypical was the occurrence of only 2 grasshopper species and 7 butterfly species

Woodlice

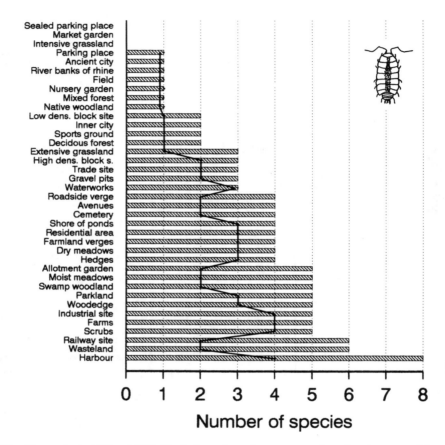

Fig. 6. Woodlice species in 1989 and 1990. The harbour shows the greatest number of species, some of them are very rare, but all of them are indigenous. The line shows the middle number of species found in each habitat type.

on dry and warm meadows. But this habitat is not natural in Düsseldorf, because its occurrence is restricted here today to embankments.

In the years of investigation 30 land snail species (Matzke 1973, Söhngen 1989) were collected (Fig. 5). Some of them, for example *Oxychilus cellarius* and the grass snail *Vallonia pulchella* occupy nearly every garden in the city of Düsseldorf. Other species, such as *Succinea oblonga* or *Zonitoides nitidus*, are seldom seen while living in special habitats like wet

→

Fig. 7. Habitat network in the western part of Düsseldorf. Beside the 'development-map' there are maps about 'evaluation' and 'status quo'. The figure shows the possibilites of conservation and development divided into: 1. protection of existing habitats, 2. expansion of areas and addition of biotope structures, 3. restoration of habitats and 4. development and rehabilitation of habitats.

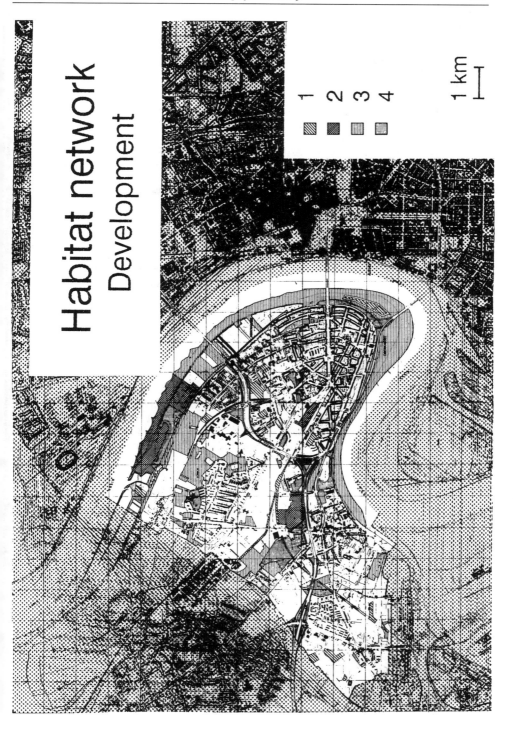

Habitat network
Development

1
2
3
4

1 km

wasteland, riverbanks or swamps. Most of the species were found under moist conditions in high biomass-production habitat types like the swamp woodlands.

A total of 11 species of woodlice (Fründ & Ruszkowski 1989, Tischler 1980) were found in 1989 and 1990 (Fig. 6). *Porcellio scaber*, *Oniscus asellus* and the pill woodlouse (*Armadilliaium vulgare*) were widespread and there was the remarkable occurrence of *Platyarthrus hoffmannseggii*, a species which lives most of the year in ant-hills. The most species were found in the harbour, an area with very different conditions in respect of humidity.

In addition there are investigations in Düsseldorf of amphibians (9 spec.), reptilians (4 spec.) (Elend et al., 1986) and birds (Gilbert 1989, Klausnitzer 1987).

In comparison with the habitat types, it is most important that all sites of abandoned land/wasteland and sites rich in biotope structures be preserved and developed first. In addition to the local town planning mitigation is an excellent instrument to protect and develop special habitats. The concept of habitat conservation and development supplements management regulations for areas in Düsseldorf.

The habitat network is a main result of the mapping project (Fig. 7). Because of genetic isolation and species death this is the only means by which a longterm conservation and development of the fauna be guaranteed. One step is the minimizing of barrier-effects, *e.g.*, from broad roads. Another is the expansion of important areas by the addition of the surrounding acres. The evaluation of the habitats is connected with the size of the sites on the one hand and their importance on the other (age, plant and animal species, rarity of species and biotopes, number and kind of biotope structures, historical continuity, whether typical for the region, etc.). Plans are in preparation for all parts of the town. Specifically there are the following activities:

1. protection of existing biotopes;
2. expansion of areas and addition of biotope structures;
3. restoration of biotopes;
4. development and rehabilitation of biotopes.

The concept of urban habitat conservation and development is part of the so called 'Grünordnungsplan' of the whole town of Düsseldorf. This plan is nearly finished and it is of importance for the town planning of the following decades. The top priority is to conserve open spaces and to protect fully the most important sites for indicator species and their communities, but not only for the threatened ones. The smaller sites should become larger, and barriers eliminated by the effects of linking corridors. The concept can only be successful, when all land-use forms even in the town itself become sustainable.

References

Baader, I., Blachnik-Göller, T., Gödde, M., Mittl, S., Rosenlehner, M. & Wächter, M. 1991. Flächendeckende Erfassung der Vegetation als Instrument der räumlichen Planung, dargestellt am Beispiel einer Vegetationstypenkarte. Raumforschung u. Raumordnung 49: 20–26.

Blab, J. & Kudrna, O. 1982. Hilfsprogramm für Schmetterlinge. Naturschutz aktuell 6, Kilda Publ., Greven.

Diesing, D. & Gödde, M. 1989. Ruderale Gebüsch- und Vorwaldgesellschaften nordrhein-westfälischer Städte. Tuexenia 9: 225–251.

Elend, A., Glaw, F. & Schütz, P. 1986. Die Amphibien und Reptilien der Stadt Düsseldorf. Town of Düsseldorf (ed.), Düsseldorf.

Fründ, H.-C. & Ruszkowski, B. 1989. Untersuchungen zur Biologie städtischer Böden. 4. Regenwürmer, Asseln und Diplopoden. Verh. Ges. f. Ökol. 18: 193–200.

Gilbert, O.L. 1989. The ecology of urban habitats. Chapman and Hall, London, New York.

Gödde, M. 1986. Vergleichende Untersuchung der Ruderalvegetation der Großstädte Düsseldorf, Essen und Münster. Town of Düsseldorf (ed.), Düsseldorf.

Gödde, M., Richarz, N., Walter, B. & Albrecht, G. 1992. Stadtbiotopkartierung. Town of Düsseldorf (ed.), Düsseldorf.

Haeupler, H. & Schönfelder, P. 1988. Atlas der Farn- und Blütenpflanzen der Bundesrepublik Deutschland. E.-Ulmer Publ., Stuttgart.

Ingrisch, S. 1980. Zur Orthopterenfauna der Stadt Gießen (Hessen) (Saltatoria, Dermaptera und Blattoptera). Ent. Ztschr. 90: 273–280.

Klausnitzer, B. 1987. Ökologie der Großstadtfauna. G.-Fischer Publ., Jena.

Lölf (ed.) 1986. Rote Liste der in Nordrhein-Westfalen gefährdeten Pflanzen und Tiere. 2nd ed., Landwirtschaftsverlag, Münster.

Matzke, M. 1973. Landgastropoden innerhalb einer Großstadt am Beispiel von Halle an der Saale. Malakol. Abh. 4: 21–38.

Petersen, M. 1984. Zur Bedeutung zweier Bodenabbaugebiete als Lebensraum für Schmetterlinge (Insecta: Lepidoptera). Natur u. Landschaft 59: 444–448.

Roweck, H., Kleyer, M. & Schmelzer, B. 1987. Lebensraumverbund Mittlerer Neckar. Landschaft + Stadt 19: 173–187.

Söntgen, M. 1989. Untersuchungen zur Biologie städtischer Böden. 3. Schnecken. Verh. Ges. f. Ökol. 18: 187–192.

Schulte, W. 1987. Zielsetzung und Konzeption von stadt- und dorfökologischen Lehrpfaden. Natur u. Landschaft 62: 299–306.

Sukopp, H. & Weiler, S. 1988. Biotope mapping and nature conservation in urban areas of the Federal Republic of Germany. Landscape and Urban Planning 15: 39–58.

Tischler, W. 1980. Asseln (Isopoda) und Tausendfüßler (Myriopoda) eines Stadtparks im Vergleich mit der Umgebung der Stadt: zum Problem der Urbanbiologie. Drosera 2: 41–52.

Wittig, R. & Schreiber, K.-F. 1983. A quick method for assessing the importance of open spaces in towns for urban nature conservation. Biol. Cons. 26: 57–64.

SURVEY, MAPPING AND EVALUATION OF GREEN SPACE IN THE FEDERAL TERRITORY OF KUALA LUMPUR, MALAYSIA

JOHN O. RIELEY[1] and SUSAN E. PAGE[2]

[1] *Department of Life Science, University of Nottingham, Nottingham, NG7 2RD, United Kingdom;* [2] *Department of Adult Education, University of Leicester, Leicester, LE1 7RH, United Kingdom*

1. Introduction

Detailed green space inventories and wildlife surveys have been made in many temperate conurbations (*e.g.*, Numata 1977, Rieley & Shepherd 1990, Shaw *et al.* 1986, Sukopp & Werner 1987, West Midlands County Council 1986). However, the Kuala Lumpur Urban Green Project launched in September 1989, was the first detailed green space survey to be carried out in a tropical city. The aims of this project were to:

a. prepare an inventory of urban green space;
b. classify the green space into types useful to end-users;
c. map the distribution of green space;
d. evaluate the urban green space resource;
e. select 'target sites' on which to carry out more detailed surveys and assess ways in which these could be used for amenity, educational and wildlife purposes;
f. prepare a synopsis of vegetation types as the basis for future detailed surveys;
g. determine site user preferences, perceptions and viewpoints on urban green space;
h. influence decision takers and policy makers in order that the importance of urban green space would be represented more positively in the political arena;
i. prepare interpretative and publicity material presenting the values of green space to the community, legislators and politicians;
j. prepare a green space planning strategy for the Federal Territory of Kuala Lumpur.

Kuala Lumpur is typical of many tropical cities in that it does not have a long historical urban tradition. It probably dates from around 1857 when large deposits of tin were discovered in the vicinity. By the end of the nineteenth century the population was only 25,000. Following independence in 1959, when Kuala Lumpur was designated the capital of Malaysia, urbanisation proceeded apace and, in 1972, in recognition of its growing status, it was declared to be a city – the second in Malaysia after Georgetown in Penang. At this time it occupied 93 km², which increased to the present 243 km² following declaration of Kuala Lumpur as a Federal Territory in 1974 (Fig. 1). The population was 1,036,900 in 1980 and is projected to reach 2,200,000 by the year 2000 (Dewan Bandaraya Kuala Lumpur 1984).

Throughout the growth of Kuala Lumpur, the former tropical, lowland dipterocarp forest ecosystem has been considerably modified: the land has been exploited for timber and tin, plantation crops introduced, and the infrastructure for Malaysia's administrative capital and commercial centre constructed. As a consequence, the indigenous vegetation has now largely been replaced by a complex assemblage of urbanised plant communities.

Urban Ecology as the Basis of Urban Planning, p. 173–183
edited by H. Sukopp, M. Numata and A. Huber
© *1995 SPB Academic Publishing bv, Amsterdam, The Netherlands*

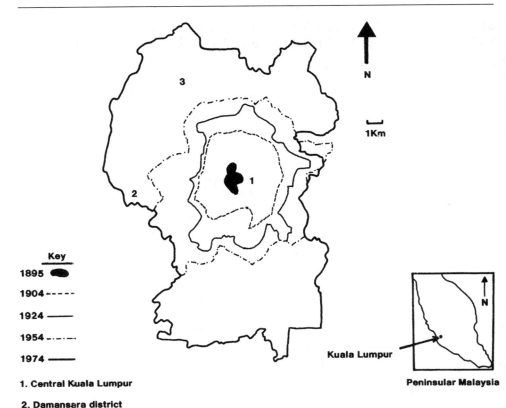

Key

1895   ●
1904 -----
1924 ———
1954 -..-..-
1974 ———

1. Central Kuala Lumpur

2. Damansara district

3. Jinjang district

Peninsular Malaysia

Kuala Lumpur

Fig. 1. The expansion of Kuala Lumpur (partly based upon information in Aiken & Leigh (1975)).

2. Methods

Field surveying and mapping were carried out during September–December 1989.

2.1. Classification of urban green space

The classification used has borrowed widely from Shimwell (1983) and Rieley & Page (1985) and is based upon the structure of the vegetation. Green space classes were selected to satisfy two main criteria: firstly, they had to have local relevance and, secondly, they had to be identifiable from aerial photographs. In addition, there was a conscious attempt to fit managed green space types into the Malaysian national land use classification scheme.

Urban green space was classified as: natural/semi-natural, managed, abandoned, and bare ground (Table 1). Natural/semi-natural areas comprise forest, scrub, coarse grassland (semi-natural, secondary communities), weed communities and wetlands. Managed areas may be one of the following: forestry, horticulture and cropland, plantations of crop trees and palms, amenity grassland (mown grassland), urban savannah (mown grassland with occasional planted, often ornamental trees) and water bodies. Areas formerly cultivated with

Table 1. A green space classification for the Federal Territory of Kuala Lumpur.

A. Natural/Semi-natural:	Forest	(a) Primary forest
		(b) Modified forest
		(c) Secondary forest
	Scrub	
	Grassland and weed communities	
	Wetland	(a) Open water
		(b) Marsh and swamp
B. Managed:	Forestry	(a) Native trees
		(b) Introduced trees
	Horticulture and cropland	
	Plantations of crop trees and palms	
	Amenity grassland	
	Urban savannah	
	Water bodies	(a) Ornamental lakes
		(b) Aquaculture
C. Abandoned:	Plantations of crop trees and palms	
	Horticulture and cropland	
D. Bare ground		

short- or long-term crops were classified as abandoned. Bare ground was also allocated to a separate green space class as it has the potential for colonisation by pioneer vegetation. Where appropriate each category was further divided.

2.2. Green space mapping

Utilising the 1987 photo-mosaic of Kuala Lumpur on the scale of 1:10,000 a preliminary, coloured map was prepared of all the green areas within the Federal Territory, comprising both semi-natural vegetation and agricultural land use types. The dominant vegetation was used to categorise the sites for mapping purposes.

Each photo-mosaic covered the same area as that of the topographic maps (also 1:10,000 scale). The Federal Territory of Kuala Lumpur was divided into blocks of 3 × 2 km² following existing grid lines. Within each block, bare areas, water bodies and green spaces of more than 0.5 ha, and with a minimum width of 20 m, were delineated on the photo-mosaics. Boundaries between blocks were checked and modified so that they integrated.

It was impossible to identify with confidence all of the green space types from the aerial photographs. Particular difficulties were encountered in separating marsh vegetation of former mining pools from grassland and in determining the difference between abandoned rubber plantation and secondary forest. Consequently, the accuracy of the aerial photograph identification was checked by ground survey and any necessary amendments were made to the base maps. In order to achieve this, every site within each of the 243 km² blocks of the Federal Territory was visited and the vegetation communities present on them were recorded; in total 1038 sites were surveyed.

2.3. Target sites

The best green spaces in terms of habitat and species diversity were designated as 'target sites' for future, more detailed study. These were considered to have potential as green space resources for amenity, education and nature conservation. Although the decision on whether or not to designate target sites was taken in the field, and was inevitably subjective, certain criteria were applied in their selection including site size; substrate type; diversity and rarity of habitats, vegetation and species; degree of disturbance; the management required to improve the green space value of the site; and importance as a wildlife reservoir, corridor or link.

3. Results

3.1. Green space statistics

The areas occupied by different types of green space in the Federal Territory of Kuala Lumpur are shown in Table 2. The different categories of green space in selected parts of Kuala Lumpur are displayed in Table 3. Green space covers approximately 45% of the Federal Territory of Kuala Lumpur. Of the total green space resource, agriculture and horticulture comprise about 28%, secondary forests 16%, coarse grassland and weed communities 17%, scrub 10% and wetlands 10%. Urban savannah, modified natural forest, amenity grasslands and bare ground occupy only 6%, 5%, 3% and 3% respectively. Within the time available it was impossible to evaluate accurately the large areas of modified forest which fringe the city. In addition, estimates were not made of the total area of private gardens or the biological micro-niches of the built environment.

The green space resource is not evenly distributed throughout the Federal Territory (Table 3). For example, it occupies about a quarter of the land area within the urban core, nearly half of the district of Jinjang, chosen as a typical example of suburban Kuala Lumpur, and about two-thirds of the district of Damansara, which lies on the urban-rural fringe and which is typical of the peripheral parts of the Federal Territory (see Fig. 1).

Managed urban savannah is the dominant green space type (27%) in the urban core where it is present as public parks and golf courses. Coarse grassland comprises 20%, a large proportion of which occurs in cemeteries. The amenity grasslands of sports stadia, race courses and playing fields also form an important proportion of the green space (11%) whilst modified and secondary forests occupy a significant 24%.

Suburban areas offer a completely different landscape to the inner city. They contain little modified or secondary forest and much of the green space is associated with former tin mining activities. Aquatic and swamp plant communities have colonised abandoned mining ponds, whereas coarse grassland, weed communities and scrub have become established on mining wastes. In the Jinjang district, aquatic and swamp, coarse grassland and weed, and scrub vegetation form 27%, 33% and 14% respectively of the green space. Market gardening (horticulture) is also a prominent green space feature of this district, especially on former tin mining land. There is no modified forest remaining in Jinjang and secondary forest now comprises only 8% of the green space.

In Damansara district, on the urban/rural fringe, plantation agriculture is the dominant green space type comprising 52% of the total. Secondary forests, some of which are abandoned rubber plantations, constitute 22% and scrub 8%. A few small stands of modified forest have persisted along streamsides and in some rubber plantations (1%). Grassland and weed communities make up 12% of the green space.

3.2. The distribution of green space types in the Federal Territory of Kuala Lumpur

3.2.1. Natural/semi-natural green space

Modified natural forests occur on undisturbed soils and are located mainly on the fringes of the Federal Territory, although there are a few stands nearer the city centre, mainly in the older, pre-1954 parts (see Fig. 1). Although very important for wildlife, these natural forests are deteriorating as a result of urbanisation and isolation as more land is cleared for housing

Table 2. Areas occupied by the principal green space types in the Federal Territory of Kuala Lumpur.

	Area (hectares)	% of total green space
Natural/semi-natural		
Modified forest	545.7	5.0
Secondary forest	1786.9	16.4
Scrub	1074.3	9.8
Grassland & weed communities	2112.9	19.4
Wetland	1041.7	9.5
Managed/abandoned		
Forestry, horticulture & agriculture	3052.2	28.0
Amenity grassland	357.0	3.3
Urban savannah	647.7	5.9
Bare ground	298.6	2.7
TOTAL AREA OF GREEN SPACE	10917.0	
TOTAL AREA OF FEDERAL TERRITORY	24263.0	
PERCENTAGE GREEN SPACE	45.0%	

Table 3. Areas occupied by green space types in three districts of the Federal Territory of Kuala Lumpur.

	Central Kuala Lumpur	Jinjang (hectares)	Damansara
Natural/semi-natural			
Modified forest	94.8	0.0	40.5
Secondary forest	222.5	82.8	676.8
Scrub	64.0	152.3	229.0
Grassland & weed communities	270.5	350.8	356.5
Wetland	142.7	281.8	23.0
Managed/abandoned			
Forestry, horticulture & agriculture	28.0	109.7	1571.3
Amenity grassland	153.0	30.0	39.0
Urban savannah	356.0	10.7	70.0
Bare ground	8.5	44.9	27.9
TOTAL AREA OF GREEN SPACE	1340.0	1063.0	3034.0
TOTAL AREA	5413.0	2347.0	4611.0
PERCENTAGE GREEN SPACE	24.8%	45.3%	65.8%

developments. All of the modified forests surveyed were classified as target sites. Secondary forest is more common than modified forest and occurs throughout the Federal Territory wherever land has been cleared of vegetation and then abandoned. After colonisation by pioneer plants and their subsequent replacement by scrub, a dense secondary forest develops dominated by trees of moderate height such as *Acacia auriculiformis* and *Dillenia suffruticosa*. There is an abundance of secondary forest in the inner parts of the city (pre-1954) and also in the older suburbs, but very little within those areas which have been developed recently or which are currently undergoing development. 50% of the secondary forests surveyed had a sufficiently high wildlife interest to be classified as target sites. Most of these were long established forest stands.

Low-growing scrub communities which precede the establishment of secondary forest occur throughout the city on disturbed soils. Scrub often dominates abandoned building sites, former tin mining areas and ground from which the top soil has been removed to provide infill for building activities elsewhere. There are very few areas of scrub within the inner city since these communities have already been succeeded by secondary forest, but scrub is a common vegetation type in the suburbs, particularly along river corridors and on tin mining waste. Twenty-six sites (24% of all scrub-dominated sites) were designated as target sites.

Natural grassland is the second largest green space category in the Federal Territory. These grasslands, and associated ruderal weed communities, occur throughout the city on derelict plots of land which were cleared for building purposes, infrastructure provision or soil removal; natural grasslands also occur in cemeteries, along electricity reserves and railway lines. Some grasslands are subject to periodic burning or cutting to prevent the establishment of scrub whilst others are undergoing succession to other green space types. There are relatively few grassland sites in the older inner city (pre-1904) whereas, in the suburbs, natural grasslands occupy many sites destined for future building development. Only 11% of the grassland sites were designated as target sites owing to their temporary nature and low species diversity.

Sites dominated by swamp and open water plant communities are located mainly in areas of former tin mining activities. The larger and deeper pools left behind by earth-moving operations remain as open water whilst smaller, shallower pools have been colonised by swamp vegetation. Although a few pools and swamps can be found outside the tin mining areas, very few occur within the older parts of the city. Wetlands are relatively new habitats within the region, yet many already have a considerable wildlife interest or the potential for greater diversification. The importance of wetlands in the green space of Kuala Lumpur is emphasised by the designation of 59 (37%) as target sites.

3.2.2. Managed green space

Very few forestry plantations were encountered in the survey. Market gardens are abundant but concentrated in former tin mining areas, especially on the northern and southern fringes of Kuala Lumpur. Within the category of plantations of crop trees and palms, orchards are abundant within the Malay Reservation along the western boundary of the Federal Territory and are also a prominent feature of some of the squatter areas scattered throughout the city. Rubber plantations are situated on the fringes of the Federal Territory, but are declining rapidly as they are cleared for new housing and commercial developments. They will continue to decrease as urbanisation of the Federal Territory proceeds. None of the sites occupied by forestry, agriculture or horticulture were designated as target sites.

Amenity grasslands occur in all parts of the Federal Territory but are concentrated mainly in the older, long-established urban areas and housing estates. Few areas of amenity grassland have so far been provided within new developments. Amenity grasslands are heavily managed by frequent mowing. As a result they have a minimal wildlife value and not one of the 213 amenity grasslands surveyed was classed as a target site. Urban savannah, *i.e.*, amenity grassland with planted trees, is more abundant in the older city areas (pre-1954) where it has achieved a degree of maturity. It is present in public parks, golf courses, other recreational areas and cemeteries. This green space type is important in the built-up parts of the city where the trees provide shade, reduce ground temperatures and older trees, especially rain trees (*Samanea saman*), support luxuriant epiphyte communities of ferns and

Table 4. Classification of target sites according to green space type.

	No. of target sites
Natural/semi-natural	
Modified forest	17
Secondary forest	49
Scrub	26
Grassland & weed communities	33
Wetland (a) open water	17
(b) marsh and swamp	42
Managed	
Urban savannah	6
Water bodies (a) ornamental	1
Abandoned	
Plantations of crop trees & palms	2
TOTAL NUMBER OF TARGET SITES	193

orchids. Six out of a total of 127 urban savannah sites were designated as target sites. There are only a few managed water bodies in the Federal Territory: some are used for aquaculture and the cultivation of plants for culinary purposes or animal food, whilst others are landscaped ornamental lakes in formal parks and gardens.

3.2.3. Abandoned land

Plant colonisation of abandoned building sites has contributed greatly to the semi-natural green space resource of Kuala Lumpur, and has favoured the development of pioneer communities, grassland, scrub and, on long abandoned land, secondary forest. In addition, some abandoned rubber plantations and small-holdings have become overgrown with shrubs, trees, climbers and epiphytes adding to the vegetation diversity of the Federal Territory. The latter may contain some species which were formerly cultivated, *e.g.*, banana, papaya or manioc. Two long-abandoned plantations were considered of sufficient structural and vegetational diversity to merit classification as target sites.

3.4. Target site statistics

Summary information on the target sites is presented in Table 4. 193 target sites were identified, all of which warrant further detailed study. Of these, 92 are forest or scrub (48%), 59 are open water or swamp (31%) and 33 support natural grassland and weed communities (17%). The survey shows that these are the most important areas for wildlife, together comprising 96% of all target sites.

4. Implications for green space planning and provision in Kuala Lumpur

In many temperate cities, informal green space provision is regarded as essential for city dwellers and workers and is now given a high priority in planning procedures (Barker 1987, Barker & Graf 1989). This recognition has come about partly through an acknowledgement of the wildlife value and community potential of undeveloped land outside of formal parks, sports and recreation grounds, and also through an acceptance of the important alternative uses that derelict and underused land can be put to, other than building construction and resource exploitation. This survey has highlighted the green space resource of the Federal Territory of Kuala Lumpur and shown it to be of considerable diversity and importance. Not only have the areas of highest wildlife interest been located but parts of the conurbation in which there is relatively little green space have also been identified. However, in order to optimise the benefits available to the community from this green space resource, it is essential to adopt a holistic approach and to integrate site improvement for wildlife and public utilisation within a green space plan for the whole of the Federal Territory.

The population of Kuala Lumpur is rapidly expanding and although at present almost 50% of the Federal Territory is green space, much of this will inevitably disappear. Consequently, a plan, in the form of a green space strategy, needs to be prepared to maintain and protect a network of green spaces which will be of continuing value to people as well as wildlife.

A green space strategy for Kuala Lumpur should include the following points. However, several of these have problems associated with their implementation which are discussed.

4.1. Maintenance of the green space resource

The green space resource of Kuala Lumpur is beneficial to both people and wildlife. Many sites have an existing or potential value for wildlife, but additional important attributes of urban vegetation include climatic amelioration, soil erosion abatement, air pollution mitigation and noise reduction (Soepadmo & Latif 1988). The most valuable areas of green space for wildlife are the modified and secondary forests, however, the truly urban pioneer and successional communities also have a value, in particular those of aquatic and wetland habitats. Maintenance of the green space resource will help to improve the quality of life for the people of Kuala Lumpur by providing attractive surroundings, helping to reduce pollution and safeguarding non-renewable natural resources. Attractive green spaces can also improve the appearance of a city and help to attract business, tourism and investment.

Constraints on maintaining the present green space resource include the high land values within the inner city which favour commercial development of sites; the requirements of a rapidly increasing human population within the Federal Territory for housing, transport, employment and recreation, all of which require land-take from the present green space resource; and the lack of appreciation amongst politicians and administrators of the alternative uses and benefits of urban green space sites. In addition, some members of the public perceive areas of unmanaged green space as unfavourable features in residential districts. They are considered as untidy, overgrown eyesores or even as a public health hazard – home to snakes, mosquitoes and other undesirable fauna. Similar problems concerning public perception of wild green space occurs even in London (Johnston 1990). Despite the above considerations, protection of green sites and development need not be incompatible if a planned approach to land management is incorporated into statutory and non-statutory planning policies.

4.2. Protection of key sites for amenity, education and nature conservation

The target sites identified in this survey could provide the framework for community integration of wildlife resources. Since many city residents never or seldom visit the countryside, urban green space can play a key role in providing social, recreational and educational opportunities. Indeed, many wild green space sites within the Federal Territory are already used for informal leisure purposes, e.g., fishing, walking, food gathering and grazing of domestic animals. Existing wildlife 'reservoirs' (i.e. large areas of green space which contain a diversity of habitats) should be protected as nature reserves (Adams & Dove 1989), with particular emphasis upon habitats which cannot be easily recreated, such as modified or secondary forests.

Some of the large expanses of former tin mining land should be used for habitat creation, leisure and amenity purposes. Although sections of these abandoned landscapes have been designated for housing and industrial development with some amenity provision, their wildlife potential, which is considerable, is not being realised. If properly planned, many of the water bodies are large enough to support a variety of multi-use facilities. However, with so many potential vested interests involved in land development, it is essential that alternative land uses, including nature areas, are incorporated at the planning stage.

4.3. Maintenance and extension of the green space network

The loss of species diversity from isolated wildlife sites can be mitigated by maintaining or creating an interconnecting system of green spaces. These are particularly valuable if (i) they provide linkages between the urban and rural environments and (ii) if they contain a number of larger 'reservoir' sites supporting a variety of habitats and species (Adams & Dove 1989). Although Kuala Lumpur still has many wildlife reservoirs, corridors and links, these will come under increasing pressure as development progresses. Efforts should therefore be made to keep them intact or provide suitable replacements. Worldwide Fund For Nature (Malaysia) has prepared a conservation strategy for Kuala Lumpur (WWF, 1989) that advocates protection of the remaining large semi-natural wildlife refuges and enhancement of the inter-connecting wildlife corridors. These measures will facilitate movement of highly mobile wildlife, for example, birds and butterflies, to and from the inner city. Most of the wildlife reservoirs identified by WWF are forests, but the linkages between the forests include river corridors, electricity and railway reserves, and formal parks and gardens.

The green space survey of Kuala Lumpur has highlighted sections of the Federal Territory which have a low proportion of green to non-green space, especially in the inner city. Positive action through the planning process should be taken to increase the amount of green space in under-provided areas by habitat creation and site enhancement, with particular emphasis upon improving green corridors. There is also considerable scope for increasing the forest resource of the Federal Territory by planting native tree species to create new 'urban forests' (Sham 1986). An effective green network can assist in the conservation of a wide variety of wildlife throughout the Federal Territory and provide an improved environment for its citizens.

4.4. Promotion of building design and land management practices to encourage native flora and fauna

The impact of buildings on the urban ecosystem should be minimised. Architects can design for wildlife by incorporating favourable features. Establishment of natural vegetation on roofs and walls, for example, should be encouraged, since this provides additional habitats for wildlife. Roof gardens also have other environmental advantages, for example building insulation and a reduction in the run-off rate of stormwater (Brownlie 1991), which could be of particular benefit in a tropical climate. Landscape design for new developments should also aim to provide semi-natural areas around buildings in order to encourage wildlife and enhance their aesthetic appeal. Landscaping schemes should take account of natural vegetation succession and, where possible, make use of on-site substrates and colonisation by natural vegetation. Sympathetic land management practices can also be applied to managed green space, for example parks and gardens.

4.5. Promotion of the study and appreciation of the urban ecosystem

In order to maintain the biological diversity and habitat quality of urban green space and to provide reasoned arguments for implementation of the above policies, the data base of site information requires constant updating; regular inspection of green spaces must also be carried out as part of the green space strategy. However, the success of any green space strategy ultimately depends upon the involvement of people. Although some limited use of urban green space by schools already occurs in Kuala Lumpur, wildlife appreciation is limited and could be greatly increased if appropriate interpretative materials were provided for teachers and other educators. The concept of urban studies has not yet been widely accepted in educational institutions in Malaysia but a green space strategy could be used to promote interest in nature conservation and to actively involve people in helping to conserve the green space resource.

5. Conclusions

The development and implementation of a green space planning strategy for the Federal Territory of Kuala Lumpur can only be achieved through the cooperation of administrators, planners, land managers, biologists, nature conservationists, architects, developers and politicians. This is a daunting task which, if successful, would lead to the improvement and protection of the urban environment of Kuala Lumpur. The city authorities have lent their support to the initial green space survey and are sympathetic to the maintenance and improvement of the managed green space resource. A National Seminar on valuing and managing the green space resource of Malaysia's towns and cities held at the University of Malaya in August 1989 was attended by administrators, planners and politicians from many Malaysian states. This seminar made proposals for a green space action programme. However, if these ideas and concepts are to become accepted widely and established in Malaysia, then a much greater degree of commitment is required locally and an input of resources from abroad is necessary. A further symposium is being planned to deal with site-based experiences and problems of implementing green space strategies. Ultimately, it is hoped that the Kuala Lumpur experience will be extended to other tropical and developing cities.

Acknowledgements

We are indebted to the British Council and the University of Malaya for providing accommodation and facilities in Kuala Lumpur. We wish to acknowledge the contributions made to this work by Professor Lim Teck Ghee, Professor Teh Tiong Sa and Dr. Chin See Chung of the University of Malaya and Dr. Peter Shepherd of the University of Nottingham without whom it would not have been possible to carry out the project in the limited time available. Mr. Peter Smithurst provided assistance with the preparation of the figure.

References

Adams, L. & Dove, L. 1989. Wildlife reserves and corridors in the urban environment. A guide to ecological landscape planning and resource conservation. National Institute for Urban Wildlife, Columbia, Maryland, USA.

Aiken, S.R. & Leigh, C.H. 1975. Malaysia's emerging conurbation. Ann. Am. Ass. Geogr. 65: 546–563.

Barker, G.M.A. 1987. Strategies for nature conservation in urban areas in Britain. In: Green plant – Proceedings of the Fairbrother Group Conference at Liverpool, October 1987.

Barker, G.M.A. & Graf, A. 1989. Principles for nature conservation in towns and cities. Urban Wildlife Now No. 3, Nature Conservancy Council, Peterborough.

Brownlie, D. 1991. Roof gardens – a review. Urban Wildlife Now No. 7, Nature Conservancy Council, Peterborough.

Dewan Bandarya Kuala Lumpur 1984. Kuala Lumpur Structure Plan.

Johnston, J. 1990. Nature areas for city people: a guide to the successful establishment of community wildlife sites. Ecology Handbook 14, London Ecology Unit.

Numata, M. 1977. The impact of urbanization on vegetation in Japan. In: Miyawaki, A. & Tüxen, R. (eds.), Vegetation science and environmental protection. Proceedings of the International Symposium in Tokyo on Protection of the Environment. Maruzen Co. Ltd., Tokyo.

Rieley, J.O. & Page, S.E. 1985. Botanical and vegetation survey of the city of Nottingham, James Davies and Partners, Nottingham.

Rieley, J.O. & Shepherd, P.A. (eds.) 1990. Wildlife sites in the city of Nottingham. Nottinghamshire Wildlife Trust.

Sham, S. 1986. Moderating urban temperatures through tree planting in the Kuala Lumpur-Petaling Jaya area, Malaysia. In: Sham, S. (ed.), A study of the urban ecosystem of the Kelang Valley Region, Malaysia, Vol. 1. Working Group on Urban Ecosystems, Malaysian National MAB Committee.

Shaw, W.W., Burns, J.M. & Stenberg, K. 1986. Wildlife habitats in Tucson: a strategy for nature conservation. School of Natural Resources, University of Arizona, USA.

Shimwell, D.W. 1983. A conspectus of vegetation types. Urban Research Unit, School of Geography, University of Manchester.

Soepadmo, E. & Latif, A. 1988. The role of plants in mitigating urban stress. In: Sham, S. & Badri, M.A. (eds.), Environmental monitoring and assessment; tropical urban applications. Collection of Working Papers 10, Universiti Kebangsaan Malaysia.

Sukopp, H. & Werner, P. 1987. Development of flora and fauna in urban areas. Nature and Environment Series No. 36. Council of Europe, Strasbourg.

West Midlands County Council 1986. The nature conservation strategy for the County of the West Midlands. West Midlands County Council, Birmingham.

WWF 1989. Proposals for a conservation strategy for the Federal Territory of Kuala Lumpur. Worldwide Fund for Nature, Malaysia.

RE-CREATION OF NEW NATURE AND REHABILITATION OF NATURAL FORESTS ON BUILDING SITES IN JAPAN

KAZUE FUJIWARA

Yokohama National University, Tokiwadai 156, Hodogaya-ku, Yokohama 240, Japan

Introduction

According to the national census of 1990, there are 21 cities in Japan with a human population of over half a million each. Of these cities 20 are located in the evergreen broad-leaved forest region. It is unfortunate that the natural environment of most areas of the evergreen broad-leaved forest region (so-called Camellietea japonicae Miyawaki et Ohba 1963, Fujiwara 1981) has been largely impaired by use for residential and industrial purposes. Even in the 'ancient capitals' of Kyoto, Nara and Kamakura, numerous housing compounds have slowly spread, demolishing the natural assets of the ancient past. Contrary to the movement to preserve the natural environment, which started in the early 1970s, the tendency is that even remaining natural and semi-natural space is being taken up as sites for buildings and transportation facilities. As for industrial sites, despite legal restrictions to preserve and restore the genuine natural environment, lawns and decorative gardens are created and huge amounts are spent on maintenance costs every year. In many instances, it is not intended to create diverse and stable forests with multiple layers and various habitats. Such structured environmental forests would bring about many advantages, involving soil and groundwater protection, habitat protection, wind abatement and so on.

With the growing sentiment toward nature preservation, the government, local municipalities, business enterprises and citizens joined efforts to control environmental pollution. As a result, advancements in research and technology made it possible to reduce pollutants in most cases. The recent energy crisis and economic recession, however, have tended to draw the peoples' attention away from environmental problems. As long as the majority of the Japanese population desire to enjoy the present or an even higher level of economic affluence, further land development, even if smaller in scale, and further increases in industrial production will be indispensable in the years to come.

On the other hand, citizens seem to want to live in a natural – especially a green – environment, and this even more as land development advances. How to maintain a balance between industrial development and the preservation, restoration and re-creation of nature will continue to be a crucial problem that awaits solution.

Re-creation and rehabilitation of environmental forests in Japan

The prototype of the environmental forest is the 'native forest', *i.e.*, the present potential natural vegetation, which has long existed around Shinto shrines and Buddhist temples, in Japanese gardens and around local residences in various places.

In Europe people have experience and a history of rehabilitating and re-creating natural forests, using pioneer trees. These forests are preserved as nature conservation areas. In Japan Professor Dr. Akira Miyawaki introduced this method in 1969 (Miyawaki & Fujiwara 1969, Miyawaki *et al.*, 1974). Then he proposed to rehabilitate natural forests as environmental protection forests for monitoring pollution and restoring natural environments. He developed the 'Miyawaki Method': The topsoil is restored on sites before potted plant seedlings of the canopy species of the local potential natural forest are planted. The species

Urban Ecology as the Basis of Urban Planning, p. 185–188
edited by H. Sukopp, M. Numata and A. Huber
© *1995 SPB Academic Publishing bv, Amsterdam, The Netherlands*

are selected on the basis of phytosociological field surveys (Braun-Blanquet 1928, 1932, 1951, 1964, Ellenberg 1968, Mueller-Dombois & Ellenberg 1974, Fujiwara 1987, Tüxen 1956). Existing natural, multistratal communities with original or semi-natural vegetation in and around the construction sites are to be kept intact. Their preservation is the most advanced method of environmental protection.

At first we planted one individual per square meter. In further research two or three individuals per square meter were tried for normal sites and six to nine individuals per square meter in severe environments. Dense plantations show faster growth and require less maintenance than plantations of individual trees. Also, recovery of the topsoil promotes the growth of seedlings without succession (succession develops topsoil). It is important that no or little maintenance is required, since Japanese officers and company people change positions every two or three years and their plantation projects must show success within this period of time.

What is the difference between the rehabilitation of native forests by Miyawaki's method and more common (forestry) plantation methods? The following can be cited:

1. The method of species selection differs from the forestry method. We select and use as many native canopy species as possible, based on the potential natural vegetation.
2. The plantations are mixed, not with only a single species. Besides, it is desired that aesthetically pleasing marginal (mantel) communities be planted linearly along the border of open vegetation zones, such as roads, bare lots and lawns.
3. Pot seedlings with well-developed root systems and a height up to 0.8 m are planted.
4. The plantations are dense, with 3–9 individuals per square meter.
5. The soil is prepared before the planting, good drainage is provided and organic fertilizers such as compost, weeds, dropped leaves, etc. are used.
6. A mulch layer of rice straw, leaves, etc. is applied for protection against soil drying and loss of nutrients.
7. After two or three years a management of the plantation is discontinued (Miyawaki 1984, Fujiwara 1984).

Beginning in 1972, Shin Nippon Steel Company (Shin Nittetsu) tried the 'Miyawaki Method' at nine factories from Kyushu to Hokkaido. Other companies followed suit and planted environmental protection forests on their sites. Local governments did likewise, either at the same time or since.

As a result of the follow-up investigation of the growth processes of the environmental forests that have been created in over 200 places since 1973, the following points have been ascertained:

1. In urban areas, trash, useless wood, broken blocks, concrete blocks, etc. are put into mounds. Mounds and slopes are useful in areas with bad drainage and high precipitation. Seedlings planted on mounds with restored topsoil grow taller and stronger than those on mounds without topsoil.
2. Acorns grow, after ten years, to be about the same height as the sixth-year saplings that were 0.5 m when planted. Acorns directly planted in the rehabilitation sites, however, need intensive and careful maintenance work when young for successful survival. The speed of growth of individual trees is about the same in either case. The locations and the level of maintenance work seem to determine the degree of growth of shrubs and herbs in the forest understorey; the tenth-year forest stands, however, which started from acorns, tend to support more undergrowth than other, planted forests.
3. The application of straw or other mulching materials immediately after planting stabilizes soil conditions and facilitates sound, strong growth of seedlings.
4. Mixed planting of several kinds of trees that are species of the potential natural vegetation, rather than planting of a single type of tree, yields better results, maintaining the balance between the competition and coexistence among individual trees.

5. In places under severe conditions, such as coastal areas that are directly exposed to salt water, or on steep slopes, the planting density should be especially high (5–6 individuals/m², among which 3–4 individuals are trees and 2–3 are shrubs). In ordinary places, the desirable density is 2–3 individuals/m².
6. The growth of seedlings is much better on slopes than on flat land. Therefore, the effects of the green mass can be improved when the environmental forest is planted on a mound.
7. Adaptation of species of the potential natural vegetation shortens the period of maintenance work. Wide varieties of canopy plant species of the potential natural vegetation are suitable for planting. The competition of individual seedlings is effective for their growth. While some species grow tall fast, others spread branches and occupy space. Therefore the selection of species needs to be diverse.
8. *Persea thunbergii*, *Cinnamomum camphora*, *Neolitsea sericea* (Lauraceae) grow fast and strong immediately after being planted in the evergreen broad-leaved forest region. In three or four years, the dominant species of the potential natural vegetation of each location rapidly exceed the growth of other species.

Conclusion

The new nature of industrial sites should be multi-functional. We can now combine our scientific knowledge with our conception of the traditional native, harmonious landscape and create balanced industrial sites. They would include the conservation and re-creation of traditional landscapes as well as the planting of green patches and corridors, according to ecological scholarship. New nature on industrial sites could be an 'eco-museum' and contribute not only to the reduction of environmental pollution but also to environmental education. It could show that the true attributes of green environments are much more than mere function in the ecosystem, for example the abatement of environmental pollution. They could foster public realization that green environments belong to everyone and need to be available to everyone as public parks, for recreation and children's playing grounds.

This effort to harmonize the coexistence of nature, industries and people, however, may not be taken as an excuse for a boundless development of industrial and residential sites. On the contrary, it is highly important to find clever ways to reduce the consumption of landscape, energy and other natural resources.

References

Braun-Blanquet, J. 1928: Pflanzensoziologie. Grundzüge der Vegetationskunde. 330 pp. J. Springer, Berlin.
Braun-Blanquet, J. 1932. Plant sociology. 439 pp. New York.
Braun-Blanquet, J. 1964. Pflanzensoziologie. Grundzüge der Vegetationskunde. 3rd edition. 865 pp. Springer-Verlag, Vienna/New York.
Ellenberg, H. 1956. Grundlagen der Vegetationsgliederung. Part 1: Aufgaben und Methoden der Vegetationskunde. 'Einführung in die Phytosoziologie' (Walter, H., ed.), vol. 4. 136 pp. Eugen Ulmer, Stuttgart.
Fujiwara, K. 1984. Investigation of the growth process of environmental forests in the industrial area in Camellietea japonicae. In: Abstracts, international symposium on urban ecosystem and environmental science, pp. 20–22. Yokohama National University.
Fujiwara, K. 1987. Aims and methods of phytosociology of 'vegetation science'. In: Plant ecology and taxonomy to the memory of Dr. Satoshi Nakanishi, pp. 607–628. The Kobe Geobotanical Society, Kobe.
Miyawaki, A. & Fujiwara, K. 1969. A restoration planning of the green environment and landscape of 'new developing area' in the western part of Fujisawa City, 38 pp. Fujisawa. (In Japanese with German summary, a vegetation map in color.)
Miyawaki, A. & Fujiwara, K. 1988. Restoration of natural environment by creation of environmental protec-

tion forests in urban areas. Growth and development of environmental protection forests on the Yokohama National University Campus. Bull. Inst. Envir. Sci. Tech. Yokohama Natn. Univ. 15: 95–102. Yokohama.

Miyawaki, A., Fujiwara, K., Box, E.O. 1987. Toward harmonious green urban environments in Japan and óther countries. Bull. Inst. Envir. Sci. Tech. Yokohama Natn. Univ. 14: 67–82. Yokohama.

Miyawaki, A., Fujiwara, K., Kimura, M. 1984. Ecological and vegetation-scientific studies on creation of environmental protection forests in the industrial areas of Japan. Yokohama Phytosoc., Vol. 22. Part II. 151 pp. (In Japanese with German and English summaries), Yokohama.

Miyawaki, A., et al. 1974. Phytosociological investigation for the creation of environmental protection forests around schools. 116 pp. Inst. Envir. Sci. Tech. Yokohama Natn. Univ. (In Japanese with German summary.)

Mueller-Dombois, D. & Ellenberg, H. 1974. Aims and methods of vegetation ecology. 547 pp. Wiley, New York.

Tüxen, R. 1956. Die heutige potentielle natürliche Vegetation als Gegenstand der Vegetationskartierung. Stolzenau/Weser. Angewandte Pflanzensoziologie 13: 5–42.

Human ecology

ANIMALS AND MAN IN THE PROCESS OF URBANIZATION

HIDEO OBARA

Department of Zoology and Humanology, Jyoshi-Eiyo University, 3-9-21 Chiyoda, Sakado-shi, Saitama, 350-02, Japan

Abstract

The present paper reports on a series of systematic approaches to ecological studies on cities and urbanized areas and on the changes in dynamics of animals in those areas. It is also attempted to establish a structural and functional model of relationships among the components of urban ecosystems, including man, based on the results of these studies.

1. Introduction

The city-dwelling human population in the next century is expected to exceed eighty percent of the total population in the world. It is of great importance in the last decade of this century to ecologically analyze various aspects of densely populated cities and to consider ideal cities for the future from both biological and ecological points of view.

A series of comprehensive studies on cities and urban ecosystems in Japan started in 1971 and have continued up to today, based on the main concept of the UNESCO's MAB program. For the studies in Japan, several special working groups were organized by Dr. Numata to carry out these studies systematically. In those studies, various elements forming an urban ecosystem, as well as relationships between them, were disclosed. As one of those relevant works, a study on dynamics of animals in cities and urbanized areas was promoted. As a result, remarkable changes in habitat sites of the observed animals were recognized at every research, in proportion to the progress of urbanization. It is suggested that these changes in habitat sites of each species depend on and are directed by the interaction with human activities.

2. The process of fundamental researches

Since 1971, five-phased interdisciplinary studies have been implemented on the structure, function and dynamics of urban ecosystems, particularly concerning Tokyo Metropolis and also Chiba and Ichihara Cities, which both are situated in the rapidly developing industrial zone along Tokyo Bay Coast to the east of Tokyo (Fig. 1). The early 1970s was just the time when urbanization had begun all over Japan.

Against this background, the first phase of the studies was carried out in order to evaluate the impact of the degrading environmental condition on living beings including man, based on biological fundamental researches. In the second phase, studies were implemented to biologically clarify the construction and function of a city and the suburbs as an ecosystem, and also to recognize the dynamics and the role of animals and man as components of the ecosystem, regarding a city as a biocentric and as an anthropocentric system.

It is generally said that each city has a common structure and function as well as its respective specifics according to geographical, historical or environmental features. In order to clear this complicated aspect that pertains to the whole ecosystem, the items to be examined were subdivided into nine groups on the basis of appropriate disciplines in the third

Urban Ecology as the Basis of Urban Planning, p. 191–201
edited by H. Sukopp, M. Numata and A. Huber
© 1995 SPB Academic Publishing bv, Amsterdam, The Netherlands

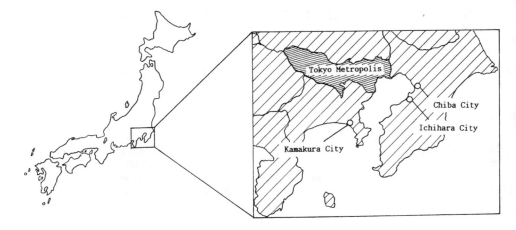

Fig. 1. Research area.

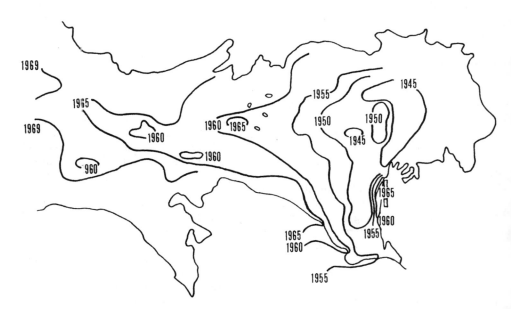

Fig. 2. Decline of the dragonfly (*Anax parthenope julius, Orthetrum albistylum speciosum, Mnais strigate, Calopteryx atrata* and the other resident species) in Tokyo from 1945 to 1969 (Y. Shinada, 1974).

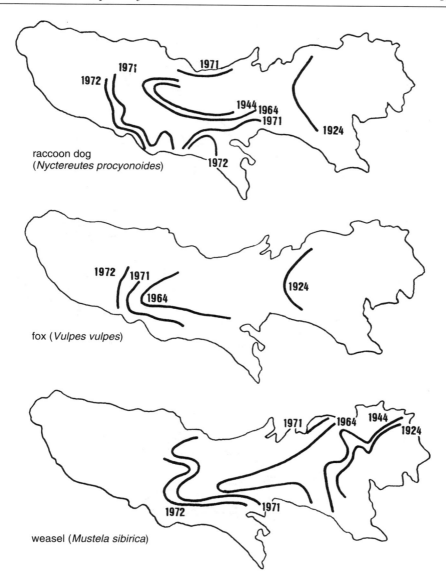

Fig. 3. Decline of mammals in Tokyo from 1924 to 1972 (1) (S. Chiba, 1972).

phase of the study. These groups are: air, water, soil, vegetation, wildlife and humans, land utilization, economy, demography and sanitation, city planning.

In the following phase, the results of each research of these items were all integrated through the item 'water' as an intermediary key-factor. This integrates several small systems into an urban ecosystem and is well qualified as an indicator, showing the change of the dynamics of an urban ecosystem and providing an overview of structure and function of the ecosystem in the various cities.

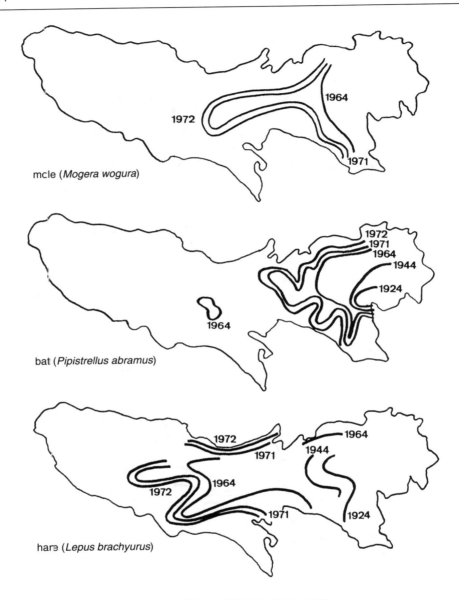

Fig. 4. Decline of mammals in Tokyo from 1924 to 1972 (2) (S. Chiba, 1972).

In general, every type of studies on cities touches on issues concerning city planning. Several measures for more effective planning, such as the image of an ideal city that is 'natural' for man, were composed in the fifth phase. These approaches were expected to give essential information for city planning in the future.

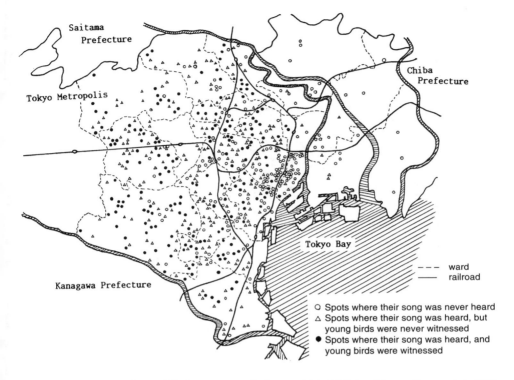

Fig. 5. The breeding condition of the Japanese great tit (*Parus major*) in 23 Tokyo Metropolitan wards in 1972 (N. Sakurai, 1974).

3. Changes in population dynamics of wild animals

In our study on animals in Tokyo, some remarkable changes in the dynamics following urbanization were recognized.

A well-known insect in Japan, the dragonfly (*Anax parthenope julius, Orthetrum albistylum speciosum, Mnais strigate, Calopteryx atrata*), used to be observed in every part of Tokyo until 1945. By 1969 when urbanization had slowly progressed, it had retreated and could be observed only in the western part of Tokyo where rural areas bordered by hills and mountains remained (Fig. 2). Its habitat had continued to decrease with the progress of urbanization.

The same kind of development is found with the mammals in Tokyo. A study of the present situation of mammals and their habitats in Tokyo shows a rapid decline of species and individuals in areas with increasing urbanization. This can be attributed to the loss of vast habitat areas as well as food sources.

The changes in habitat sites of well-known mammals, such as fox (*Vulpes vulpes*), weasel (*Mustela sibirica*), hare (*Lepus brachyurus*), raccoon dog (*Nyctereutes procyonoides*) were investigated on the basis of information provided by the residents in study areas. In an investigation in 1972, none of these species were observed anymore in the urbanized areas (Fig. 3, 4). Moles (*Mogera wogura*) and bats (*Pipistrellus abramus*), however, remained in the same area even after the urbanization (Fig. 4).

In the historic context, Japan had not only large populations but also a rich variety of wildlife in spite of her small land size. However, the process of modernization started in the

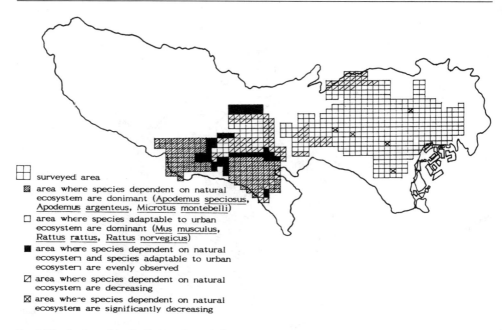

Fig. 6. Distribution of the family Muridae in Tokyo in 1976 (H. Obara *et al.*, 1977).

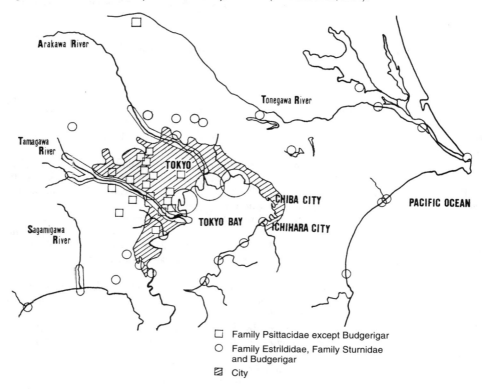

Fig. 7. The distribution of cage birds in and around Tokyo in 1981 (H. Obara, 1981).

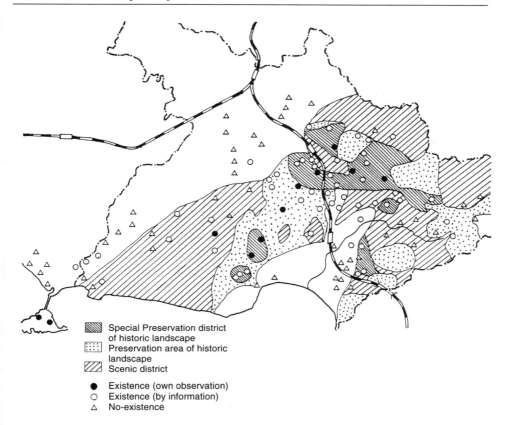

Fig. 8. The geographical distribution of Formosan squirrels (*Callosciurus caniceps thaiwanensis*) around Kamakura in 1980 (T. Shoji and H. Obara, 1981).

19th century and led to a rapid industrialization and urbanization of vast areas, especially along the coast-line. These changes drastically impacted the natural ecosystems and led to a tremendous reduction of wildlife species and their quantity. A number of mammal species have become extinct or reduced in number to an extreme degree. The situation is clearly urgent for many species in Japan, not only in terms of individual species of animals but in terms of dynamic movements (Obara 1987). The natural ecosystems in Japan were affected by human activity and have become more artificial. Habitat destruction, in turn, has brought about a decline in the distribution of medium-sized wild mammals and small wild mammals in that order. Chiba (1974) and Obara have confirmed this kind of change and elimination of species taking place in Tokyo (Obara *et al.*, 1977).

With certain wild bird species, for example, the eastern house swallow (*Hirundo rustica*), their reappearance in the urbanized areas was observed since the artificial ecosystems could be utilized in diverse ways as habitat, such as tall buildings for providing suitable nesting sites. In addition, a distribution map indicates that the Japanese great tit (*Parus major minor*) could breed even in an isolated grove or coppice with little foliage (Fig. 5). This shows that even after urbanization, these wild animals (birds) may still propagate, depending on the type of urbanization (Sakurai 1973).

The field mouse (*Apodemus speciosus*), geisha mouse (*Apodemus argenteus*) and Japanese

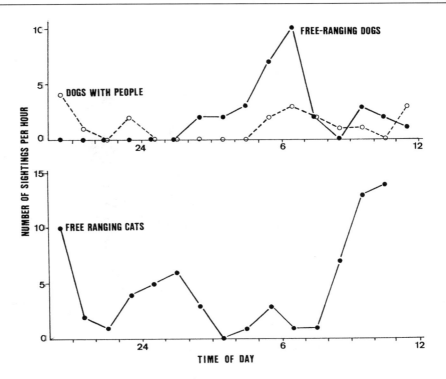

Fig. 9. Active period of dogs and cats in Goi area in 1985 (H. Hirata, 1986).

field vole (*Microtus montebelli*) belong to the declining animals in an urban ecosystem. On the other hand, the house mouse (*Mus musculus*), the roof rat (*Rattus rattus*) and Norway rat (*Rattus norvegicus*), as free-living animals, are now establishing their niche in the urban ecosystem (Fig. 6). The change in their distribution, from species dependent on natural ecosystems to the other species adaptable to urban ecosystems, was observed during the progress of urbanization. The situation is such that only house mice and rats can be found in the central parts of Tokyo and even in the suburbs.

Meanwhile, there are various kinds of pet-animals existing independently in an urban ecosystem, which have so increased that they cannot be disregarded as one of the components of urban ecosystems.

Cage birds are the one of those captive animals distributed in large population in urbanized areas (Obara 1981). Most of them have managed to survive after having escaped or having been deserted (Fig. 7).

In Kamakura City where enough coppice still remains, the exotic Formosan golden-backed squirrel (*Callosciurus caniceps thaiwanensis*) has expanded in its distribution and has established its niche in the ecosystem (Fig. 8) (Shoji & Obara 1981).

Pet animals are increasing in number of individuals and also in species in urbanized areas. An unappropriate care and desertion of pets can promote an increase of stray animals, which after all become feral animals adapted to the urban ecosystem and construct a population (Hirata *et al.*, 1981). In an investigation of pet animals, dogs (*Canis familiaris*) and cats (*Felis cactus*) were observed (Fig. 9) (Hirata *et al.*, 1986).

Generalizing the results of the above, the animals adapted to urban environments include indigenous wild species, exotic foreign wild species and domesticated pet animals. The rela-

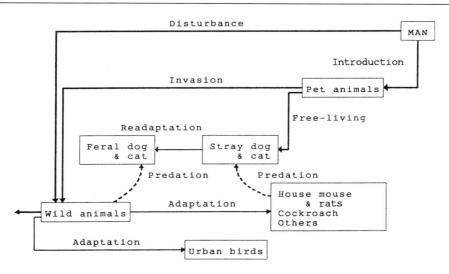

Fig. 10. Dynamism of animals in urbanization (H. Obara, 1987).

tionship between man and those animals in urban ecosystems is logically summarized as follows (Fig. 10):

1. Wild animals are disturbed and expulsed by man and their dynamics are changed.
2. Domestic animals are introduced by man and disturb wild animals, when they propagate after having been deserted and feralized.
3. Exotic wild animals invade the cities and some of them propagate.
4. New relationships and food chains are established with those animals.

In the newly constructed food chain of animals in urban habitats and the outskirts, the biosphere is separated into a natural ecosystem and an artificial ecosystem (Fig. 11). In addition, the natural ecosystem is now being involved in the artificial ecosystem which is continuously expanding.

It is evident that man has affected the original form of natural ecosystems by social activities through the development of mass-production, transportation and other systems, in the wake of urbanization (Fig. 12). This fact actually motivated us to initiate this study of anthropocentric construction and function in city planning. It is well known that man has had various impacts to the natural environment in the process of his evolution and forming of a civilized ecosystem (Fig. 13). Furthermore, man has reconstructed the civilized ecosystem into an artificial ecosystem for his habitation (Obara & Hirata 1982).

The self-habitat-making activity by man has increased quantitatively, geographically and also in space. It has diversified and become structural in the process of biological evolution of mankind. Making use of a natural ecosystem as a basis, he changed it to an artificial one by breaking it down into various elements and then reconstructing it, and also increasing the degree of artificialization more and more by the utilization of artificial materials (Obara 1981).

4. Future subjects

While we consider a structural and functional model of the reconstructed artificial ecosystem there is another important subject we should work on when regarding a whole urban

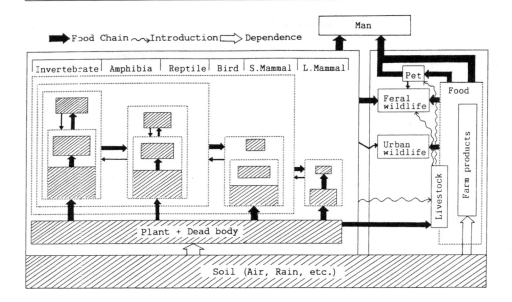

Fig. 11. Structure model of present ecosystem under urbanization (H. Obara, 1987) (natural prey-predation relation).

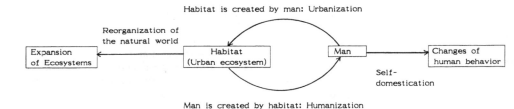

Fig. 12. Interactions between habitat and man.

ecosystem and its components. It is to define an existence of man in this ecosystem.

Man is generally defined as a social component, and as *Homo sapiens* as a biological component. The existence of man (*Homo sapiens*) in societies and cultures in each age also means its existence as a species. This kind of structure is recognized as a place where human beings live, in other words, as a habitat that is basically the same as that of animals. *Homo sapiens* makes up an artificialized and socialized habitat for himself. This aspect of human existence has remained unchanged even in every era of civilization which was brought about by tools expressing the various stages of human culture. When viewed biologically, man performs an artificial selection for himself and shows the tendency of self-domestication via the stages of self-artificial-selection and self-taming similar to the domestication of other creatures. Also it may be called social selection, for all features of human existence are integrated with a society in a wide sense and man as a species actually exists through his socialization.

From another point of view, a city is a system where human beings exist and maintain their existence as a species. The system is an artificial ecosystem consisting of and based on

Evolution of Man	Australopithecus	Homo erectus	Homo sapiens, Modern man
Diversification of production systems	Gathering	Gathering Hunting	Gathering, Hunting, Agriculture, Stock Farming, etc., Industry
Diversification of ecosystems	Natural ecosystems	Natural ecosystms Civilized ecosystems	Natural ecosystems Civilized ecosystems Artificial ecosystems

Fig. 13. Historical relationship between man and ecosystem.

artificial substance. Human existence is structured through tools and all systems developed from the tools, and this process is carried out through social production and daily life utilizing nature as materials. Tools and their derivatives are concrete matters which give man specific features as a social human being, and they define human existence and change nature. Also the artificial substance system, on which a city is built, is basically a derivative from tools (Obara 1988).

Unless we understand and regard an urban ecosystem as a total system, any research would not give the necessary bases for urban planning. The artificial reorganization of biosphere and ecosystem is now progressing in a global level. In the specific evolutionary and ecological process of self-selection of human beings, it is profitable to examine the possible directions of man's development.

References

Chiba, S. 1974. Studies in urban ecosystems. In: Numata, M. (ed.), Fundamental studies on the characteristics of urban ecosystems, pp. 27–46 (in Japanese).

Hirata, H. *et al.* 1981. An observational study of free-living dogs, *Canis familiaris*, in the cities on the bay-coast, Ichihara city, Japan. In: Numata, M. (ed.), Chiba Bay-Coast cities project (Integrated ecological studies in Bay-Coast cities, III), pp. 84–102.

Hirata, H. *et al.* 1986. Characteristics of urban dogs and cats – organization of their own societies in maintaining reciprocal relations with men. In: Obara, H. (ed.), Special research project on environmental science (Integrated studies in urban ecosystems as the basis of urban planning, I), pp. 163–175.

Obara, H. 1981. Urbanization of man and animals. In: Numata, M. (ed.), Chiba Bay-Coast cities project (Integrated ecological studies in Bay-Coast cities, III), pp. 77–83.

Obara, H. 1987. Problems of wildlife protection in Japan. The proceedings of Jyoshi-Eiyo University 18, pp. 105–115.

Obara, H. 1988. Study on urban ecosystem and foundation of urban planning. In: Obara, H. (ed.), Special research project on environmental science (Integrated studies in urban ecosystems as the basis of urban planning, III), pp. 1–7.

Obara, H. & Hirata, H. 1982. Homo sapiens as habitat-makers and the process of hominization and urbanization. In: Numata, M. (ed.), Chiba Bay-Coast cities project (Integrated ecological studies in Bay-Coast cities, IV), pp. 172–177.

Obara, H. *et al.* 1977. An aspect of the existence of mammals in urban ecosystems. In: Numata, M. (ed.), Tokyo Project, Interdisciplinary studies of urban ecosystems in the metropolis of Tokyo, pp. 173–187.

Sakurai, N. 1973. The breeding condition of the Japanese great tit in 23 Tokyo metropolitan wards. In: Numata, M. (ed.), Fundamental studies on the characteristics of urban ecosystems, pp. 123–137.

Shinada, Y. 1974. The natural history of cities. Chuo-Koronsha Press, Tokyo.

Shoji, T. & Obara, H. 1981. The movements of Formosan golden backed squirrels in the urban environment. In: Numata, M. (ed.), Chiba Bay-Coast cities project (Integrated ecological studies in Bay-Coast cities, III), pp. 103–105.

URBAN WILDLIFE AND HUMAN WELL-BEING

LARRY W. VANDRUFF[1], DANIEL L. LEEDY[2] and FOREST W. STEARNS[3]

[1]College of Environmental Science and Forestry, State University of New York, Syracuse, New York 13210, U.S.A.; [2]National Institute for Urban Wildlife, Columbia, Maryland 21044, U.S.A.; [3]University of Wisconsin, Milwaukee, Wisconsin 53201, U.S.A.

Abstract

This paper reviews our knowledge of the role that wildlife plays in human well-being in the urban ecosystem. Numerous benefits of wildlife in close association with humans relate to ecological, economic, psychological and social contributions by the native and exotic fauna and their habitats. Detrimental effects of wildlife on man usually are related to public health concerns, disturbance and annoyance, and property damage. The goals of urban wildlife programs should be anthropocentric, directed toward understanding and enhancing the amenities which wildlife can provide in the urban ecosystem and minimizing the negative impacts.

1. Introduction

The urban environment is like no other ecosystem in the magnitude of human density and influence. The structure and functions of the urban ecosystem have been aptly analyzed by Stearns & Montag (1974), Bornkamm et al. (1982), Douglas (1983), and Spirn (1984). By the year 2000, over half of the world's population will live or work in cities (Douglas 1983). In many developed countries well over half of the people already live in urban areas. Although the human species is the ecological dominant and together with domestic animals makes up the major faunal biomass, other native and exotic vertebrates exert a significant influence upon the ecosystem. The nature of wild animals — and especially their effect upon *Homo sapiens* — is the subject of this paper.

We consider urban wildlife to be the non-domestic fauna of human settlements and associated support areas (*e.g.*, airports, highways, water impoundments, etc.). Following American convention, we will exclude urban vegetation from our discussion of wildlife although with full understanding that urban vegetation provides the habitat, cover and food for most urban wildlife species. The emergence of urban wildlife as an area of ecological, social, and resource management concern can be traced in Gill & Bonnett (1973), Noyes & Progulske (1974), Euler et al. (1975), Stearns (1975), Leedy et al. (1978), Leedy (1979), Stenberg & Shaw (1986), Rodiek & Bolen (1990), and proceedings of two other recent national (USA) symposia on urban wildlife (Adams & Leedy 1987, 1991). For an international perspective, on social and biological values of wild lands, one may consult the papers of Numata (1981), Barker (1986), Deelstra (1986), and Sukopp (1990). The key feature is that urban wildlife is in daily contact with human beings and has the potential to significantly influence our well-being and ecology.

2. Detrimental effects of urban wildlife

Wild (and domesticated) animals in a man-dominated ecosystem may have various negative impacts on human well-being. These involve public health, disturbance and annoyance to humans, and property damage.

Urban Ecology as the Basis of Urban Planning, p. 203–211
edited by H. Sukopp, M. Numata and A. Huber
© 1995 SPB Academic Publishing bv, Amsterdam, The Netherlands

2.1. Public health concerns

Often of greatest concern to urbanites and of considerable interest to urban ecologists are the many potential public health problems caused by urban wildlife. The frequency of domestic and wild animal bites to humans and the number of diseases transmissible to humans (zoonoses) justify this concern. However, at least in North American cities, bites from domestic animals far outnumber those from wildlife. Urban fauna, including insects, serve as alternate hosts or vectors of the agents of serious diseases. Well over 200 zoonoses exist and new forms are still being described (Hubbert *et al.* 1975, Acha & Szyfres 1980). These diseases pose a public health problem, especially in the urban ecosystem where people, pests, and wildlife may cohabit in high densities with frequent contact.

More than one billion of the world's human population live in substandard housing often associated with urban poverty, filth, and pests. Under such conditions rats and mice (primarily Muridae), with associated insects (fleas, flies and mosquitoes), serve as important carriers and transmitters of disease. For the pest-associated zoonoses, children are more commonly affected because transmission is facilitated by hand-to-mouth behavior and intimate contact with animals. Exotic fauna may establish and become serious pests in urban environments, including the health hazards which they present to man and domestic animals. Over 60 transmissible diseases are found associated with pigeons (*Columbia livia*), starlings (*Sturnus vulgaris*), and house sparrows (*Passer domesticus*) (Weber 1979). Such international zoonotic scourges as malaria, yellow fever, filariasis, dengue, plague, rabies, and trachoma may afflict urbanites. Zoonoses of frequent mention and concern in the United States include various arboviruses, aspergillosis, chlamydiosis, cryptococcosis, histoplasmosis, leptospirosis, rabies, salmonellosis, toxoplasmosis, and tuleremia (*e.g.*, Morse *et al.* 1983). As human populations expand, so will the propensity for the transmission of serious diseases between animals and man as well as from man to man. It should be pointed out, however, that in developed countries with high standards of living, diseases and health problems attributable to wildlife are relatively minor.

2.2. Disturbance and annoyance

Urban wildlife have annoyed urban man from time immemorial; plagues of locusts and frogs are described in the Old Testament of the Bible. In modern times, insect and amphibian populations may present localized problems, numerous bird and mammal species may annoy disturb, and otherwise inconvenience human beings and disrupt the urban ecosystem.

Waterfowl may decrease the water quality of an urban lagoon. Urban waterfowl ponds, often shallow and poorly aerated, may become stagnant and eutrophic through the input of bird feces and the decaying bread and baked goods provided by the visiting public or urban resident (Heusmann & Burrell 1974, Hardin 1977). Phosphates, nitrogen, and solids in the water increase and, if left unattended, will eventually make the area unsuitable for either human or waterfowl use (Harris *et al.* 1981). Waterfowl diseases, such as botulism, are a common problem in urban areas, and moribund or dead wildlife demand attention of local authorities. Other birds, like pigeons and gulls, may become pests through annoying urban people with their droppings and their noise.

Various species of sciurids may cause problems in urban areas. The grey squirrel (*Sciurus carolinensis*) is one of the most-frequently reported nuisance wildlife species in the American urban ecosystem. Their predilection to gnaw their way into human dwellings, chew bark and clip branches from trees, destroy ornamental flowers, cause electrical blackouts, and 'rob' food from bird feeders render them a potential pest. Their activities may be exacerbated by a human penchant for feeding this sciurid rodent where it occurs in backyards, city parks and downtown areas. Manski *et al.* (1981), reporting on squirrel populations in downtown Washington, D.C., document the extreme of problems caused by this species in the urban environment.

Human preference for wildlife is frequently species-specific and based on people's encounters with the species (O'Donnell 1984). Highly visible (diurnal) species such as waterfowl, songbirds, squirrels, and chipmunks are usually liked; while nocturnal species such as raccoons, skunks, and bats are often viewed as nuisances and disliked (Dagg 1970, Brown *et al.* 1979, and O'Donnell 1984). As often-noisy nocturnal predators, coyotes (*Canis*) in western cities such as Los Angeles are disturbing to some citizens; in contrast for others the coyote is a symbolic and desirable tie to western frontier history (Gill & Bonnett 1973).

2.3. *Property damage*

The potential for wildlife damage to human dwellings, gardens, and ornamental vegetation is well-known. Much information is provided on wildlife-human diseases and on animal damage in urban areas, including that inflicted by commensal rodents and insects, in a report 'Urban Pest Management' by the National Research Council (1980).

Birds which frequent air traffic corridors, especially during spring and fall migration, may cause serious problems including damage to airplanes and occasional loss of human life (Solman 1973). Deer and other big game animals cause occasional damage to airplanes on airport runways and frequent collisions of automotive vehicles on highways and beltways.

3. The beneficial role of urban wildlife

3.1. *Ecological values*

Urban wildlife may serve an ecological role in preserving human well-being. As a tool, wildlife may alert us to conditions of the urban ecosystem. Our understanding and assessment of the impact of humans upon the urban ecosystem has been furthered using wildlife. Garay & Nataf (1982) found the microarthropod community to be a better indicator of the degree of human trampling in suburban forests than were certain physical or chemical features of the soil.

Birds serve to some extent as biological indicators, *i.e.*, they tend to reflect the ecological health of the environment. In mines, the canary has been used as an indicator of air quality because it is more sensitive than man to the level of toxic gases (*e.g.*, carbon monoxide) in the ambient air. Custer & Osborn (1977) suggest, after Thomas *et al.* (1973), that primitive man must have realized it was unsafe to drink from a water supply that did not support certain forms of life. Studies of the brown pelican (*Pelecanus occidentalis*) by Anderson *et al.* (1975) and of the peregrine falcon (*Falco peregrinus*) (Hickey 1969) have shown that the population dynamics of such species can serve as indicators of environmental perturbation. In these instances, the causes of declines observed either in reproductive success or adult numbers of the species were traced to chlorinated hydrocarbon pesticides. Pesticide residues in eggs of wading birds were found to reflect pollution patterns along the Atlantic Coast (Ohlendorf *et al.* 1974). Allen (1938) reported that urbanization was largely responsible for the loss of several colonies of the black-crowned night heron (*Nycticorax nycticorax*) on Long Island, New York. Other studies have demonstrated that birds are sensitive to habitat deficiencies in the urban environment (Williamson & DeGraaf 1981).

Leopold (1933), in his classic book 'Game Management', indicated that the creative use of the same tools that have hithertofore destroyed the habitat for such species – axe, plow, fire and gun (and we might parenthetically add urbanization and industrialization) – could be used to restore the habitat, *i.e.*, "environments can, by the judicious use of those tools employed in gardening or landscaping or farming, be built to order with assurance of attracting the desired bird." Barnes (1966) stated that "the top symbols for a suburban neighborhood would be wood thrushes, catbirds, or brown thrashers. All require an area of gracious shade trees, naturalistic plantings of smaller trees (dogwoods, thorns and the like), and many shrubs, preferably with a mulch or litter around them. Such a neighborhood would enjoy the finest of bird songs, a vocal advertisement of a place for pleasant living." He suggested that the scarlet tanager is a rather special symbol, indicative of the presence of a substantial number of mature oak trees.

Use of wildlife for the assay of environmental pollutants has been largely neglected. Bigler & Hoff (1976), examining the tissues of grey squirrels, noted that levels of heavy metals differed in squirrels from differing levels of urbanization. Another study (McKinnon et al. 1976) found significantly higher lead levels in the livers of squirrels living in low socio-economic areas of a city than those found in squirrels from more affluent city areas. The use of wildlife as an indicator of environmental quality and ecosystem perturbation will increase as our knowledge is expanded.

Although the forgoing discussion is an oversimplification, the use of wildlife as biological indicators has merit. A more holistic, ecological approach that gives consideration to the biotic and abiotic components of an ecosystem is desirable.

3.2. Economic benefits

Economic benefits to individuals and society from urban wildlife are demonstrated indirectly. Bird feeding supports an American industry variously estimated at $ 170 (DeGraaf & Payne 1975), to $ 517 million (Lyons 1982). Kellert (1980) found that 68 percent of U.S. respondents fed birds, while Witter et al. (1981) reported that 59 percent of Missourians fed birds or other wildlife near their home. Much of this feeding of birds, and other wildlife, occurs in the urban ecosystem. The production and sale of items such as binoculars, cameras, film, books and outdoor clothing used by people in observing urban wildlife represent big business.

Geist (1975) argues that the support and management of wildlife in urban areas is preventative medicine for deficiencies in public education, and for public health challenges to urban society. He presented circumstantial evidence that the presence of urban natural areas, with incipient wildlife, may lead to greater intellectual maturation of youth through the influences of environmental diversity and stimulation. As a support system, a complex ecosystem within and surrounding an urban area may be an asset to public health.

Geist (1975) also relates the importance of wildlife in degrading garbage. Anyone who has visited a fast-food eatery in a modern city or its suburbs may have observed house sparrows, starlings, crows, ravens, and gulls pecking on spilled food items or flying away with french fried potatoes. House sparrows become adept at removing insects squashed on the grill and radiator of automobiles.

3.3. Social returns

Humans in the United States have a strong affection for urban wildlife (Kellert 1984); perhaps this is universal for our species whether in urban ecosystems or elsewhere. The strong desire of urbanites to have wildlife around them and people's willingness to pay a municipal tax for management activities was clearly demonstrated in a survey of residents of Guelph, Ontario (Gilbert 1982). According to the 1980 National Survey of Fishing, Hunting and Wildlife-Associated Recreation, 54 percent or 89 million citizens of the U.S.A. reported enjoying wildlife in residential settings (Lyons 1982). Among New York State's metropolitan residents, 73 percent reported observing, feeding, and photographing wildlife at some time during the year (Brown et al. 1979). These authors found that 73 percent of their study population showed an interest in attracting wildlife to their backyards, while 96 percent of this group felt that wildlife programs were important to their children. Diverse environmental and natural conditions stimulate the brain during a child's development which may lead to high intellectual and physical development (Geist 1975). Such diverse groups as the physically impaired, mentally handicapped, and elderly gain pleasure from contact with plants and animals. Therapy using plants and animals has increased response and healing rates for these groups.

Feelings of personal satisfaction from helping wildlife was the most frequently reported reason for feeding wildlife in backyards across America (Yeomans & Barclay 1981). Among residents of Columbia, Maryland, 92% of those interviewed felt that the sight of waterfowl on urban wetlands in the area outweighed any nuisance that the ducks might create. Seventy-three percent were willing to pay more for property near water managed for wildlife (Adams *et al.* 1984). The presence of ducks in the lagoon community of Beach Haven West in coastal New Jersey were considered a benefit and source of pleasure to 95 percent of the residents. Only two percent considered the ducks a nuisance (Figley & VanDruff 1982). Visitors to urban duck ponds in the Syracuse, New York area considered the presence of ducks pleasurable and a valuable educational and recreational resource (Hardin 1977). Residents also recognize ducks as providing an efficient, natural means of mosquito control (Harris *et al.* 1981). Although animals in zoological parks are not free-ranging, public willingness to support these institutions suggests the strong interest that *Homo sapiens* has in other animals.

4. Enhancing human well-being – neglected opportunities

4.1. Resource management

The future of urban wildlife management is to maximize the positive interactions between wildlife and humans while reducing the negative interactions. Studies have shown (Brown & Dawson 1978) that people prefer to see wildlife around their homes rather than travel away from home. (Also many people do not have the means to travel.) This preference can and should be exploited by urban planners and wildlife managers. The environment most controlled by individual urbanites is the area immediately around their dwelling. Buildings themselves constitute wildlife habitat and should be so designed and constructed as to prevent use by unwelcome wildlife species like starlings, house sparrows and pigeons for nesting and roosting. As in the wild, animal pests in urban and suburban ecotopes can often be best controlled through habitat management. It is suggested that basic efforts should be directed toward attracting songbirds first, as they are highly desirable (Leedy *et al.* 1978), except perhaps English sparrows (*Passer domesticus*) and starlings (*Sturnus vulgaris*). Because native trees support more insects for predatory birds (Robinson & Bolen 1984) and are less susceptible to disease and insect pests, they should form the basis for most wildlife habitat schemes in New World temperate climes. The range of possibilities for urban wildlife management is outlined by Leedy *et al.* (1978) and is addressed in papers in Stenberg & Shaw (1986) and Adams & Leedy (1987, 1991).

Management efforts may be directed at landscape features (Adams & Dove 1988), at a habitat type (*e.g.*, estuarine marsh), the total wildlife community, a particular taxon (*e.g.*, Passeriformes, Piciformes, etc.), or at individual species. The grey squirrel is a logical selection for an urban wildlife management program since the species is diurnal, energetic and highly visible, easily attracted, often present in more than one color morph, tolerant of human activities, low in incidence of transmissible diseases, and appealing, yet with nuisance possibilities. Additionally, much is known about squirrel ecology under urban conditions (Flyger 1974, Thompson 1977, 1978, Thompson & Thompson 1980, Manski *et al.* 1981). Other likely candidate species valuable for urban wildlife management programs include the mourning dove and raccoon in America, and the rhesus monkey (*Macaca mulalla*) in India.

More efforts should be directed toward comprehensive wildlife management plans incorporating social, as well as ecological, values and goals. The comprehensive restoration and management plan developed for New York City's Central Park, may serve as a model (Hecklau 1985). The plan demonstrates the need for education of park planners, administrators and maintenance personnel; resolution of conflicts between various park user groups; and communication between these groups and park administrators and planners as one promotes wildlife as an important part of the recreational experience of park visitors. The political, social, and ecological facets of planning and implementing urban wildlife programs are included in the works compiled by Dawe (1990).

4.2. Research

To enhance human well-being in urban environments using urban wildlife, targeted research is essential. If well-designed research, possibly involving the cooperation of medical doctors and psychologists, could be conducted and such research showed convincingly that people who observe wildlife in their backyards are healthier and commit fewer crimes, funding for urban wildlife research and management probably would be increased.

We must establish the role that wildlife may play in the preservation (or restoration) of species diversity associated with urban natural area conservation. For example, the relationship between habitat and the diversity of breeding avifauna is better known (Willson 1974, Lancaster & Rees 1979, DeGraaf & Wentworth 1981, 1986, Beissinger & Osborne 1982, Figley & VanDruff 1982, Johnsen 1982, Clark *et al.* 1983, Dickman & Doncaster 1987) than are such relationships for urban mammals (Matthiae & Stearns 1981, Nilon 1986, VanDruff & Rowse 1986). Our knowledge of the habitat requirements and community relationships for urban herpetofauna is meager at best (Schlauch 1978).

4.3. Education

As the world's human population becomes more urbanized, we face an increasing struggle between human-centered value judgments and ecological value judgments. An ecological basis for our anthropocentric existence and future survival as a species can best be taught using examples and case studies from the urban environment. As an oft-appealing component in our immediate environment, urban wildlife can serve to focus attention upon conservation and human ecology. Observing the activities of wildlife is a ready entry to the mysteries of the natural world (Spirn 1984). Citizens who learn to understand and appreciate ecological principles in their backyards or local communities, will be better able to vote intelligently on conservation issues of national significance. The need to develop wildlife education programs in large cities was pointed out in Kellert's (1984) survey of urban Americans. However, the opportunities for employing urban wildlife in educational programs have barely been tapped. Aware of this, some authors have suggested possibilities for including wildlife at various levels of public education (Cotton 1982, VanWingerden 1982, Vogl & Vogl 1985, Adams *et al.* 1987). Such challenges will continue to dominate public education in the 21st Century. To quote E.O. Wilson (1984) "... To the degree that we come to understand other organisms, we will place a greater value on them, and on ourselves."

Summary

Urban wildlife has a definite role in the well-being of humans in the urban environment. Although the value of wildlife as an amenity in the urban ecosystem is recognized, opportunities to give urban wildlife greater consideration in resource management, research, and education efforts have been sadly neglected. Even modest efforts to conserve and restore natural systems, including management of wildlife species, populations and communities, will yield significant benefits to humans residing on or visiting urbanized ecosystems.

References

Acha, P.N. & Szyfres, B. 1980. Zoonoses and communicable diseases common to man and animals. Pan-Amer. Health Organ., Washington, D.C.

Adams, L.W. & Dove, L.E. 1989. Wildlife reserves and corridors in the urban environment. A guide to ecological landscape planning and resource conservation. Nat'l Inst. for Urban Wildl., Columbia, Maryland. 91 pp.

Adams, L.W., Dove, L.E. & Leedy, D.L. 1984. Public attitudes toward urban wetlands for stormwater control and wildlife enhancement. Wildl. Soc. Bull. 12: 299–303.

Adams, L.W. & Leedy, D.L. (eds.) 1987. Integrating man and nature in the metropolitan environment, proceedings of a national symposium on urban wildlife. Nat'l Inst. for Urban Wildl., Columbia, Maryland. 249 pp.

Adams, L.W., Leedy, D.L. & McComb, W.C. 1987. Urban wildlife research and education in North American colleges and universities. Wildl. Soc. Bull. 15: 591–595.

Adams, L.W. & Leedy, D.L. (eds.) 1991. Wildlife conservation in metropolitan environments. Nat'l Inst. for Urban Wildl., Columbia, Maryland. 264 pp.

Allen, R.P. 1938. Black-crowned night heron colonies on Long Island. Proc. Linnaean Soc., New York 49: 43–51.

Barker, G.M.A. 1986. The links between ecological science, local authority action and community involvement in planning and land management for nature conservation in British cities. International seminar on the use, handling and management of urban green areas. MAB-UNESCO Comite Expagnol.

Barnes, I.R. 1966. Amid brick and asphalt. In: Stefferud, A. & Nelson, A.L. (eds.), Birds in our lives, pp. 414–424, U.S. Dept. Interior, Fish and Wildlife Service, U.S. Gov't. Printing Office, Washington, D.C. 561 pp.

Beissinger, S.R. & Osborne, D.R. 1982. Effects of urbanization on avian community organization. Condor 84: 75–83.

Bigler, W.J. & Hoff, G.L. 1976. Urban wildlife and community health: grey squirrels as environmental monitors. Proc. Ann. Conf. S.E. Assoc. of Fish and Wildl. Agencies 30: 536–540.

Bornkamm, R., Lee, J.A. & Seaward, M.R.D. (eds.) 1982. Urban ecology, the second European ecological symposium. Blackwell Sci. Pub., Boston, Massachusetts. 370 pp.

Brown, T.L., Dawson, C.P. & Miller, R.C. 1979. Interests and attitudes of metropolitan New York residents about wildlife. Trans. 44th N. Amer. Wildl. & Natur. Resour. Conf., 44: 289–297.

Clark, K., Euler, D. & Armstrong, E. 1983. Habitat associations of breeding birds in cottage and natural areas of central Ontario. Wilson Bull. 95(1): 77–96.

Cotton, J. 1982. The field teaching of ecology in central London – the William Curtis Ecological Park 1977–80. In: Bornkamm, R., Lee, J.A. and Seaward, M.R.D. (eds.), Urban Ecology, pp. 321–327. 2nd European Ecological Symposium. Blackwell Sci. Pub., London, United Kingdom. 370 pp.

Custer, T.W. & Osborn, R.G. 1977. Wading birds as biological indicators: 1975 colony survey. U.S. Dept. Interior, Fish and Wildl. Service. Special Sci. Report-Wildl. No. 206. 28 pp.

Dagg, A.I. 1970. Wildlife in an urban area. Natur. Can. 97: 201–212.

Dawe, G.F.M. 1990. The urban environment – a sourcebook for the 1990s. Centre for Urban Ecology, Birmingham, United Kingdom. 636 pp.

Deelstra, T. 1986. National, regional and local planning strategies for urban green areas in the Netherlands: An ecological approach. International seminar on the use, handling and management of urban green areas. MAB-UNESCO Comite Expagnol.

DeGraaf, R.M. & Payne, B.R. 1975. Economic values of nongame birds and some research needs. Trans. North Am. Wildl. and Natur. Resour. Conf. 40: 281–287.

DeGraaf, R.M. & Wentworth, J.M. 1981. Urban bird communities and habitats in New England. Trans. N. Am. Wildl. and Natur. Resour. Conf. 46: 396–413.

Dickman, C.R. & Doncaster, C.P. 1987. The ecology of small mammals in urban habitats. I. Populations in a patchy environment. J. Animal Ecol. 56: 629–640.

Douglas, I. 1983. The urban environment. Ed. Arnold, Baltimore, Maryland. 229 pp.

Euler, D., Gilbert, F. & McKeating, G. (eds.) 1975. Proceedings of the symposium – wildlife in urban Canada. Off. Cont. Ed., U. Guelph, Ontario. 134 pp.

Figley, W.K. & VanDruff, L.W. 1982. The ecology of urban mallards. Wildl. Monog. 81. The Wildl. Soc., Washington, D.C. 40 pp.

Garay, I. & Nataf, L. 1982. Microarthropods as indicators of human trampling in suburban forests. In: Bornkamm, R., Lee, J.A. & Seaward, M.R.D. (eds.), Urban ecology, the second European ecological symposium, pp. 201–207. Blackwell Sci. Pub., Boston, Massachusetts. 370 pp.

Geist, V. 1975. Wildlife and people in an urban environment – the biology of cohabitation. In: Euler, D., Gilbert, F. & McKeating, G. (eds.), Wildlife in urban Canada, pp. 36–47. Off. Cont. Ed., U. Guelph, Ontario. 134 pp.

Gilbert, F.F. 1982. Public attitudes toward urban wildlife: a pilot study in Guelph, Ontario. Wildl. Soc. Bull. 10(3): 245–253.

Gill, D. & Bonnett, P. 1973. Nature in the urban landscape: a study of city ecosystems. York Press, Baltimore, Maryland. 209 pp.

Guth, R.W. 1979. The junk food guild birds and mammals on picnic grounds and in residential areas. Illinois Audubon Bull. 189: 3–7.

Hardin, J.W. 1977. A study of human and waterfowl usage of urban ponds in the vicinity of Syracuse, N.Y. Unpub. M.S. thesis, SUNY Coll. of Enviro. Sci. and For., Syracuse, New York. 124 pp.

Harris, H.J. Jr., Ladowski, J.A. & Worden, D.J. 1981. Water-quality problems and management of an urban waterfowl sanctuary. J. Wildl. Manage. 45(2): 501–507.

Hecklau, J.D. 1985. Wildlife in Central Park: the problems and opportunities associated with wildlife management in an urban park setting. Trans. N.E. Fish Wildl. Conf. 41: 126–137.

Heusmann, H.W. & Burnell, R.G. 1974. Park mallards. In: Noyes, J.H. & Progulske, D.R. (eds.), Wildlife in an urbanizing environment, pp. 77–86. Coop. Ex. Serv. Univ. Mass. Amherst, Massachusetts. 182 pp.

Hickey, J.J. (ed.) 1969. Peregrine falcon populations, their biology and decline. Univ. of Wisconsin Press, Madison, Milwaukee, and London. 596 pp.

Hubbert, W.T., McCulloch, W.F. & Schnurrenberger, P.R. (eds.) 1975. Diseases transmitted from animals to man, 6th ed. C.C. Thomas Pub., Springfield, Illinois. 1206 pp.

Johnsen, A.M. 1982. Urban habitat use by house sparrows, rock doves, and starlings. Unpub. M.S. thesis, SUNY Coll. of Enviro. Sci. and For., Syracuse, New York. 75 pp.

Kellert, S.R. 1980. Americans' attitudes and knowledge of animals. Trans. N. Am. Wildl. Natur. Resour. Conf. 45: 111–123.

Kellert, S.R. 1984. Urban American perceptions of animals and the natural environment. Urban Ecology 8: 209–228.

Lancaster, R.K. & Rees, W.E. 1979. Bird communities and the structure of urban habitats. Can. J. Zool. 57: 2358–2368.

Leedy, D.L., Maestro, R.M. & Franklin, T.M. 1978. Planning for wildlife in cities and suburbs. U.S. Dept. Interior Fish and Wildl. Serv., Washington, D.C. 64 pp.

Leedy, D.L. 1979. An annotated bibliography on planning and management for urban-suburban wildlife. U.S. Dept. Interior, Fish and Wildl. Serv., Washington, D.C. 256 pp.

Leopold, A. 1933. Game management. Charles Scribner's Sons, New York City, New York. 481 pp.

Lyons, J.R. 1982. Nonconsumptive wildlife-associated recreation in the U.S.; identifying the other constituency. Trans. N. Amer. Wildl. Natur. Resour. Conf. 47: 677–685.

Manski, D.A., VanDruff, L.W. & Flyger, V. 1981. Activities of grey squirrels and people in a downtown Washington, D.C. park: management implications. Trans. N. Am. Wildl. and Natur. Resour. Conf. 46: 439–454.

Matthiae, P.E. & Stearns, F.W. 1981. Mammals in forest islands in southeastern Wisconsin. In: Burgess, R.L. & Sharpe, D.M. (eds.), Forest island dynamics in man-dominated landscapes, pp. 55–66. Springer-Verlag, New York City, New York.

McKinnon, J.G., Hoff, G.L., Bigler, W.L. & Prather, E.C. 1976. Heavy metal concentrations in kidneys of urban grey squirrels. J. Wildl. Diseases 12: 367–371.

Nilon, C.H. 1986. Quantifying small mammal habitats along a gradient of urbanization. Ph.D. Thesis. SUNY Coll. of Enviro. Sci. and For., Syracuse, New York. 148 pp.

Noyes, J.H. & Progulske, D.R. (eds.) 1974. A symposium on wildlife in an urbanizing environment. U. Mass. Coop. Ext. Serv., Amherst, Massachusetts. 182 pp.

Numata, M. 1981. Integrated ecological studies in bay-coast cities. II. Chiba. 174 pp.

O'Donnell, M.A. 1984. Wildlife problems, human attitudes and response to wildlife in Syracuse, N.Y. metropolitan area. Unpub. M.S. thesis, SUNY Coll. of Enviro. Sci. and For., Syracuse, New York. 116 pp.

Ohlendorf, H.M., Klass, E.E. & Kaiser, T.E. 1974. Environmental pollution in relation to estuarine birds. In: Kahn, M.A.O. & Bederka, J.P. Jr. (eds.), Survival in toxic environments, pp. 53–82. Academic Press, New York City, New York.

Robinson, W.L. & Bolen, E.G. 1984. Wildlife ecology and management. Macmillan Pub. Co., New York City, New York. 478 pp.

Rodiek, J. & Bolen, E.G. (eds.) 1990. Wildlife and habitats in managed landscapes. Island Press, Washington, D.C. 250 pp.

Schlauch, F.C. 1978. Urban geographical ecology of the amphibians and reptiles of Long Island. In: Kirkpatrick, C.M. (ed.), Wildlife and people, proceedings, pp. 25–41. John S. Wright Forestry Conference. Purdue University Department of Forestry and Natural Resources, West Lafayette, Indiana. 191 pp.

Solman, V.E.F. 1973. Birds and aircraft. Biol. Cons. 5(2): 79–86.

Spirn, A.W. 1984. The granite garden. Urban nature and human design. Basic Books, New York City, New York. 334 pp.

Stearns, F. 1975. Urban wildlife – wildlife habitat and implications for man. From Science for Better Environment. In: Proceedings of the International Congress on the Urban Environment, pp. 243–249. HESC.

Stearns, F. & Montag, T. (eds.) 1974. The urban ecosystem: a holistic approach. Dowden, Hutchinson & Ross, Stroudsburg, Pennsylvania. 217 pp.

Stenberg, K. & Shaw, W.W. (eds.) 1986. Wildlife conservation and new residential developments. Proc. national symposium on urban wildlife. Univ. Arizona School Renew. Natur. Resour., Tucson, Arizona. 203 pp.

Sukopp, H. 1990. Urban ecology and its application in Europe. In: Sukopp, H. & Hejúy (eds.) Urban Ecology, pp. 1–22. SPB Academic Pub., The Hague, The Netherlands.

Thompson, C.C. & Thompson, P.S. 1980. Food habits and caching behavior of urban grey squirrels. Can. J. Zool. 58: 701–710.

Thompson, D.C. 1977. Diurnal and seasonal activity of the grey squirrel (*Sciurus carolinensis*). Can. J. Zool. 55(7): 1185–1189.

Thompson, D.C. 1978. The social system of the grey squirrel. Behaviour 64(3–4): 305–328.

VanDruff, L.W. & Rowse, R.N. 1986. Habitat association of mammals in Syracuse, New York. Urban Ecology 9: 413–434.

VanWingerden, W.K.R.E. 1982. The teaching of urban ecology to future teachers. In: Bornkamm, R., Lee, J.A. & Seaward, M.R.D. (eds.), Urban Ecology, 2nd European Ecological Symposium, pp. 315–320. Blackwell Sci. Pub., London, United Kingdom. 370 pp.

Vogl, S.W. & Vogl, R.L. 1985. Teaching nature in cities and towns. Urban Outdoor Bio. & Ecol., Interstate Print. & Pub., Danville, Illinois. 102 pp.

Weber, W.J. 1979. Health hazards from pigeons, starlings, and English sparrows. Thomson Pub., Fresno, California. 138 pp.

Williamson, R.D. & DeGraaf, R.M. 1981. Habitat associations of ten bird species in Washington, D.C. Urban Ecology 5: 125–136.

Willson, M.F. 1974. Avian community organization and habitat structure. Ecology 55: 1017–1029.

Wilson, E.O. 1984. Biophilia. Harvard U. Press, Cambridge, Massachusetts. 157 pp.

Witter, D.J., Tylka, D.L. & Werner, J.E. 1981. Values of urban wildlife in Missouri. Trans. N. Amer. Wildl. Natur. Resour. Conf. 46: 424–431.

Yeomans, J.A. & Barclay, J.S. 1981. Perceptions of residential wildlife programs. Trans. N. Amer. Wildl. Natur. Resour. Conf. 46: 390–395.

SUBJECT INDEX

Acarina, 72, 75, 78
aerial photographs, 72, 164, 174, 175
air pollution mitigation, 47, 180
alien species, 14, 15, 16, 27, 28, 53, 68
allergy, 33, 47
amenity grassland, 178
annual precipitation, 87
anthropogenous influence, 126
anthropozoogenous influences, 90, 91, 94, 134
apophytes, 152
apophytization, 26
archaeophytes, 53, 126, 157
azonal plants, 60

bats, 195
biological indicators, 33, 205
biomass production, 118, 121, 137, 170
birds, 197
butterflies, 163, 166

cage birds, 198
carabids, 72, 76, 78
cats, 198
cemeteries, 30, 164
city size, 24, 25, 152, 159
climatic amelioration, 180
coenoclines, 95
Collembola, 10, 72, 75, 78
competition, 8, 9, 14, 16, 17, 118, 136, 186, 187
coppicing, 121, 136
culture relics, 44
cushion shaped formations, 96

data collection, 6
decomposition of litter, 90
"deposit soils", 72
diversity, biological, 181
diversity of habitats, 152, 157, 158
diversity of species, 8, 10, 13, 14, 16, 24, 29, 31, 44, 78, 96, 102, 104, 118, 121, 122, 124, 136, 137, 157-159, 181, 208
diversity of vegetation, 30, 31, 159
dogs, 198
dry stone walls, 102, 113, 126
dynamics of animal populations, 195
dynamics of urban ecosystems, 191
dynamics of vegetation, 90, 95

earthworms, 72, 73, 78
ecological groups, 118
ecosystem, 5
ecosystem, biocoenological or community aspect, 4
ephemerophytes, 53
ergasiophytes, 157
erosion, 90
euhemerobic sites, 132, 134

euhemerobic zone, 96, 133
eutrophication, 134
extensive pastures, 96, 102, 104, 113, 115, 118, 122, 132, 134, 135

"facultative" segetal species, 105, 127
fallow lands, 127
field weeds, 104
floristic lists, 24, 25, 27, 31
forest, denudation of, 60
forest, dipterocarp, 173
forest, environmental protection forest, 185
forest, natural, 60, 176, 185
forest, re-creation of, 185
forest, secondary, 177, 178, 180
forest, urban, 181
fox, 195

gardens, 53
germination tests, 95, 115, 135
gradient analysis, 94
grasshoppers, 163, 167
grazing, 121
grazing behaviour, 93
grazing pressure, 118, 121, 123, 136
green space classes, 173, 174, 176, 178
green space network, 170, 181

habitat destruction, 197
habitat mapping, 6, 32, 164
habitat types, 29, 30, 31, 164, 165, 170
habitats, changes in habitat sites, 191, 195
hare, 195
harvested fields, 127
hemerobic stages, 134
hemeroby, 28, 90, 91, 94, 118
holism, 7, 9
human influence, 91, 118

indicator species, 29, 54, 56, 96, 119, 121, 122, 134, 136, 137, 170
indicator values, 28, 29, 30, 54, 72, 73
indicators of extreme degradation, 122
individualistic concepts, 7, 8
industrial sites, 30
integration, 5
invasion, 13, 60

landsnails, 163, 168
land-use intensity, 134
lawns, 46, 71, 72
life forms, 28, 31, 54
life strategies, 28
livestock, 91, 92
lumbricides, 72, 73, 78
"lurotopes", 151, 152

SPECIES INDEX

(Contains the scientific names of plants and animals which are mentioned in the text. Names listed in tables do not appear here.)